OLD JUBE

OLD JUBE

A Biography of General Jubal A. Early

by

MILLARD KESSLER BUSHONG, Ph.D.

Illustrations and Maps

by

Timothy T. Pohmer

WHITE MANE PUBLISHING CO., INC.

First Printing, 1955
Second Printing, 1961
Third Printing, 1985
Fourth Printing, 1988

This White Mane Publishing Company, Inc. publication is printed
by arrangement with
Beidel Printing House, Inc.
63 West Burd Street, Shippensburg, PA 17257

In respect to the scholarship contained herein, the paper used in this book meets the guidelines for permanence and durability of the Committee on Production Guidelines for Book Longevity of the Council on Library Resources.

For a complete list of available publications

Please write

White Mane Publishing Company, Inc.
P.O. Box 152
Shippensburg, PA 17257

ISBN — 0-942597-04-4 (previously ISBN — 0-932751-00-8)

PRINTED IN THE UNITED STATES OF AMERICA

To Dee

Preface

I first became interested in writing a biography of General Jubal Early while I was teaching history at the United States Military Academy, West Point, New York. The more I investigated this subject, the more I was convinced that for some unexplainable reason historians have neglected one of the great heroes of the Confederacy. In order to acquaint the reader better with one of the South's almost-forgotten generals, I undertook this study.

Since I have written this book for the general reader, I have included considerable background material that I would have omitted if I had been writing solely for historians. I have tried to describe the course of the Civil War in the East and then show how General Early fitted into the picture.

I have received a great deal of aid in the preparation of this biography, and I wish to take this means of expressing my gratitude. The Research Council of the Richmond Area University Center made several grants for travel and clerical purposes. Miss Henrianne Cabell Early of Washington, D. C. greatly facilitated my research by many helpful suggestions. Professor Woodford B. Hackley of Richmond, Virginia and Mr. John L. Reid of Staunton, Virginia read the entire manuscript and gave me the advantage of their historical and literary criticisms. My brother, Attorney Lee Bushong of Charles Town, West Virginia offered many valuable comments, besides making it possible for me to finance the initial cost of publication. Mr. Timothy T. Pohmer of Baltimore, Maryland spent many hours in drawing the maps and illustrations. Finally, my wife, Dean McKoin Bushong, has merited my special appreciation for her wise counsel, helpful attitude, and patience during the years spent in writing this volume.

I, alone, am responsible for the errors in the manuscript, and, although I have tried to reduce them to a minimum, I ask the indulgence of the reader for those that may have crept in.

Millard K. Bushong

"Arcadia", Route 2
Berryville, Va.
July 15, 1955

Table of Contents

Illustrations and Maps

CHAPTER I

Young Jube

Many years after the Civil War an old Confederate soldier mounted the steps of the United States Capitol in Washington. He had heard that the body of General Joseph Wheeler was then lying in state and that all who wished could pay their last respects to the memory of that hero of the Civil and Spanish-American wars. As this old veteran had served under Wheeler and also Jubal Early, he was very anxious to see one of his old commanders once more.[1]

With his mind directed to some of the incidents which occurred while he was fighting under the Stars and Bars nearly half a century before, the Confederate soldier approached the rotunda of the Capitol. As he came near the casket, he no doubt speculated how General Wheeler would look. He realized that, like himself, the dashing cavalry leader had probably aged considerably and would appear different from when he had commanded his troopers in the Civil War, but he expected to recognize some of the old features which had made Wheeler stand out in a group. When he finally arrived at the casket and peered at the figure within, he received a tremendous shock.

In the old soldier's reminiscences he had completely forgotten that General Wheeler had served in the United States Army in the Spanish-American War. Consequently he was unprepared to see the body of his former leader clad in the blue uniform of an American major general. Recalling what blue had meant to the boys in gray who had fought in 1861-1865, the old cavalryman, after recovering from his first shock, stammered out, "Wall, by gee, gen'ul, when you git on t'other side and Jubal Early catches you in them togs, I'm bettin' you'll git the puttiest cussin' that ever cum your way!"[2]

The preceding version of an alleged incident, which has many variations, gives a suitable introduction to the subject of this biography. Jubal Early had many unique characteristics—some desirable, some undesirable—but perhaps those most frequently

1

attributed to him by the Confederate enlisted men were his liberal
use of profanity and his undying devotion to the cause for which
he fought. They made him the butt of many jokes and told numerous anecdotes about his peculiarities. They never loved him the
way they idolized Robert E. Lee, but they respected the fighting
qualities which endeared Jubal Early to his Commander-in-Chief.

On November 3, 1816 in the Red Valley farming section of
Franklin County, Virginia, a son arrived in the family of Joab and
Ruth Hairston Early. He was the third child in a group that
eventually included ten—five sons and five daughters. The proud
parents continued a family tradition by naming their new offspring Jubal Anderson Early, for an ancestor had originated the
idea of naming children after characters in the Bible.[3] Although
Jubal's parents did not carry this custom to the extent that others
did, they named one of his brothers Joab.[4]

The family in which the newcomer found himself was a respectable and prominent one in that part of Virginia.[5] Socially,
politically, and economically, it stood high. The father, Joab, had
served at various times as Franklin County's sheriff, colonel of
militia, and delegate to the Virginia General Assembly, respectively. He owned several fine farms adjoining the one on which
he was then residing and lived comfortably for that day and age
in a rural community. In spite of the size of his family, Joab was
able to send his children to various schools and colleges. The
mother, Ruth, was the daughter of Colonel Samuel Hairston and
Judith Saunders and was likewise well descended. Her parents
were large slaveholders and enjoyed an outstanding position in
the neighborhood.[6]

The Early family in America is believed to have been founded
by John Early, who came from England to Virginia about the
middle of the 17th Century. Subsequent generations lived in
Middlesex, Orange, Culpeper, Madison, Bedford, and Franklin
Counties. One of them, Jeremiah, originated the custom of using
Biblical names for his children. Six of his nine offspring answered
to the call of Jeremiah, Joshua, Jacob, John, Joseph, and Joel,
respectively.[7] One of these sons [Jeremiah] surpassed the father
in his religious zeal, for he named his eleven children as follows:
Jacobus, Judith, Jeremiah, Joseph, John, Jenny, Jeffrey, Jubal,
Elizabeth, Sarah, and Abner Early.[8]

One of the preceding sons [Jubal] lived in Franklin County
and was married in 1790 to Mary Cheatham. To this union were
born two sons, Joab and Henry. Jubal and one of his brothers
operated the Washington Iron Works in Henry County until the

former died in 1797. His son, Joab, the father of the subject of this biography, lived in Franklin County until 1847, when he moved to Putnam County, in what is now West Virginia. As his property there was confiscated during the Civil War, he went to Lexington, Missouri, where he lived with his son Robert until his death in 1870.[9]

The youth of Jubal Anderson Early was much the same as that of country boys in the first half of the 19th Century. He had his share of hard work, as well as the simple pleasures afforded by a rural existence. He attended the neighborhood version of the "little red schoolhouse" until 1832, when he enrolled at the Danville Male Academy. At the latter institution he perfected his knowledge of the three R's but, in addition, studied Latin, Greek, and French. He likewise attended an academy in Lynchburg.[10]

Encouraged by his ability to master these subjects, Jubal applied to his friend and neighbor, Nathaniel H. Claiborne, member of the United States House of Representatives, for an appointment to the United States Military Academy at West Point. The congressman was sufficiently impressed with Early's background and general qualifications, for on November 8, 1832 he recommended the appointment. In urging the candidacy of his youthful neighbor, Claiborne wrote the Secretary of War that Franklin County had never previously had a cadet at West Point.[11]

The would-be soldier awaited with great interest the arrival of the letter notifying him of his appointment as a cadet. In April, 1833 he received it. Signed by Lewis Cass, Secretary of War, the long-awaited epistle directed him to report to the Superintendent of the Military Academy between June 1 and June 20 of that year. It further informed him that his remaining at West Point was conditional upon successful completion of the academic examinations to be given in January, 1834. Finally, the communication instructed the appointee to notify the Government of his acceptance or non-acceptance and, if he intended to enter the academy, to forward the written assent of his parents.[12]

The ambitious Jubal Early complied fully with the necessary directions, and, taking leave of his family and friends, set out for his destination high on the bluffs above the Hudson. Little did he realize that this was the beginning of a military career that was destined to obtain national prominence for him, as well as make him one of the most famous native sons of Franklin County.

and he could not play on any musical instrument on Sunday. He was restrained from playing chess, backgammon, cards, or any games and from defacing or injuring any of the academic buildings. He could not throw stones or missiles near the buildings, nor entertain citizens in the barracks during study hours. A cadet could not drink or have intoxicating liquors in his room. He could not use tobacco. He could not keep a waiter, horse, or dog. He was forbidden to behave irreverently while attending divine service or to profane the Sabbath in any way.[4] It was very obvious to Jubal Early that he was entering a life entirely different from what he had known in Franklin County, Virginia.

Shortly afterwards Early appeared before the academic board for a preliminary oral examination. His success in overcoming this obstacle was announced in an order of the adjutant dated June 15, 1833.[5] He was then assigned a tent in the summer encampment, which was established annually on the plain. This was to be his home for the next two months. In 1833 these temporary quarters of the corps bore the name of Camp Rensselaer, in honor of General Stephen Van Rensselaer who headed the academy's board of visitors for that year.[6] The purpose of the summer camp was to instruct the cadets in military drill and discipline, as well as infantry and artillery practice. Upperclassmen who were not on leave handled most of the summer instruction. Early remained in the tent city until it was dismantled on August 26 and the corps returned to the stone barracks.[7]

Early's scholastic career at West Point began on September 1 when he entered the academic building for his first class, mathematics. From eight o'clock in the morning until eleven he had ample opportunity to witness the functioning of the West Point system in the mathematics classroom. No sooner had he entered the room than he saw the instructor take the record of every absentee cadet. He could not help noticing that promiscuous cutting of classes was out of the question. He must certainly have observed that the small size of the class, or section as it was called, made possible personal instruction, which is unobtainable in large classes. He became accustomed to the frequent use of blackboards and to daily recitations by each cadet. Thus the stage was being set for the inevitable day of reckoning when the weekly grade was recorded. The fourth year [freshman] course in mathematics included the study of algebra, geometry, trigonometry, application of algebra to geometry, and mensuration of planes and solids.[8]

At eleven o'clock when the class was over Early and his fellow-plebes returned to their rooms in the barracks. At the end of an hour they attended a class in French. Here the mathematics scene was reproduced.[9]

Dinner at one o'clock interrupted the French lesson until it was resumed at two. Then followed two more hours of instruction and recitation. Although this concluded the academic class attendance for the day, it did not conclude the day's activities. There remained military instruction, which lasted from four o'clock until sunset. Here emphasis was placed on duties of the private soldier. Then followed, in turn, dress parade, roll-call, and supper. After this the cadets returned to their quarters for further study until nine-thirty. The sounding of taps at ten o'clock, followed by the extinguishing of lights, completed the day.[10]

Members of the fourth class were placed on probation for their first six months at West Point, after which they, along with the remainder of the corps, were tested by the semi-annual examinations held in January. During the course of this trial period their instructors had kept a close record of their academic proficiency and had filed weekly reports. For Jubal Early and his fellow-plebes their general examination period began on January 6, 1834 and continued for about two weeks. As a result of this mid-winter inquisition the successful cadets received their warrants, or certificates of full admission to the military academy. By January the class had accumulated enough new cadets and "turnbacks", or repeaters, to reach the total of ninety-seven members. However, the process of attrition had set in to such an extent that only eighty-four received warrants.[11] It is interesting to note that as a result of the January, 1834 examinations Jubal Early ranked nineteenth in mathematics and thirty-first in French, in a total class of ninety-seven.[12]

General examinations were also held at the end of the academic session in June. Early improved his scholastic standing to such an extent that as a result of these tests he moved up to ninth place in mathematics but still remained thirty-first in French. By this time the class roll contained only eighty-five names. In the order of general merit at the end of the fourth class year Early stood eleventh.[13]

Early's disciplinary record for his first year at West Point is as unenviable as his scholastic record is impressive. He committed enough violations of the rigid behavior code to amass a demerit score of 142. This resulted in his obtaining the undesirable rank of 203 in conduct, in a total cadet corps of 242.[14] However, in justice to him, it must be pointed out that these violations were of a relatively minor character. Nevertheless they were considered serious enough to constitute reportable offenses. In his autobiography the Virginian gives no explanation of his record in conduct at the military academy except to say that he "was not a very exemplary soldier . . . [and] had very little taste for scrubbing brass".[15] It is conceivable that many of his demerits were due to his negligence in this respect—an unpardonable sin at West Point.

In view of the life of a cadet at the military academy, especially in the early 19th Century, it is surprising that the number of demerits awarded delinquents is not larger than it is. The slightest infraction assumed major proportions and the hapless offender was doomed to walk numerous punishment tours, if he was lucky enough to get off with so light a sentence. Arrests and confinements to quarters were frequent. The post order books of this period are full of the names of cadets who were called before the superintendent or a court-martial for violations of the military code. An accurate estimate of the ease with which a cadet could be remiss in what was expected of him is afforded by the following description of Edgar Allan Poe's days at West Point in 1830-1831:

> There is a studied confusion about the incessant routine of a military academy that no haphazard method of existence can hope to equal. The method itself is beyond approach for producing a continuous series of events that perpetually threaten to make everyone late to something. As a consequence, the unfortunate young gentlemen subjected to the process are forever rushing about changing clothes or books, dashing up and down stairs, arising, going to bed, winding themselves in long sashes, buckling on swords, answering oral orders bawled through the long corridors or stampeding off the formations and yelping 'here' to their names at roll call thousands of times. The method of existence is so complicated that living is impossible.[16]

In view of these conditions, the record of Robert E. Lee, among others, who did not receive a single demerit during his entire four years at West Point from 1825-1829, is all the more remarkable.[17]

Upon the completion of the fourth class year at West Point Early and his classmates became third classmen. The principal advantage derived from this promotion was that it admitted the former plebes to the exalted position of upperclassmen and hence entitled them to special privileges, especially in regard to the incoming fourth class. This "recognition" in June is one of the main objectives to which lowly plebes aspired and to the present day it has remained an important event in the life of a cadet.

Jubal Early's rise to the rank of a third classman, no doubt, came just in time to give him the necessary encouragement to remain at West Point. Like many another cadet, he had found the first year a most trying one. The rigid discipline, the continual academic grind, the constant pressure of competition in everything that he did, plus a touch of nostalgia made the young cadet waver in his determination to see it through. When he communicated these thoughts to members of his family, they urged him to remain at West Point even if he did not intend to stay in the regular army after graduation. His brother Sam suggested that he might later study law but wrote that "your opportunities at West Point are as favourable to a preparation for a study of the law as you would meet with anywhere."[18] As a result of these and other arguments, the young Virginian decided to continue where he was.

About the middle of June, 1834 the corps left the barracks and transferred its quarters to the tents comprising the summer encampment. It was during this summer period that Early and his classmates were given the first part of the course in artillery, as well as infantry training.[19]

In Early's second academic year, which began, as usual, in September, he continued the study of mathematics and French but on an advanced scale. In addition he took a course in drawing. His course in mathematics included analytic geometry, with its application to conic sections, integral and differential calculus, and a course in perspective, shades, and shadows. The new subject, freehand drawing of the human figure, was taught by Robert W. Weir, a distinguished American painter. He had been employed by Congress to execute one of the paintings for the rotunda of the Capitol in Washington.[20]

As a result of the general examinations in January, 1835 and the weekly classroom grades, Early maintained his good scholastic record. By this time the number of cadets in his class had dropped to seventy-nine. Early's standing then was fourteenth in mathematics, thirty-first in French, and twenty-sixth in drawing.[21]

According to the military academy's library records, Early did most of his extra reading during the years 1834 and 1835. It is interesting to note that practically all of the books which he borrowed from that repository were in the field of history. Early began to read these books as soon as he had passed the January examinations in his plebe year. During the remainder of his first year at the academy he confined most of his attention to Smollett's *History of England*. When he entered upon his studies in his third class year, he became interested in his own country and started reading David Ramsay's *History of the United States*. Then he turned to Rupell's *Modern Europe*. This was followed by his reading some of the volumes in a set of books known as *Universal History*. His interest in antiquity is proved by the borrowing of Rupell's *Ancient Europe* and Rollins' *Ancient History*. Early's appetite for historical knowledge seems to have been satisfied by what he read his first two years at West Point, as there is a noticeable drop in the number of books taken from the library after that time. In 1836 and 1837 he is charged only with several volumes of Adam Ferguson's writings on Roman history.[22]

June, 1835 rolled around and brought to a close another academic year. Early had continued to climb the ladder so much that at the end of his second year at West Point he stood twelfth in mathematics, twenty-second in French, and ninth in drawing, in a total class of seventy-six members. This record enabled him to rank eighth from the top in order of general merit.[23]

Early's record in conduct was less impressive than during the preceding year, however, for he had a demerit score of 189, which ranked him 223 in the entire cadet corps of 240 men. A cadet whose demerit score exceeded 200 for any one year was subsequently declared deficient in conduct and recommended by the academic board to the War Department for discharge.[24] It may be that some of these demerits resulted from a youthful escapade in the Mess Hall during which Lewis A. Armistead struck Jubal's head with a plate. Armistead, who later died in Pickett's charge at Gettysburg, was dismissed from the academy.[25]

According to the military academy regulations, a cadet was eligible for a summer furlough after he had been present at two previous summer encampments. To obtain this welcome relief from military discipline, he must ask his parents to request it.[26] Consequently, Early applied for and received permission to be away from West Point from July 6 until August 28.[27] Presumably he spent most of the intervening time at his home in Virginia.

The resumption of academic work in September, 1835 found Early beginning his second-class year with the study of natural philosophy or physics, chemistry, and drawing.[28]

The beginning of Jubal's third academic year coincided with the initial attempts of a small, gallant band of Texans to gain

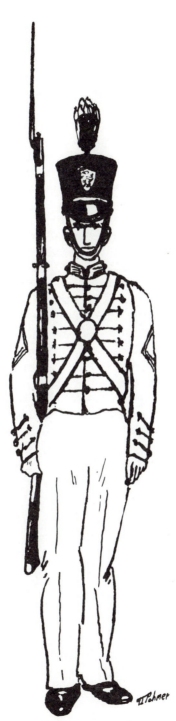

A West Point Cadet

11

their independence from Mexico. As many Americans were flocking southward to aid the hard-pressed Sam Houston, Early seriously considered joining in this fight against oppression. Accordingly, in November, 1835 he wrote his father on the subject. In seeking parental consent, he not only argued about the righteousness of the Texan cause, but he also pointed out the opportunities which would await those who helped in the struggle for independence. Jubal implored his father to borrow the money he would need for the long journey.[29] His youthful enthusiasm was not shared by the wiser Joab, who wrote his son to finish his work at West Point before thinking of other worlds to conquer. Dutiful son that he was, Jubal heeded this wise counsel.

January, 1836 eventually put in appearance and with it came the semi-annual battle of wits between the instructors and cadets. Early emerged from the lists by ranking eleventh in natural philosophy, fifteenth in chemistry, and fifteenth in drawing. By this time his class numbered only fifty-nine.[30]

Early maintained his good academic record during the June examinations also and completed his second class year by standing thirteenth in natural philosophy, nineteenth in chemistry, and eighteenth in drawing. Fifty-eight cadets comprised the class then. In order of general merit Early ranked eleventh.[31]

Early's record in conduct for his second class year remained bad. This time his demerit score reached 196, which was dangerously near the fatal 200. In the whole cadet corps of 216 ranked in order of merit in conduct Early stood 200 from the top.[32]

Early's poor showing in conduct may explain why he was never awarded a single commissioned or non-commissioned officer's rank in the cadet corps during his entire four years at West Point. As has been pointed out, in his autobiography he attributed his delinquencies to his distaste for scrubbing brass.[33] If this is the case, then he must have carried this dislike to the point of continual neglect and was demerited accordingly. It is inconceivable at a school like West Point that a cadet with a poor conduct record would be chosen as an officer in the corps, regardless of how high his academic standing might be. Jubal's relatively good scholastic record in addition to the qualities of leadership which he later displayed on the battlefield would in all probability have obtained some of the coveted cadet positions for him if his disciplinary record had been better.

About this time Early had a verbal encounter with one of his classmates, Joseph Hooker, which gives a preview of what was destined to take place when their troops met in battle years later. Before a debating society "Fighting Joe" made a scurrilous attack on Southern slaveholders in which he accused them of killing their Negroes when the latter were too old to be of use on the plantation. Although Early was not in favor of slavery, he could not resist the temptation to spring to his feet and denounce the assertion as a slanderous lie. Not content with this, he vigorously assaulted Hooker after the society had adjourned and, according to one account, obtained "results satisfactory to himself."[34]

In September, 1836 Early entered upon his final academic year at West Point. His studies for that period were engineering, ethics, and artillery.[35]

During his first-class year at the academy Early maintained practically the same scholastic standing that he formerly had. As a result of the examinations of January, 1837, in a class of fifty, he emerged sixteenth in engineering, thirty-first in ethics, and fortieth in artillery.[36]

In June, 1837 the board of visitors, led by its president, the Honorable Thomas Bennett of Charleston, South Carolina, met with the academic board to conduct the final examinations. When this supreme test was over, it was disclosed that Henry W. Benham still led his class of fifty cadets and hence had the honor of being number one man in order of general merit. Not far behind was Braxton Bragg, who ranked fifth. Farther down the list but still high enough to make a creditable showing was Jubal Early, who stood eighteenth. At about the middle of the class of 1837 was John Sedgwick, who ranked twenty-fourth. John C. Pemberton was twenty-seventh and "Fighting Joe" Hooker was twenty-ninth in the general standing. The "goat" or lowest-ranking member of the class was Franklin Saunders of North Carolina. To be more specific, in a class of fifty Early stood seventh in engineering, twenty-first in artillery, thirty-third in ethics, and thirty-fifth in tactics.[37]

In discipline it was the same old story. Even the fact that he was in his last year at West Point and hence supposed to be a sort of model to the other cadets did not deter Early from compiling the undesirable demerit score of 189. This was sufficient to rank him 195 from the top, in a total cadet corps of 211. In fact, Early's record in conduct was perhaps worse than his previous years at the academy, inasmuch as his delinquencies were serious enough to warrant his arrest on several occasions. Before his first class year there is no evidence that he was ever placed in arrest.

However, in extenuation, it should be pointed out that Early's arrests even now were still for what would seem minor offenses. Once he was arrested and confined to his room for six days because he had visited other cadets after taps and at another time he was given three days' confinement for disobeying a sentinel's orders.[38]

Future Confederate leaders who were cadets at West Point during the years 1833-1837 but not classmates of Early were the following: P. G. T. Beauregard, William J. Hardee, Edward Johnson, Richard S. Ewell, and Richard B. Garnett. Prominent Union officers also at the academy during this time were George G. Meade, William T. Sherman, Irvin McDowell, Henry W. Halleck, and George H. Thomas.[39]

Upon the successful completion of the four-year course at the military academy Early, along with his classmates, was graduated and commissioned a second lieutenant in June, 1837. Choosing artillery as his branch of service, he was attached to Company E of the Third Regiment of Artillery. As the Seminole Indian War was still in progress in Florida during the summer of 1837, the newly-commissioned lieutenants were not granted the usual leave of absence immediately after graduation. Instead, many of them, including Early, were ordered to Fortress Monroe, Virginia, to drill recruits being assembled for the Florida war.[40]

CHAPTER 3

War and Peace

The First Seminole War, which began in 1816 and lasted until 1818, was caused principally by the desire of certain Americans to capture Negro slaves and restore them to their owners. It was marked by sporadic fighting in which both sides asked for no quarter and received none. It was ended after a small army of white soldiers and Creek allies led by General Andrew Jackson destroyed the Seminole villages and captured a few slaves.[1]

The second conflict, which is that usually referred to as the Seminole War, began in 1835 and lasted until 1842. It resulted from the efforts of the United States Government to force the Seminoles to leave their Florida lands and relocate in the Indian Territory west of the Mississippi River. As the proposed new home of the Seminoles would be near that of the Creeks, the former were afraid that the tribes would be united and they would lose their separate identity. Not only did the Seminoles object to being controlled by the Creeks but they also opposed the giving up of their slaves, which they were sure the Creeks would take from them.[2]

The year 1835 witnessed the outbreak of hostilities, as well as the ambush and massacre of an American force under Major Francis L. Dade. On the way from Fort Brooke to Fort King, in western Florida, the whole group of 110 officers and men, with the exception of three, was killed.[3] This disaster caused the Americans to intensify the prosecution of the war, which continued to drag on with no decisive results on either side. The American commanders, Generals Edmund P. Gaines, Duncan L. Clinch, and Winfield Scott, were removed in turn and the thankless task of subduing the Indians handed over to Major General Thomas S. Jesup. This was the situation when Second Lieutenant Jubal A. Early appeared on the scene.

After helping to train recruits at Fortress Monroe, Virginia, Lieutenant Early and his associates sailed for Florida and arrived at Tampa Bay in October, 1837. Early then proceeded to Gary's

Ferry, on Black Creek, where he joined the body of recruits with whom he was to fight. This group, which was known as Company E, Third Regiment of Artillery, was expected to be led by Captain Elijah Lyon. However, because of the latter's incapacitation due to disease and the absence of the company's two first lieutenants on special duty, Early succeeded to the job of company commander. He continued to lead Company E through the campaign of General Jesup in the winter of 1837-1838.[4]

The failure of a group of mediating Cherokee Indians to effect a peaceful settlement with the Seminoles caused Jesup to resume military operations in the latter part of 1837. On December 18, he informed one of his subordinates, Colonel Zachary Taylor, of the breakdown in negotiations and instructed him to move against the enemy. The subsequent campaign, which included an engagement on December 25 near Lake Okechobee, resulted in the capture of a sizable group of prisoners and the seizure of Indian property, especially livestock.[5] In addition, Taylor was brevetted a brigadier general and later entrusted with the chief command in Florida.

The expedition which Lieutenant Early and his organization accompanied was that led by General Jesup himself. Leaving Fort Taylor on January 6, 1838, the commander with about 500 men advanced into the Indian country. After one of the scouting parties had encountered a small body of Seminoles, the main army arrived at the head of the St. John's River. On January 24 Jesup's force met about 100 of the enemy at a crossing of the Locha-Hatchee River and quickly attacked. In this introduction to actual warfare Early's part was inconspicuous. Despite the fact that he heard bullets whistling through the trees, he did not see a single Indian![6]

In General Jesup's report of this skirmish he emphasized the strength of the enemy position which his army attacked. In spite of some confusion in the ranks of the Tennessee volunteers, the bravery of the remaining troops was sufficient to disperse the Indians. The casualties among the whites were seven killed and thirty wounded.[7]

Crossing the river the next day, Jesup's army erected a stockade on Jupiter Bay and named it Fort Jupiter. From this base the commander sent out small detachments into the countryside, but these groups failed to achieve any success against the redskins. The nature of the country imposed severe hardships on those attempting to campaign in it, and the troops became greatly discouraged. So much dissatisfaction arose with the whole expedition that a number of officers, including General Abram Eustis, urged Jesup to conclude a truce with the Indians. These officers suggested that since the whole region of Florida was not then needed by the whites, the Indians should be allowed to withdraw into the southern part and remain there. Jesup, who was fully cognizant of increasing criticism because of his lack of success, concurred and agreed to urge the Secretary of War, Joel R. Poinsett, to approve such a plan.

Accordingly Jesup began negotiations with the Indians and dispatched a letter to Secretary Poinsett. The latter's answer reiterated the Government's intention to stick by its guns and remove all of the Seminoles to the West. By resorting to questionable methods Jesup in March, 1838 succeeded in capturing a large number of Indians near his camp.[8] This loss so disconcerted another group of the enemy that it surrendered to Taylor. Jesup was shortly afterwards removed from command of the Florida army and was replaced by Taylor. With occasional intervals of peace the war continued to drag on until 1842.

At the conclusion of the winter campaign of 1837-1838 Early's troops remained near the seacoast, inactive most of the time. As fighting had ceased temporarily, they returned to Tampa Bay and then embarked for New Orleans. They were ordered to join some other soldiers and then report to General Winfield Scott at Ross' Landing [now Chattanooga], Tennessee, to assist in the removal of the Cherokee Indians to the West. The army authorities anticipated difficulty in effecting the transfer and hence thought it necessary to reinforce Scott.

However, these fears came to naught, and Early entered a life of comparative inactivity in Tennessee. As he had not intended to remain permanently in the army, he planned to resign and re-enter civilian life. His contemplated departure from military duty was facilitated by lack of trouble with the Cherokees and the fact that the Seminole War was thought to be concluded. Accordingly he tendered his resignation, and, while awaiting action on it, obtained a leave of absence. On July 4, 1838 he left Ross' Landing for Louisville, Kentucky, en route to his Virginia home. At Louisville he read in a newspaper about an increase in the size of the army and his promotion on July 7 to first lieutenant. Early admitted that if the news of his promotion had reached him sooner, he might have withheld his resignation, but, as the latter had already been submitted, he decided to let it go forward.[9]

One strong motive for requesting a leave at this time was Early's desire to keep an appointment he had made the year before. This was with an attractive young lady from Philadelphia whom he had met previously at White Sulphur Springs.[10]

During the summer of 1837 a good-looking young second-lieutenant, riding a beautiful black stallion, appeared at the White Sulphur Springs in Greenbrier County, Virginia for a short visit. Fate had also caused a pretty young debutante from Philadelphia to choose the same resort for her summer vacation. Early had never been introduced, but he soon met her under somewhat unusual circumstances. The subsequent encounter was destined to have a lasting effect on the young army officer.

One day the debutante engaged a driver and carriage to take her for a short drive into the surrounding countryside. The same idea had also occurred to Lieutenant Early, who rode off on his black charger. Not far from the hotel at the resort was a small stream which was usually very shallow and easily fordable. However, on the day in question it was a mad, raging torrent of water swollen by heavy rains on the mountainside. When the driver reached the ford, he paused momentarily, then urged the horses forward. Before the animals had reached the middle of the stream, they were swept off their feet and, with the floating carriage, were carried downstream.

Fortunately, Jubal Early had witnessed the driver's lack of judgment and was on hand to help rescue the lady from the dangerous waters. Hesitating not a moment, the young soldier spurred his steed into the stream. With the object of his rescue screaming at her desperate plight and the carriage tossing and rolling in the water, Early managed to reach his quarry just as the carriage turned over. Catching her before she was lost, he held her tightly and urged his noble steed to the shore. Before long he had galloped up to the hotel with the almost lifeless body of the belle in his arms.[11]

The young lady's friends and relatives carried her into the hotel and helped her recover from the shock of the narrow escape. When the story of the rescue became known, Lieutenant Early was the hero of the hour. That evening he monopolized the dancing list of the Quaker belle. From that time until he had to return to army duty he was her almost constant companion. Apparently his attentions were not unwelcome for she seemed delighted and, when the time came for him to leave, promised to meet him again at the resort the following summer. She subsequently returned to her Pennsylvania home and he to his troops at Fortress Monroe.

When the spring of 1838 drew near, Lieutenant Early looked

forward with eager anticipation to the meeting. After the Florida campaign he requested and obtained the desired leave. The same mail which brought the necessary army papers also brought a Northern newspaper, addressed to him in a familiar hand. As the young officer tore open the latter, he noticed an article encircled with a heavy black mark. His heart sank as he read about the marriage of his beloved to another, and he realized for the first time that she had been toying with his affections. Greatly disappointed and deeply hurt, he, nevertheless, cut the piece from the paper, placed it in a book, kept it, and, firmly resolved never to fall in love again.[12] It is said that because of Early's disappointment over this affair he never married.

Jubal Early's resignation from the army became effective on July 31, 1838, and in the fall of that year he began the study of law in the office of Norborne M. Taliaferro, a prominent attorney of Rocky Mount, Virginia.[13] While engaged in this, he became convinced that he was training for the wrong profession. Realizing that his education at West Point was more suitable for the engineering profession than for law, he determined to seek work along the former line. As one of his former West Point schoolmates, James N. Ellis, was then an assistant engineer on the James River and Kanawha Canal project, Early wrote him inquiring about the possibility of employment as an engineer.[14] Much to his disappointment, he learned that there was nothing available.[15] When further efforts failed to uncover an opening in engineering, Early decided to continue reading law.

Finally Jubal's diligent study produced results, for on January 14, 1840 he received his shingle. To acquire this certificate, it was necessary for him to convince the Franklin County Court of his "honesty, probity, and good demeanor" and then appear before an examining board to prove his "capacity, ability, and fitness" to enter upon the practice of his profession in Rocky Mount.[16] Like many young lawyers who desire to become better known, Early became interested in politics. Identifying himself with the Whig Party, he was elected in 1841 to the Virginia General Assembly as a member of the House of Delegates and represented Franklin County for two terms in Richmond. In 1843 he was appointed Commonwealth's Attorney for his native county and continued to serve in this capacity until 1852, except in 1847-1848 when he served in the War with Mexico.[17]

Although Jubal Early was reserved in manner and never sought popularity, his force of character and intellect were such that he soon obtained the confidence of his friends and neighbors

Jubal A. Early in 1840

in legal matters. Consequently his practice began to grow. He cared nothing for money, and his days at the bar were noted for the modesty of his fees. Although he was not a man of means, he was generous and kindly disposed toward those in need of his services. He was always ready to lend an attentive ear to the problems of his poorer clients, and if they were unable to pay him, he did not refuse to aid them. He derived considerable satisfaction out of helping those in distress, and this characteristic remained with him until the day of his death. True to his friends, he cared nothing about conciliating his foes; but friends and foes alike agreed that he possessed one attribute highly desirable in a lawyer, that of personal honesty.[18] The most careful research has failed to reveal that his career both as a lawyer and soldier was anything but honest and truthful.

While Early was practicing law in the little county of Franklin, events of much greater significance were shaping up on the national stage. The infant Texas Republic, after wrenching itself loose from Mexico, had for nine long years tried to maintain itself as an independent state. Having offered itself for annexation to the United States, it had been rebuffed, and then it tried a "go-it-alone" policy. For numerous reasons this was not successful, so when the United States offered annexation in the closing days of the Tyler Administration in 1845, it was accepted. In acquiring Texas, however, the United.States fell heir to a disputed boundary with Mexico, which had never become reconciled to the loss of so valuable a region. Threats of war were uttered, and Brigadier General Zachary Taylor was ordered to march a small American army into the disputed region between the Nueces and Rio Grande Rivers.

When the Mexican authorities demanded that Taylor withdraw and the latter refused to do so, war was inevitable. Before long border incidents occurred, and in one of them some American soldiers were killed by a small enemy force north of the Rio Grande. This afforded the new President, James K. Polk, who was an ardent expansionist, an opportunity to obtain a declaration of war from the American Congress. Taylor, meanwhile, had advanced into Mexico proper, where he won some small victories.

As soon as war with Mexico became imminent, Jubal Early felt a longing to return to the colors, and, at least temporarily to become a soldier again. It will be recalled that when he was a cadet at West Point he had been interested in the valiant struggle the Texans were then waging for independence. His civilian pursuits had not dimmed his military ardor when war seemed near in 1846. His action in reentering the army was also influenced by the fact that, since he had been educated at the expense of the United States Government, even though he had left the service, he felt an obligation to offer his aid in time of emergency.

With these ideas dominating his thinking, in May, 1846 Early wrote a letter to President James K. Polk offering to serve as a commissioned officer in the United States army. In his communication the Franklin County lawyer emphasized the obligation of duty to his country and his desire to contribute to the "maintenance of its honor and just rights." Early's honesty and frankness impelled him to state that he was not seeking any political favor from the Government and that he was a member of the opposition Whig Party. He sent this letter to his friend in the House of Representatives, William M. Treadway, who was expected to forward it to the President.[19]

Not receiving an answer from either the President or the Congressman, Early wrote the latter again. This time Treadway replied. He informed the would-be officer that because the volunteers under General Taylor had done so well in Northern Mexico and because of the peacetime difficulty in decreasing the size of the regular army, he did not think that Congress would authorize its expansion. However, as a regiment of volunteers was then being organized in Virginia, the Congressman suggested that Early's services might be needed for it, and, accordingly, reminded the Chief Executive of the application submitted earlier.[20]

A few weeks later Early's patience was rewarded with the receipt of a communication from William Smith, Governor of Virginia, appointing him Major of the First Regiment of Volunteer Infantry. This organization was the Old Dominion's contribution to the War with Mexico. The newly-commissioned major learned later that its head, and hence his immediate superior, was Colonel John F. Hamtramck of Jefferson County, a West Point graduate who had served under General Zachary Taylor in the War of 1812.[21]

In January, 1847 Major Early went to Old Point Comfort, where the Virginia troops were assembling. Since Colonel Hamtramck was delayed in arriving, Early had to assume the thankless task of trying to enforce army discipline upon volunteers who a few weeks before had been civilians. No one appreciated the difficulty of his task any more than did the thirty-year old major himself who finally felt impelled to violate military propriety by writing to Hamtramck and suggesting that the older officer come to Old Point Comfort as soon as possible. In his letter, Early stated the nature of the problems he was trying to solve and pointed out the desirability of having on hand an officer whose age would entitle him to more respect and obedience from the men.[22]

Colonel Hamtramck finally arrived and for a few days relieved his harassed subordinate in order that he could go to Norfolk to attend to personal business. When Early returned to Old Point Comfort, however, Hamtramck went away again and left him again in charge of the Virginia Regiment. After combating successfully the problems caused by delayed shipping, foul weather, and considerable sickness among the volunteers unaccustomed to army life, Early was finally able to write to his father on February 27 that nine companies had already sailed for Point Isabel, Texas, and that he, along with the remaining three, would leave Hampton Roads the following morning.[23]

By March, 1847 the entire Virginia Regiment had reached the Rio Grande. Proceeding up the river, the volunteers passed Matamoros, Camargo, and a little place named China on the Mexican side of the border. They remained in the neighborhood of Monterey and Buena Vista while more decisive events were transpiring further south. Thus they saw very little active fighting except for occasional skirmishes with small Mexican scouting parties.

After General Taylor's victory at Buena Vista in February, 1847, the scene of fighting shifted to the south, where General Winfield Scott was marching from Vera Cruz to Mexico City. Although the officers and men of the Virginia Regiment made strenuous efforts to be transferred to a more active theatre, their requests were denied by General Taylor, who feared further depletion of his little force would embolden the Mexican dictator and general, Santa Anna, to strike once more in the north. Consequently, the Virginians settled down to the dull and monotonous routine of garrison duty while the outcome of the war was being determined by the overland campaign of General Scott against the Mexican capital.

Although there was little military activity in northern Mexico after the battle of Buena Vista, sometimes the Virginians would engage in scouting and patrol skirmishes. On one occasion, Early suggested to Colonel Hamtramck a move involving greater risk than the senior officer thought wise. When the major persisted, Hamtramck allowed him to take fifty volunteers and go on the expedition. As the adjutant prepared the necessary orders, he remarked, "Jubal, I can testify that you are an Early who is

never late, but I fear you will soon be known as the *late* Early."[24]
However, in spite of this dire prediction, Jubal returned unharmed
from this adventure.

Not long afterwards Major Early was appointed Military
Governor of Monterey in which capacity he served creditably for
several months. Then the Virginia Regiment was ordered to
Buena Vista where it remained for the duration of the war. Unfortunately at the latter place Early contracted rheumatism from
which he suffered the remainder of his life. It was responsible
for changing him from an erect, soldierly-looking officer into
one badly stooped. It troubled him so much at this time that he
sought a leave of absence to recuperate.

Early obtained the desired opportunity to recover his health
and spent most of his leave with his father, who was then living
in the Kanawha River Valley in present West Virginia. He remained there for some time, and, although his commanding officer
extended his leave from time to time, Early felt he should return
to his command. While he was proceeding down the Ohio River
on a steamboat, he had a very narrow escape when the ship's
boiler burst. According to one account, half of his stateroom was
carried off by the explosion and pieces of the boiler protruded
through the floor cutting and burning his feet. Fortunately he
suffered no permanent injuries from this incident and returned
to Buena Vista without further interruption.[25]

General Scott's successes in central Mexico led to the Treaty
of Guadalupe Hidalgo which was signed February 2, 1848, concluding the war. The American forces left Mexico to return to
the United States, where the volunteers were mustered out of
service. Major Early, along with the remainder of his troops, received his honorable discharge Aug. 3, 1848 at Fortress Monroe.[26]

Returning to Rocky Mount, Jubal Early resumed the practice
of law. Apparently his service in the army had not dimmed the
demand for his legal services, for he was soon occupied with
considerable litigation. One of his most important cases at this
time concerned the construction of a will and was tried in Lowndes
County, Mississippi. As a large amount of property was involved,
and he had to contend with three very able lawyers, Early was
justly gratified when he won the case.[27]

Nor did Jubal Early stay out of politics. Still identified with
the Whig Party, which was declining in the nation at large, he
unsuccessfully sought the right to represent Franklin County at
the Virginia Constitutional Convention of 1850-1851. Two years
later he was defeated for his old seat in the General Assembly.

He received some consolation, however, from the fact that his friends and neighbors retained him as Commonwealth Attorney of Franklin.[28] The new State Constitution of 1851 provided that this office would now be elective. Although still interested in political affairs, Early was not chosen for any other elective office until he represented Franklin County at the Virginia Secession Convention in 1861.

CHAPTER 4

The Terrapin from Franklin

When the critical election of 1860 resulted in the elevation of Abraham Lincoln to the Presidency of the United States, South Carolina took the lead in terminating her existence in the Federal Union. Previously Governor William H. Gist of the Palmetto State had recommended to the legislature that in case of Lincoln's election, it should take steps to summon a convention which would, presumably, take the state out of the Union. Accordingly, the legislature, without a dissenting vote, passed a law on November 13, 1860 which provided for a convention to consider "the dangers incident to the position of the State in the Federal Union."[1]

Delegates to the convention, who were chosen in popular mass meetings, met first at Columbia and later at Charleston. By the unanimous vote of 169 members on December 20 they adopted an ordinance which declared that the union between South Carolina and the other states was dissolved. At the same time they issued to the world a document giving the reasons for their action. They did this to make it clear that their state was not in rebellion but merely separating from its former political allies.[2] Within the next few months secession was completed by the states of Alabama, Mississippi, Florida, Georgia, Louisiana, and Texas. Delegates from these states, as well as South Carolina, met at Montgomery, Alabama in February, 1861 and organized The Confederate States of America.

Meanwhile the course of the lower South was not unnoticed by its sister state Virginia. A minority group led by Henry A. Wise insisted that the mere election of Lincoln would be sufficient grounds for the Old Dominion to sever its relations with the Union. The majority of Virginians, however, felt that the election of Lincoln or any other man to the Presidency was not a necessary cause for secession. This group desired to have the state remain in its normal relationship to the other states and await developments. Most Virginians admitted the right of secession under sufficient provocation, although the northwest was

26

somewhat cool to separation even then. In like manner the residents of the Old Dominion denounced the right of the Federal Government to coerce a state. Cultural and economic ties bound them closely to the lower South.[3]

Recognizing the exigency of the situation, Governor John Letcher called the Virginia General Assembly to meet in extra session on January 7, 1861. Before Lincoln's election he had promised the president of the James River and Kanawha Canal Company that he would convene the assembly to consider the company's offer to sell to a French organization. Ninety-four members of the legislature on November 7 had petitioned him to convene the assembly the first Monday in December, but the Governor deferred the meeting until the beginning of the new year.

When the assembly met, it passed resolutions denying the right of the Federal Government to coerce a state, and it adopted measures for reforming the militia. It also resolved that Virginia would support the South if all efforts at redress of grievances failed. On January 14 it called a convention to meet on February 13 in Richmond and provided for the election of delegates on February 4. At the same time voters would decide whether important decisions of the convention would be final or whether they would have to be submitted to the state's electorate in a popular referendum.[4]

In line with Governor Letcher's recommendations, the assembly invited all of the states to select delegates to meet in Washington on February 4 in what became known as the "Peace Conference." It selected five delegates to represent Virginia, among whom was Ex-President John Tyler.[5]

When Virginia voters went to the polls to select delegates to the forthcoming convention at Richmond, they were faced with the alternative of choosing "unionist" or "secessionist" men. On the face of the returns, the result was an overwhelming victory for the unionists. Likewise the proposal for submitting important decisions of the convention to the people was carried. Of the 152 delegates elected, about 120 were opposed to secession at that time and about 50 of them at any time. Thus the outright secessionist strength of the convention would be only about 32. Naturally, the unionists rejoiced in their initial victory. Their strength was principally in the western part of the state, and, according to one conservative, ". . . not a single secessionist or conditional Union man has been returned in Virginia west of the Blue Ridge."[6] In the Shenandoah Valley, for example, the two unionist candidates of Jefferson County defeated their secessionist opponents by approximate majorities of more than two to one.[7]

In Franklin County, in the southwestern part of the state, a similar struggle was taking place over the election of delegates to the Richmond convention. Although complete details about the contest are lacking, unionist delegates Jubal A. Early and Peter Saunders were chosen over Abram Booth Hancock and Hughes Dillard. According to Early's own statement, he defeated Dillard by 1061 votes, but he does not enlighten us concerning the margin by which he defeated his other opponent, Hancock.[8]

The Secession Convention which convened in Richmond February 13 was composed of a number of persons who had been active in politics. The distinguished list was headed by Ex-President John Tyler and included two former Cabinet officers, one ex-governor, two former lieutenant governors, three defeated gubernatorial candidates, and many former judges, legislators, and members of previous constitutional conventions. While not a body of great political sagacity, its membership was probably above the average state assembly of this type. According to the Richmond *Examiner,* it was made up of "old fogies who had not represented Virginia in the past thirty years."[9] Conspicuous by their absence were leading politicians such as James M. Mason and R. M. T. Hunter.

As no vote for judging the delegates' feelings about secession was taken until April 6, it is difficult to group them accurately at the opening of the convention. From the statements made by the candidates during the campaign and from the views of contemporary writers, it appears that there were three distinct groups, with each merging into the other. The first group, known as secessionists, consisted of about thirty-two members from the Tidewater, Piedmont, and southwest. They believed that the doctrine of secession was right, that community of interest bound Virginia to the lower South, and that their commonwealth should follow the course of the cotton states as soon as possible. Since this group included less than one-fourth of the delegates, it decided to follow a course of agitation until the arrival of a favorable opportunity to take Virginia out of the Union. It was led by Henry A. Wise, former governor, and Lewis E. Harvie, an able politician who had been connected with the "Southern Rights" wing of the Democratic party in Virginia.[10]

A larger group known as the moderates consisted of states' rights Whigs, Stephen A. Douglas Democrats, and a few supporters of John C. Breckinridge. Their strength varied from time to time but usually included about seventy delegates, most of whom were from the Valley, the upper Piedmont, and Potomac counties. Among their leaders were R. Y. Conrad, R. E. Scott, W. B. Preston, and James Barbour, although the latter went over to the secessionists in early March. In the main the moderates accepted the doctrine of secession but felt that it should be resorted to only after every other means had failed. As the moderates were never strongly united and as their plans depended largely upon the chances of compromise, it is not surprising that when conciliation failed they lost most of their members in March, and in early April their "party" disintegrated.

The unionist group consisted of about fifty delegates coming largely from the Trans-Allegheny and Valley counties. Led by George W. Summers and Alexander H. H. Stuart, most of this body denied the right of secession but opposed the enforcement of Federal laws in a seceded state. Willing to cooperate with the moderates to gain a compromise with the North, these unionists would continue to oppose dissolution of the Union.[11]

The convention held its first session in the hall of the House of Delegates on February 13 but the next day moved to Mechanics Institute, where it continued to meet until its work was finished. Its organization seemed favorable to the unionists, who elected one of their number, John Janney, chairman of the convention and dominated the most important committee, that on Federal Relations. The membership of this committee consisted of ten moderates, seven unionists, and four secessionists.

The Committee on Federal Relations did not proceed at once to the business at hand but instead concerned itself with resolutions and petitions while it awaited the Peace Conference report and Lincoln's inaugural address. The Peace Conference or Convention consisted of delegates from twenty-one states who assembled in Washington. Its recommendations to Congress on February 27, however, received little support. In the meantime the Virginia Secession Convention was marking time, listening to orations concerning the Old Dominion's contributions to the Union, coercion, and secession. Commissioners from the states of South Carolina, Georgia, and Mississippi made effective and interesting speeches and succeeded in winning over some of the wavering delegates. They said, in effect, that if Virginia would join the Southern Confederacy, she would be assured a position of influence, prosperity, and security. Thus, she would be to that government what New England had long been to the United States.[12]

Because of the favorable impression made by the visiting commissioners throughout Virginia and the failure of the Peace Conference, the secessionists gained in strength. Their cause was further strengthened by Lincoln's inaugural address in which the President declared his intention "to hold, occupy, and possess the property and places belonging to the Government."[13] However, in spite of these gains, the secessionists were unable to take Virginia out of the Union at that time.

Jubal Early did not lose any time in demonstrating to the convention at Richmond how he felt about secession. Being a man of strong convictions and having been elected by Franklin County to help keep Virginia in the Union, he was determined to do so. The persistence, stubbornness, and tenacity which he displayed in the resulting debates caused his opponents to refer to him as "The Terrapin from Franklin."

The convention had been meeting only a week when William M. Treadway of Pittsylvania County offered a resolution instructing the Committee on Federal Relations to investigate the report that the United States Government was moving arms and men to forts bordering on or in Virginia. On February 20 Early spoke against this resolution and pointed out that it was giving too much importance to the constitutional right of the President to protect public property. He stated that he was satisfied the President had no intention of intimidating the citizens of Virginia and that they were in no danger from these guns "unless they may foolishly run their heads into the mouth of one of them."[14] The delegates thereupon voted to table the resolution.

Several days later Early rose to his feet again, this time in defense of Major Robert Anderson, the Federal commander at Fort Sumter. Replying to the statement that the guns of Fort Sumter had been for days pointing at the bosoms of the women and children of Charleston, Early said that there was no danger. He pointed out that he had known Anderson when they were both in the regular army and that "in his veins runs true Virginia blood," for his father was originally from the Old Dominion. According to Early, if Major Anderson ever had to direct a gun against the bosom of any countryman "every shot will wring his own heart." The delegate from Franklin pointed out that Anderson was a soldier, nevertheless, and would do his duty, however painful that might be.[15]

When Lincoln's inaugural address reached the ears of the delegates in Richmond, the President was criticized for his announced intention to execute the Federal laws in all the states.

Although Early did not approve of the inaugural, he defended Lincoln in a speech to the convention on March 6. He pointed out that if the states of the lower South had not already seceded, then Lincoln's determination to execute the laws would have been hailed throughout the country as a guarantee that he would perform his duty. Defending the stand that minority rights could be asserted under the Federal Constitution, Early pleaded for a peaceful solution of the problem rather than a resort to force.

At the same time Early rebuked John Goode, Jr., a delegate from Bedford County, for telling the convention that Early's course was contrary to that desired by his Franklin County constituents. Goode claimed to have received letters from prominent residents of Franklin stating that secession sentiment was increasing there and that if another election were held, Early would be defeated. Early defended his stand and revealed that one of the residents whom Goode referred to was the same Colonel Dillard whom Early had decisively beaten at the polls for a seat at the convention. The delegate from Franklin surmised that the other resident mentioned by Goode was a newcomer to the county, since he had never heard of him.[16] In a letter written to Early the next month by a certain P. Smith from Shady Grove, in Franklin County, the writer informed him that his course in the convention had given entire satisfaction to his friends and that he had heard nothing to the contrary.[17]

With the tide at the convention favorable, the moderates were able to control the Committee on Federal Relations. It made a preliminary report on March 9 and a supplemental one ten days later. Although vague about the right of secession, these reports condemned the use of force by the Federal Government against a state. The committee recommended calling an immediate conference of the border states and a national convention. It was assumed that Virginia would await the outcome of these proposals before resorting to extreme measures, and hence this victory lay with the moderates.

The moderates hoped that Secretary of State William H. Seward would be able to prevent President Lincoln from doing anything that would provoke hostilities. The critical condition of Major Robert Anderson's garrison at Fort Sumter made the sending of supplies imperative, but the South Carolina authorities had no intention of allowing anything to reach that Federal outpost. Toward the end of March rumors were circulating that the President intended to relieve Fort Sumter and that Seward could no longer restrain him. Although the convention secessionists could muster only 45 votes in favor of secession on April 4 while their opponents collected 88 votes to defeat the proposed ordinance, their cause was gaining in strength rapidly. Moderates were afraid to adjourn for fear that the radical assembly, still in session, would call another convention to meet at once.[18]

The firing upon Fort Sumter on April 12 and Lincoln's call for 75,000 volunteers to enforce the laws of the United States created a panic in Richmond. As a result the secessionists gained control of the convention. Public opinion in the Old Dominion would not allow the state to send its quota of militia to fight against the Cotton States and demanded that Virginia cast her lot with them. As bad as secession was, it was better than fighting against one's own people. Consequently on April 17, by a vote of 88 for, to 55 against, the Virginia Convention adopted an ordinance of secession. The ordinance was to be effective when ratified by the people at their regular spring election, which came that year on May 23.[19]

To the last Jubal Early had stuck by his guns. He had continued to oppose the rising tide of secession in the convention with all the strength at his command. In an address to that body on April 12 he presented the views of the tobacco-growers and manufacturers of his section, both slaveholders and nonslaveholders. Refuting the statement that all of Virginia's interests lay to the south, he declared that the state was dependent upon Northern capital to carry on the manufacture of tobacco. He stated that Franklin County was then suffering because its tobacco manufacturers were unable to draw upon the commission merchants in the North. Consequently there was not enough money to pay the planter for his tobacco, and both planters and manufacturers were in distress.

The "Terrapin from Franklin" then proceeded to show that the principal market for Virginia tobacco was the North, especially the cities of New York and Baltimore. From these points, he declared, it was distributed all over the country. Since there were more persons in the North than in the South, it stood to reason that more tobacco was consumed by the section with the larger population. He estimated that the North and West consumed two-thirds of the manufactured tobacco of Virginia. If Virginia seceded, the United States could be expected to encourage tobacco production in what remained of the Union, especially in the states of Ohio, Indiana, and Illinois. A protective tariff would then exclude Virginia tobacco and since the Southern Confederacy would be unable to take up the slack, financial ruin would be the fate of Virginia's tobacco-growers and manufacturers.

Early also tried to disprove the statement that Virginia's interest lay southward by citing the commercial relations of the Old Dominion with the state of Tennessee. He pointed out that in the past three or four years southwest Virginia had been importing considerable supplies of corn from her neighbor to the west. A series of droughts ruined the corn crops in Virginia so much that it was necessary to depend upon outside sources. He cited the Virginia and Tennessee Railroad as an important connecting link and said that the proposed links with the Kentucky and Ohio regions would bring Virginia a trade of tremendous proportions.[20]

Even after Confederate batteries in Charleston had fired on Fort Sumter Early was not ready for the withdrawal of Virginia from the Union. The attack occurred on April 12, and on April 13 he addressed the Virginia Convention as follows:

> I must confess that upon this day my heart is bowed down with sorrow, not so much that the flag of my country has been compelled to give way to another; not so much that a gallant friend and comrade of mine in former times has been compelled to yield to the force of over-ruling numbers, as that I find Virginians ready to rejoice in this event. I had fondly hoped, however we might disagree as to the course to be pursued towards these Confederated States, that the heart of every Virginian would appreciate the gallant devotion to duty which had characterized that man, who, if reports be true, was lately the commander, and is now the hero of Fort Sumter. . . .
>
> Now, sir, when a man in whose veins every drop of blood that flows is that of a Virginian; when the son of an officer of the Revolution, who fought for our liberties—yes, sir, fought for South Carolina—when, I say, the son of that man, with a handful of starving men, has been fired into, and has been compelled, at the cannon's mouth, to lower the flag of his country, I confess that my heart is bowed down with sorrow to find Virginians ready to rejoice at such an event. . . .
>
> Mr. Chairman, this act has done nothing to advance the cause of the Confederate States. In my humble opinion, it has placed a gulf between them and the people of Virginia. The mass of the people will never be found sanctioning their cause. We are threatened with having an army marched through the State of Virginia to Washington; and I see by the papers this morning that a son of Virginia has stated in Charleston that the very moment a blow was struck, Virginia would go out of the Union. If there be any Virginians who advise or encourage the idea of marching an army from the Confederated States through our borders to Washington, they mistake the tone and temper of our people. I trust that the issue may never be forced upon us; but when it does come,

mark it. that the invasion of our soil will be promptly resisted. The spirit of manhood has not deserted the sons of
Virginia.[21]

On April 15 President Abraham Lincoln gave his answer
to the attack on Fort Sumter. In a proclamation which pointed
out that the Federal laws were being disregarded by the states
of the Confederacy, he called upon those remaining in the Union
to furnish 75,000 militia to "cause the laws to be duly executed."[22]
This proclamation was issued by Secretary of State William H.
Seward.

When unofficial word of Lincoln's call for troops reached
Richmond, the convention was still in session. On the very day
of the President's proclamation Jubal Early rose to his feet to
oppose precipitate action on the part of that body, pending official
confirmation of the call for troops. He refused to believe that such
a course had been taken by responsible Washington authorities.
Describing Secretary of State Seward as "a statesman—able,
prudent, and discreet," Early could not believe he had signed his
name to any such document. He doubted the legality of Lincoln's
right to call out the militia without first issuing a warning proclamation. Only in case that should fail did Lincoln have the right
to call on the military to aid the civil authority. Early also thought
it strange that Lincoln, in the same proclamation calling for
troops, would assemble Congress on a distant day [July 4]. In
conclusion Early declared that if the proclamation had been issued as reported, it was evidence that the Lincoln administration
had "lost all prudence, discretion, and good sense."[23]

Events moved swiftly in Richmond. As has been pointed out,
the convention voted 88 for, to 55 against, when the vote on secession was taken on April 17. Early was one of those voting in the
negative even after Lincoln's call for troops was found to be
official. Even then he hoped that the collision of arms might be
avoided and some satisfactory adjustment made. In spite of the
fact that the adoption of that ordinance wrung from him bitter
tears of grief, he felt it his duty to yield to the decision of the
majority. He was a Virginian and, like many others, although he
was opposed to secession, if Virginia chose to join the Southern
Confederacy, he would cast his lot with her.[24]

Although Early had voted against secession, once the ordinance had passed, he later signed it. Apparently most of the
unionists attached their signatures, as did many delegates later
elected to the convention. As a result there were 143 names on

the ordinance. According to one account, the legalistic Early expressed his feelings as follows:

Abraham Lincoln, President of the United States, having set aside the Constitution and laws and subverted the government of the United States, and established in lieu thereof a usurped government, founded upon the worst principles of tyranny, the undersigned has, therefore, determined to sign the Ordinance of Secession adopted by the Convention on the 17th of April last with the intention of sustaining the liberties, independence and entity of the State of Virginia against the said Abraham Lincoln, his aiders and abettors, with the hope or desire of a reconstruction of the old Union in any manner that shall unite the people of Virginia with the people of the non-slave states of the North.[25]

Early's decision to defend his state against external aggression was undoubtedly a popular one with most of his friends. One of them, John Otey Taylor of Lynchburg, wrote that he had been defending Early's reputation in that city and that he had been trying to assure other friends that Jubal would be willing to lead Virginia troops against the foe.[26] Taylor was attempting to induce him to come to Lynchburg to take charge of soldiers who had assembled there. Another friend, G. B. Greer of Rocky Mount, informed Early that the people of Franklin County were looking to their delegate for leadership.[27]

In the meantime another exchange of communications had taken place. Secretary of War Simon Cameron, attempting to recruit the desired 75,000 volunteers, wrote to Governor John Letcher requesting that Virginia furnish 2,340 troops as her quota. Cameron asked that these men be detached from the state militia and mustered into the service of the United States. To this request Letcher replied as follows:

Executive Department
Richmond, Va. April 16th, 1861

Hon. Simon Cameron, Secretary of War.

. . .

In reply to this communication I have only to say, that the militia of Virginia will not be furnished to the powers at Washington, for any such use or purpose as they may have in view. Your object is to subjugate the Southern States, and a requisition made upon me for such an object—an object, in my judgment, not within the purview of the Constitution, or the act of 1795—will not be complied with. You have chosen to inaugurate civil war, and having done so, we will meet it, in a spirit as determined as the Administration has exhibited towards the South.

Respectively
John Letcher[28]

The Call to Arms

It will be recalled that the secession ordinance would not be effective until it had been ratified by the people of Virginia in their regular spring election, which fell that year on May 23. However, ratification was taken for granted after the ordinance had been adopted by the convention. In an effort to check war preparations in the North by showing that the South was united, former staunch unionists campaigned for ratification. Among the soldiers in camp a vote against ratification would have been considered treason. Intimidation was undoubtedly resorted to by both sides and usually the counties were either solidly for or solidly against the ordinance. On April 24 the Virginia Convention entered into a league with the Confederate States in which Virginia agreed to place her entire military forces at the service of the Confederate President. Consequently, when May 23 arrived, the war was on in earnest, and the Old Dominion's voters approved the secession ordinance by large majorities.[29]

As for Jubal Early, there remained but one more thing to do and that was to tender his services to Governor Letcher. Before leaving Richmond to return to Franklin County in order that he might put his private affairs in shape, he wrote to the Governor offering his services with the troops in the field. Having done this, he went to Rocky Mount and awaited the call to duty.[30] He had not long to wait. He soon received a commission appointing him colonel in the Virginia militia. Upon reporting to General Robert E. Lee, he was directed to proceed to Lynchburg to take command of all Virginia volunteers mustered into service there and to organize them into regiments.[31]

CHAPTER 5

In the Nick of Time

Colonel Jubal Early took command of the Virginia volunteers at Lynchburg on May 16, 1861, succeeding Lieutenant Colonel Daniel A. Langhorne. While there, he organized and armed the following three regiments: 28th Virginia (Colonel R. T. Preston) and 24th Virginia (his own), both as infantry, and the 30th Virginia (Colonel R. C. W. Radford) as cavalry. The latter regiment subsequently became known as the 2nd Virginia Cavalry.[1] Returning to the convention at Richmond, he signed the secession ordinance on June 14 and then rejoined his regiment, which had been transferred to Manassas. Evidence that his presence was needed is afforded by letters which he received from friends informing him that his troops were very anxious for him to resume command. His acting successor, Lieutenant Colonel Peter Hairston, was making himself unpopular with the soldiers, according to one report.[2]

After returning to his troops at Manassas, Early soon received charge of a brigade consisting of the 7th and 24th Virginia regiments, as well as the 7th Louisiana. His commanding officer was Brigadier General Gustave Toutant Beauregard, the hero of Fort Sumter.

After preliminary skirmishing on July 18 at Blackburn's Ford, Early's brigade awaited the main attack of the enemy, which subsequently became known as the First Battle of Bull Run. A Federal force led by Major General Irvin McDowell, a former classmate of Beauregard at West Point, had left the defenses of Washington to march against the Confederates. Neither McDowell nor his superior at Washington, Lieutenant General Winfield Scott, felt that the Federal troops were sufficiently trained for an offensive campaign, but the Northern newspapers and public demanded that the "on to Richmond" slogan be made a reality. Then, too, there was the fear that the three-months volunteers would finish their term of enlistment before accomplishing anything. Hence it was desirable to use them as soon as possible.

38

As a matter of fact, one of the Federal regiments and a battery claimed their discharge on the very day of the Battle of Bull Run and "marched to the rear to the sound of the enemy's cannon."[3]

Prior to the first battle of Bull Run, a strong Confederate army had been sent to Winchester, in the lower Shenandoah Valley. The commander of this force was General Joseph E. Johnston, who was confronted by a somewhat larger Federal force under Brigadier General Robert Patterson. Orders from Richmond, where President Jefferson Davis was trying to direct the armies in the field, written on July 17, suggested that Johnston join forces with Beauregard at Manassas. Leaving militia to guard Winchester, Johnston gave Patterson the slip, marched to Piedmont Station on the Manassas Gap Railroad, and embarked on trains for Manassas. This movement had been so completely masked by the cavalry of Colonel J. E. B. Stuart that it was not suspected by Patterson until the 20th. By the afternoon of that day Johnston had joined Beauregard with the bulk of his army, which included a brigade led by Brigadier General T. J. Jackson as well as some Georgia regiments.[4]

Although Johnston was Beauregard's senior in rank, he recognized the fact that his subordinate was more familiar with the local situation at Manassas and he, therefore, approved Beauregard's plan of attack. By directing the latter to undertake its execution, Johnston, in effect, waived the seniority of command.

On July 21 Beauregard's ambitious plans for attacking McDowell on the Federal left flank were disrupted by his opponents who seized the initiative on the Confederate left, where he was weakest. After shifting some reinforcements to his left, he still planned to go ahead with the offensive on his right. However, upon being informed that the enemy's right flank had crossed Bull Run in force, he shifted additional troops to his left. If the Federals succeeded in bringing an overwhelming force against the Confederate left, they might turn Beauregard's flank, double it up, seize Manassas Junction, and cut off Johnston's army from its line of supply.[5]

Not suspecting that the Federal attack on his left along the Warrenton turnpike might turn his flank, Beauregard issued orders for the left of his line to hold its position at Stone Bridge. He then directed the Confederate center and right to advance, cross Bull Run, and attack the Federal left and rear at Centreville. The order to Brigadier General Richard S. Ewell, whose brigade was to lead the Confederate advance on Centreville, mis-

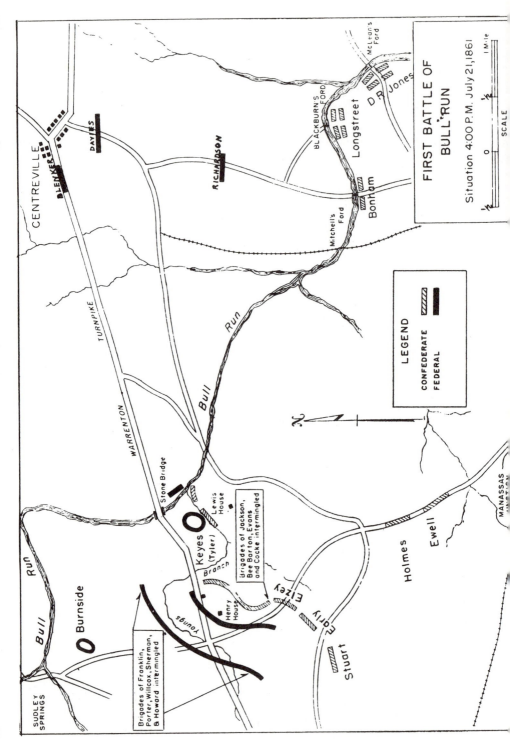

FIRST BATTLE OF BULL RUN

Situation 4:00 P.M. July 21, 1861

SCALE

1 Mile

LEGEND

CONFEDERATE

FEDERAL

McLean's Ford

BLACKBURN'S FORD

D R Jones

Longstreet

Bonham

Mitchell's Ford

CENTREVILLE

BLENKER

DAVIES

RICHARDSON

TURNPIKE

Bull Run

WARRENTON

Stone Bridge

Lewis House

Brigades of Jackson, Bee Barton, Evans and Cocke intermingled

Keyes (Tyler)

Branch

Henry House

Youngs

Elzey

Early

Stuart

Holmes

Ewell

MANASSAS JUNCTION

Burnside

Bull Run

SUDLEY SPRINGS

Brigades of Franklin, Porter, Wilcox, Sherman, & Howard intermingled

40

carried. Since this brigade was to head the movement, none of the others advanced.

By half-past ten Beauregard received word that his center and right had not advanced. Although the firing was becoming more audible on his left, he still did not suspect that he was being outflanked. Fearing that Federal progress on this side would hinder the proposed Confederate attack, Beauregard ordered the brigades of Brigadier Generals D. R. Jones, James Longstreet, and Richard Ewell to make a strong demonstration all along their front on the other side of Bull Run. He also directed the brigades of Brigadier General T. H. Holmes and Colonel Jubal A. Early, with some other regiments, to reinforce the Confederate left. He and Johnston then set out for the spot where the heaviest fighting seemed to be taking place.

Colonel N. G. Evans, who had been guarding the Confederate position at Stone Bridge on the left flank, received word from Captain E. Porter Alexander that Federals were crossing Bull Run beyond his flank. Evans did not wait for orders but notified Colonel Philip St. George Cocke, on his right, that he would move upstream to engage the enemy. Learning that Evans was being attacked by an overwhelming force, Brigadier General Barnard E. Bee took his two regiments and two from Colonel Francis S. Bartow's force and marched to Evans' support. Later these Confederate defenders were joined by Colonel Wade Hampton's 600 South Carolinians. Vigorous prosecution of the Federal attack forced the troops of Evans, Bee, Bartow, and Hampton to withdraw to the position known as Henry House Hill. As they were retiring, they had been reinforced by the brigade of Brigadier General Thomas J. Jackson.[6] It was while Bee was trying to reform his broken line that he referred to Jackson's brigade standing "like a stone wall." Only the arrival of Jackson, the spirited fighting of the Southern infantrymen, and the accurate fire of artillerymen saved the Confederate army from disaster.

Beauregard's position was rapidly becoming more serious. Johnston had left him to go to the Lewis House, where he would be able to hurry forward reinforcements. Colonel C. F. Fisher's 6th North Carolina regiment arrived and took position on the extreme left. When some of the North Carolinians joined others in falling back, one of their chaplains who temporarily headed a regiment rallied them. In referring to this incident later on, the chaplain, a Scotch Presbyterian, remarked that he hoped the Lord would forgive him, but he had to swear once or twice at the boys to make them come back.[7]

Other troops came up. Brigadier General E. Kirby Smith's brigade from Johnston's Army of the Shenandoah arrived and although its commander was wounded as soon as he came within range, it gave a good account of itself under the leadership of Colonel Arnold Elzey, one of Jubal Early's West Point classmates. As the enemy was still extending his lines in an outflanking attempt, another Confederate brigade was needed to fall in on the extreme left.

While Beauregard continued his efforts to bring up reinforcements to prevent the Federals from outflanking his left side of the line, it will be interesting to note the part which the brigade of Colonel Jubal A. Early was playing in the drama then being enacted.

At the beginning of the battle Early's brigade was held in reserve, in about the center of the Confederate line but to the rear, so he could support Generals Longstreet or Jones if necessary. Receiving Longstreet's request for troops, Early obliged by sending them to Blackburn's Ford. Longstreet then ordered Early to cross Bull Run at McLean's Ford with his remaining regiments. Before this maneuver could be completed, Early received word that Beauregard had ordered all Confederates on the north side of Bull Run to recross to the south side. This command, of course, included Longstreet's troops also. Early reformed his brigade south of the stream and remained in that vicinity until about noon, when he received orders to report to Beauregard.

Unfortunately Beauregard did not remain at a central headquarters, and Early encountered considerable difficulty locating him. The commander's note did not reveal where he wanted his subordinate to go. However, since Early knew that Beauregard had originally been located near Mitchell's Ford, to the west, he moved his brigade in that direction. Receiving word that Beauregard's headquarters would be located at the Lewis House, still farther west, Early headed for that objective.[8]

About three o'clock in the afternoon Early reached the vicinity of the Lewis House but did not find Beauregard. Instead he encountered a stream of stragglers, who brought news from the battlefront on the Confederate left. Stating that everything was lost and that it was useless for the brigade to go on, the discouraged soldiers tried to dissuade the officers from leading their men toward almost certain failure. Early's efforts to rally some of these stragglers failed, for the most part, as he was able to persuade only one of them to continue fighting.

Upon learning that the elusive Beauregard had gone to the

front, Early sought Johnston, who was in that vicinity. The latter directed him to take position on the extreme left of the Confederate line and then attack the Federals. While the two officers were talking, more stragglers appeared. Upon receiving Johnston's command to use bayonets to compel these Confederates to re-enter the fray, Early passed the order on to Colonel James L. Kemper. However, Early soon realized the futility of trying to make these cowards fight when there was no fight left in them and consequently ordered Kemper to move on to the front.[9]

Meanwhile McDowell had been pressing the Federal attack on the Confederate left flank. He determined to keep the initial advantage he had gained and to assault the enemy on the Henry House Hill. Although he had allowed Colonel Ambrose E. Burnside to withdraw his brigade on the plea of fatigue, he still had available for the attack the brigades of Brigadier Generals Andrew Porter, O. B. Willcox, W. B. Franklin, and William T. Sherman. In addition, he had a squadron of regular cavalry and four batteries of artillery. Sherman's brigade of Brigadier General Daniel Tyler's division had already crossed Bull Run by a ford a mile or more above the Stone Bridge and had forced the Confederates to flee in confusion across Young's Branch. Tyler, with the brigade of Brigadier General Erasmus Keyes, crossed Bull Run at the same ford but after a short advance against the enemy, he "marched down Young's Branch, out of sight of the enemy, and took no further part in the engagement."[10]

Advancing across the valley of Young's Branch, the Federal right flank moved up the hill toward the Henry House. When it encountered fire from the Confederates, it pushed out beyond the dwelling. McDowell sent forward the batteries of Captains James B. Ricketts and Charles Griffin, which were planted near the Henry House. Although these batteries were supported by the 11th (Fire Zouaves) and 14th (Brooklyn) New York regiments of infantry, a charge by Confederate cavalry under Stuart drove off the infantry. At the same time the 33rd Virginia infantry came into sight. Griffin was about to meet it with a charge of canister when Major William F. Barry, the chief of artillery, convinced him that the approaching soldiers were Federals sent by Brigadier General S. P. Heintzelman to support the battery. The true identity of the regiment was revealed when it opened fire at close range. The resulting damage caused the loss of most of the batteries, although Federal reinforcements recovered them and drove the 33rd Virginia regiment back.[11]

Fighting continued on this part of the battlefield. The two

Federal batteries were captured and recaptured. About three o'clock the Unionists were strengthened by the arrival of the brigade of Colonel O. O. Howard. They were extending their lines in another effort to outflank the opposing Confederates. After Beauregard had committed Kirby Smith's brigade, he realized that he needed still another one to prevent his flank from being rolled up. Looking anxiously toward the southwest, the Confederate general saw a marching column. While trying to establish the identity of these soldiers, he received a dispatch from the signal corps informing him that a large force was approaching from the very direction toward which he had been looking. The signalmen believed these were Federal troops of Patterson's Army in the Valley, which had finally come to reinforce McDowell at Manassas.

Despondently Beauregard turned his glass toward the marching troops. At their head was their flag, but in the absence of a strong breeze one could not tell whether it was the Stars and Stripes or the Stars and Bars. Beauregard had determined to pull in his left flank and retreat if the unknown troops proved to be Federals. Suddenly the suspense was ended. A breeze swept across the field and revealed the flag to be Confederate. At the head of the approaching column rode Jubal Early with his whole brigade ready to plug the hole in the Southern line.

The effect of Early's appearance on the other Confederates was electrifying. Suddenly the whole line became infused with the spirit of the newcomers. As Early's brigade deployed, Beauregard used it to rally his battle-weary soldiers. This time it was the enemy's right flank which was being enveloped. All along the line Confederates rushed forward.[12] Federal soldiers broke ranks and fled. In spite of strenuous efforts by their officers to rally them, they continued to retreat. Captain James B. Fry, McDowell's assistant adjutant general, has given us the following description of the Federal retreat:

> There was no panic, in the ordinary meaning of the word, until the retiring soldiers, guns, wagons, congressmen, and carriages were fired upon, on the road east of Bull Run. Then the panic began, and the bridge over Cub Run being rendered impassable for vehicles by a wagon that was upset upon it, utter confusion set in: pleasure-carriages, gun-carriages, and ammunition wagons which could not be put across the Run were abandoned and blocked the way, and stragglers broke and threw aside their muskets and cut horses from their harness and rode off upon them. In leaving the field the men took the same routes, in a general way, by which they had

reached it. Hence when the men of Hunter's and Heintzelman's divisions got back to Centreville, they had walked about
25 miles. That night they walked back to the Potomac, an
additional distance of 20 miles; so that these undisciplined
and unseasoned men within 36 hours walked 45 miles, besides fighting from about 10 A. M. until 4 P. M. on a hot and
dusty day in July.[13]

The battle had been won and there remained the important
decision whether or not there would be any pursuit of the disorganized and demoralized Federals. Stuart's cavalry pursued
by the Sudley Springs road and Colonel R. C. W. Radford's
squadron by the Warrenton turnpike, but these cavalry forces
were not strong enough to do much good. Beauregard might have
used the brigades of Brigadier Generals T. H. Holmes and Richard
S. Ewell, but when he received a report that a large Federal force
was moving against his depot at Manassas, he sent these troops
in that direction. Later the report was discovered to be false.
There were still other fresh Confederate troops available for the
pursuit. Longstreet had four regiments and Brigadier General M.
L. Bonham had three which had not fired a shot. Between the
hours of five and six these generals were ordered to advance upon
Centreville so that they could cut off the Federal retreat by way
of the Stone Bridge. Time was lost when Bonham asserted his
seniority of rank and marched his regiments ahead of Longstreet's.
Meeting with some enemy resistance and becoming apprehensive
of an attack made after sundown, Bonham gave orders to withdraw to the south side of Bull Run. Longstreet reluctantly followed, and the opportunity to achieve the utmost from the
Confederate victory was lost. Not until July, 1864 was a Confederate army, under the command of Jubal Early, able to get
so close to Washington.

Meanwhile Early's infantry brigade, with the 19th Virginia
in support, had attempted to pursue the fleeing Federals. When
the Confederates moved forward into the valley of Young's
Branch, they lost sight of the enemy and were unable to establish
contact. They continued advancing until they found themselves
on the same ground on which Evans had fought so vigorously
that morning. Still not seeing any Federals and having moved
into unknown territory, Early decided to halt. He was also
influenced by the fact that his men had been marching and fighting since morning and consequently were very tired. Noticing
President Jefferson Davis on the battlefield, Early informed him
of the general condition of things, stated that he was without
orders from his superior officers, and asked for instructions. The

President suggested that he form his men in line near where he was and then await orders. There Early's brigade spent the night and part of the next day.[14]

After the battle Early's brigade remained in the Bull Run vicinity until the latter part of August when it was ordered to move toward Fairfax Station. With the exception of a few skirmishes with the enemy, it did no important fighting. Consequently it passed the winter in this region in a relative state of inactivity. Meanwhile Early received notice of his promotion to brigadier general, with his new rank dating July 21. His brigade at this time consisted of the 24th Virginia regiment, the 5th North Carolina State Troops led by Colonel Duncan K. McRae, and the 23rd North Carolina regiment. The latter organization was led by Colonel John Hoke. Later Early's brigade was augmented by the addition of a company of cavalry led by Captain W. W. Thornton and a battery of artillery led by a Captain Holman.[15]

After the first battle of Bull Run there was no more important fighting in Virginia during the remainder of the year 1861. The three-months Federal volunteers went home, and the three-months chapter of the war ended. McDowell was relieved of command and was replaced by Major General George B. McClellan, a West Point graduate who had been earning military laurels in western Virginia. The new Federal commander realized that the task of coercing the Southern Confederacy was too great to be accomplished with only 75,000 volunteers enlisted for three months. He proceeded to reorganize the defeated army of McDowell and to give it such thorough training that it would be well prepared for the tremendous task ahead. What he did with this force is told by the events occurring in 1862.

CHAPTER 6

On the Peninsula

The Peninsula campaign of 1862 reflected the character of Major General George B. McClellan, the Federal commander, in the same manner in which its counterpart, the Shenandoah Valley campaign, bore the stamp of its Confederate leader, Major General Stonewall Jackson. Because Jubal Early's brigade did not serve under Jackson in winning laurels in the Valley, that part of the military picture will not be included in this volume. Instead, Early's part in the defense of Richmond from the east will be discussed.

The selection of George B. McClellan to replace the discredited McDowell after the first battle of Bull Run was one that was popular with the Northern people, the newspaper press, and the Federal army. Up to this time McClellan had been successful in every major undertaking he had tried. In the West Point class of 1846 in which Stonewall Jackson was graduated seventeenth and George E. Pickett fifty-ninth, McClellan had ranked second. Entering the Corps of Engineers in the United States army, he served with distinction under General Winfield Scott in the War with Mexico. When the Crimean War broke out in Europe in 1854, he was selected to be one of the United States Government's observers. Shortly afterwards he was appointed a captain in the 4th United States Cavalry. Resigning from military service, he entered private business and upon the outbreak of the Civil War had become a railroad president.[1] His military operations in western Virginia in 1861 are usually credited with saving that section for the Union.

Though the first battle of Bull Run was a Confederate victory, it was indecisive and produced no great gain militarily for the South. According to Joseph E. Johnston, the Confederate army was "more disorganized by victory than that of the United States by defeat."[2] The failure of Confederate leaders to pursue McDowell and thus reap the full benefits of their victory resulted in controversies full of charges and counter-charges. The success of

47

the South in this first major engagement encouraged the belief
that the war was practically over and hence resulted in a relaxation of the military effort.

On the other hand, the Northern reverse at Bull Run convinced the Federal officials of the magnitude of the task before
them. They realized the impossibility of coercing the Confederacy
without a tremendous struggle, and they determined to take the
necessary steps to assure victory. The House of Representatives
voted for the enlistment of 500,000 volunteers, and by the middle
of October more than 100,000 new men had enlisted in the Federal
army in and around Washington.

Upon the retirement of General Winfield Scott on November
1, 1861 McClellan became general-in-chief of the Army of the
United States. Even before this date he had addressed himself
to the two great tasks for which he was especially fitted, that of
erecting adequate defenses for the protection of Washington and
of drilling and organizing the new levies into an effective fighting
force. He showed himself a brilliant organizer and the Army of
the Potomac, which he created, reflected his character throughout the entire war. Unfortunately McClellan's preoccupation
with his task of drilling and equipping an army delayed a forward
movement until the spring of 1862, by which time he had lost
some of his original popularity in the North. His inactivity even
made President Lincoln wonder about his new choice of commander.[3]

McClellan's first plan for winning the war was to move
against Johnston's army at Centreville. Although he outnumbered
Johnston more than two to one, he was deceived by the report
of his own secret-service department into believing that Johnston's
army was twice its real size. Instead of depending upon his
cavalry to obtain information about the enemy, McClellan relied
upon Pinkerton detectives, which were usually a poor substitute.
This characteristic of exaggerating the strength of the enemy
while minimizing his own strength was to make McClellan cautious
almost to the point of timidity. He never wanted to attack without
a superiority which would give an absolute assurance of victory.
Since he was never satisfied that he had this superiority, he usually failed on the offense, though he was admirable on the defense.
In spite of Lincoln's approval of the proposal to move against
Johnston at Centreville, McClellan changed his plans and decided
to make Richmond his objective.

The new Federal course was for McClellan to remove his
army by water to Urbanna on the lower Rappahannock River and

A Confederate Officer

then make an overland dash of fifty miles to capture Richmond. The Union officer thought he could complete this movement secretly and get to the Confederate capital before Johnston could move to its protection. As Washington was well fortified by this time and McClellan proposed leaving a small force to defend it, he did not believe the Federal capital to be in danger. In fact, he did not think Johnston would dare attack Washington while Richmond was threatened. However, this plan came to naught because of Lincoln's concern for the safety of Washington. Neither the President nor his advisers favored any proposal which would remove the main Federal army from between the principal Confederate force and the capital of the Union.[4] This obsession which Lincoln and his advisers had for the safety of their capital was time after time to handicap the operation of Federal armies in the field. Realizing this, Confederate generals made their plans accordingly.

The advent of winter with its accompanying bad roads delayed the expedition against Richmond. While the Federal army remained in its camp at Washington, the Northern people became more and more impatient. With their newspapers demanding an advance and Lincoln having difficulty prodding McClellan to action, the President in January, 1862 issued the first of his famous "war orders." This directed that the Federal army should advance against Johnston's Confederates on or before February 22—Washington's birthday. This date was probably chosen for sentimental reasons. Although McClellan now outnumbered Johnston three to one, he paid no attention whatsoever to the President's order. Nor could two other "war orders" induce McClellan to move until he was ready. When that time came, he ignored Lincoln's hopes for a direct movement against the enemy and instead decided upon an oblique advance to Richmond by way of the Peninsula between the James and York rivers. Accordingly, McClellan transferred the Union army by water to Fort Monroe, which was to be the first base of operations. This fortress was then in possession of a Federal garrison. By May 1 McClellan's army of 112,000 effectives was safely on the Peninsula.[5]

As soon as McClellan moved into the field, Lincoln issued an order which relieved him of his position as commander of all the Union armies and restricted his control to the Army of the Potomac. The pressure of McClellan's opponents, as well as the reorganization of the army under corps commanders, was responsible for this move by the President. Lincoln's withholding of McDowell's corps from the peninsula army was destined to have an important effect on McClellan's entire campaign against Richmond. The President's exasperation with his slow-moving commander of the Army of the Potomac was apparently increasing, judging from the following communication:

Executive Mansion
Washington, May 1, 1862

Major-General McClellan:
Your call for Parrott guns from Washington alarms me, chiefly because it argues indefinite procrastination. Is anything to be done?

A. Lincoln[6]

As soon as the Confederate authorities learned of McClellan's plan to attack Richmond from the east, President Davis, in consultation with Joseph E. Johnston, ordered the Southern general to march his army to the Peninsula to join the defending forces of Major General John B. Magruder. Magruder had taken up position at Yorktown, about twenty-five miles up the Peninsula. Johnston's army arrived there a few days after McClellan had begun to move against the Confederate defenses. As Johnston was the ranking officer, he assumed command.

McClellan's plan was to move up the Peninsula and try to seize a point between Yorktown and Williamsburg, where he might be able to cut off the retreat of the Yorktown garrison and prevent the arrival of reinforcements.[7] The advance, which began on April 4 in two columns, was stopped the following day by the Confederate works in front of Yorktown and the Warwick River. Magruder had caused several dams to be erected on the latter stream, which made it unfordable throughout most of its length. This natural defense line, strengthened by strategically located Confederate batteries, extended for thirteen miles entirely across the Peninsula. Concluding that it could not be carried by assault, the Federal commander decided on siege operations. After obtaining the necessary siege guns and mortars, he was ready to order the cannonade to begin when he learned that the Confederates had withdrawn from his front on May 3.

In anticipation of such a retirement from Yorktown, Magruder had constructed a strong line of defense about two miles east of Williamsburg. Fort Magruder was near the center of this line and was connected with deep creeks on either side by a string of redoubts. The attempt of the Confederate rearguard under Major General James Longstreet to hold this line so that the main army could get away brought on the engagement at Williamsburg on May 5.

In the subsequent fighting in front of Williamsburg the Federals attacked so vigorously with skirmishers and artillery that Longstreet determined to reinforce the troops of Brigadier General Richard H. Anderson, which were receiving the brunt of the assault. Accordingly, he ordered Brigadier Generals Ambrose P. Hill and Cadmus M. Wilcox to take their brigades back to Fort Magruder. As the fighting became more general, the Southern leader sent for his reserves, the brigades of Brigadier Generals R. E. Colston and George E. Pickett. Anderson used these reserve brigades to strengthen his right.[8]

Toward the end of the afternoon the Federals seized a redoubt on the left of the Confederate line which the defenders had failed to occupy. Quickly bringing up guns, the bluecoats began to pour artillery fire into Fort Magruder. Realizing this danger, Longstreet requested Major General Daniel H. Hill to send a brigade from the latter's division. It was Longstreet's intention to use these reinforcements to strengthen his left wing if necessary.

The brigade detached from Hill's division was that led by Brigadier General Jubal A. Early. It consisted of Early's original command, the 24th Virginia regiment, which had performed such gallant service at Bull Run, and three inexperienced regiments, the 5th and 23rd North Carolina and 38th Virginia. In addition the 2nd Florida Infantry and 2nd Mississippi battalion were operating temporarily with Early. This brigade had been in the rear of the main Confederate army retreating from Williamsburg toward Richmond and had spent the night of May 4 about two miles west of that town. Because provisions had not been received and the men had consumed the rations brought from Yorktown, Early's troops were hungry. A rainy night increased their discomfort. Expecting to resume the retreat toward Richmond early on the morning of May 5, they had been delayed by the bad condition of the roads. Thus, they were ready to go when word came from Hill to move, although this time it was over the ground they had traversed the preceding day.[9]

After reporting to Longstreet, Early was directed to move toward Fort Magruder, where he expected to find Anderson. He sent his brother and aide, Lieutenant Samuel H. Early, to carry advance word of his approach. Not finding Anderson at the fort, Old Jube reported to Brigadier General J. E. B. Stuart, who was in charge there. Longstreet then appeared and told Early to post his brigade to the left and rear of Fort Magruder and then await orders. Before Early could carry out these commands, he complied with another Longstreet request that he send two regiments to strengthen the Confederate right. In doing this, Early relieved himself of the Mississippi battalion and the Florida regiment. Then he took the four remaining regiments to the position assigned him, which was on a ridge in a wheat field. Directly in front from 200 to 300 yards away were some woods which obscured the enemy. However, artillery fire from that direction told Early that Federals were not far away.

Although anxious to attack the Federal battery, Early did nothing until he had talked the matter over with his divisional commander, D. H. Hill. The latter agreed with Old Jube that an attack on the rear of the Federal position afforded the best chance of success. Approval of Longstreet and Johnston was obtained. Ordering Brigadier General G. J. Rains to form his brigade in the rear of Early's men, Hill posted some field-pieces to cover the Confederate retreat in case their attack failed. The advance was to be made in a single line on brigade front and was to be from north to south. Farthest to the east, on the left was placed the 24th Virginia, while on its right was the 38th Virginia regiment. Next to the latter was placed the 23rd North Carolina, while on the extreme Confederate right was located the 5th North Carolina regiment. Hill, a North Carolinian, took charge of the two Carolina regiments, while Early led the Virginians. Because Old Jube thought his old brigade, the 24th Virginia, would come in contact with the enemy first, he accompanied it. According to one prominent authority, there was a rivalry between Hill and Early in which each desired the troops under his command to capture the Federal guns.[10]

When Early saw Hill's North Carolinians advancing on his right, he ordered his Virginians to do likewise. The 24th Virginia responded with alacrity and marched quickly across the wheat field into the woods, but the 38th was somewhat slower getting started. This tardiness may have been due to its lack of experience. At any rate Early found it necessary to order the 38th to double-quick until it caught up with the other regiments.[11] However, by the time it was brought up the 24th was so far ahead that contact with it was lost. When Hill's Carolinians found their advance slowed up by the thick underbrush, the division commander halted them until he could learn Early's position.

Without waiting to see whether or not the troops on his right were keeping pace with him, Old Jube shouted, "Follow me," put his spurs to his horse, and set out across the open field in front.

Old Jube in 1862

54

The 24th Virginia made directly for the Federal battery which had been its initial objective. In spite of heavy enemy fire, Early forced the Federals to withdraw into the nearest redoubt and the woods behind. While attempting pursuit, Early received a severe wound in the shoulder from a Minié ball. He was hit twice. At about the same time his horse was shot through both eyes. He continued to urge his men forward and sent for the other regiments to come to the aid of the 24th since it was receiving the brunt of the Federal fire. The 5th North Carolina alone did so but was so far to the right that it required some time to come up. By this time Early was suffering so much from his wounds and was feeling so faint from loss of blood that he had to retire to one of the redoubts held by his side.[12]

The wounded general then left the field and entered the hospital at Williamsburg. An examination revealed that he had been struck twice but that one of the wounds was a mere scratch. The other was more serious. The ball had struck him near the place where the arm joins the shoulder and had run around his back to the opposite shoulder blade. Early later believed that if the ball had not been turned when it encountered a bone, he would have been killed. The force with which he was struck is revealed by the fact that after the ball was removed from his body, it was found to have been flattened out. Although the wound was very painful at the time Early was hit, there resulted no serious fracture. Nevertheless it removed the pugnacious and daring brigade commander from duty in the field for several months.[13]

After leaving Williamsburg, he reached the James River near Charles City Courthouse, where he obtained transportation on a steamer to Richmond. He arrived at the Confederate capital on the 8th, after which he went to Lynchburg. Recovering sufficiently to travel on horseback, Early rode to Franklin County, there to remain until he would be able to resume active duty in the field.[14]

Meanwhile, back on the battlefield Colonel D. K. McRae had succeeded to the command of Early's brigade when his senior was wounded. McRae had been in charge of the 5th North Carolina regiment, which, it will be recalled, had advanced to the support of the 24th Virginia. These North Carolinians had been on the extreme right of Early's command when it attempted to advance in brigade front. Before the 5th North Carolina could form a continuous line with the 24th Virginia, it had to go a long distance. This was because the intervening regiments of the brigade, the

23rd North Carolina and 28th Virginia, had not yet come out of the woods. This space which normally would have been filled by two regiments was now the front of the 5th North Carolina.

After vainly trying to get his two missing regiments into line, General Hill returned to the field where his other troops were engaging the enemy. The 24th Virginia and 5th North Carolina were still advancing toward the Federal line but were losing men fast. It was quite obvious that they would have to be reinforced in order to sustain the attack. Confusion in the bringing up of additional troops arising mainly from lack of drill and discipline caused Hill to order the brigade to withdraw. The 24th Virginia retired into the woods on its left, but the 5th North Carolina had to recross the field under heavy fire. Consequently, this regiment suffered severely.[15]

Early's brigade sustained about 600 casualties in this engagement, which represented about 38 per cent of the entire Confederate losses for the day's fighting. The attack was one of the most gallant of the entire war, and, like many of the others, failed to accomplish enough to compensate for the relatively heavy losses. According to the official report of Brigadier General Winfield S. Hancock, who commanded the defending Federal brigade, his troops were retiring because of lack of reinforcements when Early's brigade attacked.[16] On the entire battlefield, the other Confederate forces had repulsed Federal attacks on their center and right. Only a small part of Johnston's entire army participated in the Battle of Williamsburg. Since the Confederates desired to hold back the enemy until they could move their wagons over the almost impassable roads in the retreat to Richmond, the Southerners may be said to have accomplished their objective. Because of a lack of transportation, some of their wounded had to be left in Williamsburg, but the main army made good its escape and took position in the defenses of the Confederate capital.[17]

CHAPTER 7

In Defense of Richmond

It is not the purpose of this volume to give a detailed account of all the important battles of the Civil War but only to deal with those which concern Jubal A. Early. Since he was wounded in the fighting at Williamsburg on May 5 and did not return to field duty until June 29, he missed some of the engagements in the defense of Richmond.

As the Confederates retired up the Peninsula toward Richmond, they evacuated Norfolk and its important navy yard. They also had to destroy the valuable ironclad "Merrimac," renamed the "Virginia," for, in spite of its success against the Federal fleet in the Battle of Hampton Roads, it was in no condition to escape by putting to sea. Unfortunately for the South, it drew too much water to enable it to proceed very far up the James River.

Major General George B. McClellan established his base and headquarters at White House Landing on the Pamunkey River. The White House was the property of General Robert E. Lee's son, W. H. F. Lee, more familiarly known as "Rooney." As usual, McClellan planned to advance cautiously and asked for reinforcements. Reporting only 80,000 effectives available for the capture of Richmond, he desired the cooperation of Washington authorities and especially the concentration under his command of all available Federal forces in Virginia. Unfortunately this cooperation was lacking. President Lincoln and Secretary of War Stanton placed their knowledge of military strategy ahead of that of their commander on the Peninsula. With their usual concern for the defense of Washington, they insisted that McDowell's corps of 40,000 be kept near Fredericksburg. In vain could McClellan argue that Washington was virtually being defended by his army on the Peninsula and that he needed the support of McDowell in an all-out offensive against Richmond.[1] Actually on three distinct occasions McDowell was ordered to join McClellan, and each time the orders were rescinded before they could be obeyed because of some new activity on the part of Major General Thomas J. Jackson.[2]

When McClellan was overruled, the ensuing contest was one which pitted Lincoln and Stanton against two of the ablest soldiers America has ever produced—Lee and Jackson. Using brains, audacity, and celerity of movement, these two Southern generals made the most of their interior lines and McClellan's caution. To Jackson was given the task of operating in the Shenandoah Valley so as to threaten Washington by way of Harpers Ferry. With a force estimated to number no more than 16,000 he successfully opposed Federal armies numbering collectively 45,000. His strategy was to fall upon each of his Union opponents singly, create fears for the safety of Washington, and thus prevent the sending of reinforcements to McClellan.[3] After having succeeded in this, he was secretly withdrawn from the Valley and used to reinforce Lee before Richmond. At the same time nearly half of the Union army was standing by at various places to be ready for Jackson's next move in the Valley.

By June, 1862 McClellan had accumulated about 105,000 men on the Peninsula. In addition, there were about 40,000 elsewhere in Virginia. To oppose this formidable army the Confederates had about 85,000 troops. The first great battle for the Confederate capital was the engagement at Seven Pines (Fair Oaks), on May 31-June 1. Johnston attacked McClellan's forces astride the Chickahominy River but in the bloody encounter which followed was repulsed and driven toward Richmond. In addition, he was severely wounded. Because he was unable to remain in command, he was replaced by General Robert E. Lee, who had been acting as President Davis' military adviser. In spite of many mistakes which Davis made in regard to military appointments, his choice of Lee for this important command was destined to be one which silenced the President's noisiest critics.

After Jackson had joined Lee for the defense of Richmond there began the series of engagements known as the Seven Days' Battles from June 25 to July 1. Individually these conflicts were known as the battles of Mechanicsville, Gaines' Mill, Savage Station, Frayser's Farm, and Malvern Hill. During the course of this fighting McClellan changed his base from the White House on the Pamunkey to Harrison's Landing on the James. While this change was being made, the White House mansion was burned. The last of the Seven Days' Battles, that at Malvern Hill on July 1 in which Lee's army suffered a bloody repulse, was the only one in which Jubal A. Early participated.[4]

One can imagine the impatience with which Old Jube watched his wound slowly heal. Whatever his critics had to say about him later on—and they had plenty to say—they never accused him of not wanting to be in the midst of hostilities. The old soldier was a born fighter and was rarely afraid of attack. His part in the Battle of Williamsburg has been called reckless and perhaps foolhardy by some, but it illustrates his aggressive nature. Perhaps a better example of his pugnacity is given in an anecdote told by Brigadier General A. R. Lawton.

According to the account, Stonewall Jackson once called his generals to a council of war which was held in a nearby farmhouse. Early came to the meeting and took his seat in a corner. With his head leaning down on his breast, he was soon sound asleep. Jackson opened the council by explaining the position of the enemy, after which he said: "We can take a certain road to the left and strike them in their right flank; or we can take this road to the right and hit them in their left flank; or, by going a more circuitous route, we could strike them in the rear or avoid a conflict altogether. Now, gentlemen, I have called you together to get your opinion as to what is best to be done under the circumstances."

Since Early was the ranking general present with the exception of Jackson, someone suggested that he be heard from first. This caused the officers to look toward Old Jube, who was still fast asleep and snoring. General Lawton then punched Early with his elbow, saying: "General! General! General Jackson wants to know what we must do."

Arousing from his slumber, Old Jube lifted his head, rubbed his hand across his face, and replied, "Do? Why fight 'em! Fight 'em!"[5]

Finally, on June 26, General Early was released from the hospital at Lynchburg.[6] Although still incapacitated to the extent that he could not mount his horse without assistance, he reported for duty with Lee's army on June 28. He arrived at the Confederate chieftain's headquarters at Gaines' house, north of the Chickahominy, that evening, but as it was too late to see him then, Early waited until the next day. During his absence from the Army of Northern Virginia, as Lee's force was called, a reorganization of the divisions and brigades had taken place. Consequently Early's old brigade had been broken up, and the regiments assigned to other brigadier generals. Lee informed Early that no new arrangement could be made in the presence of the enemy and advised him to return to Richmond and await a vacancy.[7]

Old Jube had no intention of waiting long. The day after he returned to Richmond he called on the Secretary of War, George W. Randolph. The latter gave him a letter to Lee, suggesting that he be assigned to the temporary command of the brigade of Brigadier General Arnold Elzey of Ewell's division. Elzey had been severely wounded. On the first of July this was done and Old Jube found himself in command of a brigade once more, this time attached to the command of Stonewall Jackson. Ewell's division was in the rear of Jackson's column. Early's new brigade consisted of the remnants of seven regiments, namely: the 13th Virginia, 25th Virginia, 31st Virginia, 44th Virginia, 52nd Virginia, 58th Virginia, and the 12th Georgia regiments. The whole brigade numbered 1,052 officers and men.[8]

The day that Early received his new command was the day on which the Battle of Malvern Hill was fought. McClellan had retreated to this naturally strong position and had placed his artillery in position to withstand any assault Lee would make. With one flank protected by Western Run and the other by Turkey Run, as well as Federal gunboats on the James, McClellan's position was practically impregnable. He placed his artillery on a commanding plateau where it would be able to sweep all approaches. An open space, 300 to 400 yards wide, was immediately in front of the Federal line, beyond which was wooded ground traversed by a swamp.

Lee's plan was to mass his artillery in positions from which it would be able to bring heavy fire upon the Union lines. This was to be followed by charging columns of infantry. Unfortunately for the Southern side, because of defects of the artillery organization, inefficiency of the staff, ignorance of the ground, and general confusion, the artillery attack failed. Most of the division batteries came into action separately and were quickly put out of action by the concentrated fire of the Federal guns on Malvern Hill. Not a single shot was fired by the Confederate reserve artillery, which consisted of four battalions containing the best guns.[9] According to Major General D. H. Hill, some idea of the power of the Federal rifled pieces may be obtained from the fact that on one occasion he observed a Confederate soldier seated comfortably behind a very large tree, considering himself safe. Shortly afterwards a shell passed entirely through the huge tree and took off the soldier's head.[10]

In spite of the failure of the Confederate artillery, the infantry

Confederate Battery Defending Richmond

was ordered to attack. The troops of General D. H. Hill assaulted the center of the Union line but were repulsed with tremendous losses. Although Jackson ordered two divisions to Hill's assistance, they arrived too late. An attack on the Union left by Major General Benjamin Huger, supported by Major General John B. Magruder, likewise was repulsed with heavy loss. Other Confederate attempts to dislodge the Federals met with the same results.

Early's brigade remained in the rear until it was ordered to the support of D. H. Hill . Accompanied by Major General Richard S. Ewell, or "Old Bald Head" as his men called Ewell, Early moved through the woods in the rear of Hill's position. Federal artillery shells were constantly bursting in the trees above. Ewell made a reconnaissance, after which he directed Lieutenant Colonel J. H. Skinner of the 52nd Virginia regiment to lead Early's brigade to a certain position. At the same time the division commander told Old Jube to accompany him by another route. In the subsequent confusion Early became separated from most of his regiments. By the time he had found them again, it was too late to help Hill. In fact both Hill and Magruder had retired from the battlefield. They ordered Early to hold the position he then occupied and not to advance. His men spent the night in the open field there but could not sleep because of the cries and groans of the wounded.

The next morning Early observed a small body of Confederate troops nearby, about ten or twelve in number. He rode up to the group and found that it consisted of Brigadier General Lewis A. Armistead, of Huger's division, with a few men of his brigade. When Old Jube inquired where Armistead's brigade was, the general replied, "Here are all that I know anything about except those lying out there in front."[11]

Although the failure of the Confederate assaults at Malvern Hill was disastrous, McClellan made no counter-attack. In spite of the fact that his losses in killed and wounded were only about one-third as great as the Confederate total of 5,000, the Federal commander withdrew the next day, July 2, to Harrison's Landing, where he took up a strongly fortified position. Lee advanced to the vicinity of McClellan's new position, where he became convinced of the futility of another assault. Consequently he returned to his former camp near Richmond.

McClellan's strength at the beginning of the Seven Days' Battles consisted of about 105,000 men, while Lee had from 80,000 to 90,000 effective troops. Federal losses for the same battles amounted to a total of 15,849 in killed, wounded, or missing. On the other hand, the Confederates lost 20,135 during the same time.[12]

McClellan was still a formidable opponent and was making plans to move against Richmond from the south by way of Petersburg. Thus he anticipated the plan which General Ulysses S. Grant was later to use successfully. However, he did not have an opportunity to carry them out. President Lincoln visited McClellan at his headquarters on July 9 and asked a number of questions concerning the failure to take Richmond. As a result of his interrogating numerous Federal generals, he came to the conclusion that McClellan still had an effective fighting force of 75,000 or 80,000 men and that although Confederates were only four or five miles away, the Union army was probably "safe" with the help of the navy. In spite of the fact that Lincoln's interference in preventing McDowell's corps from joining McClellan had hindered the principal Federal effort against Richmond, the President decided that he needed a new commander. Submitting to the Radical clamor, he reduced McClellan to a subordinate position. At the same time, he united the forces of Generals John C. Frémont, Irvin McDowell, and N. P. Banks and placed this combined force under the command of Major General John Pope. Simultaneously he restored the rank of general-in-chief of the Union armies and conferred this office upon General Henry W. Halleck, who established headquarters at Washington.[13]

Naturally McClellan was disappointed. Deprived of command of his army, overruled in his suggestion about taking Richmond from the south, and disgraced in the eyes of some Northerners, he could do nothing but yield to fate. The tradition grew in the North that he could easily have taken Richmond. When the war was over, Lee was asked whether this was possible. His answer was that McClellan could not have entered Richmond at this time, "that he [Lee] had taken every precaution to prevent it, . . . that it [Richmond] could not have been taken unless his own men had acted much worse than he had any reason to expect they would . . . , and that he was much stronger then than when Grant was before Richmond."[14] Lee later faced Grant with only 45,000.

Perhaps the answer why McClellan failed to take the Confederate capital is furnished in the following conversation reputed to have occurred between President Abraham Lincoln and Lieutenant General Winfield Scott:

According to the story, Lincoln once asked Scott the question:

"Why is it that you were once able to take the City of Mexico in three months with five thousand men, and we have been unable to take Richmond with one hundred thousand men?"

"I will tell you," said General Scott. "The men who took us into the City of Mexico then are the same men who are keeping us out of Richmond now."[15]

CHAPTER 8

Recommended for Promotion

Headquarters Army of Virginia
Washington, D. C., July 14, 1862

To the Officers and Soldiers of the Army of Virginia:

By special assignment of the President of the United States I have assumed the command of this army. I have spent two weeks in learning your whereabouts, your condition, and your wants, in preparing you for active operations, and in placing you in positions from which you can act promptly and to the purpose. These labors are nearly completed, and I am about to join you in the field.

Let us understand each other. I have come to you from the West, where we have always seen the backs of our enemies; from an army whose business it has been to seek the adversary and to beat him when he was found; whose policy has been attack and not defense. In but one instance has the enemy been able to place our Western armies in defensive attitude. I presume that I have been called here to pursue the same system and to lead you against the enemy. It is my purpose to do so, and that speedily. I am sure you long for an opportunity to win the distinction you are capable of achieving. That opportunity I shall endeavor to give you. Meantime I desire you to dismiss from your minds certain phrases, which I am sorry to find so much in vogue amongst you. I hear constantly of 'taking strong positions and holding them,' of 'lines of retreat,' and of 'bases of supplies.' Let us discard such ideas. The strongest position a soldier should desire to occupy is one from which he can most easily advance against the enemy. Let us study the probable lines of retreat of our opponents, and leave our own to take care of themselves. Let us look before us, and not behind. Success and glory are in the advance, disaster and shame lurk in the rear. Let us act on this understanding, and it is safe to predict that your banners shall be inscribed with many a glorious deed, and that your names will be dear to your countrymen forever.

Jno. Pope,
Major-General, Commanding.[1]

65

This was the greeting which Major General John Pope extended to his newly created "Army of Virginia" in the reorganization of the Federal armies following McClellan's failure to take Richmond. The new leader received command of the armies of Major Generals Banks, Frémont, and McDowell, which had failed so miserably in attempting to trap Stonewall Jackson in the Shenandoah Valley. Pope thus enjoyed a unity of command which had been denied his troops a few months previous. Having gained a reputation by his capture of New Madrid and Island No. 10 in the Mississippi region, he was transferred to the Virginia scene. Since McDowell, Banks, and Fremont had all three ranked him, they were not altogether pleased with the changed situation whereby they would be under Pope. Frémont's dissatisfaction was so great that he refused to serve under him and resigned. He was succeeded by Major General Franz Sigel. Altogether Pope's "Army of Virginia" numbered about 47,000.[2]

The new commander established headquarters in Washington and proceeded to make plans for carrying out the three-fold objective of the Army of Virginia. This was to protect the city of Washington from attacks coming from the direction of Richmond, to assure the safety of the Shenandoah Valley, and to operate against the enemy's communication lines in the vicinity of Charlottesville and Gordonsville. If the latter move were successful, it might draw off Confederate troops from Richmond and thus allow McClellan's Army of the Potomac to move against the capital. Accordingly Pope proceeded to assemble the widely separated parts of his army at some central position and ordered Banks and Sigel to move to the vicinity of Sperryville and Little Washington [in Va.]. At the same time he ordered the division of Brigadier General James B. Ricketts, of McDowell's corps, to advance to Warrenton. After this was accomplished, Pope instructed Banks to send his cavalry to occupy Culpeper and to send out pickets toward Gordonsville.[3]

It will be recalled that the reorganization of the Union army at this time brought Major General Henry W. Halleck from Mississippi to Washington, appointing him General-in-Chief of all the land forces in the United States. Halleck had received popular acclaim for Union successes in the West, although his subordinate in that theatre of operations, General Ulysses S. Grant, deserved most of the credit. Halleck arrived in Washington on July 23 and the next day left to confer with McClellan, who was still in charge of the Army of the Potomac with its base at Harrison's Landing on the James. Although McClellan had failed to take Richmond, he was still at the head of a powerful, well-trained army and was willing to resume active operations. Unfortunately he continued to minimize his own strength and, relying mostly on Pinkerton detectives instead of his own army intelligence, he estimated the Confederate army around Richmond to be about twice as large as it actually was. Consequently, in spite of his already sizable force, McClellan asked Halleck for 30,000 reinforcements. As large numbers of additional troops were not available, Halleck determined, against McClellan's protest, to withdraw the Army of the Potomac from the Peninsula and to unite it with Pope's Army of Virginia.[4]

On August 3, 1862 the order was issued for the withdrawal of McClellan's army. From that date on, the principal role in the ensuing campaign was destined to be played by Pope's Army of Virginia. McClellan's Army of the Potomac was relegated to a position that was distinctly secondary.

While Pope was ordering the concentration of his Army of Virginia in the vicinity of Sperryville and Little Washington and his cavalry was threatening the Virginia Central Railroad at Gordonsville, Stonewall Jackson was leaving Richmond to meet this new threat. Lee hoped that a Confederate advance against Pope, whose army, it will be recalled, was entrusted with the defense of Washington, would cause Lincoln to order McClellan's withdrawal from the Peninsula to reinforce Pope. In spite of the fact that 16,000 of McClellan's army of 90,000 were sick, and "Little Mac" would probably not assume the offensive without many reinforcements, the fact that he commanded such a large force so close to Richmond had to be considered. Since Jackson's Valley campaign earlier that year had drawn off troops that might have been used against Richmond, so likewise perhaps another advance by Jackson in the summer of 1862 would remove the menace of McClellan's large army.[5] It must be recalled that Lee was counting on Lincoln's and Stanton's fears concerning the safety of Washington to cause the demand for McClellan to unite with Pope.

Since Confederate strategy demanded protection of the Virginia Central Railroad, Jackson moved an army consisting of his own and Ewell's divisions from Richmond to Beaver Dam and Fredericks Hall. After learning that most of Pope's Unionists were north and west of Culpeper, he led his Army of the Valley on July 19 to Gordonsville. While awaiting developments at the latter place, he maintained the discipline of his troops by providing frequent drills. To reinforce him, Lee dispatched from his own army the Light Division of A. P. Hill and the Second Brigade of

Louisiana Volunteers. In the communication announcing these reinforcements, Lee said:

> . . . I want Pope to be suppressed. . . . A. P. Hill you will, I think, find a good officer, with whom you can consult, and by advising with your division commanders as to your movements much trouble will be saved you in arranging details, as they can act more intelligently. I wish to save you trouble from my increasing your command. Cache your troops as much as possible till you can strike your blow, and be prepared to return to me when done, if necessary. I will endeavor to keep General McClellan quiet till it is over, if rapidly executed. . . .[6]

Although McClellan knew Lee's army had been diminished by the detachment of Jackson, he remained inactive. It was believed at his headquarters at Harrison's Landing that Jackson's strength consisted of 60,000 to 80,000 troops and 3,000 to 4,000 cavalry.[7] This was considerably in excess of the actual figure of about 24,000 including Hill's division.

Since Jubal Early was still in charge of Elzey's old brigade of Ewell's division, he was with Jackson's army in its march toward Gordonsville. Glad to be back in the field after his enforced period of inactivity because of his wound at Williamsburg, Old Jube was fretting. His complaint, which was expressed in a letter written in camp on July 23, was that he had not been given a permanent command, in spite of the fact that almost four weeks had elapsed since he had reported for duty after being released from the hospital. He expressed regret that his old brigade had been broken up in the reorganization of the army preceding the Seven Days' Battles and its regiments assigned to officers who were junior in rank to him. Manifesting concern that the return of Elzey to field duty would find Early without any command, Old Jube wanted to know if the Confederate authorities had lost confidence in him. If so, he planned to offer his services to the State of Virginia. He concluded by stating that it almost seemed as if his having been wounded at Williamsburg was being treated as a crime.[8]

General Lee was not long replying to his complaining subordinate. His letter to Early reads in part as follows:

> . . . I regret that you consider yourself unassigned to a command. I had hoped that your present command was agreeable to you. The service is important, requiring an officer of intelligence and capacity, and I know of no one to whom the brigade could be better intrusted than yourself. I con-

sider, too, from your knowledge of the country and people, that you were peculiarly qualified for the duty, and congratulated myself that you were available. From the many changes constantly occurring in the service, arising from causes beyond my control, it is difficult for me to consider any position more permanent than another. Your present brigade, it is true, was last commanded by General Elzey, and upon his restoration to duty it may be considered proper to assign him to it. But you surely would be considered entitled to another command. . . . I can only assure you that confidence in your zeal and ability has been increased instead of diminished by your service, and that the honorable wound you received at Williamsburg in the defense of your country is viewed as a badge of distinction and claim for high consideration instead of crime, as you suppose.[9]

When Confederate spies informed Jackson at Gordonsville that only a part of Pope's army was at Culpeper, he determined to march against it and destroy it before the Federal commander would be able to bring up the remainder of his forces. Accordingly, he gave the necessary orders and the Army of the Valley left its camp near Gordonsville on August 7. Although the distance to Culpeper was only about thirty miles and the "foot cavalry" in Jackson's army had previously covered this much ground in one day, it was unequal to the task this time. Because of slow marching and confusion resulting from Jackson's failure to give clear orders to his division commanders and take them into his confidence, not much progress was made. His advance did not reach Cedar or Slaughter Mountain, seven or eight miles south of Culpeper, until about noon on August 9.

This surprising tardiness on the march at a time when sound strategy demanded maximum speed displeased Jackson. Unusually hot weather on the 8th might account for some of the delay, but the chief reason was a "combination of poor planning, bad staff work, and unnecessary reticence on Jackson's part."[10] He failed to inform Hill of a change in plans and in spite of Lee's suggestion that he take the divisional commander into his confidence, he did not do so. Although he assumed some of the blame for the delay himself, he felt that Hill was not beyond censure, and he became doubtful of the ability of the commander of the Light Division to conduct a march. This feeling which Jackson acquired toward his subordinate boded ill for the future.

Although Halleck had instructed Pope to be very cautious until he had more troops on the line of the Rappahannock River, the commander of the Army of Virginia decided to advance Banks' corps, supported by the cavalry of Brigadier General George D. Bayard, to a position near Cedar Mountain. It is interesting to note that Pope's orders to Banks were sent by Colonel Louis Marshall, a nephew of General Robert E. Lee, who was a Federal officer.[11]

Believing that only the advanced units of Pope's army had reached Culpeper, Jackson determined to push on toward that place. Confederate cavalry under Brigadier General Beverly H. Robertson led the advance, followed by Early's brigade of Ewell's division. Although still so incapacitated by his wound that he could not mount his horse without assistance, Old Jube was spoiling for a fight. His part in the forthcoming engagement was destined to be so conspicuous that he was recommended by General Ewell for promotion.[12]

As Early's brigade advanced, 1500 strong, to take position behind Robertson's Confederate cavalry in front, Old Jube detached some of his men to picket both sides of the road. This was to guard against an enemy cavalry attack. The remainder of Ewell's division, consisting of the brigades of Brigadier General Isaac R. Trimble and Colonel Henry Forno, followed. Forno headed the brigade of Brigadier General Harry Hays, who was absent. After Ewell's division came Jackson's old division, which was led by Brigadier General Charles S. Winder, although that officer was so sick he was brought to the field in an ambulance. He soon mounted a horse, however, and rode at the head of his troops. Brigadier General W. B. Taliaferro, who headed the Third Brigade, was second in command of this division. The other brigades were led by Colonel Charles A. Ronald, Colonel Leroy A. Stafford, and Lieutenant Colonel Thomas S. Garnett, respectively. Jackson's third division, that of A. P. Hill, then followed. Its brigades were headed by Brigadier Generals L. O'B. Branch, James J. Archer, Charles W. Field, William D. Pender, and Colonel Edward L. Thomas.[13]

The dominant feature of the terrain in this vicinity was Cedar Mountain, whose ridges covered the Confederate right and commanded the Federal left. Because a man by the name of D. F. Slaughter lived on the eastern slope, this was sometimes called Slaughter's Mountain. When Jackson was informed that Union forces were in front, he determined to use this natural feature to turn the Federal left flank. Consequently, he ordered Ewell to take two brigades over the shoulder of the mountain and strike the enemy's left flank. Early was to advance up the Culpeper road and was to be supported by Winder's division on his left.

Hill's division was kept in reserve.

Since General Early was ordered not to begin the movement up the Culpeper road until he received word that Winder's division was ready to follow, he had to wait a short while. He made good use of this time, for, accompanied by General Robertson, he reconnoitered the ground in front. His purpose was to find out how he could advance his brigade without being seen by the Federals until he would be close enough to deliver a surprise attack. He discovered a small branch, a tributary of Cedar Run, and a thick woods directly ahead. Between the woods and Cedar Mountain he saw a valley containing open fields.[14] As the Union cavalry was visible in this valley, Early determined to form his brigade in a meadow to the left of the road, where it could not be seen by the enemy. From this meadow he planned to advance obliquely across the road against the Federal horsemen in the field. After this reconnaissance Old Jube returned to his troops, where he found a courier from General Winder with the information that the supporting division was ready.

About two o'clock in the afternoon, Early began the movement Forming his regiments in the meadow he had discovered previously, he led them across the road. He ordered the 13th Virginia regiment to deploy skirmishers to cover the front and left flank of the brigade. As soon as the Federal cavalry saw the approaching Confederate infantry, it withdrew. Early's command then reached a ridge in its front. When it advanced over the crest, it received such an accurate fire from the Union artillery that Old Jube ordered it back to the south side of the ridge, where his men would have some cover. Then after sending word to Winder to move up promptly, he made another study of the terrain. He found that he was now in an open field, with a dense woods on his left and Cedar Mountain a mile distant on his right.[15]

After he had dispatched his brother and aide, Lieutenant Sam H. Early, to General Winder for reinforcements, General Early likewise felt the need for artillery. He had no sooner requested some batteries than he noticed some already on the way. Apparently Major A. R. Courtney, Ewell's Chief of Artillery, had anticipated Early's need for some heavier guns and had already sent Captains W. D. Brown and W. F. Dement with several pieces.[16] When these guns began firing, Early ordered the 12th Georgia infantry regiment to the right in order to support them and also to help protect that flank.

Winder arrived on Early's left shortly afterwards and ordered his artillery to support Early's guns. As Ewell's batteries on

Slaughter Mountain now got into action, a brisk cannonading took place. The Federal guns replied in kind, and it looked as if an artillery duel would continue for some time. Because General Early had an excellent view of the whole battleground, except in one place, where a ridge obscured the Federal infantry, he saw an opportunity for Confederate infantry to move on the left, under cover, and take the Federal batteries in flank. Accordingly, he so informed Winder. However, shortly afterwards he noticed the glistening bayonets of the enemy infantry moving toward the Confederate left flank. To warn Winder of this new threat, Early sent his brother again.[17]

General Winder had placed himself with his artillery and was enjoying the effect of the Confederate fire. He noticed with satisfaction that some of the Union batteries were changing position. While attempting to give instructions to one of his gunners, Winder was struck by an enemy shell that passed through his left arm and side, mangling him terribly. While he lay on the ground in great agony, Sam H. Early galloped up with the warning that Federal infantry were moving through the woods toward the Confederate left.

Brigadier General William B. Taliaferro succeeded Winder in command of the division, but, like most of Jackson's subordinates, he had not been taken into Stonewall's confidence. Consequently he knew little about the Confederate plan of attack, except what he could see from the position he had been occupying before Winder's removal. When he became acting commander of the division, he made a reconnaissance to the left. He detected no signs of Federals there, although his field of vision was obscured by the woods. What was more alarming, perhaps, was his discovery of enemy infantry in a cornfield in front of Early.

On the extreme Confederate right, the other brigades of Ewell's division, those led by Generals Trimble and Forno, had reached a position from which they might have been able to turn the Federal left flank. Unfortunately, they could not advance further because the field ahead was swept by Confederate fire.[18]

While the artillery duel was going on, General A. P. Hill decided to send some of his batteries to reinforce those firing from the Confederate center. Accordingly, he ordered his Chief of Artillery, Lieutenant Colonel R. Lindsay Walker, to dispatch to the front the long-range guns of the Light Division. In attempting to carry out these orders, Walker found the Culpeper road so blocked with ambulances and wagons that only a few of his batteries got through. Leading the way and not taking time to re-

Taking a Short Rest

connoitre, Colonel Walker rode into the open field in front in an exposed position on Early's left. Although a Federal line of skirmishers was only 150 yards away and these Confederate guns had no infantry support, they were soon getting ready to fire.

Immediately Old Jube saw the Federal infantry rise up and advance to capture the exposed guns. Realizing that if he did not act at once, they would soon be in possession of the enemy, he ordered his brigade to advance at the double quick to the rescue. His troops responded with a yell and a volley. They reached the batteries first and checked the advance of the bluecoats. The guns were thus saved and began to add their shells to those of the other Confederate batteries. The Union artillery continued to reply until about five o'clock when the firing on both sides slackened.[19]

Less than an hour later the Federal infantry, which Early had noticed previously moving toward the Confederate left, attacked the positions held by the brigade of Early and those held by Taliaferro and Garnett. Taliaferro counter-attacked at once. Early attempted to straighten his line. About this time the brigade of Colonel Edward Thomas, from A. P. Hill's division, moved to reinforce Early's right. This was the support which Jackson had promised to help fill in the gap between Early's right and Cedar Mountain. These additional troops arrived just in time, for the Federals were overlapping Early's right flank. Thomas' brigade succeeded in checking the Union advance, after which Old Jube rode to see what was happening on the Confederate left.

Arriving there, Early discovered that it had given way completely before the Federal infantry attack. Taliaferro's left flank had broken so much that it seemed impossible to rally the dispirited men. His right was assailed in both front and rear and compelled to fall back. This exposed the left flank of Early's brigade. The bluecoats got possession of the woods and poured a destructive fire into the rear of Old Jube's regiments, causing them to retire in disorder. The situation was critical. The only Confederate organizations which seemed able to stand were the brigade of Colonel Thomas and three regiments of Early's brigade, the 12th Georgia, 52nd Virginia, and 58th Virginia. The latter two Virginia regiments were not intact for some of their companies had retreated. The remainder of Jackson's Valley Army seemed routed.[20]

Jackson himself realized the gravity of the situation. His fine Valley Army was about to be defeated by a smaller number of Federals led by the despised Major General Nathaniel P. Banks. This was the same general who had formerly served as Speaker of the United States House of Representatives and who more recently had been derisively dubbed "Commissary" Banks because Jackson had captured so many of his supplies. Stonewall himself rode into the middle of the confused mass of humanity exposing himself recklessly in an effort to rally his men. He ordered his batteries to the rear, lest they fall to the enemy. Federal artillery, firing over the heads of its own infantry, added to the general confusion.

The famous Stonewall Brigade, which was led by Colonel Charles A. Ronald and which had been in reserve, attacked and drove back the Federals. Other Confederate units, including Colonel James A. Walker's 13th Virginia regiment of Early's brigade, pressed the attack. Ronald learned for the first time that both flanks of the Stonewall Brigade were in the air. The 27th Virginia regiment of this unit gave way and fled to the rear. It seemed as if not even the famed Stonewall Brigade could avert disaster.

Then, just in the nick of time appeared more Confederate reinforcements. They were North Carolina troops belonging to the brigade of General L. O'B. Branch, a part of A. P. Hill's division, which had been held as a general reserve. Jackson had ridden to the rear to find reinforcements and had met this unit which was Hill's leading brigade. The North Carolinians were veteran troops and were equal to the emergency. Advancing into the woods, Branch's men allowed the retreating Stonewall Brigade regiments to pass through their lines. The Carolinians continued to press on into the woods and pushed the Federals back. Other units followed their example and soon the Confederate line was restored. The tide of battle had turned, and Jackson's men were now advancing over the very same ground that they had formerly yielded.[21]

The Unionists made one final effort to redeem the day. After sunset, they launched a desperate and courageous cavalry charge down the Culpeper road. Although the Southerners were much scattered in advancing, and their line was somewhat irregular, they greeted the horsemen with a sharp volley. This reception caused the head of the column to turn, after which a raking fire from Branch's North Carolinians forced the cavalry to beat a hasty retreat.

A general Confederate advance all along the line drove the Federals entirely from the field. Desiring to exploit to the fullest his hard-fought victory, Jackson ordered the division of General A. P. Hill to press the pursuit toward Culpeper. Hill took the lead but had not gone far before darkness fell. There was some skirmishing and even a minor artillery duel, but Jackson decided to call a halt to the pursuit. He had learned that an entire second corps of General Pope's army had arrived in his front. Exhausted, he had no desire to engage it, and he therefore gave orders to the weary troops to bivouac.[22]

The day following the Battle of Cedar Mountain, August 10, was spent burying the dead, sending the wounded to the rear, and collecting the arms and booty which fell to the Confederates. The next day the Federals requested a truce for the purpose of burying their dead, which was granted. Early went to the battleground to superintend the burial of some Confederates. He noticed a number of fine Union rifles which some Confederates apparently had stacked but neglected to take away. When he saw the bluecoats helping themselves to these rifles, he not only made them desist but even made them return those they had already taken from the field. In this way he acquired six full wagon loads of arms which he sent to the rear.[23]

At a time when the Confederate Government was having difficulty supplying its soldiers with guns, ammunition, clothing, and even shoes, a victory was usually the occasion for gathering every usable article the enemy left behind. Sometimes prisoners were forced to trade articles of wear with their captors, and Confederates were not averse to divesting a dead Federal of his uniform or shoes. The story is told about a Negro boy named Sandy who was hired by a Confederate officer to serve as hostler. Desiring a new pair of shoes, Sandy was told that none were available but that he could obtain a pair simply by following directions. The officer suggested that he follow along at a safe distance behind the Confederate army after a battle and take the shoes off the first dead Federal he saw. Sandy was impressed, but when he failed to get the new shoes after several engagements, the officer asked him why he hadn't obtained the desired footwear. To this question Sandy is said to have replied as follows:

> Now, boss, I'se gwine to tell ye de God's trufe. I done just as ye told me, and when I clum ober de first line of bresworks I see a big dead Yank layin' flat on his back with blood all over his face. He had on bran' new boots, and I says to myself, 'Dem's my boots for shore!' So I picks up one foot and begins to pull off de boot sorta easy like; but Oh, my goodness gracious! he jist riz up on one elbow and says, 'You black imp of h——! 'What you doin' here?' Well, sur, I drapt dat boot, tuck to my heels, and nebber looked back tell I got to de wagon camp. No, sir-ee, no dead Yank's boots for me.[24]

In comparing the numbers involved in the Battle of Cedar Mountain, it appears that Jackson had approximately 20,000 troops within reach, whereas Banks had less than half that number. Jackson's casualties numbered 229 dead and 1047 wounded, making a total of 1276.[25] His Federal opponents lost 2381, including 400 prisoners.[26] Thus in comparing the number engaged with the number of casualties, it appears that Jackson lost about six per cent of his force, while Banks lost almost thirty per cent.

The Battle of Cedar Mountain greatly added to the laurels of General Jubal A. Early. He had been in the thick of most of the fighting and had distinguished himself time and again. He made a careful reconnaissance whenever he had the opportunity before he committed his troops; he showed much skill in the placing and handling of his men. At the time when everything else seemed lost, his right flank stood its ground. Jackson does not pay him much tribute except to say that his right "held its position with great firmness."[27] Early's divisional commander, General Ewell, was more lavish in his praise. In his official report he not only referred to Old Jube's "gallant and effective service" but he also recommended him for promotion to the rank of major general.[28] Undoubtedly this display of confidence by Ewell in Early helped make Old Jube more contented with his lot than he had been before the Battle of Cedar Mountain.

CHAPTER 9

Another Bull Run

After the engagement at Cedar Mountain, General Lee decided to try to destroy the army of General Pope before the latter could be reinforced by the troops of General McClellan. The Federal authorities had ordered McClellan to withdraw from the Peninsula and to send his troops to Aquia, near Fredericksburg. From Aquia these Unionists could be sent to reinforce Pope. General Halleck, maneuvering all the Federal armies in Virginia from his Washington headquarters, instructed Pope to "fight like the devil" until McClellan arrived.

When McClellan began leaving his base at Harrison's Landing on the Peninsula, Lee moved most of his troops from Richmond to the vicinity of Gordonsville. He left two brigades to protect the Confederate capital. Arriving at Gordonsville on August 15, Lee, in consultation with Jackson, Stuart, and Longstreet, planned the destruction of Pope. The Federal commander was then occupying an exposed position between the Rapidan and Rappahannock rivers. Lee determined to cut Pope off from his base at Fredericksburg by sending Confederate cavalry to his rear to cut the main railroad bridge across the Rappahannock. If he could do this, he should be able to destroy most of Pope's army.[1]

Unfortunately for Lee's plan to attack Pope south of the Rappahannock, the Confederate cavalry was not concentrated. Brigadier General Wade Hampton was with General D. H. Hill watching the withdrawal of McClellan. The brigade of Brigadier General Beverly Robertson was dispersed, part of it being with Jackson at Gordonsville. The division commander, Major General J. E. B. Stuart and his junior brigadier general, Fitzhugh Lee, were at Hanover Court House. Stuart and Fitz Lee went to Davenport's Bridge on August 16, from which place Stuart left by train over the Virginia Central Railroad to join the main Confederate army. Before leaving, however, the cavalry commander instructed Fitz Lee to march to Raccoon Ford on the Rapidan. Apparently the subordinate did not realize the urgency of getting to Raccoon

78

Ford as soon as possible, and his failure to do so nearly caused the capture of his chief.

After Stuart had reported to General Robert E. Lee, he and his staff rode to Verdiersville, where they spent the night. This little village was about ten miles from Raccoon Ford and was on Fitz Lee's line of march. Not understanding why Fitz Lee should be late in covering the thirty-two miles from Davenport's Bridge to the Rapidan ford, Stuart sent two of his staff to find out. Instead of meeting Confederate troopers, these officers ran into a patrol of Federal cavalry. Alarmed by the ensuing shots, Stuart barely had time to escape capture. As it was, he lost his cloak, his famous plumed hat, and, what was more important to the enemy, his haversack. The latter contained information that would be of great advantage to the Federals. By capturing an officer on Stuart's staff sent to find Fitz Lee, these Federal cavalrymen came upon correspondence which revealed the Confederate scheme to trap Pope. When the Union commander was thus informed, he withdrew his army behind the Rappahannock before Lee could carry out his plan.[2]

Although disappointed at the failure of his first effort to defeat Pope before McClellan could join him, Lee advanced to the Rappahannock. He then decided to strike at Pope's communications by a turning movement to the left. Accordingly, he dispatched Stonewall Jackson's wing and Stuart's cavalry to carry out this movement. They numbered about 24,000 men. With his remaining army of 25,000 to 30,000 men Lee planned to confront Pope on the Rappahannock.

Leaving behind all wagons except those necessary for ordnance and medical supplies, Jackson's wing started on the morning of August 25. His soldiers had received three days' rations with orders to cook them before leaving, but, unfortunately, some failed to complete their cooking. As a result, some of the food had to be eaten half-raw or had to be thrown away when it began to spoil. With Ewell's divisiion in front, A. P. Hill's in the middle, and Taliaferro's bringing up the rear, the gray columns passed through Amissville and then reached the Rappahannock. The Confederates crossed this stream, marched on past Orlean, and finally reached Salem [now Marshall], near which place they bivouacked. They had covered twenty-five miles since morning.[3]

General Jubal Early's brigade, it will be recalled, was attached to Ewell's division and hence participated in the march described in the preceding paragraph. These troops had previously been sent north of the Rappahannock to an exposed position but had subsequently been withdrawn to the south side. Early was much concerned about the welfare of his troops in their exposed position and felt greatly relieved when they retired. He had no desire to face most of Pope's army with his one brigade.

After spending the night near Salem, Jackson's troops set out again on the morning of August 26. They passed through White Plains, Thoroughfare Gap in the Bull Run Mountains, and Gainesville. Hays' brigade, led by Colonel Henry Forno, headed the advance and arrived at Bristow Station on the Orange and Alexandria Railroad just before sunset. Encountering a small force of Federal cavalry, Forno drove them off and then proceeded to capture several empty trains.

Jackson had hoped to obtain badly-needed supplies from the captured trains and consequently was greatly chagrined when he discovered they were empties. His disappointment was relieved when some of the natives of Bristow informed him that a great Federal base of supplies had been established at Manassas Junction—several miles to the north. Generals Stuart and Trimble with their commands pushed on to this base, where they drove off the Federal guard, and found their efforts rewarded with the greatest accumulation of supplies they had ever seen. According to General Hill, there was an "immense amount of commissary stores and about two miles of loaded freight cars."[4] It is needless to add that the Southerners made the most of this opportunity to enjoy the captured supplies. According to one account, when Jackson ordered all liquor not needed for medical supplies to be dumped from barrels, some thirsty Confederates even attempted to refresh themselves with what they could recover from pools and ditches.[5]

Jackson ordered three brigades of Ewell's division, including the one led by Jubal Early, to remain at Bristow Station to check any advance which Pope's army might make along the railroad. As the Confederate leader did not desire a general engagement at this time, he instructed Old Bald Head to retire toward Manassas Junction in the event the Federals appeared in large numbers.

Major General Joseph Hooker, a former West Point classmate of Early's, led the Union attack on Ewell's position at Bristow and pressed it with vigor. "Fighting Joe" commanded a division of the Third Army Corps of the Army of the Potomac. Although the Confederates outnumbered their opponents in this phase of the fighting, Ewell had no desire for a major battle, and, after resisting for an hour, retreated to Manassas in accordance with Jackson's orders. Early's brigade comprised the rear guard. By the time it arrived at Manassas Junction most of the captured booty had been seized or destroyed and Old Jube's men had to be content with filling their haversacks with hard bread and salt meat.

Realizing that Jackson's entire command was at Manassas Junction, Pope made plans for cutting it off and, if possible, capturing or destroying it. He, therefore, issued orders for a concentration of his scattered soldiers. Apparently he took no notice of the remainder of Lee's army, which was but a long day's march behind Jackson and which spent the night of August 27 at White Plains.[6]

Since Stonewall Jackson had no intention of waiting at Manassas to be destroyed, on the night of August 27-28 he began moving his men northwestwardly to the vicinity north of Groveton. In taking a new position, Jackson caused Hill's and Ewell's divisions to take roundabout routes so as to mislead Pope. How well he succeeded is illustrated by the fact that when Pope arrived at Manassas at noon on August 28, he could not ascertain where Jackson's force was. Learning later that Hill had passed through Centreville, he concluded that the main Confederate army was near that place, and he promptly ordered all the Federals there. Pope made the mistake of thinking that Jackson would move southwestwardly toward Hooker, whereas the Confederate marched northwestwardly to rejoin Lee. While the division of Brigadier General Rufus King of McDowell's corps was marching along the Warrenton-Centreville turnpike to concentrate at the latter place, it was fired upon by Jackson's artillery from the north near Groveton. This was about five-thirty o'clock on the afternoon of August 28.[7]

This affair at Groveton was fought by the Confederate divisions led by Taliaferro and Ewell, whereas the single Federal division of General King did most of the fighting for the Union. King's men, who were largely westerners, were excellent troops, well led and well equipped. Although their opponents had the advantage of high ground and good positions and, in addition, a numerical superiority of 4500 to 2800, the Federals fought stubbornly and with great courage. When finally forced to retire, they did so in good order.

In the fighting at Groveton Ewell ordered Early to take charge of his own and Hays' brigade and form them in line of battle. Later Jackson called upon Old Jube for reinforcements, which were sent. In moving forward, Early's men encountered an unfinished railroad cut, which was so deep that they had to move to the right in order to cross. While reforming their battle lines, they were exposed to a galling fire of canister and shrapnel. When darkness came, it was impossible to tell friend from foe and the Confederates, having driven off the enemy, lay on their arms all night.[8]

Although the Southerners had forced the Federals to retire, they had gained a costly victory. Brigadier General Isaac R. Trimble had been wounded by a Belgian explosive bullet, Brigadier General Charles W. Field and Colonel Henry Forno had been shot, Colonel J. Foster Marshall had been mortally wounded, and Major General Richard S. Ewell had been severely wounded. Leading some of the regiments on foot, Ewell was recognized by some of General Lawton's Georgians, with whom he was popular. Their encouraging remark, "Here's General Ewell, boys," was followed immediately by a Federal fusillade. A ball went through the Confederate general's right knee, shattering that member so severely that it was later amputated. Early had great difficulty persuading his superior to go to a hospital, so reluctant was Ewell to leave the field. Thus the Confederacy lost temporarily one of its better division commanders.[9]

After the fight at Groveton the Confederates had the general strategic advantage, for Pope became convinced that Jackson was trying to fall back to Thoroughfare Gap. Accordingly, he began concentrating his forces for pursuit on August 29. This was exactly what the Southern leaders wanted for they would be able to draw up their army in line of battle and await Pope's assaults.

Pope's inability to understand the general strategic situation resulted in so much confusion among his troops that on the morning of August 29 they were worn out by marching and counter-marching. In addition, they were badly scattered. At that time the only Federal soldiers near Jackson's position were those belonging to the corps of Major General Franz Sigel and the division of Brigadier General John F. Reynolds. They were located two miles east of Jackson's position on Bull Run. Other Union soldiers were at Bristow, Manassas, and Centreville. Ricketts' division of McDowell's corps had attempted to halt Longstreet's wing of Lee's army at Thoroughfare Gap on the 28th but had been outflanked and forced back. As this division marched on to Bristow, there was no Federal force to prevent Longstreet from passing through Gainesville to unite with Jackson.[10]

The Second Battle of Bull Run began early on the morning of August 29 with Pope attempting to pursue an army drawn up in line of battle. Jackson had selected a strong position. His left rested on Bull Run at Sudley Ford, his center occupied Stony Ridge, and his right rested on Stuart's Hill, where Longstreet's wing eventually took position. In front were the cuts and fills of an unfinished railroad. He could bring up reinforcements from the rear which would be unseen by the enemy in front. He could assemble troops in a wooded area and then rush them forward at the opportune moment for a counterattack. The bewildered Pope was so afraid that Jackson was retreating and would escape that he ordered McDowell's two divisions [Ricketts and King] to block Jackson's retreat on the Warrenton pike.

In accordance with Pope's plan, Sigel's Germans and Reynolds' Pennsylvanians, coming from the Henry House Hill, attacked Jackson's lines. The Federal troops were slightly inferior in number. Later the corps of Major Generals S. P. Heintzelman and Jesse L. Reno joined them. In spite of the gallantry of these attacks, all failed to break Jackson's lines. Instead of having one coordinated vigorous assault, the Federals relied on piecemeal attacks. First a division or part of a division would charge, then it would fall back and its place would be taken by another. Although the weak part of Jackson's position was his left flank, Pope made no attempt to turn it but resorted to frontal attacks instead.

General Early's part in the battle on August 29 began when General Jackson ordered him to take Hays' brigade and his own, along with a battery of artillery, to a ridge north of the Warrenton pike. The purpose of this movement was to prevent the turning of Jackson's right flank. This possibility was removed when the leading division of Longstreet's wing, commanded by Brigadier General John B. Hood, put in appearance and took position on the right of Jackson's line. In the afternoon Early received a request for aid from General A. P. Hill, on his left. One of Hill's brigades had almost exhausted its ammunition in attempting to fight off a Federal attack. Old Jube did not wait for orders but quickly advanced in the proper direction. In the ensuing engagement his brigade, aided by a Louisiana regiment, pushed back the enemy for a distance of several hundred yards. Since Hill made it clear that Jackson did not desire a general advance, Early drew his brigade back and took position behind the railroad cut. As the relieved brigades of

Hill's division had gone to the rear to replenish their ammunition and did not return, Old Jube remained in position all night with his men lying on their arms.[11] In this Federal attack on Hill's lines one of Hill's brigade commanders, Brigadier General Maxey Gregg, sent the following message to his chief: "Tell General Hill that my ammunition is exhausted, but that I will hold my position with the bayonet,"[12]

General Pope did not know until the end of the day that Lee's other wing, under Longstreet, had arrived and taken position on Jackson's right. Consequently, he had ordered the commander of his Fifth Army Corps, Major General Fitz-John Porter, to attack Jackson's right.[13] Porter, realizing that Longstreet's whole command stood between him and Jackson, replied that his force of 10,000 was not strong enough for this task. Although Pope then angrily ordered an immediate attack, Porter did not comply. By this time it was dark. In this exchange of notes Pope used the following strong language in writing to his subordinate:

> Immediately upon receipt of this order, the precise hour of receiving which you will acknowledge, you will march your command to the field of battle of today, and report to me in person for orders. You are to understand that you are expected to comply strictly with this order, and to be present on the field within three hours after its reception, or after daybreak tomorrow morning.[14]

Afterwards Pope preferred charges against Porter for not obeying the order to attack Jackson on August 29. As a result of the court-martial Porter was later dismissed from the Federal service, and the Union was thus deprived of one of its better general officers. According to a high-ranking Confederate officer, "The ex-Federal Confederates who had known Porter considered this result as one of the best fruits of the victory."[15]

In this fighting on August 29 Pope was not the only army leader having difficulty with a subordinate. General Lee, seeing an opportunity of rolling up General Porter's left flank, wanted the commander of his right wing, Longstreet, to do so. After reconnoitering the ground, Longstreet reported that the opportunity was not inviting.[16] Although Lee still wanted him to attack, Longstreet wasted so much time looking for favorable ground that darkness set in. As the Federals advanced over the same terrain in an effort to obtain a good position for renewing the battle the next day, the two sides met. However, darkness prevented full-scale activities. Longstreet's reluctance to carry out orders of which he disapproved was displayed the next year at

Studying the Terrain

Gettysburg. Unlike General Pope, Lee did not order a court-martial but overlooked his subordinate's shortcomings. This forgiving attitude which Lee had toward disobedient subordinates was a serious military weakness.

During the night the Confederates withdrew from the advanced position they had reached after they had repulsed the Federal attacks. In retiring they resumed their original line of battle. Pope, as well as two of his corps commanders, Generals McDowell and Heintzelman, thought Lee had retreated toward Gainesville. Accordingly, the Federal commander on August 30 ordered McDowell to pursue the Confederates. When the Federals began to advance, they realized that the Southerners were not retreating but instead were awaiting attack in a strong defensive position. Confederate artillery was located in a high position from which it had a clear line of fire against the oncoming bluecoats.[17] Pope had 65,000 to throw against the enemy's 50,000 troops, but the Confederates had much the advantage of position, as well as leadership.

In order to hold the Union left flank and prevent the Confederates from attacking there and thus cutting his line of retreat, Pope placed troops under Brigadier General John F. Reynolds on Bald Hill. He also stationed soldiers on Henry House Hill. In the center General Porter attacked Jackson's position but encountered such a hot artillery and infantry fire that he had to withdraw. In the attack on that part of the Confederate line along the unfinished railway embankment a mounted Union officer, with his sword held high, was seen leading the assaulters. At that part of the center where men were being cut down by the hundreds this gallant figure on horseback seemed to lead a charmed life. Alone, ahead of his men, conspicuous because he was mounted, he rode on. The blue lines about him wavered at the hot reception they were receiving from the Southern artillery and infantry fire. Finally this brave leader rode straight up the embankment and in the midst of cries of "Don't kill him! Don't kill him!" fell into the Confederate lines—wounded.[18]

After Porter's repulse Pope continued his efforts to break the Confederate lines. Wave after wave of brave Federal infantrymen dashed itself to pieces against their opponent's strong position. Instead of trying to win by one combined assault, with a quick succession of attacks so that the threatened Confederates would not have time to recover, Pope let each unit taste defeat before the next one advanced.[19]

Ewell's division had been posted in the center of Jackson's

lines with Hill's division on its left and Jackson's old division on its right. Jubal Early expected his brigade to take its proper place in the battle line, but when Brigadier General A. R. Lawton moved his brigade into position, there was space left for only three of Early's regiments, the 44th, 49th, and 52nd Virginia units. Leaving these in battle-line under Colonel William Smith of the 49th, Old Jube withdrew the remainder of his brigade to the rear. That part of his command left on the battle-line participated in the Federal repulse, as well as in the Confederate counterattack. As soon as the line advanced, Early moved the remainder of his brigade into the position just vacated.[20]

About this time Longstreet advanced and captured Bald Hill, which had been depopulated of Federal troops to support Porter. The First Army Corps, commanded by Major General Franz Sigel, which had been held in reserve, attempted to retake this hill from the Confederates but was unsuccessful. Union soldiers of Reynolds' division and Sykes' brigade of regulars took position on the Henry House Hill, where they successfully resisted Confederate efforts to drive them off. However, when Stonewall Jackson attacked the Federal right all along the line, the Unionists were unable to hold and were forced from the field. Their retreat over Bull Run by the Stone Bridge and nearby fords was made possible because their gallant comrades had managed to hold Henry House Hill.[21]

On the day following the battle General Pope concentrated his army on the heights of Centreville, where he was joined by the Second Army Corps, under General Banks, which numbered 9,000. This part of Pope's army had not participated in the battle but had protected the Federal wagon train on its retreat to Fairfax Court House. At Centreville Pope was also joined by the corps of Generals Franklin and Sumner, which had come from Alexandria.

As soon as General Lee was informed by General Stuart that the Union army was at Centreville, the Confederates determined to turn the Federal right by the Little River turnpike. Accordingly, on August 31 Jackson's wing moved through Sudley Springs to Pleasant Valley, four miles west of Chantilly, where it spent the night. The other wing of Lee's army, commanded by Longstreet, followed later and bivouacked near Sudley Springs.[22]

Pope suspected Lee's intention to turn his flank and dispatched an infantry brigade to reconnoiter. Since he had no cavalry fit for service, he was forced to rely upon foot-soldiers for this type of work. Learning that the Southerners were on the move, he instructed McDowell to take his corps to Fairfax Court House and occupy Germantown. He also sent two brigades under Major General Isaac I. Stevens to take position across the Little River turnpike to check the Confederates. In the ensuing engagement at Chantilly or Ox Hill Stevens met Jackson's forces and in the desperate fighting which followed, the Union officer was killed. Major General Philip Kearney then arrived with his division but was unfortunate enough to mistake the enemy for his own troops in a woods and was shot trying to escape. When darkness fell, the Federals, greatly outnumbered, retired from the battlefield of Chantilly.[23]

General Jubal Early's brigade had marched to the vicinity of this engagement, along with the remainder of Ewell's division. Three regiments of the brigade participated in the main fighting and helped repulse the Federals. The other regiments had moved to the support of Brigadier General William E. Starke, commanding Jackson's old division, when Starke requested reinforcements. These troops of Early's apparently did not become heavily engaged. Early then united his regiments and, upon retirement of Starke's division, took over that part of the Confederate battleline. The other brigades of Ewell's division helped to cover the front where Starke's men had been.[24] Old Jube could not refrain from commenting on the work of his unit, for in his official report of the Battle of Chantilly he wrote as follows:

> . . . I hope I may be excused for referring to the record shown by my own brigade, which has never been broken or compelled to fall back or left one of its dead to be buried by the enemy, but has invariably driven the enemy when opposed to him and slept upon the ground on which it has fought in every action, with the solitary exception of the affair at Bristoe Station, when it retired under orders covering the withdrawal of the other troops.[25]

After the Battle of Chantilly the Union army withdrew to Germantown and Fairfax Court House. With the exception of the regulars, who, fighting bravely, fell back in good order, it was on the verge of disintegration as an effective fighting force. Badly demoralized, lacking confidence in its commander, and feeling the futility of trying to fight under these conditions, the Union army was in such poor shape that even strong reinforcements would not restore its shattered morale. What it needed was a complete reorganization. The commanding general himself, Pope, shared some of this despondency, as is evidenced by the following report he sent General Halleck on the evening of September 2:

> . . . As soon as the enemy brings up his forces again he will again turn me. I will give battle when I can, but you

should come out and see the troops. They were badly demoralized when they joined me, both officers and men, and there is an intense idea among them that they must get behind the intrenchments. . . .

The straggling is awful in the regiments from the Peninsula. Unless something can be done to restore tone to this army it will melt away before you know it. . . . You had best at once decide what is to be done. The enemy is in very heavy force and must be stopped in some way. These forces under my command are not able to do so in the open field, and if again checked I fear the force will be useless afterwards.[26] . . .

Another account of the demoralization of the Federal army at this time is given by Brigadier General John P. Slough, who commanded volunteers at Alexandria. In a dispatch dated September 2 which he wrote to Secretary of War Edwin M. Stanton, General Slough reported as follows:

Thousands of stragglers, singly and in squads, are coming to this vicinity. Most all of the officers show authority from general officers, or are manifestly sick. Many of the men claim to be guards of trains or baggage. It is next to impossible to keep them within guard after they are collected. Can I have one of the forts in this vicinity in which to confine and reorganize them? If so, which?[27]

In order to reorganize the Union army General Halleck, acting upon Pope's recommendation, on September 2 ordered the Federals to retire to the intrenchments protecting Washington. Thus Pope's campaign in Virginia ended in an inglorious manner. The pill was particularly bitter to swallow, in view of Pope's braggadocio at the beginning of the campaign in which he referred to seeing only the "backs of our enemies." As for that unfortunate commander himself, he was transferred far from the scene of his failure—to the Northwest Department, with headquarters at St. Paul [Minnesota].[28] He later partially redeemed his reputation by commendable service against the Indians of that region.

As a result of Pope's failure at Manassas, the following anecdote has appeared: A very outspoken old Virginia gentleman was riding on a train in the vicinity when the conductor called out the name of the station. He could not help hearing a distinguished-looking Northerner in the same coach remark to the other passengers, "Manassas, Manassas! What memories that name brings back! Just where along here did General Pope make his stand?"

This was too much for the old Virginian who replied, "Stand, hell, he never made a stand. He ran all over this whole damn country."

CHAPTER 10

Old Jube Heads a Division

After the Confederate victory at the Second Battle of Bull Run General Lee determined to carry the war to the enemy's country by fording the Potomac into Maryland and then crossing Mason and Dixon's Line into Pennsylvania. The reasons for this decision are not hard to find. Aggressive by nature, Lee wanted to retain the initiative by a vigorous offensive campaign. He did not subscribe to the theory held by Jefferson Davis that the Southern armies should refrain from fighting on Northern soil. Lee knew that the only hope of the South for winning the war lay in striking hard at the Federals where it hurt the most — in Union territory. He realized that if the South contented itself with remaining on the defensive, eventually the overwhelming resources of the North would result in a Confederate surrender. The general over-all strategic situation forced the South to be on the defensive most of the time, but it did not prevent its aggressive generals from fighting on enemy ground whenever opportunity presented itself.

Lee believed that the presence of his victorious legions on the soil of Maryland would influence many Southern sympathizers to join his army. It is true that thousands of Marylanders were then enrolled in the Army of Northern Virginia just as thousands were to be found fighting for the Union. The belief prevailed in Southern circles that but for President Lincoln's use of military force to frustrate Maryland secessionists, the Old Line State would have joined the Confederacy. Hence Lee's expedition would free them from the "despot's heel." Besides, Lee hoped to destroy the Baltimore and Ohio Railroad, which followed the Maryland shore of the Potomac River until it reached Harpers Ferry, where it crossed into Virginia. Another important transportation system which followed the Potomac Valley—on the Maryland side— was the Chesapeake and Ohio Canal. If successful against these Lee might enter Pennsylvania to disrupt communication on the Pennsylvania Railroad. With these two railroad systems and the canal put out of commission there would remain only one line of communication between the East and the West, which was the circuitous route by the Great Lakes. After accomplishing these objectives the Southern leader hoped to turn his attention to Philadelphia, Baltimore, or Washington, depending on circumstances.[1]

Lee also believed that the presence of a strong Confederate army north of the Potomac would alarm the Union authorities and cause them to draw forces from every quarter for the defense of their capital Thus, the pressure on other parts of the Confederacy might be relieved. In addition he desired to give Virginia a respite from warring armies, and he hoped to obtain supplies from a region where they were plentiful. Finally, Lee felt that a Confederate victory on Northern soil would tip the scales in favor of foreign intervention in behalf of the South. The recognition of Southern independence by England and France might result in an end of the Union blockade of Southern ports.

Lee's army was not in the best of condition at the beginning of the Antietam campaign. Numbering only 55,000, it was too weak to breach the strong defenses of Washington and defeat a Federal garrison twice its size. Its morale, however, was excellent and its confidence in the victorious leaders undiminished. Unfortunately, the supply system of the Confederacy was inadequate for the job. It could not provide the soldiers with sufficient food, which meant that they usually subsisted on green corn, apples, beef, or anything else obtainable in the country through which they were passing.

Another defect of the supply system was its failure to provide the men with shoes. Almost every official report made by Confederate officers on this campaign contains some mention of this deficiency. In a letter written to General D. H. Hill long after the war General Jubal Early referred to this fact as follows: " . . . you remarked to me that it had been represented that, in the Revolutionary War Washington's men marched with bleeding feet but that you did not believe that they suffered as you had seen our men suffering on that march. There were many of them, as I had seen also, who had their feet tied up in rags which were clotted with blood. The marching on the McAdamized pike was terrific."[2] Because they did not have shoes, many of Lee's men were unable to maintain their position in line of march and hence straggled badly. This naturally weakened his fighting strength.

After General Pope had been relieved of command of the Federal forces in Virginia, the Washington authorities turned once more to General George B. McClellan. Both President Lincoln and General Halleck were reluctant to entrust McClellan with this important command, but he was the best-trained general then available to head the Federal army in the East. Lincoln's request that McClellan take charge of all the Federals in the Washington area was merely a verbal one, and "Little Mac" was subsequently accused of assuming command without authority. He later stated that he "fought the battles of South Mountain and Antietam with a halter around [his] neck" and if he had been defeated he "would probably have been condemned to death."[3] The Federal commander was more of a favorite with his men than with his superiors, as is shown by the following description of McClellan's popularity by one of his soldiers:

> As each organization passed the general, the men became apparently forgetful of everything but their love for him. They cheered and cheered again, until they became so hoarse they could cheer no longer. . . . A great crowd continually surrounded him, and the most extravagant demonstrations were indulged in. Hundreds even hugged the horse's legs and caressed his head and mane.[4]

The Confederate army crossed the Potomac River at White's Ford, near Leesburg, on September 5 and soon afterwards made its way to Frederick. Three days later General Lee issued a tactful address to the people of Maryland. Pointing out that the Southerners sympathized with the Marylanders in the alleged "wrongs and outrages" to which they had been subjected by the Federal authorities, Lee tried to show that the Confederacy wished to aid in "throwing off this foreign yoke" and to "assist you with the power of its arms in regaining the rights of which you have been despoiled."[5] The people of the Old Line State were more impressed by the rags and bare feet of Lee's veterans than by his addresses and but few of them enlisted in his army at this time.

In order to threaten Washington and keep alive Union fears for its safety, Lee had marched east of the Blue Ridge Mountains. However, since his line of communication was close to the Potomac and hence exposed to Federal cavalry attacks, he determined to move it farther west where it would run the length of the Shenandoah Valley. As strong Federal garrisons occupied Harpers Ferry and Martinsburg, which were athwart this new line, the Confederate commander decided to send General Jackson against them. This would necessitate the dividing of his army in the presence of the enemy, which principle was frowned upon by Napoleon Bonaparte as being contrary to one of the great maxims of war. Apparently Lee felt that the cautious McClellan would not be able to cause any trouble for the Army of Northern Virginia even though Jackson's corps was detached.

Consequently, on September 9 at Frederick Lee issued the famous "Special Orders No. 191," directing that the army begin marching the following day. Jackson's corps, with the exception of D. H. Hill's division, was to proceed to Martinsburg and Harpers Ferry. The encirclement of the latter town was to be completed with the divisions of Generals Lafayette McLaws and R. H. Anderson crossing Crampton's Gap and then marching to Maryland Heights while the division of Major General John G. Walker was to go to Loudoun Heights. By obtaining possession of both Maryland Heights and Loudoun Heights, while his main body attacked from the west, Jackson would have the Harpers Ferry garrison in a trap. Lee's orders directed Longstreet's corps to proceed to Boonsboro, there to await the arrival of Jackson after he had captured Martinsburg and Harpers Ferry. Finally, General D. H. Hill's division was to act as rear guard for the main army, and Stuart's cavalry was to be still farther behind.[6]

Unfortunately for the Confederates a copy of "Special Orders No. 191" fell into McClellan's hands. On September 13 a Union private, B. W. Mitchell of the 27th Indiana Infantry, found a paper wrapped around three cigars. The Federals occupied the same camp site in Frederick which had been used by D. H. Hill's Confederates. When Private Mitchell looked at his find more closely and saw that it was a copy of Lee's "Special Orders No. 191," he showed it to his superiors, who recognized it to be genuine. Thus the carelessness of a Confederate staff officer presented McClellan with the opportunity of a lifetime. The Union commander had before him Lee's plan which showed the detachment of Jackson for the capture of Harpers Ferry. An excellent opportunity was presented for the destruction of the two units of Lee's army before they could unite again.[7]

While the Confederate army was leaving Frederick at this time, the Barbara Frietchie incident is alleged to have occurred. Persistent denials have failed to disprove entirely the story as told by John G. Whittier in his famous poem. Perhaps the best evidence that Barbara did not wave her Union flag while Stonewall Jackson passed by is contained in the following account by Major Henry Kyd Douglas of Jackson's staff. Referring to the Barbara Frietchie story, Major Douglas has this to say: " . . . As for Barbara Frietchie, we did not pass her house. There was such an old woman in Frederick, in her ninety-sixth year and bedridden. She never saw Stonewall Jackson, and he never saw her. I was with him every minute while he was in the town, and nothing like the patriotic incident so graphically described by Mr. Whittier in his poem ever occurred."[8]

General Jubal Early, while not at Jackson's side on the march through Frederick, also refuted the authenticity of the story. He stated that as his brigade was passing through Frederick, he saw a young girl of ten or eleven wave a small United States flag and shout at the same time, "Hurrah for the Stars and Stripes! Down with the Stars and Bars!" Some Confederate soldiers laughed and joked about the event but, according to Old Jube, none made any rude or unpleasant remarks to the girl.[9]

General Early's brigade, with the remainder of Ewell's division, accompanied Stonewall Jackson's corps in the expedition against Harpers Ferry. These Confederate soldiers left Frederick on September 10, moved across South Mountain at Boonsboro Gap, and then marched through Boonsboro to Williamsport. At the latter place they recrossed the Potomac into Virginia and approached Martinsburg, only to find that its Federal garrison had retired to Harpers Ferry. By the morning of September 13 Early's men had reached the Charles Town-Harpers Ferry turnpike, near Halltown. There, in full view of the Federals on Bolivar Heights, the Confederate troops bivouacked and awaited word of the progress made by Generals McLaws and Walker in their respective assaults on Maryland and Loudoun Heights.[10]

On Sunday, September 14, Confederate artillery on both Loudoun and Maryland Heights opened fire on the Federal position on Bolivar Heights. In the late afternoon Southern infantrymen moved forward from the direction of Halltown. As they advanced toward the point where the Shenandoah and Potomac Rivers unite, A. P. Hill's division was on the right, Ewell's division in the middle along the Harpers Ferry-Halltown turnpike, and one briged of Jackson's division was on the left. The remainder of Stonewall's troops were held in reserve. Hence, Early's brigade, as part of Ewell's division, was in the center. By the time the Confederates had completed their investment of the Federals in Harpers Ferry, darkness had forced an end to the firing.

Promptly at dawn on the morning of September 15 a furious cannonade was begun by Jackson's batteries in the rear of Harpers Ferry, supported by those on Maryland and Loudoun Heights. At the same time the guns which had been placed on the east side of the Shenandoah River at the foot of Loudoun Heights raked the

Federals with a destructive enfilading fire. Although the Unionists on Bolivar Heights replied as well as they could, their leaders realized the futility of resistance and, after an hour's fighting, raised the white flag. The Federal officers unanimously favored surrender if reasonable terms could be obtained.

Unfortunately, the Confederates could not notify their most distant batteries of the capitulation for some time, and shells continued to fall upon the Federals. One of them struck Colonel Dixon S. Miles, the Union commander, in the leg and inflicted a mortal wound. The surrender was completed by Brigadier General Julius White, who had commanded the Martinsburg garrison before it fled to the Ferry. The terms were lenient, as the men were allowed to retain their overcoats and blankets, were permitted two days' rations, and were paroled.[11]

When General White approached with his staff to meet General Jackson and arrange for the surrender of Harpers Ferry, the Federal commander was handsomely mounted on a black horse, attractively uniformed, and equipped with a staff similarly attired. He must have been somewhat surprised to find in General Jackson "the worst-dressed, worst mounted, most faded and dingy-looking general he had ever seen anyone surrender to, with a staff, not much for looks or equipment."[12] No wonder when Jackson later rode down into Harpers Ferry, he aroused the curiosity of the Union soldiers. One of them went so far as to remark, "Boys, he's not much for looks; but if we's had him, we wouldn't have been caught in this trap."[13]

Jackson's capture of Harpers Ferry gave the South more than 11,000 prisoners, 73 pieces of artillery, 13,000 stands of small arms, and large numbers of wagons and other military supplies. He did not wait to carry out the details of surrender but hurried to join the main Confederate army which was congregating at Sharpsburg.[14] He instructed General A. P. Hill to remain in Harpers Ferry, complete the surrender, and then join him.

A noteworthy achievement in connection with the capture was that of Colonel B. F. Davis of the Eighth New York Cavalry. Realizing before the surrender that his force of 2,500 horsemen would be of no use in the forthcoming engagement at the Ferry and not having forage for his mounts, he requested permission of Colonel Miles to attempt escape by cutting his way out of the town. At a council the cavalry commanders decided to make the effort across the pontoon bridge over the Potomac and then take the route to Sharpsburg. On the night of September 14 they sallied forth and not only escaped the fate of those remaining in the town, but they also captured and destroyed an ammunition train belonging to Longstreet's corps. They intercepted this near Antietam Creek, shortly before they joined McClellan's army.[15]

While Jackson was engaged in the Harpers Ferry campaign, Major General D. H. Hill was attempting to hold McClellan in check until the divided Confederate forces could unite. On the night of September 13, General Stuart informed Lee that General McClellan had a copy of his Order No. 191 and that the Unionists were at the eastern foot of Turner's Gap in South Mountain. Accordingly, Lee ordered Longstreet and D. H. Hill to dispute the passage of the gaps in the mountain. The Battle of South Mountain was fought on September 14 chiefly by D. H. Hill's division, as Longstreet's men did not reach the ground until the late afternoon. As the Federals succeeded in enveloping both flanks of the Confederate line, they forced Hill to withdraw. However, Hill's stubborn resistance had gained one whole day for Jackson to capture Harpers Ferry and Lee to reunite his scattered forces at Sharpsburg.

As soon as Lee received word that Jackson had captured Harpers Ferry and was on his way to rejoin him at Sharpsburg, the Confederate chieftain decided to give battle near that town from heights overlooking Antietam Creek. Thus he would meet McClellan in Maryland, north of the Potomac.[16]

On the afternoon of September 15, General A. R. Lawton, in charge of Ewell's division, received orders from General Jackson to move his men from Harpers Ferry to Sharpsburg. He was instructed to cross the Potomac at Boteler's or Blackford's Ford, about a mile and a half below Shepherdstown. Because of the necessity for obtaining rations, Early's brigade did not begin the march until after dark. The next day the whole division crossed the river.

Although the Potomac is shallow enough ordinarily for one to wade across at Boteler's Ford, there are some holes in which the water is over one's head. According to one account of the Confederate crossing of this stream, a little Irish soldier from a Mississippi regiment plunged very boldly into the water. In spite of his short stature, he did not hesitate but, holding his gun, cartridge box, and shoes on his head, started across. When he was within about twenty yards of the opposite shore, he called out, "Boys, I'm over dry shod!" Before the words were scarcely out of his mouth he slipped into a deep hole and went under, head and ears, gun and all. As he arose, he continued, quietly, as if

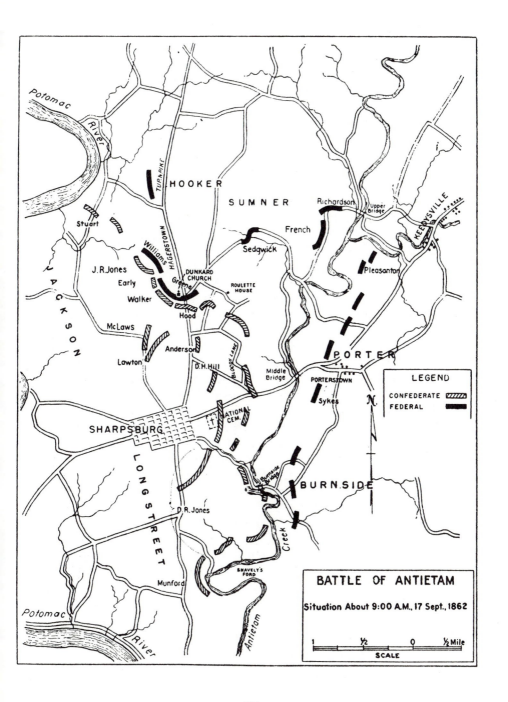

Potomac River

HOOKER

Stuart

SUMNER

Richardson
Upper Bridge
KEEDYSVILLE

French

Sedgwick

Williams

Pleasanton

J.R.Jones

Early

DUNKARD CHURCH
Greene

ROULETTE HOUSE

Walker

Hood

McLaws

Anderson

Lawton

D.H.Hill

BLOODY LANE

Middle Bridge

PORTER

PORTERSTOWN

Sykes

N.

LEGEND

CONFEDERATE

FEDERAL

SHARPSBURG

NATIONAL CEM.

LONGSTREET

D.R.Jones

Burnside Bridge

BURNSIDE

Munford

SNAVELY'S FORD

Antietam Creek

Potomac River

BATTLE OF ANTIETAM

Situation About 9:00 A.M., 17 Sept., 1862

1   ½   0   ½ Mile

SCALE

he were merely completing his remark, "After I get on some dry clothes."[17]

The Confederate line of battle at the beginning of the Battle of Antietam on September 17 was as follows, from left to right: On the extreme left was Stuart's cavalry. Next were the divisions of Brigadier Generals A. R. Lawton and John R. Jones. Since Early's brigade was attached to Lawton's division, Old Jube's men had a position on the left of the Confederate line. Hood's division was next in line, after which came that of D. H. Hill. Farther to the Confederate right and south of Sharpsburg were stationed D. R. Jones' division and Evans' brigade. Behind the right flank, in reserve, was located Walker's division.[18]

Hostilities on the 17th began with a Federal artillery barrage, after which the troops of Major General Joseph Hooker's First Corps moved against the Confederate left. To protect his threatened line, Jackson moved Early's brigade to serve as the flank infantry element. Hooker's attack was so vigorous that he succeeded in driving the Confederate line back. The Southern position became so critical that General Lawton, in charge of Ewell's division, requested Hood's division to come to its rescue. These Texas troops had been temporarily relieved to enable them to cook rations, but they had hardly begun to do so when they were summoned to help drive off the assaulting Federals.

General Jackson directed Jubal Early to lead his brigade to the assistance of Hood. Upon the wounding of General Lawton in Hooker's attack, Old Jube, as the ranking brigadier, assumed command of Ewell's division. The advancing bluecoats of Hooker's corps soon found themselves deep in a pocket, with Early on their right flank, Hood in their front, and D. H. Hill on their left. They were repulsed and then forced to retire. Their place as the attackers was taken by the Union Twelfth Corps commanded by Major General Joseph K. F. Mansfield. This assault was also repulsed by Hood's veterans but at great cost. Infantry action gave way to an artillery exchange. Hood's shattered division withdrew to the Dunkard [or Dunker] church to rest and obtain additional ammunition.[19]

While Hood was withdrawing, General Walker's division arrived and engaged the Unionists. It was aided by General Richard H. Anderson's division. By this time McLaws' division had arrived and was being engaged by the Federal Second Corps, led by Major General Edwin V. Sumner. Although these Federal troops were fresh on the field, McLaws managed to drive them back.

In this fighting on the Confederate left Jubal Early's men had been active participants. After Old Jube had been directed by Stonewall Jackson to assume command of Ewell's division because of the wounding of General Lawton, he turned the leadership of his own brigade over to Colonel William Smith of the 49th Virginia regiment. He then rode to see how the remaining brigades of the division were faring. He soon learned that they had been badly cut up and, accordingly, had passed to the rear. Their place in line of battle had been taken by Hood's Texans. When Early found out that his own brigade was the only part of Ewell's division left on the field for him to command and that Hood's division was being overwhelmed, he rode to inform the corps commander, Stonewall Jackson.[20]

Early found Jackson in the rear of the Dunkard Church and, after explaining the critical situation to his superior, obtained a promise of reinforcements. He then returned to his own men to help them repulse the Federal attack. His brigade had formed line of battle in a woods west of the Sharpsburg-Hagerstown turnpike. As there were many limestone ledges among the trees, his men were able to conceal themselves. While the bluecoats advanced into the same woods, Old Jube sent an urgent plea for Jackson to hurry the promised reinforcements. Just about this time Greene's division of Mansfield's corps advanced to the vicinity of the Dunkard Church and thus threatened to cut Early off from the remnants of Hood's division which had withdrawn to a position on his right. Fortunately for Old Jube's brigade it was not seen by the Federals.

Not for long were Early's men to remain inactive. Discovering that Greene's bluecoats were moving to the rear of the Dunkard Church and thus threatening to take the whole Confederate line in reverse, Old Jube gave orders for an attack. His brigade needed no urging. With the 49th Virginia regiment leading the advance, the other troops joined in. The brigade attacked so vigorously that it drove the Unionists entirely out of the woods. This advance put the Southerners in a position where they were exposed to another Federal column on their left. When Early perceived an additional body of bluecoats moving to the same position, he ordered the brigade to retire, change front, and meet the new threat. As soon as he had reformed his line, he was reinforced by some brigades from McLaws' division and together they repulsed the new Federal assault. Early then reformed his brigade and placed it in position to withstand any new Union effort. Reinforced by additional troops from McLaws' division, he remained in position the remainder of the day, as well as that night and the following day |September 18|.[21] There was little fighting on the Confederate left, as the tide of battle had turned toward the center of the battlefield.

This last attack had been very costly to both sides. Although the Confederates had succeeded in restoring their line so that it was in practically the same position where it had been that morning, now the line was held only by scattered fragments. In addition, it was almost destitute of artillery. As for the Federals, they had lost 2,200 officers and men within a few minutes. General Mansfield had been killed and General Sedgwick had been wounded three times.[22]

After the repulse of Sedgwick's division two other divisions of Sumner's Second Corps advanced against the Confederate center. These were commanded by Brigadier General William H. French and Major General Israel B. Richardson. Crossing the Antietam by a ford below the Upper Bridge, French's troops attacked the Confederate line held by D. H. Hill's division near the Roulette house. Richardson's men attacked on the left of French's position. Out-numbered, the Southerners fell back to the sunken road more familiarly known as Bloody Lane. When the Federals extended their line to the left, they were able to enfilade the Bloody Lane. A misunderstanding between Confederate officers had caused the command "about face and forward march" to be issued to the Southern defenders of the sunken road. When other troops thought that the position was being abandoned, they retired. Finally the whole Confederate line gave way, and the troops fled in the utmost confusion. The Unionists were thus left in possession of Bloody Lane and the nearby hills to the south.[23]

Although French's and Richardson's divisions had suffered casualties of 2,900 or more, they had not suffered as much as the Confederates who opposed them. Without a single fresh regiment in reserve and with practically all of their infantry forces in that part of the battlefield badly used up, the Southerners could not have resisted another determined Union assault. Their artillery was still firing but was suffering heavily from Federal guns across Antietam Creek. One more assault on this part of the Confederate line would probably have resulted in a decisive Union victory and perhaps have destroyed Lee's army, but the timid McClellan let the golden opportunity pass.[24]

Yet the Union commander had plenty of troops available for this knockout blow. Major General William B. Franklin's Sixth

Corps had arrived on the field from nearby Pleasant Valley, and the Fifth Corps under Major General Fitz-John Porter, which formed the general reserve, was available. In addition, the First, Second, and Twelfth Corps, which had already participated in much hard fighting, were capable of doing more. As if these were not enough, McClellan also had the cavalry under Brigadier General Alfred Pleasonton and some regular battalions of Sykes' infantry division, which were idle. Although General Franklin pleaded with his chief to let him attack with the fresh Sixth Corps, McClellan refused to do so.

Once again the scene of battle shifted to the Confederate right —this time to the extreme right flank in the vicinity of the Burnside Bridge over the Antietam. McClellan had ordered Major General Ambrose E. Burnside, commanding the Ninth Army Corps, to attack this part of the Confederate position and as early as seven o'clock in the morning of September 17 had notified his subordinate to prepare for the assault. Three hours later McClellan instructed Burnside to attack.[25] This bridge was defended by Toombs' brigade of Brigadier General David R. Jones' Confederate division. Toombs' men were stationed on the bluffs above the bridge and were assisted by artillery placed in east Sharpsburg where the National Cemetery is now located.

General Burnside immediately prepared for the attack. He sent Brigadier General Isaac P. Rodman with his division and a brigade from Cox's division to cross the Antietam at the fords, below the bridge. He then instructed Brigadier General Samuel D. Sturgis to send his division and Crook's brigade of Cox's division to cross at the Burnside Bridge. He kept the division of Brigadier General Orlando B. Willcox in reserve. After two fruitless attempts to carry the bridge, the Federals tried again and this time succeeded. After crossing the creek, they formed their line for assaulting the Confederates on the bluffs above. Four brigades of David R. Jones' division, numbering only 2,000, fought valiantly but were gradually forced back. They retreated up the slope of Cemetery Hill and into the edge of the town of Sharpsburg. With the capture of a Confederate battery, it seemed as if the Union army was about to gain the decisive victory it was seeking.

However, fate decreed otherwise. Just about the time that Burnside's men appeared to have won the day, the Confederates received reinforcements which enabled them to beat off the attack. A. P. Hill's division, which had been left to complete the surrender details at Harpers Ferry, arrived on the Antietam battlefield in the nick of time. Realizing the critical situation on the Confed-

erate right, Hill threw his men against the left flank of the attacking Federals and drove them toward the Burnside Bridge where
they bivouacked for the night.[26] Thus the Battle of Antietam
ended.

Both armies remained on the field of battle the following day,
September 18, watching each other. That night the Army of
Northern Virginia recrossed the Potomac at Boteler's Ford, and
was once again on the soil of the Old Dominion. Lee's chief of
artillery, Brigadier General William N. Pendleton, was ordered to
place a group of guns on the Virginia bluffs, but before he could
prepare this line, Federal skirmishers crossed and captured four
pieces of artillery. The loss so disgusted Jackson that he dispatched A. P. Hill to oppose the enemy. On the morning of September 20 Hill formed his troops on the north side of the present
Shepherdstown-Moler's Cross Roads pike advancing northward
and facing the ford. He then sent three brigades to the front
but was unable to bring up his artillery because of the lack of time.

Union soldiers formed their lines on the high bluffs above the
river, facing southward, where they awaited Hill's attack. While
they were being assaulted on the front and on both flanks, the
order came to withdraw. The attempted retreat soon developed
into a rout, and each Federal tried to save himself as best he could.
Some of the soldiers tried to escape by the ravine, others were
driven back northward over the precipitous bluff and killed or
mangled, while still others were shot crossing the river. The
bluffs over which some of them fell are at places from fifty to
eighty feet high. The following quotation is taken from Hill's
official report of this phase in the fighting: "Then commenced the
most terrible slaughter that this war has yet witnessed. The broad
surface of the Potomac was blue with the floating bodies of our
foe. But few escaped to tell the tale."[27]

The 118th Pennsylvania Volunteers, known as the Corn Exchange Regiment, suffered the greatest losses in this fighting.
According to its own figures, the organization had 269 killed,
wounded, or missing, out of an original total of 739.[28]

General Jubal Early detached Lawton's brigade from Ewell's
division to assist General Pendleton in defending the south bank
of the Potomac in this engagement. With the remainder of the
division Old Jube moved toward Martinsburg.

Shepherdstown, Virginia witnessed the retreat of Lee's army.
Before the Battle of Antietam was over, Confederate wounded began streaming into the town. Every available shelter was thrown
open to the Southern troops, and even then there were not enough.

After the supply of private homes proved insufficient, the town's six churches, the schoolhouses, the Odd Fellows' Hall, and the council room were filled to capacity. Rough boards were thrown across the beams of the unfinished town hall, and it was soon filled. Then it became necessary to use the stone warehouses in the ravine by the river and a dilapidated building known as the "old blue factory." Broken, mangled bodies were everywhere.[29]

The Federals put a battery on the Douglas hill, opposite the town, and sent shells screeching across the river. Soon pandemonium prevailed. Roads leading out of the place were jammed with wagons, ambulances, caissons, horsemen, footmen, and civilians. The most pitiful picture was presented by the hundreds of wounded Confederates who were able to move. They did not want to spend the remainder of their days in Northern prisons, and, therefore, made every possible effort to escape. One witness described the scene as follows:

> Men with cloths about their heads went hatless in the sun, men with cloths about their feet limped shoeless on the stony road; men with arms in slings, without arms, with one leg, with bandaged sides and backs, men in ambulances, wagons, carts, wheelbarrows, men carried on stretchers or supported on the shoulder of some self-denying comrade—all who could crawl went and went to almost certain death. They could not go far, they dropped off into the country houses, where they were received with as much kindness as it was possible to ask for; but their wounds had become inflamed, their frames were weakened by fright and over-exertion: erysipelas, mortification, gangrene set in; and long rows of nameless graves still bear witness to the results.[30]

As for the results of the Battle of Antietam, there is no general agreement. Undoubtedly, Lee's first invasion of the North was checked and his army was greatly weakened. With a total force not exceeding 40,000 men, he had suffered casualties of 8,000 or more, while inflicting losses of about 12,410 on McClellan. With an army just about half as large as McClellan's, Lee had managed to fight the Unionists to a standstill. McClellan claimed that he defeated Lee in the battle but in the words of one commentator, "it is hard to say which should reflect least credit upon the Union commander, not to have defeated Lee's army, or not to have destroyed it if he defeated it. Truth to tell, McClellan did neither."[31]

CHAPTER 11

Jubal's Boys Get Hill Out o' Trouble

After General Lee's first invasion of the North had been checked at the bloody Battle of Antietam, the Confederate army went into camp along Opequon Creek, near Winchester. The Southerners needed time to recover from their losses and to augment their forces with thousands of stragglers who had not crossed to the north of the Potomac. For the first time the Army of Northern Virginia was now definitely organized into the First and Second Corps, under the leadership of Generals Longstreet and Jackson, respectively. These two officers had been promoted to the rank of lieutenant general.[1]

As other promotions were in order, General Early wondered whether or not a grateful Confederate Government would recognize his military prowess exhibited at Antietam by making him a major general and putting him in command of Ewell's division. According to Dr. Douglas S. Freeman, Old Jube was one of the "heroes of the battle of September 17. As surely as at Cedar Mountain, and with the issue more critical, he showed himself tenacious, cool and hard hitting. At one time he was facing the Federals on three sides, but he made his dispositions shrewdly and he held his ground."[2]

Early's chances for promotion received a boost when General Lee, in his official report on Antietam, complimented his aggressive subordinate by stating that " . . . General Early attacked with great resolution the large force opposed to him."[3] General J. E. B. Stuart, who had been in a favorable position to observe events on the Confederate left, likewise had words of praise for Early. In his official report of Antietam the cavalry commander stated " . . . Early behaved with great coolness and good judgment, particularly after he came in command of his division."[4] Finally, even the reserved Jackson commended Old Jube with the observation that " . . . General Early attacked with great vigor and gallantry the column on his right and front."[5] However, Jackson's tribute to

104

Early was somewhat offset by his recommending for promotion General I. R. Trimble instead.

On October 27 Lee submitted his suggested promotions to the Confederate authorities, and on the list of proposed major generals he included the names of both Trimble and Early. The former was to be assigned to the command of Jackson's division, whereas Early was to head Ewell's division if a successor to Ewell was necessary, and General Edward Johnson was still unable to serve in the field. However, by the time the Confederate Government yielded to pressure from all sides, Lee's list was changed and neither Trimble nor Early received the coveted post of major general.[6]

While the main Union and Confederate armies remained inactive in northern Virginia, General J. E. B. Stuart made a raid through Maryland and Pennsylvania, entirely around the Federal army. Crossing the Potomac on October 10, three brigades of Confederate cavalry passed through Mercersburg, Chambersburg, Cashtown, Emmitsburg, and Hyattstown. The command recrossed the Potomac near the mouth of the Monocacy on the 12th and rejoined Lee. McClellan sent Federal troops to intercept the raiders, but they were unable to prevent their escape. Stuart's troopers had destroyed some stores and carried off horses, but, except for the glamor of the exploit, they did not accomplish much. In fact the results obtained were hardly worth the risk, for the Confederate leader might have had his whole force cut off north of the Potomac and captured.[7]

Nevertheless, Stuart's raid around the Union army, added to disappointment with McClellan in general, strengthened the movement to remove the Federal general. With other Union leaders, Rosecrans and Buell, winning successes in the West, Lincoln and Halleck thought the time ripe for activity in the East. However, the slow and cautious McClellan could not be prodded into action, and the fine fall weather in October gradually slipped away. On the 26th he did cross the Potomac, but it was not until November 4 that he reported his cavalry advance at Piedmont and his infantry at Upperville. Finally, Lincoln's patience was exhausted, and on November 7 Brigadier General Catharinus P. Buckingham, acting as courier, rode to McClellan's headquarters at Rectortown and informed him of his removal. His successor was to be Major General Ambrose E. Burnside, who had conducted the Federal attack on the Confederate right flank at Antietam.[8]

The new Union commander decided to make Aquia Creek, near Fredericksburg, his headquarters and, after trying to deceive

Lee, he moved his whole force to Fredericksburg. From the latter place he expected to drive on to Richmond. In order to facilitate the accomplishment of this plan General Burnside reorganized the Army of the Potomac into three Grand Divisions and a Reserve Corps. He grouped the Second and Ninth Corps into the Right Grand Division and placed Major General Edwin V. Sumner in command. He then formed the Third and Fifth Corps into the Center Grand Division and designated Major General Joseph Hooker as commander. Finally, he organized the First and Sixth Corps into the Left Grand Division, with Major General William B. Franklin as its head. The Reserve consisted of the Eleventh Corps commanded by Major General Franz Sigel. When this army took position on the northern bank of the Rappahannock River, opposite Fredericksburg, it numbered about 122,000 strong.[9]

General Lee had considered the possibility that Burnside might move on Fredericksburg and when Stuart informed him on November 18 that such was the case, the Southern leader ordered Longstreet's corps thence from Culpeper. The entire corps had arrived at Fredericksburg by November 21. Lee's other corps, that commanded by Stonewall Jackson, had remained in the Shenandoah Valley. However, when Lee suggested that his dependable subordinate join him at Fredericksburg, Jackson did so and by November 30 the reunited Army of Northern Virginia, numbering about 78,500 was ready for Burnside's next move.

General Jubal Early, in charge of Ewell's division, left the Valley along with the rest of Jackson's Second Corps. Marching southward, he led his men through New Market, across Massanutten Mountain, then across the Shenandoah River and the Blue Ridge Mountains, finally arriving at Madison Court House.

On this march Stonewall Jackson informed Early that "the Lieutenant General Commanding desires to know why he saw so many stragglers in rear of your division today." Old Jube's answer gave the facts that most of the stragglers were from the other divisions ahead of him and then concluded with the revealing observation that "the reason the Lieutenant General Commanding saw so many stragglers in rear of my division was because he rode there."[10] According to one Confederate veteran, "Nobody but Old Jube would have presumed to flip Stonewall that way."[11]

Another anecdote which was said to have happened about this time concerned Stonewall Jackson and a bridge builder called "Old Miles." Because bridges along the line of march were continually being swept away by floods or destroyed by the Federals, a good bridge builder was a necessity. "Old Miles" had the reputation of being able to complete a bridge in the time it would take another man to make the measurements. On this particular occasion when a bridge across the Shenandoah had been destroyed, Jackson called his subordinate to him and said: "You must put all your men to work, Miles, and must keep them at it all night, for I've got to have a bridge across this stream by morning. My engineers will draw up the plans for you."

Early the next morning Jackson, very much worried, met Miles. "See here," he said dubiously, "how about that bridge? Did the engineer give you the plans?"

Taking his cigar from his mouth and flipping the ashes, Miles replied, with a sneer," General, the bridge is done. I dunno whether the picter is or not."[12]

When Early arrived at Fredericksburg, Jackson ordered him to move his division to Guiney's depot, on the Richmond, Fredericksburg, and Potomac Railroad. Several days later the corps commander directed him to move to the support of D. H. Hill at Port Royal, about twenty miles below Fredericksburg on the Rappahannock. According to General Hill, General Halleck had originally ordered Burnside to cross the river in this vicinity instead of at Fredericksburg, but the presence of Early's division forced Burnside to change his plans and to make the crossing and attack at Fredericksburg instead.[13] Early took position near a place named Skinker's Neck, on the Rappahannock between Port Royal and Fredericksburg.

Having decided to force a crossing of the Rappahannock in front of the strong position occupied by Lee's army, Burnside collected his troops. Because the Union artillery commander, Brigadier General Henry J. Hunt, had massed powerful batteries of 147 guns on Stafford Heights, on the northern side of the Rappahannock, the Federals were able to dominate the ground occupied by the town of Fredericksburg. Also, Lee's position on Marye's Hill was too far away for him to contest successfully the Federal crossing of the river. The real fight was to occur after the Northerners had gained the southern bank.

Accordingly, on the night of December 10 Burnside revealed his plan to cross the Rappahannock. He contemplated spanning the river with five pontoon bridges, three of which would be located opposite Fredericksburg and two farther downstream, just below the mouth of Deep Run. With Hooker's Grand Division remaining on the northern bank of the Rappahannock as the general reserve, Burnside planned to send Sumner's Grand Division across by the upper bridges and Franklin's by the lower ones. The Federals assumed their places during the night and, although annoyed by Confederate sharpshooters across the river, succeeded in laying two bridges by noon of December 11. They were aided by a dense fog which made it difficult for the Southerners to see them. These bridges were constructed near the mouth of Deep Run.[14]

The Federal commander encountered considerably more difficulty in trying to lay the bridges opposite Fredericksburg. A brigade of Mississippians under Brigadier General William Barksdale, strongly posted in cellars and behind brick walls, contested vigorously the Federal bridge-building efforts. In attempting to remove this obstacle, Burnside ordered Hunt's artillery to shell the town of Fredericksburg. In spite of this destruction Barksdale's men held fast, and it was not until Federal infantry crossed in boats and attacked them that the Confederates withdrew. Not long afterwards Burnside's engineers succeeded in laying their bridges.

By December 12 Burnside had his main army south of the Rappahannock, and he then discussed the plan of attack with his subordinates. Because the Confederate left flank rested on Marye's Hill overlooking the town of Fredericksburg, the Federals decided that the Confederate right was the weaker side. This was in the vicinity of Hamilton's Crossing, a road which crossed the tracks of the Richmond, Fredericksburg, and Potomac Railroad. Although the Confederate right flank did not rest on any natural obstacle, it was strengthened by abatis and earthworks. Furthermore, it was defended by Stuart's cavalry and horse artillery, which guarded the space between Hamilton's Crossing and the Massaponax River, farther south. Nevertheless, the Federal leaders agreed that the main attack would be launched by Franklin in the Hamilton's Crossing sector and that the secondary effort would be undertaken by Sumner against the Confederate left.[15]

Although General Franklin expected the command to attack at daybreak, he did not obtain the order until seven o'clock on the morning of December 13. In addition to this delay the Federal officer was confronted with an order which was not clear to him. General Burnside had apparently changed the original plan without consulting him and had decided to order General Sumner's troops to seize the heights on the Confederate left flank. Franklin was directed to send a division to obtain possession of the heights near Hamilton's Crossing but was to "keep your whole command in position for a rapid movement down the old Richmond road."[16]

Noticing the Federal troop movements and receiving reports from his scouts, General Lee was able to guess successfully Burnside's plan. Accordingly, he recalled the forces of D. H. Hill from

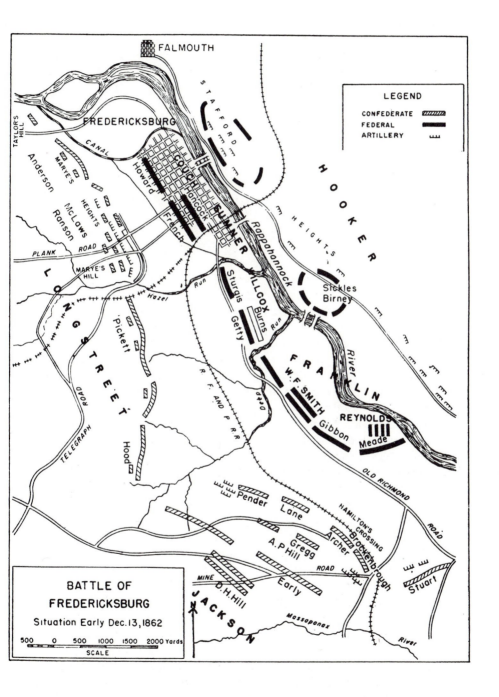

FALMOUTH

LEGEND
CONFEDERATE
FEDERAL
ARTILLERY

TAYLOR'S HILL

FREDERICKSBURG

STAFFORD

H O O K E R

CANAL

Anderson

MARYE'S

Marye's

HEIGHTS

McLaws

Ranson

COUCH
Howard
Hancock
French
SUMNER

Rappahannock

HEIGHTS

PLANK ROAD

MARYE'S HILL

L O N G S T R E E T

Hazel

Run

Sturgis

WILLCOX

Burns

Getty

Run

Sickles
Birney

Pickett

R. F. AND P. R. R.

Deep Run

F R A N K L I N
W. F. SMITH

River

TELEGRAPH ROAD

Hood

REYNOLDS
Gibbon
Meade

OLD RICHMOND

Pender

EEEE

Lane

HAMILTON'S CROSSING

ROAD

Gregg
A. P. Hill

Archer

Brocketbough

Stuart

MINE

ROAD

D. H. Hill

Early

J A C K S O N

Massaponax

River

BATTLE OF
FREDERICKSBURG
Situation Early Dec. 13, 1862

500   0   500   1000   1500   2000 Yards
SCALE

109

Port Royal and Jubal Early from Skinker's Neck. They arrived on the battlefield in support of the Confederate right flank on the morning of December 13. The two corps of the Army of Northern Virginia were thus at full strength to resist the Federal attack. Lee placed the First Corps under Longstreet in position to defend the Confederate left on Marye's Hill, and the Second Corps under Stonewall Jackson where it would defend the right flank, near Hamilton's Crossing.

While Early's men were moving to the front, the following event is said to have taken place. It concerned Early and one of his chaplains. As the Confederates were advancing toward the enemy, they were met by artillery shells which burst among them, killing men and horses. Old Jube met one of his chaplains going to the rear as fast as his legs would carry him and in an abrupt and commanding manner ordered him to halt. In response to Early's inquiry where he was going, the chaplain replied, "General, I'm going to a place of safety in the rear." Whereupon Old Jube responded as follows: "Chaplain, I have known you for the past thirty years, and all of that time you have been trying to get to Heaven, and now that the opportunity is offered you are fleeing from it. Sir, I am surprised!"[17]

Interpreting Burnside's vague order as best he could, Franklin sent several divisions to seize the heights near Hamilton's Crossing. One of these groups, commanded by Major General George G. Meade, pressed forward into swampy ground between the Confederate brigades commanded by Brigadier Generals James J. Archer and James H. Lane, which were part of A. P. Hill's Light Division. This swampy region, about 500 to 600 yards wide, which separated these two Confederate brigades, was supposed by the Southerners to be impassable. Hence it was undefended except for the brigade of Brigadier General Maxey Gregg, located behind the swamp in the second line of defense. The first notice that Gregg received of the proximity of the attacking Federals was the sight of soldiers immediately in front of him. Believing himself secure in his second-line position, Gregg had allowed his men to stack arms and take things easy.[18]

When the bluecoats burst upon the surprised Southerners, the utmost confusion resulted. Many of the latter were unable to reach their stacked weapons, and, consequently, were shot by the enemy. A few more fortunate ones managed to grab rifles and fire into the Federals. More confusion resulted when General Gregg, believing the Unionists to be retiring Confederates, rode among his men ordering them not to fire. That unfortunate officer was shot from his horse, and some of his men fled precipitately from the battle-field. However, other regiments of Gregg's brigade stood their ground and, aided by reinforcements, checked the Union advance.

One of the obstacles in the way of this Federal penetration into the Confederate lines was Jubal Early. His division had been held in reserve, in the rear of Gregg. About noon a courier from the hard-pressed Archer, seeking General A. P. Hill, met Early and stated that Archer needed reinforcements badly. While Old Jube was reflecting upon this situation, a staff officer appeared with an order from Stonewall Jackson to hold his division in readiness to move to the right because of a demonstration which the Federals were making there.[19] When Early tried to decide what to do, an artillery officer from A. P. Hill's division rode up with the statement that there was "an awful gulf" between Archer and Lane. He added that if it were not closed and the enemy driven back, the Confederates would lose all their batteries on the right.

In spite of unfamiliarity with the ground in front of him General Early hesitated no longer. This new crisis would not allow delay. Accordingly, he moved his men to the support of the Con-federates in front. As these reinforcements advanced on the dou-ble-quick to aid the men in Hill's division, they showed their pride in their commander by shouting to their hard-pressed comrades: "Here comes old *Jubal!* Let old Jubal straighten that fence! Jubal's boys are always getting Hill out o' trouble!"[20] The effect of the appearance of these fresh forces on Archer's brigade can readily be surmised. Their arrival was the first tangible evidence that the men in the front lines had strong second line support. Aided on its flanks by other Confederates, Early's division attacked vigor-ously. It rolled back the advancing bluecoats, closed the gap be-tween Archer and Lane, and even pressed beyond the Richmond, Fredericksburg, and Potomac Railroad tracks. In fact, Old Jube had difficulty holding his men back. Some advanced so far that when they were directed to withdraw in order to stabilize the lines, they suffered heavily from enemy fire.[21] When the Southern-ers retired across the railroad, the Unionists, though reinforced, were not strong enough to recapture the woods.[22]

Jackson attempted a counterattack but was forced to give it up when the Federal batteries made such a move ill-advised. Except for artillery exchanges the fighting on the Confederate right flank almost ceased. Burnside had failed to achieve a suc-cessful breakthrough there and was now advancing his men in a direct frontal attack on the strongest part of the Confederate line—the left flank defended by Longstreet's corps.

General Burnside himself directed the Union attack against the strong Confederate left. When the fog lifted, at eleven o'clock, Confederate artillerists spotted thousands of bluecoats massed in the streets of Fredericksburg. Soon afterwards the Southern guns began to shell the town. With the division of Brigadier General William H. French in advance, followed by that of Brigadier General Winfield S. Hancock, the Federals moved against the enemy lines. In spite of great gaps torn in their ranks by Confederate artillery, the attackers came right on. When they were within two hundred yards of gray-clad infantry hidden behind a stone wall at the base of Marye's Hill, they were exposed to a terrific musketry fire. Despite this rain of destruction, some of them pushed on until they were within sixty yards of the Confederate position. After a single discharge they were forced to withdraw, leaving a third of their number on the ground.[23]

The failure of French's division did not deter the one following it, which was led by Hancock. Passing their fallen comrades, these bluecoats advanced to within thirty or forty yards of the stone wall before they retreated. By this time the Southern defenders had been reinforced until they were firing in four ranks. The Federal divisions commanded by Brigadier Generals Oliver O. Howard, Samuel D. Sturgis, and George W. Getty, respectively, then attacked with the same result. The defeated Unionists fell back to whatever cover the ground in front of the Confederate lines afforded.[24]

An interesting event relating to the fighting in front of the stone wall has been preserved and is repeated here because it is typical of that feeling of humanitarianism which was exhibited toward the foe at various times by both the Blue and Gray. This particular occurrence concerns a Confederate soldier named Richard Kirkland, who was a member of Company E, of the Second Regiment, South Carolina Volunteers, belonging to Kershaw's brigade. When the attacking Federals of Meagher's brigade, Hancock's division, were repulsed before the stone wall, they left hundreds of dead and dying soldiers on the field. The cries of their wounded for water made a deep impression on Kirkland, who is described as a "boy soldier." Finally, unable to withstand this appeal for help, he went to his commanding officer, Brigadier General Joseph B. Kershaw, and sought permission to give water to the wounded Union soldiers in front. Telling him that he would certainly be killed for attempting such a foolhardy project, Kershaw refused to allow him to do so. However, when Kirkland persisted, his commanding officer relented and gave an affirmative answer.

Kirkland thereupon obtained a dozen or more canteens filled with water and leaped across the stone wall. Federal soldiers saw him and, supposing his purpose was to rob the dead and wounded, fired upon him. As soon as they saw him raise the head of a bluecoat and give him a drink from a canteen, they withheld their fire. As Kirkland continued his Samaritan efforts, both friend and foe cheered him. He then returned to his own lines and prepared to defend the stone wall against further attacks. He continued to serve in the Confederate army in Longstreet's corps until he was killed on the field of Chickamauga.[25]

In order to divert attention from the Confederate left, Burnside ordered Franklin to attack with his whole force. He also directed Major General Joseph Hooker, who commanded three reserve divisions, to renew the assault on the Confederate left — against the stone wall. However, after consulting Hancock and French regarding the strength of the Confederate position, Hooker was convinced that "it would be a useless waste of life to attack with the force at my disposal."[26] He then went to Burnside to try to dissuade him but was unsuccessful.

Complying with orders from his superior, General Hooker prepared for the attack. He first directed the Federal artillery to shell the Confederate position behind the stone wall, at the foot of Marye's Hill. By this time the Southerners had placed four brigades behind the wall and in some places the firing line was six ranks deep. At four o'clock in the afternoon Hooker sent Brigadier General Andrew A. Humphreys' division against the foe, but it was thrown back as its predecessors had been. When Getty's division then launched an unsuccessful assault upon the end of Marye's Hill and twilight settled on the battleground, Hooker withdrew. He remarked, "Finding that I had lost as many men as my orders required me to lose, I suspended the attack."[27] This ended the battle.

The next day General Burnside issued an order to resume the attack but subsequently rescinded it. He later stated that when General Sumner had protested against such action and had informed him that the higher Union commanders were unanimously against it, he had given in.[28]

Lee had hoped that Burnside would renew the attack on December 14 and strengthened his lines accordingly. However, that day and the day following passed with no renewal of the engagement. Burnside withdrew his men to the north bank of the Rappahannock on the night of December 15.

According to one account, on the day following the battle of Fredericksburg Generals Lee, Hampton, and Early were together, looking at the Federals before them. Early remarked that he "wished they were all dead." Lee is alleged to have rebuked his outspoken subordinate and to have said that he "did not wish that they were dead but that they would go home and mind their own business." However, as soon as Lee had left, Old Jube added, "I not only wish them all dead but I wish them all in Hell!"[29]

CHAPTER 12

Old Jube Helps Defeat Hooker

After the Battle of Fredericksburg General Early's division went into winter quarters in the vicinity of Port Royal, about twenty miles down the Rappahannock River from Fredericksburg. As the Federals established a line of cavalry pickets on the opposite bank of the river, the Confederates erected fortifications, paying special attention to those places where the enemy might cross the stream. The Southerners also busied themselves constructing roads in order to facilitate ease of communication.[1]

In recognition of General Early's fine leadership of Ewell's division, he was promoted to major general, with his new rank beginning as of January 17, 1863.[2] He was also assigned to the permanent command of the division which he had been leading and the name of that organization was changed to that of its new leader. General Ewell was still unable to resume active duty in the field because of his wound at Groveton. Early's brigade commanders were Brigadier Generals R. F. Hoke, William Smith, A. R. Lawton, and Harry T. Hays.[3]

There was very little activity on the Union side of the Rappahannock during this time. The lack of confidence in General Burnside was not improved by the ill-fated "Mud March" in January, 1863, in the course of which the Federal commander wanted to cross the Rappahannock in order to move around the Confederate left. He soon had to abandon this project, however, because of heavy rains which made the Virginia back roads impassable. Some of them had to be corduroyed before they could be used at all.[4] Dissension in the ranks of the Unionists was revealed when Burnside issued an order dismissing Major General Joseph Hooker and several other high-ranking general officers from the Federal army. Giving President Lincoln the alternative of supporting him in this move or accepting his own resignation, Burnside learned that the President had decided to let him go. In his place as the new commander of the Army of the Potomac was Joseph Hooker.[5]

Although General Early's Confederates were not bothered by

the enemy, they were by no means inactive. Old Jube has given an interesting account of.how his troops occupied themselves on one occasion. The winter of 1862-1863 provided Virginians with much snow and once when it lay deep on the ground, Hoke's brigade challenged Lawton's to a battle with snowballs. The offer was quickly accepted, and the two brigades took their positions. General Hoke led his men, while Colonel Evans headed their opponents. Since Hoke's men were the challengers, they attacked Evans' troops, who had taken position in defense of their camp. Colonel Evans had the larger force but, unfortunately, his soldiers were Georgians who were not as accustomed to snow as Hoke's North Carolinians. Consequently, when the more experienced snowballers attacked vigorously, giving the Confederate yell, and pelting the "enemy" unmercifully with hard balls, the Georgians retired in a complete rout. Their camp fell into possession of the assaulters.

However, Evans' men could not look on unconcerned while their successful opponents helped themselves to the spoils in the captured camp. They soon reformed their lines and counterattacked with great vigor. They were so determined that they succeeded in forcing Hoke's band to flee. Pushing ahead all along the line, the Georgians sent the North Carolinians reeling back to the latter's camp. To complete the picture, they even managed to capture General Hoke. After wallowing him in the snow, they released him on parole.[6] On other occasions similar snow battles often provided the soldiers with relief from the monotony of the routine while an army was in winter quarters.

When President Abraham Lincoln decided to offer command of the Union Army of the Potomac to Major General Joseph Hooker, he felt impelled to give his new selection some words of advice. Accordingly, he addressed the following letter to the Federal general:

Executive Mansion
Washington, D. C., January 26, 1863

Major-General Hooker:

General:

I have placed you at the head of the Army of the Potomac. Of course I have done this upon what appears to me to be sufficient reasons, and yet I think it best for you to know that there are some things in regard to which I am not quite satisfied with you. I believe you to be a brave and skillful soldier, which, of course, I like. I also believe you do not mix politics with your profession, in which you are right. You have confidence in yourself, which is a valuable, if not an indispensable, quality. You are ambitious, which, within reasonable bounds, does good rather than harm; but I think that during General Burnside's command of the army you have taken counsel of your ambition, and thwarted him as much as you could, in which you did a great wrong to the country and to a most meritorious and honorable brother officer. I have heard, in such a way as to believe it, of your recently saying that both the Army and the Government needed a dictator. Of course, it was not for this, but in spite of it, that I have given you the command. Only those generals who gain successes can set up dictators. What I now ask of you is military success, and I will risk the dictatorship. The Government will support you to the utmost of its ability, which is neither more nor less than it has done and will do for all commanders. I much fear that the spirit which you have aided to infuse into the army, of criticising their commander and withholding confidence from him, will now turn upon you. I shall assist you as far as I can to put it down. Neither you nor Napoleon, if he were alive again, could get any good out of an army while such a spirit prevails in it. And now beware of rashness. Beware of rashness, but with energy and sleepless vigilance go forward and give us victories.

Yours, very truly,

A. Lincoln[7]

In spite of the President's fears concerning the spirit of the Army of the Potomac, the appointment of "Fighting Joe" Hooker revived the morale of the army. The new commander abolished the awkward Grand Divisions of Burnside and reorganized the army into corps. Instead of keeping the cavalry attached in fragments to infantry divisions, he consolidated it into a Cavalry Corps under the leadership of Brigadier General George Stoneman. When the latter part of April, 1863, rolled around, Hooker had what he called "the finest army on the planet."[8] At this time it consisted of approximately 122,000 infantry and artillery, included 400 cannon, and boasted 11,000 cavalry.[9] It was posted on the northern side of the Rappahannock River, opposite the town of Fredericksburg, and sprawled in both directions along the river.

General Hooker's main antagonist, the Confederate Army of Northern Virginia commanded by General Robert E. Lee, had remained on the southern bank of the Rappahannock, behind the town of Fredericksburg. Its entire complement of men was no more than about 60,000, which included 6,500 cavalry. Lee's artillery numbered about 170 guns.[10] Its lines stretched from Banks' Ford on the left to Port Royal on the right.

Burnside's disastrous repulse at Fredericksburg the preceding December had convinced Hooker of the futility of attempting to attack Lee's whole army on Marye's Hill and the adjoining heights. The Federal commander then determined to move around Lee's flanks instead of making a suicidal assault on the Confederate front. Because the terrain seemed more favorable, he planned to turn Lee's left. To do this, it would be necessary to move up the north bank of the Rappahannock, cross at one of the fords, and push on to Chancellorsville. At the same time the main force was to make this march, part of the Federal troops were to be left behind on Stafford Heights to watch the Confederates opposite them, and, if possible, to attack them. Hooker planned to send most of his cavalry on a raid to destroy Lee's lines of communication with Richmond and Gordonsville and, if Lee should retreat, to hold or delay him.[11]

As soon as General Lee became aware of General Hooker's plan, he prepared to attack one of the separate wings of the Federal army, even though each wing was almost equal to his entire force. He decided to leave General Jubal Early's division and General William Barksdale's brigade, together with the reserve artillery, to "contain" the Federals left behind at Fredericksburg. Then, with the remainder of his force Lee planned to assault Hooker's main army in the vicinity of Chancellorsville.

That wing of the Union army which had been left behind at Fredericksburg consisted of the First and Sixth Corps commanded by Major General John Sedgwick. This force included about 40,000 troops, supported by an additional 19,000 in reserve from the Third Corps. To oppose this large army Early had only 9,000 men and fifty-six guns.[12]

After the principal Union and Confederate armies had left the Fredericksburg vicinity, General Sedgwick received an order from General Hooker to move through Fredericksburg, drive Early away, and then advance to Chancellorsville. Sedgwick was further instructed to be ready at daybreak on the morning of May 3 to attack Lee's rear while Hooker assailed the front. Although it was almost midnight on May 2-3 when Sedgwick received this order, he advanced almost at once to Fredericksburg.

According to the instructions he had received from General Lee, Early was expected to try to hold Sedgwick if at all possible; if not, to retire toward Guiney's Depot on the Richmond, Fredericksburg, and Potomac Railroad, so as to protect Confederate supplies gathered there. In the event that the Federals disappeared from his front or materially weakened their force in that location,

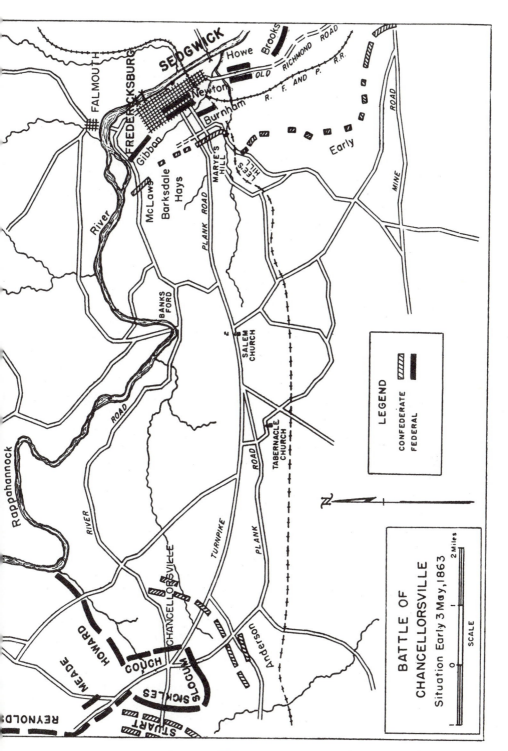

BATTLE OF
CHANCELLORSVILLE

Situation Early 3 May, 1863

LEGEND

CONFEDERATE

FEDERAL

SCALE

2 Miles

SEDGWICK

FALMOUTH

FREDERICKSBURG

Howe

Brooks

OLD RICHMOND ROAD

R. F. AND P. R.R.

Newton

Burnham

Gibbon

MARYE'S HILL

LEE'S HILL

Early

McLaws

Barksdale

Hays

River

PLANK ROAD

MINE ROAD

BANKS FORD

SALEM CHURCH

TABERNACLE CHURCH

ROAD

Rappahannock

RIVER

PLANK ROAD

TURNPIKE

CHANCELLORSVILLE

Anderson

HOWARD

COUCH

SLOCUM

SICKLES

MEADE

STUART

REYNOLDS

119

Early was ordered to join the main Confederate army at Chancellorsville. However, if he did unite with Lee, Old Jube was to leave behind at Fredericksburg a force which would be strong enough to protect the town.[13] According to Dr. Douglas S. Freeman, " . . . if someone had to remain at Fredericksburg, and Jackson had to go and Longstreet was absent, Early, all in all, was the division commander best qualified to guard the heights and to protect the rear of the Confederate forces that were moving against Hooker."[14]

When the Federals opposite the Confederate right began to withdraw on the morning of May 2, Early was hopeful that he would soon be able to lead part of his small army to join Lee at Chancellorsville. Before he made this move, he learned from his subordinates on the Confederate left that Sedgwick's men were assembling at Falmouth, across the river from the upper end of Fredericksburg. As it seemed likely the enemy was planning to cross the stream there and attack the Confederate left flank, reinforcements for Lee from Early's small command were out of the question.

While Old Jube discussed the situation with his subordinates defending the Confederate left, Brigadier Generals William Barksdale and William N. Pendleton, he received a visit from Colonel R. H. Chilton, Lee's Chief of Staff. Colonel Chilton brought verbal orders from Lee that Early was to advance toward Chancellorsville with his entire force, except for Pendleton's artillery and one brigade of infantry. He was further directed to leave a few artillery pieces to support the infantry but to send the bulk of the guns to a safe place in the rear. If the force left behind was unable to defend its position against Federal assaults, it was to retreat toward Spotsylvania Court House.[15]

Both Early and Pendleton were considerably surprised by Chilton's message and questioned the latter to be sure there could be no mistake. Old Jube told him that he could not possibly retire without being seen by the enemy, who was using balloons to observe Confederate movements. He also pointed out that the Federals would undoubtedly take possession of Fredericksburg, as well as the surrounding heights. Chilton replied that Lee had presumably taken all these facts into consideration and that it was more important for his commander to have a stronger force at Chancellorsville than to continue to leave so many troops at Fredericksburg. If successful in defeating Hooker at Chancellorsville, he would be able to retake Fredericksburg. Noticing the large Federal force at Falmouth, Chilton remarked that it was probably on the way to join Hooker at Chancellorsville. Upon being requestioned by Early and Pendleton, Colonel Chilton said there could be no mistake in his orders.[16]

General Early was still not convinced that Colonel Chilton had interpreted General Lee's orders correctly, and he pointed out that the Union force which he was confronting at Fredericksburg was much larger than any he could expect to defeat in the Wilderness. However reluctant he was to abandon his position at Fredericksburg, Early was a good enough soldier to know that orders were orders, and he prepared to move. He assumed that his commander knew more about the situation than he, himself, did.

He soon had most of his army in motion on the Plank Road to Chancellorsville. He left the covering force, as instructed, and pulled his troops out of their positions. Just before dark, he received another messenger from Lee's headquarters who informed him that Chilton had misunderstood his commander's previous orders. The new instructions, which were written, reiterated the original ones Lee had given Early, that is, Old Jube was not to leave Fredericksburg if a withdrawal could not be safely made and if, by remaining there, he could neutralize a large enemy force.[17]

In spite of this confusion of orders, Early determined to continue the march toward Chancellorsville. He reasoned that in all probability the Federals had occupied the positions he had evacuated and that he could not expect, with his small force, to drive them out. Thus he would deprive Lee entirely of the use of his troops, at a time when the Confederate chieftain might need them most. Accordingly, the column continued along the Plank Road for about a mile, when Early was overtaken by another messenger. This one was from Barksdale's brigade, which had been following Early's division. This courier brought the alarming news that the Federals were advancing against the heights back of Fredericksburg in great numbers and that unless the small Confederate defending force had immediate assistance, all the artillery which Early had left behind would be captured. The messenger also stated that Barksdale had reversed his column to march back to Fredericksburg.

This threw a new light on the situation. Old Jube could not afford to lose all of his artillery, nor could he divide his little army in the presence of such a large enemy force. His whole command would either have to continue the march to Chancellorsville or return to Fredericksburg. He decided to try to save the artillery and gave orders for his men to about-face. There was still a possibility that the Federals had not occupied the positions which Old

Jube's men formerly held, although the enemy would undoubtedly do so the next day. Great was Early's relief when he reached his former lines late in the evening and discovered them untenanted by Federals! Colonel Chilton's misunderstanding of orders, while exasperating to say the least, had apparently resulted in no permanent damage. Only General Pendleton, in charge of the artillery on the Confederate left, appeared weakened. In compliance with orders, he had sent many of his guns to a safe place far away, and he would thus have to make the best fight with what guns remained.[18]

The battle opened at daylight on the morning of May 3 with the Federal artillery and infantry attacking Early's left. The defending Southerners beat back two assaults. Old Jube thought the main Federal attack would be against his right flank, which was not as strongly fortified by nature as his left was.[19] But Sedgwick had determined to try to penetrate the Confederate lines defending Marye's Hill. This was the same position against which Burnside had sent his troops in vain the previous December.

At about eleven o'clock the Unionists sent a whole division, supported by a brigade, against Marye's Hill. Although the defenders in Barksdale's brigade were so spread out they had only one infantryman to about five feet of parapet, they beat off this third attack. Then the Federals under a flag of truce requested permission from Colonel Thomas M. Griffin, commanding the immediate line of defense, to take care of their wounded. The Confederate officer very graciously received the enemy flag-bearers, who were thus unsuspectingly given an opportunity to see just how weak the defense was. Hurrying back, the flag-bearers reported this to their own side with the result that a furious Union attack overwhelmed the defenders and enabled the bluecoats to gain possession of Marye's Hill.[20]

As soon as the Unionists broke through the left of his defense line, Early prepared to form another, in the rear. He was driven back about two miles before he found defensible ground, near what was known locally as Cox's house. By the middle of the afternoon he had drawn up his little force in a defensive manner, awaiting the next Federal move. His infantry losses in this engagement were not great, but his artillery did not fare so well. The Federals succeeded in capturing ten Confederate guns, although the Southerners managed to retake two.[21] The horses belonging to these guns had been taken to a safe place in the rear and could not be brought up in time to save them.[22]

While Early had been confronting Sedgwick at Fredericksburg, Lee's main part of the Army of Northern Virginia had been outmaneuvering Hooker in the Wilderness. While it is not the purpose of this book to describe in detail the events taking place in the Chancellorsville region, it is necessary to state briefly the principal events transpiring there. Lee's plan to trap Sedgwick, after Hooker had been disposed of, called for participation by Early's division.

After Hooker took position in the neighborhood of Chancellorsville, he surrendered the initiative to Lee's inferior force. The Confederate commander and his principal subordinate, Jackson, worked out a daring plan whereby Lee would divide his army so as to send Jackson on a flank march to attack the Federal right and rear. The scheme worked admirably. Early on the morning of May 2, Stonewall's men began their march. Because Hooker had sent most of his cavalry off on a raid far to the south, the Union leader was not kept well informed of his adversary's moves. On the contrary, Stuart's cavalry apprised Lee of Hooker's activities. Because they had to take a circuitous route in order to be invisible to the Federals, Jackson's troops did not arrive in position to assault the Federal right until late in the evening. When they had gained their objective, they attacked and drove back the unsuspecting Federals in confusion.

About this time Jackson rode ahead of his lines to reconnoiter and, upon his return, was mistaken for the enemy and wounded three times. He died about a week later from pneumonia after an arm had been amputated to save his life. The wounding of Jackson at Chancellorsville, followed by the wounding of A. P. Hill, caused suspension of the Confederate assault. However, it was resumed on the morning of May 3 by J. E. B. Stuart, who had succeeded to command of the infantry forces even though he was a cavalryman.

At the same time that Stuart was attacking the Federal right, Lee was assaulting its front. The Confederates managed to reunite their lines and by mounting an offensive all along the line obtained possession of Chancellorsville and the field of battle. Hooker withdrew to new positions nearer the Rappahannock. Lee prepared to renew the attack when he received word that Sedgwick had captured Marye's Hill and was advancing on the Plank Road toward Chancellorsville. The Southern leader then made dispositions to meet this new threat. The resulting engagement was known as the Battle of Salem Church.

General Lee sent Major General Lafayette McLaws down the Plank Road to meet the advance of Sedgwick and then ordered Early, in conjunction with McLaws, to attack the bluecoats.[23] Old

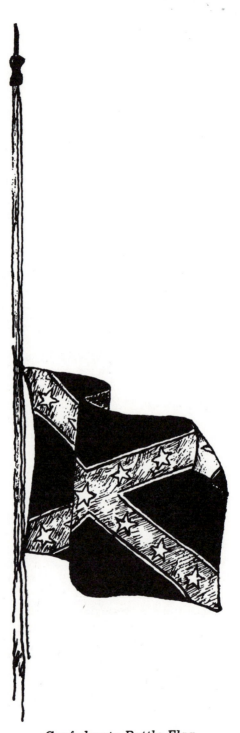

Confederate Battle Flag

Jube sent word to McLaws that he would concentrate his troops that night [May 3] and would move against the enemy early the next morning. The aggressive Early informed his colleague that he would drive the Federals from Lee's and Marye's Hills and that, while advancing, he would connect with McLaws' right.[24]

At daybreak on the morning of May 4 Early began the advance. He sent Brigadier General John B. Gordon, who now led Lawton's old brigade, along the Telegraph Road until he reached Lee's Hill which he found unoccupied. Taking possession of this eminence, Gordon pushed on toward Marye's Hill. In order to reach it he had to drive off a force of Federal infantry which was moving along the Plank Road. Gordon's successes cut Sedgwick off from the town of Fredericksburg.

Early then directed another of his brigade commanders, Brigadier General William Smith, to move against the Federals who were still in possession of some of the nearby heights to the northward. However, when the enemy appeared too strong to be dislodged, Old Jube called off the assault. Two of Smith's regiments suffered the loss of part of their strength when about ninety men took refuge in a house at the foot of a hill and remained there until captured by the Federals. Early then communicated his day's activities to McLaws, whom he requested to attack at once, for Old Jube had not discovered any evidence of offensive action by his colleague.

Early selected one of his staff members, Lieutenant A. L. Pitzer, to carry this information to McLaws. The latter was at Salem Church, on the Plank Road about six miles from Fredericksburg. When Pitzer brought Old Jube's request for cooperation in an attack, McLaws was inclined to wait. He was not familiar with the terrain in his front, nor did he know the strength of his opponent. Also, he had received word from Lee that the division of Major General Richard H. Anderson was moving from Chancellorsville to reinforce the Confederates at Salem Church. McLaws instructed Pitzer to inform Early that he would not advance until Anderson joined him. Then, the signal for the general attack would be three guns, fired in rapid succession.[25]

Before the signal was given, Lee arrived on the scene. Apparently he had decided that the threat from Sedgwick demanded the attention of the commanding general himself, and he abandoned Hooker in the Wilderness. Meeting Early, Lee went over the situation with him and then decided that McLaws should demonstrate in front of the Federals and that Old Jube, along with Anderson, should begin the attack. Once the advance got under way, Lee planned to send in the troops of Brigadier Generals W. T. Wofford and Joseph B. Kershaw.[26]

When the signal for the attack was heard, Early put his brigade in motion against Sedgwick's left flank. Everything went according to plan until Brigadier General Robert F. Hoke received a wound which caused him to fall from his horse. Unfortunately, none of his subordinates knew the brigade's mission. As they pushed forward, they came into contact with Hays' men, with the result that both organizations were thrown into a bad state of confusion. Their advance into a woods made it almost impossible to restore order. Although they had been driving the Federals before them, they at last arrived at a place where the enemy had rallied. Receiving a warm reception from this quarter, the Southerners withdrew. Early reformed their lines along the Plank Road, but darkness interfered with the continuance of the attack. That part of Sedgwick's force which received this assault was the division of Brigadier General Albion P. Howe.[27]

McLaws, on the Confederate left, had not been in contact with Early, on the right, and consequently was ignorant of what his colleague had been doing. Two of McLaws' brigades, Kershaw's and Wofford's, advanced across the Plank Road and pressed on toward Banks' Ford. Anderson's division, in the center of the Confederate line, had reached the Plank Road about dark. Nightfall prevented the Southerners from cutting Sedgwick off from his escape route, which proved to be Banks' Ford across the Rappahannock. During the night he crossed that stream by means of a pontoon bridge and thus escaped.

Lee still believed a large Federal force to be in Fredericksburg and ordered Early there during the night. As Old Jube was also directed to leave two of his brigades in line on the north of the Plank Road, he had only two with which to reinforce Barksdale at Fredericksburg. That night Barksdale thought the Federals were reoccupying the town in force, and therefore, he requested reinforcements from Early. To this demand Old Jube replied that he had none to send and that he thought Barksdale was in error about the Federals reoccupying the town in force. He thought that the morrow would find the enemy had withdrawn across the Rappahannock. Early's guess was correct. When the morning of May 5 broke, Sedgwick had removed his entire force north of that stream.[28]

That same day Lee directed Early to leave Barksdale at Fredericksburg and to proceed with the remainder of his force up the Plank Road toward Chancellorsville. Old Jube advanced as far

Old Jube's Men at Fredericksburg during the Battle of Chancellorsville

127

as Salem Church, where he was halted. Later he was ordered to return to his old position at Fredericksburg. Having disposed of Sedgwick at the Battle of Salem Church, Lee now planned to finish off Hooker. To do so, however, he would have to reunite his scattered forces. He spent most of May 5 getting ready to attack Hooker at daybreak on the sixth. However, in this he was disappointed. As his skirmishers advanced, they discovered that Hooker, like Sedgwick, had withdrawn and put the Rappahannock between his own army and that of Northern Virginia.[29] Thus Hooker, like his predecessors, McDowell, McClellan, Pope, and Burnside, had failed utterly to destroy Lee's army, and Old Jube again played a prominent part in defeating the Federal plans.

Several years after the war had ended, the Union General William T. Sherman was conversing with one of Hooker's veterans who had fought at Chancellorsville. While the soldier from the Army of the Potomac was describing that engagement, Sherman asked, "Did the rebels run?" Whereupon the veteran replied, "Did they run? Did the rebels run? Great Scott! I should say they did run. Why, General, they run so like thunder that we had to run three miles to keep out of their way; and if we hadn't thrown away our guns, they'd run all over us, sure!"[30]

CHAPTER 13

Old Bald Head and Old Jube Cooperate

After General Hooker's failure at Chancellorsville the Army of Northern Virginia and the Army of the Potomac resumed their positions on opposite sides of the Rappahannock River in the Fredericksburg region. Since both forces needed rest and reorganization, there was little aggressive activity during the remainder of May, 1863. As might be expected, Union morale suffered another setback as a result of the Confederate victory at Chancellorsville. On the other hand, General Lee's army felt itself equal to any task its beloved leader might ask it to perform. It is not an exaggeration to state that the *esprit de corps* of the Army of Northern Virginia was never as high as it was on the eve of the Gettysburg campaign.

Besides having a fine fighting spirit, the Confederate army increased its numbers. It was strengthened by the arrival of two divisions of Longstreet's corps, which had not participated in the Battle of Chancellorsville. They had been detached from the main army prior to that engagement for a minor enterprise against Suffolk. Furthermore, the Army of Northern Virginia was aided by the operation of the Confederate draft act, which brought in a large number of conscripts. By May 31 it boasted a grand total of approximately 76,000 officers and men, and 272 pieces of artillery.[1]

The death of Stonewall Jackson on May 10 posed a serious problem regarding a successor to lead the renowned Second Corps. Lee had a number of able officers still in service but, as events were later to prove, none was capable of measuring up to Jackson's standards as a subordinate. Because of the increased size of his force, Lee reorganized his infantry into three corps, instead of the two he had formerly employed. The corps were led by Lieutenant Generals James Longstreet, Richard Ewell, and A. P. Hill. Each one consisted of three divisions and most of the latter had four brigades. Since each corps possessed five battalions of artillery, it was a complete little army in itself, except that it lacked a complement of cavalry. It is interesting to note that the general organization of the Confederate corps was practically the same as is used today.

In the reorganization of Hooker's Army of the Potomac the average strength of army corps and divisions was only about half that of Lee's force. The Federal army was commanded by many officers whose rank was not commensurate with their responsibilities. The United States authorities throughout the Civil War displayed a reluctance to bestow adequate rank upon their higher commanders. Although each Union corps and division was numerically inferior to its Confederate counterpart, the Army of the Potomac had many more than the South so that its overall strength exceeded that of the Army of Northern Virginia. According to one report, the Army of the Potomac on June 30 had approximately 115,000 officers and men, as well as 362 guns.[2]

The Confederate authorities at Richmond decided to use their reorganized Army of Northern Virginia for a second invasion of the North. Lee, ever aggressive, knew that the South could never expect to win the war by remaining strictly on the defensive. It might postpone ultimate defeat by repelling Union attacks, but, unless war weariness in the North forced the Lincoln administration to make peace, the enemy's superior resources were bound to tip the scales in the end. However, if the South would abandon its defensive state of mind and would advance into Northern territory, it might win a great victory there. The scene of conflict would not only be shifted to the enemy's land and thus Virginia would be given a respite from the fighting, but foreign recognition of Southern independence might result from a victory on Northern soil. It was also hoped that a successful invasion of Pennsylvania would ease the pressure which U. S. Grant was exerting on John C. Pemberton at Vicksburg and W. S. Rosecrans, on Braxton Bragg in East Tennessee.

In execution of the proposed offensive, Lee planned to use the favorite route of the Shenandoah Valley, cross the Potomac at Williamsport or Shepherdstown, enter Maryland, and then proceed northward via the Cumberland Valley. He hoped to replenish his inadequate supplies from the well-stocked farms in Pennsylvania. If he used the route of the Shenandoah, he could maintain his communications by holding the passes of the Blue Ridge and South Mountains. In order to prevent Hooker from concentrating all of the Union strength against him in the North, Lee proposed that Beauregard organize an army "even in effigy" at Culpeper Court House. The failure of the Richmond authorities to create this army removed a threat to Washington from that quarter and enabled Hooker to advance his whole army northward to meet Lee.[3]

In the reorganization of Lee's army Jubal Early's division was attached to the Second Corps, now commanded by "Dick" Ewell. The latter had recovered from his serious wound at Groveton and, although minus a leg, was ready for the long march to Pennsylvania. Besides Early's division, Ewell's corps included the divisions led by Major Generals Edward Johnson and Robert E. Rodes. The brigades which comprised Early's division were headed by Brigadier Generals Harry T. Hays, John B. Gordon, Isaac E. Avery [Hoke's brigade], and William Smith.[4]

Ewell's corps left its position along the Rappahannock on June 4 and marched toward Culpeper Court House, which it reached three days later. Learning that Federal cavalry was active near Brandy Station on June 9, Ewell sent Early's division to support the Confederate troopers of General J. E. B. Stuart. Although Stuart was taken by surprise at this aggressive movement by the despised Federal horsemen, he succeeded in driving off the attackers after much fighting. Hence it was not necessary for Early's infantrymen to aid Stuart's proud squadrons, and Old Jube's men returned to their camp.[5]

The corps resumed the northward march June 10 and, crossing the Blue Ridge Mountains at Chester Gap, reached Front Royal two days later. As Old Bald Head Ewell approached Winchester, he detached Rodes' division, supported by cavalry, to move against a Federal force at Berryville and then to advance toward Martinsburg. He planned to attack Winchester with his remaining strength which consisted of Early's and Johnson's divisions. This famous town located in the northern end of the Shenandoah Valley was then defended by Major General R. H. Milroy, who had a force estimated by Ewell to number from 6,000 to 8,000.[6]

General Ewell closed in on the Federals defending Winchester. He sent Early to Newtown [Stephens City], from which village Old Jube was directed to proceed along the Valley pike toward the principal objective. At the same time the corps commander directed General Edward Johnson to approach Winchester along the Front Royal road. With Rodes' division operating east and northeast of the doomed city, Ewell hoped to trap the Federal garrison if Milroy did not retire before the investment was complete. General Henry W. Halleck in Washington had already directed that the Federal troops in Winchester be withdrawn to Harpers Ferry, but Milroy had failed to comply.[7]

In carrying out his part of the plan, Early found a Federal

force opposing his movement. After a sharp skirmish he drove it back toward Winchester. He then moved his division by a circuitous route to Little North Mountain, an eminence to the west. From here he planned to shell the Federal forts on that side of town. After a reconnaissance on the morning of June 14, Ewell had expressed complete approval of Old Jube's proposed activities.[8]

Before Early launched an attack against the Federals west of the town, he reconnoitered the ground in his front. He discovered an old orchard and a corn-field—excellent positions from which his twenty artillery pieces would be able to fire upon the enemy's fort. He then directed Brigadier General Harry T. Hays to prepare to make the initial assault with his brigade after the artillery had opened. Posting his remaining troops so that they could protect the artillery and support the infantry advance, Early then ordered the guns to begin firing.

After a cannonading which lasted almost an hour, Hays' brigade advanced against the Federal fort. Although it had to ascend a steep slope and pass through a defense of felled trees, it captured the enemy fortification. Gaining possession of several rifled pieces, it proceeded to turn them upon their former owners, who were preparing to counterattack. Early then sent forward his supporting force so that the recently-won position would not be lost. When he reached this post, Old Jube was delighted to confirm his earlier suspicion that it dominated the other Federal positions in the area, especially the main work, which was called the Flag Fort. However, by the time he had moved his troops into the captured position, it was too late in the evening to assault the Flag Fort. Consequently, Early indulged in an artillery exchange and in making preparations for continuing the offense on the morrow. He then sent a courier to notify Ewell of his success.[9]

General Ewell had already learned how well Old Jube had accomplished his mission, for he had been able to watch the progress of his subordinate from the Corps Headquarters on the Millwood road. He now wondered if General Milroy would attempt to withdraw his whole force from Winchester to Martinsburg or Harpers Ferry. Early's courier had reported that Old Jube expected the Federal leader to retire during the night, and Ewell himself came to the same conclusion. After all, Milroy's division could hardly expect to oppose successfully the entire Second Corps of the Army of Northern Virginia!

As Milroy's probable line of retreat, if he decided to withdraw, would be the Valley Pike to the north, Ewell directed Edward Johnson to lead his division to a point where it could intercept the Federals. The best place for carrying out this objective seemed to be Stephenson's Depot, about four miles north of Winchester. From this station on the Winchester and Potomac Railroad Milroy could flee northeastward in the direction of Harpers Ferry or could remain on the Valley Pike and proceed to Martinsburg. Johnson arrived there early in the morning of June 15, just in time to encounter the head of Milroy's column which was seeking that avenue of escape from Ewell's trap. He made the necessary dispositions for an immediate attack but was denied that privilege, as it was the Federals who attacked first.[10]

Milroy's attempt to break through Johnson's lines by a direct frontal attack failed, whereupon he tried to outflank the Confederates. He almost succeeded as Johnson's infantrymen had used up most of their ammunition and had no time to replenish their supply. However, at this point the famous Stonewall Brigade, now led by Brigadier General James A. Walker, arrived on the scene and promptly attacked. It checked the escape of the Federal infantry and forced its surrender although the Union cavalry, including Milroy, succeeded in getting away.

As soon as Jubal Early discovered that the Federals in the Flag Fort, opposite him, had evacuated, he ordered his whole command, except for the 13th Virginia regiment, forward in pursuit. He left the latter force behind to guard the wagons and other property which the retreating Federals had abandoned. When he came to the spot where Johnson had intercepted Milroy, he found that the fighting was over and that Johnson had captured a large number of prisoners. Realizing that further pursuit on foot was useless, Old Jube halted his division and encamped near Stephenson's Depot.[11]

With Winchester now securely in his possession and with its Federal garrison either captured or driven off, General Ewell took stock of his victory. According to his official report of this engagement, he acquired 23 pieces of artillery, most of which were rifled pieces, 4,000 prisoners, 300 loaded wagons, more than 300 horses, as well as a large amount of commissary stores. Such a bag of men and supplies was not to be minimized, especially when it cost Ewell a total loss of only 269, including killed, wounded, and missing.[12]

Although Ewell was anxious to press on into Pennsylvania, he remained in Winchester to attend a celebration on June 16. Some of the ladies from the Valley town called on him for a speech, whereupon he replied. "I can't make a speech to ladies. I never made a speech to but one lady in my life. My friend General Early

[pointing to Old Jube] can speak. He will address you, ladies."
The bachelor Early, however, could go Ewell one better, for he
answered, "I never have been able to make a speech to one lady,
much less to so many."[13]

As for General Halleck in Washington, he was so disgusted
with Milroy's failure to obey orders and evacuate Winchester
while he still had time to escape with his supplies, that Halleck
could only wire General Robert C. Schenck at Baltimore as follows: "Don't give General Milroy any command at Harper's Ferry;
we have had enough of that sort of military genius."[14]

CHAPTER 14

In the Enemy's Country

After the capture of Winchester Ewell's corps, leading the Confederate advance into the North, crossed the Potomac below Shepherdstown and moved into Maryland. It quickly occupied Sharpsburg and Hagerstown while the cavalry brigade of Brigadier General Albert G. Jenkins marched toward Chambersburg to obtain supplies. The other two corps of the Army of Northern Virginia, led by Generals Longstreet and A. P. Hill, were also on the march northward, so that practically all of Lee's army, except for isolated commands, was preparing to invade Pennsylvania.[1]

In order to understand General Lee's ignorance of the whereabouts of General Hooker's Federal army it is necessary to point out that during the march into Pennsylvania Lee was deprived of the services of his principal cavalry force, that led by General J. E. B. Stuart. This dashing cavalier had been given the task of operating on the right of Longstreet's corps in order to screen the movements of the infantry and to keep posted on the activities of the Federals. Unfortunately for Lee, Stuart, through some misunderstanding, decided to make another one of his famous raids around the Union army. Leaving two cavalry brigades to guard the passes in the Blue Ridge Mountains, Stuart took three brigades on this expedition. He expected to move around the Federals and then rejoin Lee in Maryland, but the activity of the enemy forced him so far east that he forded the Potomac within twenty miles of Washington. After capturing a Union wagon train of 125 wagons and teams, he entered Pennsylvania but did not rejoin Lee until July 2 at Gettysburg.[2]

In the meantime the Federal Army of the Potomac had changed commanders again. General Hooker had remained in charge after his defeat at Chancellorsville, although he had lost the confidence of President Lincoln and his military advisers. Hooker had ordered the Federal garrison at Harpers Ferry to withdraw and unite with the Twelfth Corps in order to cut Lee's communications and harass his rear. When he was overruled by

General Halleck at Washington, Hooker asked to be relieved from command. His request was granted, and on June 28 Major General George G. Meade took his place.[3]

General Jubal Early led his division of Ewell's corps across the Potomac below Shepherdstown into M a r y l a n d and then through Sharpsburg and Boonsboro into Pennsylvania. Crossing Mason and Dixon's famous line, he reached Waynesboro June 23 and then proceeded to Greenwood on the Chambersburg-Gettysburg turnpike. At the latter town he left his troops in camp while he rode to Chambersburg to consult his corps commander, who directed him to cross South Mountain and then advance on Gettysburg and York. As the Northern Central Railroad, which united Baltimore and Harrisburg, passed through York, Old Jube was ordered to cut it. If possible, he was to destroy the bridge across the Susquehanna River at Wrightsville, after which he was to rejoin Ewell at Carlisle.[4]

Before leaving Greenwood, Early ordered the iron works of Thaddeus Stevens to be burned. This establishment consisted of a furnace, a forge, and a rolling mill, as well as a saw mill and storehouse. Inasmuch as Federal officers had destroyed similar works in the South on the grounds that such property was a legitimate objective of war, Old Jube felt no hesitation in retaliating. As neither General Lee nor Ewell knew he would encounter Stevens' iron works, Early destroyed them on his own responsibility. In view of the fact that Stevens was a member of the United States House of Representatives and after the death of Lincoln became the directing hand in punishing the South, it is doubtful if Old Jube's act of destruction in this regard was wise. Certainly it increased the hatred and vindictiveness which the Northern Congressman displayed toward the South when the war was over.[5]

Generally speaking, this Confederate invasion of Pennsylvania was almost without parallel in history when one considers the limited amount of molestation of private property and persons. Armies invading the enemy's country are usually not so scrupulous about respecting private rights as Lee's gray-clad veterans were on this occasion. The commanding general himself had issued very strict orders against plundering and destroying. Of course the Confederate army made requisitions upon the Northern populace for the purpose of replenishing its supplies, but these were usually paid for in Confederate money or other kinds of notes. It is true that some of those good, thrifty German farmers in the beautiful valleys of Pennsylvania were reluctant to part with a prize beef or horse in exchange for paper money issued by a government whose survival was by no means certain. On occasion it was necessary to remind the owner that this was war and unusual things happened in wartime.

Brigadier General John B. Gordon, who commanded one of Early's brigades, is the source for several accounts in which the Confederates did not follow the full spirit and letter of Lee's directive. On one occasion when his troops went into camp in an open country after dark, they sought permission to use a few fence-rails for firewood to cook their supper. Apparently, except for the wooden fence rails, that necessary element for fire was entirely lacking. After looking at the fence, Gordon concluded that it would still be high enough if only the top layer of rail were removed, and he, therefore, gave his men permission to use the top rails. When morning arrived, he noticed that practically the whole fence had disappeared, but when he questioned his men, Gordon was informed by each man that he had taken only the top rail! Too late the general realized how his men had outwitted him.

On another occasion General Gordon related an amusing experience when some of his troops attempted to enforce the Confederate conscription law in Pennsylvania. This act had been passed by the Confederate Congress to conscript into the army able-bodied Southerners, but Gordon's men saw no reason why it should not apply equally to the gathering of able-bodied horses in the North. In an effort to enforce this law on a "Pennsylvania Dutchman," as those farmers were usually called, Gordon's quartermaster encountered some difficulty. The farmer in question apparently had been in the United States but a short time and consequently had not mastered all the intricacies of the English language. He attempted to save a favorite mare from the Confederates by argumentation. In the course of his remarks he made a comparison of values between his mare and his "t'ree vifes." According to General Gordon, the climax of the argument was reached when the farmer asserted: "I've been married, sir, t'ree times; and I vood not geef dot mare for all dose voomans!"[6] He was allowed to keep the mare.

In pursuance of Ewell's orders Early sent most of his wagons to Chambersburg and then marched eastward toward Gettysburg. Having learned that a Union force was in the Gettysburg neighborhood, he laid plans to capture it. When he drew closer to the town, he discovered that the enemy force consisted of the 26th Pennsylvania Militia regiment, which fled the battlefield when Confederate cavalry approached. However, the Southerners were able to capture 175 prisoners, whom they subsequently paroled. Early then attempted to conscript supplies from the Gettysburg citizens but was only partly successful. As he planned to move upon York the next day, he did not have time to see whether or not his demand for supplies could be met. Before he left Gettysburg, though, he destroyed a few freight cars and also a railroad bridge. He ordered Gordon's brigade to march to York while he, himself, with the rest of the division, moved on a parallel line slightly to the north of the York-Gettysburg turnpike.[7]

General Gordon found York undefended and entered it ahead of his chief. The town authorities met him near the corporate limits to surrender and seek protection for life and property. Gordon assured them that they had nothing to worry about from his men. As he was riding along one of the streets, a little girl ran up to his horse and handed him a large bouquet of flowers. In the center of this token of affection the surprised Confederate leader found a note written in a delicate handwriting. Upon reading it, Gordon discovered that it contained the number and position of the Union forces defending Wrightsville, his next objective. Later when he drew near to Wrightsville, his own reconnaissance corroborated the contents of the note, and he utilized this knowledge to good advantage. He never knew to whom he was indebted for this timely assistance, as the note bore no signature.[8]

When General Early arrived in York, on June 28, he established headquarters in the courthouse and declared martial law. He then made a requisition on the authorities for 2,000 pairs of shoes, 1,000 hats, 1,000 pairs of socks, three days' rations, and $100,000 in money. He received most of the supplies but only $28,600 in money. Ignorant of the fact that most of the bank deposits had been removed from the town for safekeeping and, believing the authorities had not made a serious effort to raise the whole amount, Old Jube directed that the citizenry be assembled for a public meeting in the courthouse.[9]

When the Yorkists answered the summons sent out by the courthouse bell, they filled the large court room. With the Stars and Bars flying from the flagstaff of the courthouse, Early reminded his listeners that the town was under martial law and he expected full compliance with his orders to produce the remainder of the money. The town's representatives protested that York could not possibly raise an additional $72,000, for the money was not there. It later developed that the money could have been collected from some private citizens, but since this fact was concealed from Early, he had no way of knowing whether or not the additional amount could be raised.[10] Believing that the authorities had made an honest effort to collect the whole amount, he did not take any strong measures to enforce his demand but left the town indebted to him for the remainder. Old Jube distributed the shoes, socks, and hats to his troops, who were badly in need of them. The only consolation which the thrifty Pennsylvanians had in place of their missing supplies was a promise to repay them after the independence of the Confederacy had been established.

Before leaving York to rejoin Gordon, who had marched to Wrightsville, Early attempted to wage a bit of psychological warfare. He could not resist leaving behind the following proclamation for the inhabitants of York to consider:

York, Pa., June 30th, 1863

To the Citizens of York:

I have abstained from burning the railroad buildings and car shops in your town, because after examination I am satisfied the safety of the town would be endangered; and, acting in the spirit of humanity which has ever characterized my government and its military authorities, I do not desire to involve the innocent in the same punishment with the guilty. Had I applied the torch without regard to consequences, I would have pursued a course that would have been fully vindicated as an act of just retaliation for the many authorized acts of barbarity perpetuated by your own army upon our soil. But we do not war upon women and children, and I trust the treatment you have met with at the hands of my soldiers will open your eyes to the monstrous iniquity of the war waged by your government upon the people of the Confederate States, and that you will make an effort to shake off the revolting tyranny under which it is apparent to all you are yourselves groaning.

J. A. Early
Maj. Gen'l., C. S. A.[11]

Meanwhile Early had sent the gallant Gordon to Wrightsville in an effort to secure the long bridge across the Susquehanna River. Using the knowledge gained from the unexpected note in York, General Gordon laid his plans. He determined to march down a ravine near town to the river, seize the bridge, and cross to the Columbia side. Then he hoped to move on through Lancaster toward Philadelphia so as to force General Meade to detach part of his army for the defense of the City of Brotherly Love. However, he was unable to get across the Susquehanna.[12]

As Gordon approached Wrightsville, he found it defended by a line of bluecoats, who promptly retreated across the bridge, fired it, and then took position across the river in the town of Columbia. In vain the Confederates attempted to save the burning bridge. Gordon requested the citizens of Wrightsville to furnish his men with buckets and pails but none of these utensils could be found. He could only stand by and watch the flames frustrate his bold plan to push on. The bridge, which had been prepared for destruction, burned furiously, and the flames finally reached a lumber yard near the Wrightsville end of the bridge. When the burning lumber fired the town and the villagers saw their homes endangered, Gordon was amazed at the number of tubs and pails and pans that appeared almost like magic. The Confederate officer estimated that there were enough of these utensils to equip the whole Army of Northern Virginia with fire-fighting apparatus, had it been present.

As the fire was threatening to destroy the whole town, Gordon's Confederates joined with the villagers in forming a bucket brigade from the river to the flames. At a late hour that night the Southern invaders succeeded in checking the flames and thus prevented the total destruction of Wrightsville.[13]

General Early was greatly disappointed that the Susquehanna River bridge had been destroyed, for he had to abandon the ambitious plan he had formulated to operate east of the river. As events turned out, however, he would doubtless have been unable to pursue his aggressive intentions east of the river even if the bridge had been saved. For, unknown to him, General Meade was moving north with a large Federal army to check the Confederate invaders. As soon as Lee received information concerning Meade's activities, he dispatched a courier with a note to inform Ewell. The latter sent his aide, Captain Elliott Johnston, with a copy of this note to Old Jube. As the commanding general of the Army of Northern Virginia had directed Ewell to concentrate his corps on the west side of South Mountain, Ewell gave Early verbal instructions concerning the part his division would play in the assembling of the corps.

Old Jube did not lose any time putting his division into motion. Moving in the direction of Heidlersburg by way of Weigelstown and East Berlin, he left York at daylight on the morning of June 30. Ewell had proceeded as far north as Carlisle and his cavalry had even reached the outskirts of Harrisburg before he received Lee's orders to concentrate his scattered corps. He moved with his usual celerity to Heidlersburg, where he met Early. Ewell then informed him that the Confederate strategy was for the corps to gather at Cashtown, on the Chambersburg-Gettysburg turnpike. While Early was marching toward Cashtown, Ewell sent him a note saying that A. P. Hill's corps was moving from Cashtown to Gettysburg and directed Early to lead his division to Gettysburg instead. Old Jube accordingly changed his course and moved on the direct road from Heidlersburg toward Gettysburg, which he reached on July 1.[14]

While marching to Gettysburg, the Confederates experienced several amusing incidents. On one occasion Early reported that he noticed a number of persons making mysterious signs at his troops as they passed through the rich Pennsylvania countryside. Upon inquiring the reason for this, he was informed that some enterprising individuals had preceded his division on the highway and had sold the inhabitants "protection" from the Confederates. These persons, whom Old Jube identified as "Yankees," had received payment for revealing certain signs, which, if made to the approaching invaders, would assure the purchaser immunity from molestation.[15]

At another time, according to one account, a Confederate regiment was camped on the outskirts of a small Pennsylvania town. The men, who were weary from marching over the hot, dusty roads, saw with eager anticipation that there was a small river near their camp. Before long they were nakedly refreshing themselves in its cool, clear waters. They had noticed that there were no houses in the immediate vicinity, but that on a hillside, about half a mile away, there was one dwelling which they later learned was occupied by a spinster. However, they expected to enjoy their swimming unmolested and, consequently, were greatly annoyed when a little later a boy came into camp bearing a note from the spinster to the commanding officer. The Confederate swimmers learned that the note read as follows: "Dear Sir: I wish you would order your men out of the river. I can see them plainly through my brother's field glasses."[16]

Meanwhile Lee had been advancing into Pennsylvania with the corps of Longstreet and A. P. Hill, in total ignorance of the whereabouts of the main Federal army. As has been pointed out, Stuart, instead of operating between the Confederate army and its opponent, was beyond the Union forces and in no communication whatsoever with Lee. The Southern commanding general had halted Longstreet and Hill near Chambersburg until he could locate Stuart. As the cavalry leader could not be found and as Lee had no way of learning Meade's dispositions, he supposed the Federals still to be south of the Potomac. In fact, he didn't know that Meade had succeeded Hooker until a Confederate spy brought this important information to Longstreet on the night of June 28. What was more important was the alarming news that the Union army had crossed the Potomac and was then occupying Frederick, Maryland.[17]

The Confederate chieftain quickly gave the orders necessary to meet this new challenge. He recognized the need for an immediate concentration of his whole army and for holding Meade east of the mountains. If he could succeed in the latter objective, he could secure his line of retreat. Lee hoped to assemble his army in the Cashtown-Gettysburg vicinity and there have Meade attack him on ground of his own choosing.

The preliminary maneuvering of the Battle of Gettysburg began when some Confederate infantrymen from Pettigrew's brigade of Heth's division, A. P. Hill's corps, approached the town of Gettysburg to obtain a supply of shoes. Meeting a force of Federal cavalry under the command of Brigadier General John Buford, Pettigrew withdrew to Cashtown—eight miles westward. Buford recognized the strategic importance of holding Gettysburg because of its location and posted his pickets to the west and north of the town. As the main Federal army was not at hand, he informed Generals Meade and John F. Reynolds of the situation.[18]

The strategic importance of Gettysburg was due to the fact that it was a point from which great roads diverged in all directions. One ran westward through a pass over South Mountain, which would presumably be Lee's main line of retreat in the event of failure, while another ran northward and eastward toward Harrisburg and other places along the Susquehanna River. Still another important highway stretched southeastward to Baltimore and Washington.

The town of Gettysburg is in a small valley and is surrounded by low hills. About half a mile west is a wooded elevation known as Seminary Ridge because of the Lutheran Seminary located on it. Across the Gettysburg-Emmitsburg turnpike and directly south of the town is another somewhat higher series of hills known as Cemetery Ridge. Entering this elevation from the south and traveling along it northward, the visitor will see such well-known locations as Round Top, Little Round Top, and Cemetery Hill. Then if he continues on a lower ridge toward the east, he will come upon Culp's Hill. Briefly a line extending from Culp's Hill along the ridge to Round Top might be said to resemble a fishhook, with its point at Culp's Hill bending around Cemetery Hill, its shank along Cemetery Hill and Cemetery Ridge, and its eye at Round Top. The fighting on the first day occurred west and

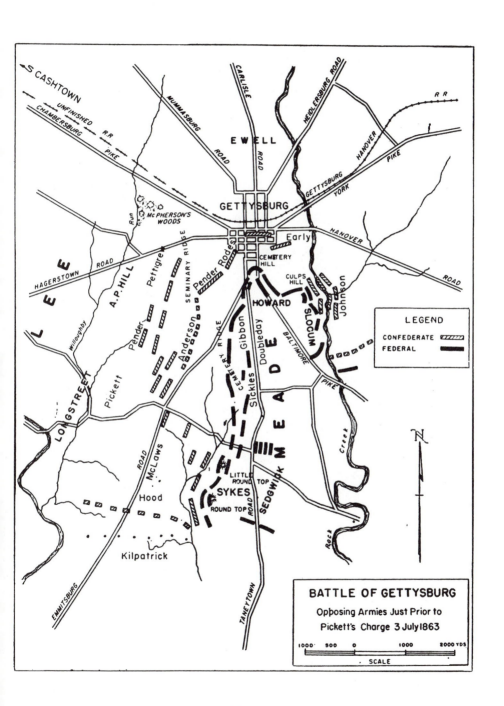

BATTLE OF GETTYSBURG

Opposing Armies Just Prior to
Pickett's Charge 3 July 1863

143

north of the town, whereas on the second and third days it was mainly centered on the ground between Seminary Ridge and Cemetery Ridge. After the first day's fighting Lee's main line was along Seminary Ridge, while Meade's rested on Cemetery Ridge.

The Battle of Gettysburg began early in the morning of July 1 when the divisions of Major Generals Henry Heth and William D. Pender, belonging to A. P. Hill's corps, approached Gettysburg from Cashtown. They soon discovered that General Buford had dismounted his cavalrymen and had formed them in a line west of Gettysburg, behind a stream called Willoughby Run. Heth's division, leading the Confederate advance, attacked vigorously, but Buford's troopers held their ground until relieved by Federal infantry belonging to the division of Brigadier General James S. Wadsworth, which was part of Reynolds' First Corps.[19]

During this phase of the battle the Confederate brigade led by Brigadier General James J. Archer entered a woods where it collided with the enemy. The Southerners could not prevent the bluecoats from enveloping their right flank and were subsequently driven back, leaving behind a number of prisoners, among whom was General Archer. The Union advantage in this respect was somewhat offset by the death of the First Corps commander, Major General John F. Reynolds, who was shot through the head and instantly killed. He was succeeded by Major General Abner Doubleday, who reformed the Union lines. As Heth was likewise reorganizing his command preparatory to renewing the attack with his other two brigades, there was a lull in the fighting.

Later in the day additional Federal troops came upon the battleground and formed their lines. The other two divisions of the First Corps were among this number, as were those belonging to the Eleventh Corps commanded by Major General Oliver O. Howard. While the Eleventh Corps was extending the Union line along Seminary Ridge, General Buford reported that Ewell's Confederate corps was approaching from the direction of Heidlersburg and was threatening the right flank of the Federals facing Hill's corps. In order to meet this new challenge Howard ordered his troops to change their front so as to face Ewell. At the same time he notified Major Generals Daniel E. Sickles and Henry W. Slocum, commanding the Third and Twelfth Corps, respectively, to come to his aid.[20]

Ewell had received instructions from Lee that if the Federals were in force at Gettysburg, he was not to bring on a general engagement until the whole Confederate army had arrived.[21] However, by the time Ewell read this message from his commander, Hill's corps had already been engaged with Union forces west of Gettysburg and some of Ewell's artillery had opened fire. As it was too late to avoid an engagement without relinquishing the advantages already gained, Ewell decided to push ahead. He advanced Rodes' division first and it soon became hotly engaged. The Federals began moving large bodies of infantry from the town and, according to Ewell, "Affairs were in a very critical condition, when Major General Early . . . opened a brisk artillery fire."[22]

Early sent Gordon's brigade forward first to support Rodes' left flank, after which he ordered the remaining brigades to form in line of battle. Uttering the famous Rebel yell, Gordon's men rushed upon the bluecoats and were soon engaged in a furious hand-to-hand struggle. The Union troops, which belonged to Howard's corps, could not face such determined assaults and soon gave way. Gordon noticed a brave Federal officer, amid the hail of bullets, vainly trying to rally his men. Not long afterwards, he saw that this courageous enemy had fallen. Advancing with his men, Gordon soon came upon this man who was lying on the ground. Playing the part of a Good Samaritan, the Confederate general dismounted and went to the aid of his late adversary, whom he discovered to be Major General Francis C. Barlow, commander of the First Division of Howard's Eleventh Corps. Gordon gave the wounded Federal a drink of water from his own canteen and then noted that a Minié ball had entered his body in front and had passed out near the spinal cord. As this caused a paralysis in both arms and legs, neither Barlow nor Gordon thought there was much hope.[23]

Making General Barlow as comfortable as possible and ordering some Confederate soldiers to carry him to the shade in the rear, General Gordon pressed on with his men. Before he left, he promised Barlow that he would send word to the wounded general's wife telling of her husband's death. The Confederate officer sent the promised message and thought no more of the matter, as he supposed Barlow had passed away. However, it was later revealed that the Confederate bullet had struck no vital point and that Barlow slowly recovered. As Gordon had a relative with the same name and initials who was killed near Richmond the next year and Barlow read the announcement of his death, the Federal general thought this was the same Gordon who had befriended him at Gettysburg. Imagine the surprise, as well as the joy, when the principals in this unusual incident met fifteen years later at a dinner in Washington, for each had thought the other was dead![24]

Early sent Gordon's brigade on until it crossed Rock Creek,

passed over some open fields, and finally arrived at a low ridge, where the Federals had drawn up a second defense line. He ordered the brigade to be halted here, while he advanced the troops of Hays' and Avery's [Hoke's] brigades. The onward rush of these additional soldiers forced the bluecoats to abandon their second line and retreat into the town of Gettysburg. While the Southerners were engaged in this movement, they were subjected to a fire from Federal batteries on Cemetery Hill.[25] Early's and Rodes' divisions had succeeded in driving the Unionists out of the north end of the town and had captured over 4,000 prisoners, as well as three pieces of artillery.[26]

When the firing had subsided somewhat, Generals Ewell and Gordon rode through the streets of Gettysburg. As has been related, Ewell had suffered the loss of one of his legs in the fight at Groveton and was now using a wooden substitute. While the two Confederate officers approached some buildings on the town's outskirts, they were greeted by a fusillade from Federal sharpshooters. Several Confederates fell and Gordon heard the thud of a Minié ball which had struck Ewell. Upon inquiring whether his superior had been hurt, Gordon received the following answer from Ewell, "No, no, I'm not hurt. But suppose the ball had struck you: we would have had the trouble of carrying you off the field, sir. You see how much better fixed for a fight I am than you are. It don't hurt a bit to be shot in a wooden leg."[27]

Unfortunately for the Southern cause, Ewell did not seem to be equal to the responsibility of commanding a whole corps at this stage of the engagement. In spite of the fact that he had driven the Federals back to the slopes of Cemetery Hill, he could not decide whether to press on the attack and thus follow up his advantage or follow Lee's orders strictly and not bring on a general engagement until the whole Confederate army had arrived at Gettysburg. Every minute that passed saw additional bluecoats appearing, for Meade's army was quickly concentrating.

Gordon had been halted while pursuing the retreating Federals and was impatiently awaiting orders to move on. Ewell learned from a courier that Johnson's division, which he had sent west of the mountains to guard his wagons, was approaching Gettysburg and could go into action on its arrival. When Gordon heard this, he suggested that he could join Johnson in attacking Cemetery Hill and, together, they should be able to dislodge the Unionists from its crest. Ewell, however, was unmoved. Another Confederate officer, Major General Isaac R. Trimble, who was temporarily serving as volunteer aide, rode up and urged Ewell to attack at once. Still Old Bald Head could not make up his mind to push on.[28]

The corps commander determined then to consult his subordinate, Jubal Early, to discuss the use to be made of Johnson's division. As usual, Old Jube displayed his aggressive tendencies, for he urged that Johnson's force be sent immediately against Culp's Hill, which was to the east of Cemetery Hill and, apparently, was unoccupied by the enemy. He also stated that, in his opinion, Cemetery Hill could likewise be taken then if Ewell would attack from the North and A. P. Hill from the West. Early felt it was imperative that the two corps unite to drive the Federal defenders from Cemetery Hill, for the latter eminence had become the rallying point for Union troops.

Ewell appeared inclined to adopt this view and ordered Johnson to move through Gettysburg and go into position as soon as he came up. He also dispatched an officer to Lee to obtain the necessary support from the West. However, the commanding general sent regrets at not being able to support the attack, for he added that all of his forces had not yet come up. Hence, if the Union position on Cemetery Hill were to be taken, Ewell would have to rely entirely on his own corps. After considering the arguments for and against such action, he concluded not to attack until Johnson's division arrived.[29] Thus he lost the golden opportunity to assault the bluecoats on Cemetery Hill before the arrival of Meade's whole army.

At dusk Lee rode over to Ewell's headquarters to discuss the general situation on the Confederate left. Old Bald Head sent for Early and also requested Rodes to remain. As it was too late to think of making an attack that evening, the Confederate officers debated the best possible action for the morrow. Lee wanted Ewell's corps to assault Cemetery Hill at daybreak. However, Early, Ewell, and Rodes persuaded the commanding general that an attack against the Round Tops farther south, would be more likely to succeed. When the meeting had ended, the Confederate plan for the next day included an early morning attack by the Southern right against the Round Tops and a demonstration by Ewell on the left. If Ewell succeeded in dislodging the Federals, he was to press on the attack and cooperate with the remainder of Lee's army on his right.[30]

Considerable speculation has arisen over whether or not Ewell could have taken Cemetery Hill if he had followed up his first successes and pressed on vigorously before the Federals had fortified the heights. Dr. Douglas S. Freeman is somewhat critical of Ewell and blames him for not being able to make a decision. He thinks that if the commander of the Second Corps had displayed the initiative and determination on the afternoon of the first day at Gettysburg that he had formerly shown as a division commander, he might have won a glorious victory.[31]

On the other hand, Professor Kenneth P. Williams, who has made the most exhaustive study of the Army of the Potomac that has been attempted, thinks that Ewell was justified in not assaulting the Union positions on either Cemetery Hill or Culp's Hill on July 1. According to this author:

> One can . . . assert that by 4:00 P. M. the position was secure; for by that time the Twelfth Corps was within reach as a strong counterattacking force, and under the direction of Hancock and Howard it could have smashed any regiments that Ewell could have placed on the brow of the hill, quite as effectively as the First Corps had thrown back the advance of Heth in the morning with very heavy captures from the brigades of Davis and Archer.[32]

The field of battle for the second and third days of the contest at Gettysburg was south of the town and lay between Willoughby Run on the west and Rock Creek on the east. After the fighting of the first day Lee's line extended in a concave manner for about six miles along the crest of Seminary Ridge, through the town, and thence eastward on the Hanover road.

Meade's line was a convex one which occupied positions for about four miles on Culp's Hill, Cemetery Hill, Cemetery Ridge, and the Round Tops. General Meade was unfamiliar with the topography of the land in this region, for he had not expected to give battle here. His capable subordinate who commanded the Second Corps of the Army of the Potomac, Major General Winfield S. Hancock, had, upon examination, been greatly impressed with the defensive strength of the Cemetery Ridge position. Accordingly, he had recommended that the Union army occupy it, and Meade had given the necessary orders for this to be done.

It will be recalled that after General Lee had consulted with the officers of Ewell's corps during the evening of the first day, he had decided to send his right wing against the Round Tops in the principal assault. He had also instructed Ewell, on the Confederate left, to demonstrate when he heard the guns on his right, and, if possible, advance against the Union positions on Cemetery and Culp's Hills.

Since General Early was not to be part of the main show on July 2 but was concerned with the lesser Southern effort, it is not necessary to dwell at length upon the failures on the Confederate right. It is sufficient to point out that this attack against the Round Tops was entrusted to the First Corps of the Army of Northern Virginia, commanded by General Longstreet. Unfortunately for the South, Longstreet was not in accord with Lee's offensive strategy at Gettysburg and, to put it mildly, failed to cooperate properly. The attack, which was to have been delivered early in the morning, did not get under way until three o'clock in the afternoon, and thus the Federals had plenty of time to put their troops in proper position. As the bluecoats were continually arriving on the battleground, the longer the Confederates delayed, the more opposition they were bound to encounter. When the attack was finally delivered, it consisted of separate piecemeal attempts to dislodge the Federals. In spite of great bravery and gallantry on the part of both officers and men, the assault achieved only minor success.[33] In fact, success is hardly the word to use in this connection, for the general result was failure.

Over on the Confederate left flank Ewell's corps had been waiting impatiently for the part it was to play in the unfolding drama. Lee had ridden over in the morning to confer with the Second Corps commander but had returned to Seminary Ridge to find out what was delaying Longstreet. Ewell and Early spent part of the morning trying to find a good position from which artillery could throw shells against the bluecoats on Cemetery and Culp's Hills.[34]

After learning that Longstreet's attack would begin in the afternoon, Early made his dispositions. He selected Gordon's brigade as his reserve and sent it to the rear, near the Gettysburg-Hanover Railroad. He then posted Smith's brigade far out on the York Road to guard against Federals who were reported to be approaching from that direction. Early did not believe these reports, but, because they persisted, he felt he could not leave his left flank and rear unprotected. To assist Smith on this flank was Stuart's cavalry, which had finally arrived on the battlefield although too worn out to be of much immediate use. Old Jube planned to use his remaining two brigades, those led by Hays and Avery, for the attack.[35]

As soon as Ewell heard Longstreet's guns, he ordered his own artillery to begin firing. When Federal batteries on the opposite heights promptly replied, he determined to launch an infantry assault. He instructed Johnson to lead his division against Culp's Hill, Early to push up Cemetery Hill, and Rodes to cooperate by attacking on Early's right flank.[36] Ewell also sent a staff officer to the nearest division of A. P. Hill's Third Corps, in order to get help on Rodes' right.

Johnson's division, which was attempting to capture Culp's Hill, encountered many difficulties. Not only did the Union position possess great natural strength but it was also strongly defended with field-works, not to mention the brave bluecoated infantrymen of Slocum's Twelfth Corps on its slope and crest. Only three of Johnson's brigades succeeded in crossing Rock Creek and when they entered the woods at the foot of the hill, darkness had descended. One brigade seized some trenches which the enemy had vacated, while the other two were checked on the side of the hill by concentrated fire from the top.[37] They remained on this slope until the next day.

A little before dusk, as soon as Johnson became warmly engaged, General Early ordered Hays' and Avery's brigades to assault East Cemetery Hill. He expected Rodes to send his division forward at the same time, for Rodes had agreed earlier that they should launch their attacks simultaneously.[38] Early's men advanced gallantly in spite of heavy artillery fire and moved against enemy infantry posted behind stone and plank fences on the slope of their objective. Capturing some prisoners and driving the other defenders before them, the Southerners fought their way to the top of the hill. There they gained possession of more prisoners, several artillery pieces, and some colors.

After a quiet interval of several minutes the Confederates on the crest heard the sound of infantry to the south. Not knowing whether this long line was friend or foe, they withheld their fire. As Early's men had been expecting cooperation in the attack from Generals Johnson, Rodes, and Longstreet, they thought that the advancing infantry might belong to any of these commands. Only after the approaching troops had delivered several volleys and had come uncomfortably close was it apparent that their uniforms were blue. Thereupon the Southerners fired in reply. Although they succeeded in checking the first line, they perceived two more in the rear of it and, realizing that their position was untenable in the face of such opposition, Early's men withdrew to the stone wall at the foot of the hill. Later they fell back to a fence about 75 yards from the wall.[39]

Although Early had Gordon's brigade in reserve, he did not send it to reinforce the two brigades which had fought their way to the top of the hill. He had planned to do so but was deterred when he realized that Rodes' division had not advanced on his right as agreed upon. Fully aware that without this additional aid his two brigades, even if supported by Gordon, would be unable to hold the captured ground, Old Jube ordered Gordon to halt. In this attack on the Federal position he was deprived of the services of Colonel Isaac E. Avery, who was mortally wounded while leading Hoke's brigade.

As soon as Old Jube realized that Rodes had not advanced with his division, he rode over to learn the reason. He came upon Rodes just as this officer was getting his brigades into position to move. Rodes informed Early that there was no indication he would receive aid on his right from the nearest division of A. P. Hill's Third Corps but that he would attack anyway, alone, if Old Jube thought it advisable.

By this time Early had learned that his own two brigades which had reached the top of the hill had been forced to withdraw, so he informed Rodes it was too late to do any good. Consequently, Rodes did not attack. In extenuation of Rodes' seeming tardiness in getting ready, it should be pointed out that his men had to travel twice as far as Early's and had to fight their way through part of the town before they could form for the assault on Cemetery Hill. This quite naturally delayed them.[40] Thus the second day's fight at Gettysburg ended.

Among the Jubal Early Papers in the Manuscript Division of the Library of Congress is a letter which throws an interesting sidelight on the fighting by Early's men during the second day at Gettysburg. It was written to General Early by Colonel D. F. Boyd, who at that time [1891] was Superintendent of the Kentucky Military Institute. Boyd related he had been told by a Captain Samuel Gaines, who had fought at Gettysburg, of the seriousness of Early's assault on Cemetery Hill. Gaines reported he had learned from a Union officer that Early's two brigades had passed in rear of General Meade's headquarters and had temporarily cut off the Federal commanding general from his army. The Union officer, who had likewise fought at Gettysburg, ventured the opinion that if Early's men had been supported on their right and thus enabled to maintain their positions on Cemetery Hill, General Meade and his whole headquarters staff would have been made prisoners![41] Whether or not this would have changed the course of the battle is idle speculation, but it is an interesting detail of one of the most decisive engagements on the American continent.

From the Confederate point of view, the second day's fighting was a series of badly coordinated, tardy, and unsupported attacks. Pickett's division had not yet arrived on the field and three other divisions, as well as four brigades, had hardly fired a shot. On the Federal side, Meade had conducted a well-planned, though strictly passive defense, and had by promptly bringing up reinforcements been able to repel every Confederate assault.

Believing that he must either win a decisive tactical victory or retreat to Virginia, General Lee decided to renew the attack the following day, July 3. As Pickett's division of Longstreet's corps came up during the night of July 2-3 and as Stuart's weary troopers had finally arrived at Gettysburg, the Confederate chieftain had practically his whole army at hand. He had left two brigades of cavalry behind to cover the line of retreat.

Fighting began on July 3 when early in the morning Geary's division of the Federal Twelfth Corps returned to its trenches on the right of Meade's line, to the east of Culp's Hill. Geary's force, which had been withdrawn from its position the day before, found part of Johnson's Confederate division in its trenches. Ewell dispatched two brigades from Rodes' division and one from Early's [Smith's brigade] to reinforce Johnson. After some slight successes at first Johnson found himself exposed to a heavy artillery fire from the heights above, while the largest gun he could bring into action was a rifle. The rugged terrain made it impossible for him to bring up artillery. Finally, when he perceived that the Federals were moving heavy columns of infantry to turn his left, Johnson fell back. The Union troops promptly regained their positions, and the fighting practically ended on the Confederate left.[42] Smith's brigade was the only part of Early's division to participate in the fighting on the third day.

The principal assault on July 3 was made by Pickett's division, with supporting brigades, against the left center of the Federal position on Cemetery Ridge. The charge of those brave Confederates across open fields to the very mouths of the Union guns is too well-known to warrant repeating in detail here. It is sufficient to say that the determined attack was met by an equally determined defense, with the result that Lee's last supreme effort to break Meade's lines by direct frontal assault ended in failure. The only alternative left to the commanding general was to get out of Pennsylvania and return to Virginia as quickly as possible. His tactical defeat at Gettysburg had left him with terrific gaps in his regiments, a scarcity of ammunition, and constantly diminishing supplies of all kinds.

After the failure of Pickett's charge Lee withdrew his shattered brigades back to Seminary Ridge and prepared for the counterattack he thought Meade might launch so as to make the

Federal triumph at Gettysburg even more decisive. Although Lee remained in position all day on July 4, Meade refrained from making a serious effort to dislodge him.

Accordingly, Lee organized his army for the retreat. On the night of July 3-4 he moved Ewell's Second Corps from the Confederate left to the Cashtown Road.[43] He had selected it to serve as the rear-guard on the long retreat back to the Potomac. About four o'clock in the afternoon of July 4 he started the train of wagons filled with wounded. Protected by General John D. Imboden's cavalry brigade, the column moved along the Chambersburg pike. A very heavy rain had fallen at noon and had drenched practically everyone in the Army of Northern Virginia; even the unfortunate wounded in the wagons suffered from the elements.

General Imboden protected the train from Federal cavalry and succeeded in bringing most of the wagons to the Potomac. As the column was passing through Greencastle, Pennsylvania the next morning, it was attacked by about forty citizens who, armed with axes, cut the spokes out of about a dozen wheels and thus caused the wagons to be dropped to the streets. Imboden stopped this practice by sending some troopers who captured the hostile civilians and treated them as prisoners of war. After a few more skirmishes with Federal cavalry the escort brought most of the train to Williamsport—on the Potomac—on the afternoon of July 5. The remainder arrived the next day.[44]

Because of the confusion resulting from the rainstorm, the mud, and, finally, the approaching darkness, the main part of the Army of Northern Virginia did not begin the retreat as soon as Lee had hoped. However, the men finally got into line and, with Ewell's corps acting as rear guard, began moving. The delay postponed Ewell's departure until about noon on July 5. The commander of the Second Corps entrusted the job of protecting the rear of the column to Early's division, assisted by Lieutenant Colonel E. V. White's battalion of cavalry. Old Jube had to beat off a Federal attack at Fairfield, a few miles southwest of Gettysburg, after which the column halted for the night. The next day, July 6, Ewell designated Rodes' division to act as rear-guard, in accordance with his policy of rotating this hazardous job. He moved Early's division to the front of the corps.[45]

Continuing the retreat, Early and his men passed through Monterey Springs, Waynesboro, Leitersburg, and Hagerstown, reaching the outskirts of the latter place on July 7. Old Jube halted here several days until he received orders to occupy a line defending Hagerstown from the southwest. Because of flood waters on the Potomac and the destruction of Lee's pontoon bridge by Federal cavalry, the Confederates were delayed almost a week from entering Virginia. Finally, however, on July 14 the waters had subsided and Early's division got across the stream. The brigades of Gordon, Hoke, and Smith forded it above Williamsport, while that of Hays, with Jones' battalion of artillery, used a newly-constructed bridge at Falling Waters. Passing through Martinsburg, the division arrived at Darkesville, where it went into camp on July 16.[46] The remainder of Lee's army likewise recrossed the Potomac, either at Williamsport or Falling Waters, and was once again on the friendly soil of the Old Dominion.

CHAPTER 15

Commanding the Second Corps

After the return to Virginia from the ill-fated Gettysburg campaign Lee's Army of Northern Virginia began the job of reorganization. Confederate casualties, particularly among the officers, had been heavy, and it became necessary to promote the more promising younger officers and give them new responsibilities. Morale in the Southland received a double setback in July, 1863 because the bad news from Gettysburg was supplemented by equally disturbing reports that Vicksburg—the last main stronghold on the Mississippi—had been captured by Major General Ulysses S. Grant on July 4. Jubal Early's West Point classmate, Lieutenant General John C. Pemberton, allowed Grant to bottle him up in Vicksburg and starve him into surrender.

In order to retrieve Confederate fortunes in the Western theatre of the war, Lee sent Longstreet with part of the First Corps to reinforce General Braxton Bragg, who was opposing Major General William S. Rosecrans near Chattanooga. Longstreet's presence, and especially that of Hood's division of the First Corps, enabled the South to claim a victory at Chickamauga on September 19 and 20, 1863. However, Bragg did not follow up his success and the victory became a somewhat barren one. With Lee thus weakened by the transfer of Longstreet's corps, he was unable to assume a full-scale offensive in Virginia. Meade likewise detached two corps from his army and sent them under Hooker to reinforce Rosecrans.

Although Meade's Army of the Potomac, even without the two detached corps, was much stronger than Lee's without Longstreet's corps, the Federal victor at Gettysburg surrendered the initiative to his active opponent. In order to find out Meade's strength, Lee began to move his army around the Union right on the night of October 8. With A. P. Hill's corps taking the lead and Ewell's troops following, the gray columns left camp on the upper Rapidan and passed through Orange, Madison, and Culpeper. Meade, who had taken position on a ridge north of Culpeper, re-

155

treated across the Rappahannock, and Lee continued to advance. When the Confederates approached Warrenton, Meade withdrew toward Manassas.[1]

At Bristow Station on the Orange and Alexandria Railroad General Hill boldly attacked a Federal force which, he learned later to his cost, was the Second Corps of the Army of the Potomac commanded by Major General G. K. Warren. The Federals handled the brigades which Hill threw into the fight so roughly that the commander of the Third Corps was glad to break off the engagement. He had failed to determine the enemy's strength by proper reconnaissance, and in his official report of the contest Hill stated: "I am convinced that I made the attack too hastily, and at the same time that a delay of half an hour, and there would have been no enemy attack. In that event I believe I should equally have blamed myself for not attacking at once."[2]

Early's division, at the head of Ewell's corps, was ordered to advance against some enemy troops and wagon trains moving toward Bristow. However, Old Jube was unable to find Federals in that direction. Consequently, he decided to attack a force near the railroad station at Bristow. Nightfall forced postponement of further activities and when he prepared to move the following day, October 15, he discovered his opponents had withdrawn. Leaving most of his division behind, Old Jube, with a regiment, reconnoitered as far as Manassas Junction. As a result he discovered the enemy posted across Bull Run. Except for some skirmishing by Confederate cavalry, there was no serious attempt to bring on a general engagement.[3]

After the affair at Bristow Station the Confederates withdrew to the south side of the Rappahannock River. Most of Early's division camped in rear of Brandy Station, but one brigade, Hays', was detached to protect the Rappahannock bridge crossing of the Orange and Alexandria Railroad. The Confederate authorities had decided to keep a small force at this place, on the north side of the river, in order to make difficult a Federal surprise movement farther down the river at Kelly's Ford.

The earth fortifications on the northern bank of the stream had been originally constructed by the Federals, but, after seizure by the Southerners, they had been changed so that they faced north instead of south. General Early considered them poorly laid out and constructed. At the rear of the position was a pontoon bridge connecting the outpost with the south side of the river. As the railroad bridge had been destroyed and as the stream was too deep for fording, this pontoon bridge afforded the only means of

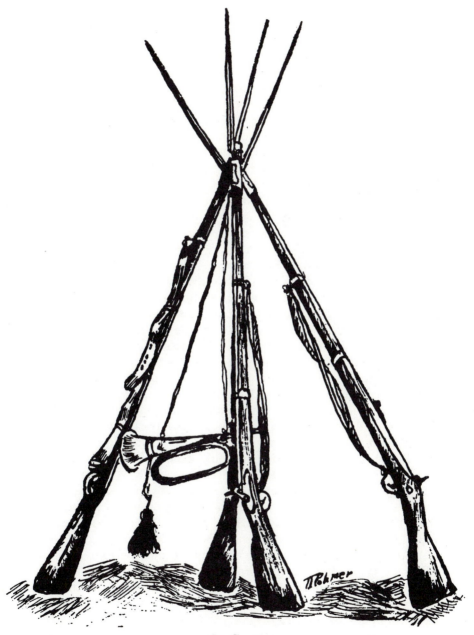

In Camp

communication with the southern bank and the only route of
escape in the event of trouble.[4]

The engagement at Rappahannock Bridge or Rappahannock
Station began on November 7, 1863 when a strong Federal force
pushed across the river at Kelly's Ford. General Rodes, who defended this part of the Confederate line, resisted the enemy advance and notified his superior officers of the impending contest.
As soon as General Early heard about the crossing at Kelly's Ford,
he moved his division to a position opposite the Rappahannock
Bridge outpost but on the south side of the river. He then crossed
on the pontoon bridge to determine if the Federals were threatening the earthworks occupied by one of his brigades.

Upon Old Jube's arrival on the north bank of the Rappahannock he discovered that General Hays was absent attending a
court-martial but was expected to return momentarily. While he
was away, one of his regimental commanders, Colonel D. B. Penn,
was in charge. Noticing that a strong Federal force—subsequently
identified as two corps—was approaching the redoubt, Early recrossed the river to hurry forward reinforcements. He encountered
most of Hoke's brigade, now led by its senior colonel, Archibald
C. Godwin, while General Hoke was on detached duty with one of
his regiments in North Carolina. Both Generals Early and Lee
thought the addition of Hoke's brigade would enable Hays' fighting Louisianians to repel the enemy. In fact, Lee directed Early
to keep the remainder of his division on the south side.[5]

Hearing the sound of more Federal guns on the north bank of
the river and wondering what it meant, Early sent a staff officer,
Major Samuel Hale, to find out. That individual saw both Hays
and Godwin, who thought they could hold their positions in the
face of the enemy attack although the assault was being made in
much greater force than had been anticipated. As Hale was returning over the bridge, he met some of Hays' men who informed him
their lines had been broken. However, he did not believe these
reports to be true.

Although Early was likewise inclined not to believe this account of Hays' lines being broken, he dispatched another staff
officer, Major John Daniel, to ascertain the truth. At the same
time he ordered Brigadier General John Pegram, who had succeeded to command of Smith's brigade, to take his men near the bridge
in order to throw back any Federal attempt to cross the river.
Major Daniel had not proceeded far before he met General Hays,
who informed him that the Federal attackers literally overpowered
his brigade with superior numbers and that Colonel Godwin's

command had probably met the same fate. Most of Hays' brigade had been captured and he himself taken prisoner but had escaped, amid a hail of bullets, when his horse became frightened and ran away. Early subsequently learned that most of Godwin's force had been taken prisoner, including its fighting commander.[6]

Old Jube was quite anxious to help his men across the Rappahannock, but the approach of darkness, as well as the strength of the enemy, deterred him. He could not even use artillery for fear of damaging friend as well as foe. He could only stand helplessly by and listen to the cheers of the Federals as they captured a great number of his men. As soon as the escapees had crossed to the south side of the stream, Early ordered that the bridge be destroyed to prevent the Federals from crossing. He particularly regretted the loss of Colonel Godwin, who had fought bravely until overpowered, and he requested that the Confederate Government try to have him exchanged.[7]

Early stated his losses in this affair as 1,630 officers and men killed, wounded, and captured. In his official report of the defeat he wrote as follows:

> The immediate causes of the disaster were the weakness of the position owing to the defective engineering, the want of sufficient bridges, the want of sufficient artillery in suitable positions on the south bank of the river, and the superior force of the enemy, which consisted of two army corps under Sedgwick, as since ascertained, the attack of the enemy being favored by the darkness and the high wind.[8]

According to Dr. Douglas S. Freeman, the real reason for the Federal success at Rappahannock Bridge was the fact that the Union army had formulated and courageously executed a sound plan of attack. Major General John Sedgwick had sent the Fifth and Sixth Corps against the Confederate position protecting the northern approach to the bridge. He had placed his artillery where it could do the most damage and had handled his infantry so well that his capable subordinates were able to occupy the first line of rifle-pits without even having to fire a shot.[9]

After the Federals had obtained possession of the northern approach to the destroyed Rappahannock bridge and had crossed the stream at Kelly's Ford, farther downstream, the Army of Northern Virginia had no choice but to withdraw and take up a new defense line farther south. On November 8 it took position in rear of Brandy Station but, except for a cavalry attack against part of A. P. Hill's line, no further fighting occurred. Because the terrain in the Brandy-Culpeper area was not well suited for defense purposes, Lee withdrew his army still farther south until it occupied its old positions just across the Rapidan River. Meade moved his army up, and the two forces confronted each other with that stream in between.

Near the middle of November General Ewell's health seemed worse, and he departed from the Second Corps for a few weeks' rest in Charlottesville. The stump of his amputated leg had been giving him much pain, and there appeared some symptoms of blood poisoning. Besides, he suffered from chills and fever.[10] While he was recuperating in Charlottesville, the command of the Second Corps devolved upon General Early.

Toward the end of the same month General Meade planned to turn the Confederate right flank and force Lee to give battle on new ground. Therefore, on November 26 he started the Army of the Potomac across the Rapidan in the vicinity of Germanna Ford. He had not proceeded far before he found his advance contested by the Army of Northern Virginia. The ensuing engagements were known by the names of Payne's Farm and Mine Run, respectively.

In order to prevent the Federals from getting too far in his rear, General Lee determined to advance against them. Since the Second Corps occupied that part of the Southern line nearer the enemy, he directed its temporary commander, General Early, to move his men first. He then instructed General A. P. Hill to follow with the Third Corps.[11]

Early in the afternoon of November 27 the Confederates belonging to Rodes' and Early's divisions came upon the Federals near Locust Grove, about seven miles southwest of Wilderness Church. Lee decided to await the arrival of Johnson's division before launching an attack.

The engagement at Payne's Farm began when General Johnson's ambulances were fired upon. Soon Brigadier General George H. Steuart's brigade was skirmishing with the bluecoats. Johnson formed his remaining troops in battle line and soon became heavily engaged. After repulsing two attacks, he assumed the offensive but, because of the wooded terrain, this proved to be very difficult. The men became badly separated from their commands. After exhausting most of their ammunition, they withdrew to a fence line, where they repulsed enemy efforts to dislodge them, until nightfall ended the fighting. Early reported that the nature of the country was such that he was unable to see any portion of the troops of the Second Corps engaged.[12] He felt that Johnson had acquitted himself creditably and had even saved the whole corps from disaster. He was afraid if the Federals had been successful at Payne's Farm, they could have attacked the rear of the other divisions of the Second Corps at Locust Grove.[13]

General Early was convinced by the fighting at Payne's Farm that General Meade's whole army was at hand, and he therefore decided to move the corps to a better defensive position on the west side of Mine Run. He gathered the Confederate wounded and dead, as far as the darkness permitted, and formed his divisions in battle line across the stream. He noted with satisfaction the arrival of Anderson's division of A. P. Hill's corps and communicated his plans to General Anderson, who took position on the right of the Second Corps.

The operations at Mine Run continued on November 28 when Meade occupied a strong position on the east bank of the stream. Both armies erected entrenchments but there was no fighting except for occasional skirmishing. Perhaps the rain, which fell all day, and the low temperature discouraged offensive movements. The next day the Southerners noticed that Meade seemed to be concentrating for an attack on the Confederate right, and they prepared to repel it. However, the Federals contented themselves with an artillery barrage which lasted about an hour and some minor skirmishing. When Meade failed to attack on November 30 or December 1, Lee assumed the offensive.[14]

The Confederate chieftain transferred two divisions to the right so that they could turn the Federal left flank, but when daylight broke on the morning of December 2, he discovered that the Federals had retired during the night. Lee then directed Early to send two divisions in pursuit and one to Morton's Ford across the Rapidan. Old Jube dispatched his old division along with Rodes' in pursuit and sent Johnson's troops to the ford. Because Meade had moved off his artillery and trains the previous day, his infantry was able to retire swiftly, and Early's men encountered only a few stragglers. Not having any cavalry, the temporary commander of the Second Corps was forced to give up the pursuit and consequently occupied the former position along the banks of the Rapidan.[15]

Old Jube's handling of the Second Corps during Ewell's absence was creditable. He displayed ability to think in terms of the corps as a whole instead of a single division. Of course he had lost sight of Johnson's division while it was fighting, and this deficiency as a leader was probably due to his inability to master the features of the terrain over which he was to operate. In other words, he had a poor sense of direction.[16] Except for this, his elevation to the responsibility of heading an entire army corps instead of only one division was marked with enough display of military ability to warrant his being entrusted with the Second Corps for a more important role in 1864.

At the conclusion of the Mine Run campaign Ewell returned to head the Second Corps, and Old Jube resumed his position as the commander of his division.[17]

CHAPTER 16

Early Forms a Dislike for Cavalry

On December 8, 1863 a Federal cavalry force under the able leadership of Brigadier General William W. Averell began a long raid across the Allegheny Mountains to the Virginia and Tennessee Railroad. In order to divert Confederate attention, Brigadier Generals Eliakim P. Scammon and Jeremiah C. Sullivan were ordered to send troops against New River and Staunton, respectively.[1] As Southern forces in the Shenandoah Valley were inadequate to meet these new threats from the West and North, General Lee sent General Early with reinforcements and with orders to assume command of all Confederates in the Shenandoah Valley.

Old Jube arrived in Staunton early on the morning of December 16 and was soon discussing the local situation with a cavalryman, Brigadier General John D. Imboden, who had been commanding the Southerners in the Valley. Imboden informed him that a force of about 5,000 Federals was confronting his troops behind Bull Pasture River, west of Staunton. Shortly afterwards Early received word from Lee in Richmond that Averell was at Salem and that he should try to capture the bold Union cavalryman.[2] Averell had left a small infantry force under Colonel Joseph Thoburn to confront Imboden while he led his troopers against the Virginia and Tennessee Railroad at Salem.

Passing through New Castle, the Federal raiders arrived at Salem in the morning of December 16. They came upon a considerable amount of flour, wheat, corn, oats, meat, and other military supplies stored at the depot, which was undefended. They lost no time putting the torch to everything that could be burned and destroying that which could not. They drove off a train from Lynchburg filled with Confederate soldiers and tore up the track and telegraph lines. In all this work of destruction General Averell took care that no private property was harmed.[3]

Roanoke College is located at Salem and during the war the school authorities, in order to be allowed to keep open the doors of the institution, had promised the Confederate Government that students would cooperate by helping repel Federal raids in that vicinity. Although the militia company had been drilling on the campus for two years, it was caught unawares when the real test came. When Averell's troopers arrived in Salem, the student company caused them no more trouble than that required to make prisoners of some of the collegians.

The Federal commander retired to Mason's Cove, nearby, where he planned to spend the night and interrogate his young captives. The following morning he commanded that the Roanokers be brought before him so that he might ask a few questions. After finding out where each of his prisoners came from, Averell inquired what they thought of the Confederacy and its chances of survival. When some of the students replied that they thought it was doing very well, the Federal officer answered, "O now, boys, you know it is most played out. You all go back to your books and study your best." He then ordered their release.[4]

In order to intercept Averell's troopers on their retreat, Early decided to send Imboden's brigade to Covington. Because of a very heavy rain which fell during the night of December 16, the Southern cavalry leader could not take the direct road to Covington, which was down the valley of the Little Calf Pasture River. This route necessitated several crossings of this and other streams, which were now impassable because of the high waters, Therefore, Early ordered Imboden to lead his cavalrymen through Brownsburg and Lexington. Since it was impossible for his infantry to keep up with the horsemen, Early sent his foot-soldiers to Staunton, so they would be able to intercept Averell if he should attempt escape by that route. A small Confederate force of about 500 dismounted cavalrymen under Colonel William L. Jackson was at Jackson's River Depot, the western terminal of the Virginia Central Railroad.[5]

Old Jube returned to Staunton, where he met Major General Fitzhugh Lee, who headed another cavalry brigade. At the same time he received word from Lynchburg that Averell was retreating over the same route by which he had advanced but had been stopped not far from Salem by high waters. Accordingly, he ordered Fitz Lee to proceed to Lexington and Colliertown, where he was to unite with Imboden. The combined cavalry force was directed to go to Covington. Early also gave Fitz Lee discretionary orders to the effect that if he received new information about Averell, he could go wherever it would be necessary to catch the wily Federal.

Unfortunately for Early's plans, he now received a dispatch

from Lynchburg that Averell had been unable to cross Craig's Creek and had returned to Salem. As he had no reason to doubt the veracity of this report, he relayed it to Fitz Lee by courier. The cavalry leader obtained this latest information at Colliertown, where he had met Imboden and, after consulting the latter officer, Fitz Lee decided to change his plans and move to Buchanan instead of Covington. When Early later received information from Lynchburg that the report of Averell's return to Salem was erroneous, it was too late to reach Lee.[6]

In spite of the false information which had caused Early's cavalry to be sent on a wild goose chase, Old Jube did not give up hope of heading off the Union raiders. Having nothing left at Staunton but infantry, he tried to send Thomas' brigade to reinforce the small body of dismounted troopers under Colonel William L. Jackson, who had taken position at Jackson's River Depot. The soldiers boarded a train on the Virginia Central Railroad but because of destroyed bridges, heavy grades, and poor condition of the railroad's rolling stock, they were unable to reach the western terminal at Jackson's River Depot.

Although unable to take his brigade to reinforce Jackson, Brigadier General Edward L. Thomas established telegraphic communication with the cavalry leader. He soon learned that Averell's advance had progressed on an obscure road into the Jackson's River Valley and had engaged the Confederate troopers posted there. Averell captured an important bridge and crossed the Jackson River. He thus escaped with most of his force but reported losses of some wagons and 129 officers and men, most of whom were captured by Jackson's troopers.[7]

When Fitz Lee reached Buchanan, he learned that Averell was not coming that way. Consequently, he rode to Fincastle, where he ascertained the correct escape route. Continuing the pursuit through Covington and Callaghan's, he realized that his quarry had made good his escape and he therefore ended the chase.[8]

During the night of December 19 while Averell was getting away safely after his successful raid, General Early learned that another Federal force had advanced southward in the Shenandoah Valley and had passed through New Market. This was a body led by Colonel George D. Wells, which was supposed to distract Confederate attention from Averell. Old Jube ordered Walker's brigade, which he had left at Staunton, to meet this new threat by advancing to Mount Crawford. At the same time he directed the return of Thomas' brigade to Staunton.

When Early joined Walker at Mount Crawford, he learned that the Federals were in Harrisonburg. Because of this information, he ordered an advance early the next morning. However, when daybreak came, he noticed that the bluecoats had retired. Although he attempted pursuit, he was handicapped by not having an adequate cavalry force, and the Federals retreated safely farther down the Valley.[9]

The other Union force which was supposed to cooperate in this winter campaign, commanded by Brigadier General Eliakim P. Scammon, did not accomplish much. It did attack a small body of Confederates at Lewisburg on December 12 and drove it across the Greenbrier River. Scammon, becoming somewhat alarmed by reports of guerrilla activity in his rear and enemy reinforcements in his front, retired to the Kanawha River prematurely.[10]

After General Averell's escape into West Virginia General Lee left Old Jube in temporary command of the Shenandoah Valley forces. There was little activity to require his return to the Army of Northern Virginia, and the Confederates were badly in need of supplies. Learning that the South Branch Valley of the Potomac, in the present state of West Virginia, possessed many things needed by the Southern army, Lee ordered Early to obtain as much as he could. The Confederate chieftain mentioned that he was particularly anxious to acquire cattle, sheep, horses, hogs, cloth, and leather. He instructed Old Jube to buy from those willing to sell and to take from those not inclined to do so. In the latter cases, though, Early was to give certificates to the owners. Lee further instructed his subordinate to operate only in those regions under enemy control, for in Confederate-held territory Lee's ordinary agents could obtain supplies. Lee made it very clear to Early that in carrying out these instructions Old Jube would leave enough behind for the subsistence of the people.[11]

General Early prepared to execute these orders. He decided to employ his cavalry for the raid and directed General Fitz Lee to bring his troopers to the vicinity of New Market, give them a few days' rest, and then cross the North Mountain into Hardy County. After entering the present limits of West Virginia, Lee was expected to drive away a Federal infantry force at Petersburg, cut the Baltimore and Ohio Railroad at the mouth of the South Branch of the Potomac, and collect as many supplies as he could.

On December 31, 1863 Fitz Lee left Mount Jackson by way of the Orkney Springs road, crossed North Mountain, and rode to Moorefield. He had an artillery and wagon escort at the beginning, but because the mountain roads were covered with ice, he had to send his large guns and wagons back to Early. The weather was very cold and caused considerable discomfort to both men and horses. Only by dismounting and leading their horses were Lee's cavalrymen able to move along the dangerous mountain roads.[12]

In order to divert attention from Fitz Lee's expedition, Early sent Imboden's cavalry brigade and Thomas' infantry force down the Shenandoah Valley to Fisher's Hill, near Strasburg. Old Jube accompanied this expedition and shared in the hardships caused by two heavy snows and extremely cold weather. He kept these troops in the Strasburg vicinity until the return of Fitz Lee, after which he moved them further south.

Meanwhile General Fitz Lee's troopers had been very active. They marched from Moorefield to Burlington and along the way captured a Federal wagon train consisting of forty wagons loaded with ammunition and hides. In addition, they obtained 250 cattle but lost about half of them in driving them at night over the mountains. They captured some prisoners and additional supplies at Burlington and on January 5 attempted to cut the Baltimore and Ohio Railroad at New Creek Depot but were forced to desist because of the suffering of the men caused by the extremely cold weather. General Lee then determined to yield to the elements and led his men back through Romney and Brock's Gap to Harrisonburg.[13]

General Early decided to make another attempt to gain the badly needed supplies for Lee's army and planned this expedition for the latter part of January. General Fitz Lee's cavalrymen returned to the eastern side of the Blue Ridge Mountains and were replaced by the brigade led by Brigadier General Thomas L. Rosser. Old Jube planned to use Rosser's brigade of cavalry, Thomas' brigade of infantry, and McClanahan's battery of artillery for this second raid into the South Branch Valley. He ordered General Imboden to divert Federal attention from the main raid by marching down the Shenandoah Valley to demonstrate in the Winchester neighborhood.

Old Jube and his men left New Market on January 28, crossed North Mountain, and entered the Lost River Valley. They reached Moorefield the following day, from which place Early sent Rosser's cavalry against a Federal wagon train moving from New Creek to Petersburg. Although the train was strongly guarded by about 800 infantry and a smaller force of cavalry, Rosser attacked it boldly, drove off its protectors, and captured ninety loaded wagons, as well as a few prisoners. Because some of the wagons were badly smashed in the fight, he was able to bring off only fifty of them.[14]

After this engagement Early sent his entire force against the Federal garrison at Petersburg, which had erected strong entrenchments. Believing discretion the better part of valor, the bluecoats evacuated the town during the night of January 30-31. The Confederates obtained a few supplies left behind by the enemy's withdrawal. Upon the capture of Petersburg, Old Jube sent Rosser against the Baltimore and Ohio Railroad. Because of the approach of a large Federal cavalry force to Romney, Rosser had to retire to Moorefield, but not before he had destroyed bridges over Patterson's Creek and the North Branch of the Potomac.

Having partially succeeded in his mission and not wanting to run the risk of losing what he had captured, General Early decided to return to the Shenandoah Valley. His expedition had proceeded only a short distance from Moorefield when a strong enemy cavalry force with some artillery appeared on the Romney road. He made his dispositions to meet the expected attack, but one was not forthcoming. Instead, the Federals contented themselves with cautious maneuvers in front of the Confederates, who returned to the Shenandoah Valley on February 5 without further molestation.

In his official report of this raid General Early listed his captures as follows: 50 wagons with their teams, 1,200 cattle, 500 sheep, 78 prisoners (including four officers), and some commissary stores. He stated that his men obtained all the cattle they could find but were deprived of further success because a number of the South Branch farmers had driven their cattle into Maryland, ahead of the Confederate advance. He also commented upon the kindness and hospitality which the people of Moorefield and vicinity showered upon his men. In forwarding this report to the Secretary of War, General Robert E. Lee commended the work of Early and Rosser, as well as their commands.[15]

During General Early's occupancy of the Shenandoah Valley in the winter of 1863-1864 he developed a dislike that he never relinquished for the cavalry branch of service. This prejudice against the troopers was extremely unfortunate as it handicapped Old Jube in his operations in the Valley during the summer of 1864. It involved him in many disputes with Generals Rosser, Imboden, and others, and caused mutual recriminations which did nothing to bolster the Confederacy during the final year of the war.

When General Early made his official report of the unsuccessful attempt to capture General Averell, he concluded with a reference to General Rosser's troopers which was anything but complimentary.[16] Later in January, 1864, he expressed his dissatisfaction with Imboden's brigade when he wrote a letter to General Robert E. Lee.[17] As Imboden was away from his men part of this time, the command devolved upon Colonel George H. Smith. The Confederate cavalry had for some time displayed more independence and less regard for discipline than the other branches of the service and although Colonel Smith tried his best to tighten up on discipline, he was not entirely successful. Early's chief criticism of Imboden's horsemen was that because they did not make the necessary reconnaissances, he could not ascertain the enemy's whereabouts. Consequently, he felt his operations were greatly impeded by the failure of the cavalry. Apparently, General Lee also shared some of these ideas about his troopers for he believed a thorough reorganization was necessary.[18]

Matters began to work toward a climax when Old Jube learned that a lieutenant in Imboden's brigade had killed a sergeant in the streets of Staunton. As Imboden was still absent, Early rebuked Colonel Smith for such lax discipline. In explaining the affair to General Lee, Old Jube denounced Imboden's brigade in very strong terms. He stated that this command was so badly lacking in discipline that he would hate to have to rely upon it in an emergency. He believed that the principal reason for this condition was the fact that a large number of Imboden's men were deserters from other branches of the army.[19]

When General Imboden upon his return to duty learned about the derogatory remarks which Early had been making concerning the troopers, he wrote a letter of protest to General Lee. In this official communication the cavalry leader stated that Early had used disparaging language in referring to the cavalry, had indirectly criticized him, and had said it was generally known in the Valley that Imboden's brigade was "wholly inefficient, disorganized, undisciplined, and unreliable."[20] Imboden concluded with the request that Lee order a court of inquiry to investigate the charges Old Jube had made and then to publish in the Valley the findings of this investigative board.

As Imboden's protest had to be sent through channels, it reached the hands of Early, who forwarded it on to Lee with a note of his own. Early defended himself by stating that he had not spoken disparagingly in public of Imboden's brigade but had expressed himself in private, especially to its temporary commander, Colonel Smith. He repeated his lack of confidence in it and joined Imboden in requesting the court of inquiry in the hope that "it may result in materially improving the condition of the command."[21] General Lee felt that the charges and countercharges which would result from a court of inquiry would do more harm than good and, accordingly, refused to convene one.

Early's previous unfavorable opinion of Rosser's cavalrymen was mitigated somewhat by that officer's fine work in the January raid into the South Branch Valley. Earlier Old Jube had complained to Lee about one occasion when Rosser had gone to Staunton to see his wife. However, in a letter to Lee which Old Jube wrote in February, 1864, he stated that he had formed a very high opinion of Rosser, and he strongly urged that the cavalry leader be promoted to the rank of brigadier general.[22] Rosser had already been recommended, but his promotion had been delayed by the Confederate Senate.

About the middle of February, 1864 General Early requested a leave which would enable him to spend a few days in his native Franklin County. In his communication to General Lee, he pointed out that he had not been home since he was wounded in June, 1862 and that private affairs there needed some attention. He also revealed that there was a decline in support of the Confederate cause in Franklin County, which he hoped his presence would check. The request was granted, and thus Old Jube received a brief respite from the grim business of war. Incidentally, this was the only leave of this kind asked for or received by him during the entire four years of the war.[23]

General Early returned to his old division near the Rapidan River about the middle of March, 1864. His corps commander, General Ewell, was still suffering from the loss of his leg. The wooden substitute was so poorly made it could not be relied upon and caused its wearer extreme discomfort. As Old Jube was the senior major general in the Second Corps, he would probably be elevated to its command if Ewell were incapacitated to the extent of not being able to serve in the field. There is no doubt that he felt fully capable of handling this additional responsibility and would have welcomed the opportunity.

The normal pleasant relations that had existed between Ewell and Early were strained somewhat by an incident which occurred in April, 1864. The affair was hushed up so much that diligent research has failed to reveal any details. Whatever the circumstances were, Ewell found it necessary to put Old Jube temporarily under arrest on April 27 for what was described as conduct "subversive of good order and military discipline."[24] When the incident came to the attention of General Lee, he restored Old Jube to his command but noted that Early's conduct was inexcusable. The commanding general felt that the good of the service demanded harmony among the higher-ranking Confederate officers, and that they should attempt to patch up their differences, in view of the threat that was then beginning to develop—a threat which events were to prove would result in the end of the Confederacy.[25] This new menace to Southern independence was the transfer of Major General Ulysses S. Grant from the Western theatre, where he had cut the South in two, to the Eastern sector.

CHAPTER 17

Early Misses a Golden Opportunity

March 9, 1864 was a momentous day for the United States of America — for on that date President Lincoln handed Ulysses Simpson Grant his commission as lieutenant general. This rank had just been revived by Congress after its disappearance following the death of General George Washington in 1799.[1] What was more important, Lincoln appointed Grant general-in-chief of all the Union armies and assured him complete cooperation from the Executive Department. Thus the Federal war effort was for the first time to enjoy that unity of command which is so essential to success.

General Grant's transfer from the Western theatre, where he had been remarkably successful, brought to the Eastern sector exactly the type of individual needed to organize and put to the best use the overwhelming resources of the North. Grant planned the strategy that called for the simultaneous and concerted movement of all the Federal armies toward a single objective — the destruction of the only two large organized armed bodies the South still had in the field. These were Lee's army in Virginia and Joseph E. Johnston's force in northwestern Georgia.

Since the new Federal commander had expressed himself dissatisfied with the work which had been performed by the Union cavalry, he instituted a great change in that branch. Accordingly, he transferred Major General Philip H. Sheridan from General William T. Sherman's army in Georgia to the main Federal force in Virginia and gave him command of the Cavalry Corps. Grant attached himself to the Army of the Potomac, still commanded by General George G. Meade, in Virginia and entrusted the defeat of Joseph E. Johnston's Southern army to his able lieutenant, Sherman. These changes were to prove very successful.

In reorganizing his army in Virginia for the important work ahead, Grant consolidated the five corps of the Army of the Potomac into three. Those retained were the Second, Fifth, and

Sixth Corps, commanded by Major Generals Winfield S. Hancock, Gouverneur K. Warren, and John Sedgwick, respectively. The Ninth Corps, headed by Major General Ambrose E. Burnside, was not incorporated into the Army of the Potomac until May 24 although it served with that body through the Wilderness and Spotsylvania campaigns. Exclusive of the Ninth Corps, which numbered about 19,000 present for duty on April 30, 1864, Grant's army in Virginia boasted approximately 102,000 officers and men.[1] Since the Ninth Corps operated with the Army of the Potomac, Grant thus headed a force of 121,000 well-trained and well-equipped soldiers.[2]

General Lee's Army of Northern Virginia in the spring of 1864 was still organized as it had been during the Gettysburg campaign, that is, into three corps commanded by Lieutenant Generals James Longstreet, Richard Ewell, and Ambrose P. Hill, respectively. Longstreet had brought his two divisions back from East Tennessee, where he had contributed to the Confederate victory at Chickamauga, and was now ready to take his place as Lee's "Old War Horse." The Confederate authorities were unable to find many recruits for Lee's depleted ranks, so that when the crucial campaign began in the spring of 1864, the Army of Northern Virginia mustered only about 64,000 effectives of all arms.[3]

The latter part of March General Grant established his headquarters at Culpeper Court House, where he would be in position to move against his opponent, General Lee, who had located his command at Orange Court House. Lee had assumed a strong defensive post south of the Rapidan River, which was well protected by entrenchments. Since Grant's main objective was Lee's army and this army occupied a position that was unassailable in front, the only recourse left to the Federal commander was to turn one of the Confederate flanks. By doing this, Grant could force his wily opponent to come out of his entrenchments and fight or allow himself to be attacked from the rear.[4]

General Grant then determined to turn Lee's right flank, cross the Rapidan, and get out of the Wilderness before Lee could discover his plans. If he could get Lee to come out and fight in the open country to the south and east, the Federal commander could use his numerical superiority to better advantage than he could in the Wilderness. In order to appreciate the difficulties involved in the Battle of the Wilderness, it is necessary to understand the nature of the country.

The Wilderness was the name given to that wooded section of land south of the Rapidan forming a rectangle approximately fourteen miles long and ten miles wide. As a number of iron mines had been worked in this region for some time, most of the original timber had been cut as fuel for the furnaces. Consequently most of the vegetation consisted of second-growth cedar, pine, black-oak, and other kinds of underbrush which made an almost impenetrable thicket. There were few clearings and roads, although there were numerous narrow trails that seemed to go off in almost every direction. Naturally the movement of large bodies of men through this region, as well as observation of the enemy's dispositions, would be extremely difficult.[5]

Traveling as light as possible, the Army of the Potomac left its camp at midnight on May 3. It crossed the Rapidan at Ely's and Germanna Fords and approached the old battlefield of Chancellorsville. Because it was necessary to have a wagon-train for the ammunition and rations, the troops were not able to make as good time as otherwise. Shortly after noon on May 4 they encountered Confederates moving from Orange Court House toward New Verdiersville on the Plank Road.

General Lee had anticipated the Federal move and refused to be misled by feints against his left flank. He set his army in motion in order that it might strike Grant's troops in flank before the Federals could get out of the Wilderness. By evening of May 4 Ewell's corps was at Locust Grove on the Orange-Fredericksburg Turnpike and only about five miles from Warren's corps which had camped at Old Wilderness Tavern. Farther south, on the Plank Road, the leading division of Hill's corps was only seven miles from Federal cavalry at Parker's Store. Apparently none of the approaching troops were aware of the presence of their adversaries.

Ewell's corps, with Jubal Early's division bringing up the rear, was the first Confederate body to make contact with the enemy. In the morning of May 5 it encountered Warren's Federal corps moving on the Germanna Plank Road across its front. Ewell immediately formed his men in line of battle. Grant and his subordinate, Meade, sent Griffin's division against the Southerners and ordered Robinson's, Wadsworth's, and Wright's divisions to support the attack.[6]

Griffin's division struck Johnson's Confederate division with such force that it forced the Southerners back. Not content with this, the bluecoats turned on the supporting brigade, that led by Brigadier General Cullen A. Battle of Rodes' division, and threw it into confusion. With the contest going against him and a near-catastrophe becoming imminent, Ewell galloped to the rear for help. As Early's division had been following the other two, the corps commander spied Old Jube's able brigadier, John B. Gordon, and addressed him as follows:

"General Gordon, the fate of the day depends on you, sir."

Whereupon Gordon replied, "These men will save it, sir."[7]

Suiting action to his words, Gordon sent one regiment against the onrushing Unionists while he got the rest of his brigade into position. With the utterance of the famous Rebel Yell, these Confederates fought so bravely that they not only checked the Federal advance but even forced the bluecoats back. In fact, Gordon's brigade drove so far forward that it was in danger of being swallowed up by the Federals on both sides. Not to be overcome by the strange turn the fighting had taken, Gordon sent his men against the enemy's flanks. He succeeded admirably in rolling up the troops on both sides of the gap he had created by his breakthrough and, with some support from Confederates who had rallied, checked the whole Federal advance in that sector and captured many prisoners.[8]

Not long after Ewell's corps had become engaged with Warren's Federals, A. P. Hill's corps, advancing on a parallel route along the Orange Plank Road, met Getty's division of the Federal Sixth Corps. This corps, it will be recalled, was commanded by Major General John Sedgwick. Meade ordered Hancock's corps to the support of Sedgwick's men. Desperate fighting ensued, and the fortunes of war see-sawed back and forth. First one side would advance and then the other. The contest lasted until eight o'clock that evening, with no decisive gains made by either side.[9]

Sedgwick's Federals renewed the attack along the Plank Road at five o'clock in the morning of May 6. As the tired Confederates of Heth's and Wilcox's divisions had borne the brunt of the fighting in this sector the day before, they were in no condition to dispute the advance. Expecting to be relieved by Longstreet's corps, they had not established strong lines of defense and soon scattered before the Federal assault. Fortunately for the Confederacy, Longstreet's veterans from the First Corps came upon the scene in the nick of time. Inspired by the example of their courageous leader, they not only checked the Federal onslaught but also drove back the bluecoats to approximately the same position they had had when hostilities began that morning.

Not content with what his men had done, Longstreet conferred with Lee regarding the possibility of pressing the advantage by rolling back the Federal left flank. Both Confederate officers agreed the time was at hand to take the initiative, and Longstreet accordingly gave the necessary orders. His subordinates were successfully executing them when he, himself, was seriously wounded by a Confederate bullet. Just the year before, the same thing had happened to Stonewall Jackson in that same region.[10]

The loss of the corps commander threw the First Corps into some confusion which even General Lee could hardly straighten out. By the time the Confederate chieftain succeeded in reestablishing order among the troops, the enemy had strengthened his position so much that he was able to repel all efforts to dislodge him.

Meanwhile, fighting had resumed on the other part of the battlefield, along the Orange-Fredericksburg Turnpike where Ewell's corps had been confronting Sedgwick's soldiers. On the night of May 5-6 that enterprising brigadier in Early's division, John B. Gordon, ordered scouts to try to locate the enemy facing him. Early's division occupied the left of the sector defended by Ewell's corps, and Gordon's brigade held the extreme left of the divisional sector. When Gordon's scouts returned, they brought the exciting news that the right flank of the whole Federal army was in front and that it appeared to be unprotected or "in the air." If their reports were true, Meade and Grant had committed the same blunder that Hooker had made a year previously.[11]

Somewhat skeptical of this first report, General Gordon sent out a second scouting party. This group not only confirmed the findings of the other scouts but added the welcome information that there was not a supporting force within several miles of the Federal flank, except that which was on the main battle line. Still unconvinced that the Federals could be guilty of such a military blunder, Gordon went to see for himself. What he saw was to convince him that fortune had really smiled on him. For not only did he observe that there was no line of soldiers guarding the Army of the Potomac's right flank, but the Federals in the front line were eating breakfast on the edge of the rifle-pits, entirely unsuspecting. As Gordon's own lines overlapped those of his opponents, here was the opportunity of a lifetime. If he could obtain the necessary permission and cooperation from his superior officers, he might achieve an outstanding success.[12]

After he had carefully laid out his plans, General Gordon rode to corps headquarters to get the necessary permission. As it was then about nine o'clock in the morning, he had the whole day to consummate his brilliant strategy. Unfortunately on this day, May 6, Gordon's usually bold and aggressive division leader, Jubal A. Early, was disposed to take a pessimistic and cautious view of the brigadier's daring plan. Old Jube opposed the scheme as being too risky. He overlooked the reconnaissance that Gordon had made and argued that Federal supports were near their right flank and would be in position to inflict tremendous damage on Gordon's exposed brigade. Although General Early had not sent out scouts to ascertain the truth, and Gordon had, this made no difference. Old Jube refused to be convinced of his error, and the golden opportunity would be lost unless higher authority intervened.[13]

General Ewell as corps commander could have overruled General Early, but he was inclined to adopt Old Jube's views. Ewell had heard rumors that Federal troops were approaching the left flank of the Second Corps and also that Burnside's Ninth Corps was near at hand. Instead of sending scouts to prove or disprove these rumors, Ewell assumed they were true and believed Gordon's scheme too risky. In a situation similar to that at Gettysburg the year before, the commander of the Second Corps could not make up his mind to take a chance and refused Gordon permission. Meanwhile, the hours came and went, while Gordon saw his ambitious plan for rolling back Grant's right flank dashed to pieces. Ewell contented himself with deciding to make a personal reconnaissance later on.[14]

This indecision and relative inactivity on the Confederate left flank remained until five-thirty in the afternoon. At that time General Lee himself rode over to Second Corps Headquarters to see if something could not be done to relieve pressure on the Confederate right flank, which had experienced most of the day's fighting. Fortunately General Gordon was still at hand, and restraining himself as much as he could in the presence of his superiors with whom he disagreed, he informed the Confederate chieftain of his discovery that morning.

Again General Early opposed General Gordon's plan. He still maintained that the proposed assault was fraught with danger and, if attempted, might result in disaster for the whole army. Gordon argued just as vehemently that Old Jube was mistaken concerning the proximity of Federal reserves. When Lee inquired why an attack had not been launched, in view of the disclosures made by Gordon's personal reconnaissance, Early's reply was so weak that Lee expressed his feelings by remaining silent and looking completely disgusted. He immediately determined to use the remaining daylight to begin an assault that should have been delivered that morning.[15]

With Lee assuming responsibility for the offensive, Ewell and Early supported it with all their resources. Old Jube directed Gordon's brigade to form in line near the Federal right flank and Robert D. Johnston's brigade from Rodes' division to act as support. Ewell had previously attached the latter brigade to Early's division temporarily. In addition, Early posted his adjutant general, Major John W. Daniel, where he could maintain contact with Gordon and keep the division commander informed of the success or failure of the attack. Old Jube remained where he could hurry forward his other brigades if Daniel informed him that Gordon needed them.[16]

The results of the belated attack on the Federal right flank were just as Gordon had anticipated. The bluecoats were completely surprised to find themselves assaulted on their flank, and many deserted their trenches and fled. In spite of brave efforts by their commanders to get them to change front and check Gordon's troops, the Federal commands were broken up and scattered. Only the advent of darkness in the dense woodland forced Gordon to halt his men. He, himself, believed that if he had been allowed one more hour of daylight, he would have captured a considerable part of Sedgwick's corps.

A recapitulation of the Union losses in this phase of the Wilderness fighting reveals that the Federals who were killed numbered almost 400, including one brigade commander. In addition, the bluecoats lost several hundred prisoners, including two brigade commanders, Brigadier Generals Truman Seymour and Alexander Shaler. General Gordon reported his own losses at about 50.[17] Major John W. Daniel of Early's staff received a bullet which shattered his thigh-bone. Although the wound was very painful, it was not fatal, and he lived to represent Virginia in the United States Senate in the post-bellum era. Because of this wound, however, he was maimed for life.[18]

The following day, May 7, witnessed only a little skirmishing with no serious fighting. When Lee discovered that Grant was trying to outflank him by moving to Spotsylvania Court House on May 8, the Confederate chieftain set the Army of Northern Virginia once more in motion. The Battle of the Wilderness was ended and that of Spotsylvania was in the offing.

It has been shown that General Early was mistaken in his notion concerning the proximity of Federal reserves when Gordon wanted permission to try to outflank Grant on May 6. No doubt he and Ewell gave too much credence to unfounded reports that Federals were threatening their flank and other bluecoats were in support of the main line. Old Jube erred when he relied upon mere rumor instead of facts, and he was negligent in not sending out scouts or reconnoitering himself to learn the true state of affairs. Since Gordon based his recommendations on what he and his scouts had learned from observation and since he was a dependable officer, both Early and Ewell should have given Gordon's findings the consideration they deserved.

General A. P. Hill had been sick during the fighting in the Wilderness and when he became unable to remain on active duty in the field, General Lee appointed General Early temporary commander of the Third Corps. Old Jube turned command of his division over to General Gordon and on May 8 entered upon his new responsibility.[19] As General Grant was trying to outflank the Confederates by moving to Spotsylvania Court House ahead of them, General Lee ordered the Army of Northern Virginia to forestall him. Lee had appointed Major General Richard H. Anderson to lead the First Corps while General Longstreet recovered from his wound. As Anderson's men occupied that part of the Confederate line nearest Spotsylvania Court House, Lee moved them first. They arrived at Spotsylvania just in time to defend it against Grant's attack.

Lee ordered Early to lead the Third Corps to Spotsylvania as soon as the Federals confronting them had departed. Not far from Shady Grove Church Old Jube sent Mahone's division against an enemy force of cavalry and infantry. General Mahone succeeded in driving the bluecoats back after a somewhat spirited engagement. Early learned from this encounter that the Federals occupied the road ahead in force so he changed his line of march in order to move to Spotsylvania more quickly.[20]

When Lee believed the Federals to be planning a move against the Confederate left flank on May 9, he ordered Early to send troops to meet this threat. In the ensuing fight the Third Corps accomplished its objective. Indecisive skirmishing occurred the next few days. Heavier fighting took place on May 12 during which Old Jube sent reinforcements to Ewell's Second Corps, which received a spirited Federal assault. The Confederate artillery had been withdrawn during the night and hence was not available to fire into the close-marching Federals, who broke Ewell's lines and captured about 4,000 prisoners, including Generals Edward Johnson and George H. Steuart. This was a disaster of the greatest magnitude and only by Herculean effort did Generals Wilcox and Gordon succeed in reestablishing a shorter and more defensible line. Wilcox headed a division in the Third Corps.[21]

In order to relieve pressure on Ewell's corps, Early sent Lane's and Mahone's brigades to attack the flank of the victorious Federals. In attempting to execute these orders, Lane's men encountered a portion of Burnside's Ninth Corps, which was moving into position against the Confederate Third Corps. General Lane captured about 300 prisoners and contributed to the repulse of Burnside.[22] Other elements of the Third Corps helped throw back the attackers. As the Federals then erected strong entrenchments in front of Early and as the terrain was not suitable for fighting, Old Jube refrained from further attacks. A few days later he was directed to restore command of the Third Corps to General Hill, whose health had improved, and to return to his old division in Ewell's corps.[23]

As Ewell's command had moved toward Hanover Junction, Early rode southward and caught up with his division on May 22. Because of the capture of General Edward Johnson at Spotsylvania, a vacancy had occurred in one of Ewell's divisions. It was filled by promoting John B. Gordon to major general and transferring his old brigade to the division which he now headed. Early's division now consisted of Pegram's, [Robert D.] Johnston's, and Hoke's brigades. The latter body had just rejoined the division from Petersburg. Because Ewell's Corps had seen so much of the recent fighting in the Wilderness and at Spotsylvania Court House, Early's brigades were far below their normal strength.

In spite of Grant's failure to outflank Lee in the Wilderness, and at Spotsylvania, the aggressive Federal commander was not deterred from maintaining the initiative. Some of his enemies in the North had begun to complain about the great number of casualties without conpensating gains, but President Lincoln stuck by his recent choice. His reply to many Northerners who demanded Grant's removal was the laconic, "He fights!"

In a third effort to go around the Confederate right flank and thus get between Lee's army and Richmond, Grant moved down the north bank of the Pamunkey River on May 27. At the same time Ewell became so ill that he had to ask Early to lead the Second Corps.[24] Two days later Lee relieved him and placed Old Jube in temporary command. Although Ewell tried to remain active in the strenuous field campaign, his health would not permit, and on June 14 Lee placed him in charge of the defenses of Richmond.[25]

The new commander of the Second Corps, acting on orders from General Lee, moved his men southward and eastward to the vicinity of Mechanicsville. As Lee believed Grant was trying to extend his left flank until it reached the Chickahominy River, he hoped to prevent this by allowing Early to attack vigorously enough to frustrate the Federal plans. On May 30 near Bethesda Church Old Jube assaulted the enemy lines in great strength but sustained a bloody repulse. He had not coordinated his attack with Anderson's First Corps, nor had he made proper reconnaissance. Early's brigades had not discovered the Federals were entrenched until they had advanced close to the breastworks. In this unsuccessful effort Old Jube lost several able officers, as well as many enlisted men.[26]

General Grant continued to extend his lines to the left, and Lee countered by moving his troops to oppose the Federals. On June 2 two of Early's divisions, those commanded by Generals Rodes and Gordon, assisted by Heth's division of the First Corps, attacked the bluecoats near Bethesda Church and drove them back a short distance. In addition, the Confederates captured several hundred prisoners. However, Early lost another valuable officer when Brigadier General George Doles, of Rodes' division was killed.[27]

In carrying out his determination to "fight it out on this line if it takes all summer,"[28] Grant moved to Cold Harbor, where on June 3 he committed a costly blunder. Although Lee's men were protected by strong entrenchments, the Federal chieftain hurled three corps against their position. After suffering thousands of casualties in this futile attempt to break Lee's lines, Grant withdrew his men and gave them a brief respite from such arduous activity. It is said that in this engagement at Cold Harbor many of the Federals had written their names and addresses on pieces of paper which they pinned to their coats in order that their dead bodies might be more easily identified.[29]

In the Federal attack at Cold Harbor two of Early's divisions helped drive off the assaulters. Rodes' division was engaged more heavily, although Gordon's division was involved in heavy skirmishing.

After the Battle of Cold Harbor, Grant evacuated his position opposite the front held by the Confederate Second Corps. No sooner had he done this than General Early made two attempts to attack the Federal right flank and rear. Both failed, largely because of the unfavorable terrain on which the Second Corps was operating. Streams and swamps abounded. In addition, Grant had taken the precaution of throwing up elaborate entrenchments covering his front, flank, and rear. Hence it was very difficult to cause him any damage by offensive operations. Early then moved his men to the vicinity of Gaines' Mill, where, on June 12, he received orders to transfer the Second Corps to the Shenandoah Valley to meet a Federal invasion force led by Major General David Hunter. This severed his connection with the campaign around Richmond, although his success in the Valley later relieved some of the pressure on Lee's weary troops.[30]

Having failed to break Lee's lines north of Richmond after forty days of tremendous losses, Grant now determined to revise his original plans. In the fighting from the Wilderness to Cold Harbor he had suffered casualties of 55,000 in killed, wounded, missing, or captured.[31] In the new strategy which Grant developed for winning the war he decided to transfer his whole army south of the James River and approach Richmond from the south. He began this new movement on June 12 and by the 17th had his army in front of the Confederate defenders of Petersburg—the key to the gates of Richmond. Lee moved his army to the south likewise, and the old antagonists were facing each other once again, this time in and around Petersburg.[32]

CHAPTER 18

Savior of Lynchburg

While events were moving toward a climax in the titanic struggle in front of Richmond and Petersburg, another part of the Federal strategy for ending the war began to unfold in the Shenandoah Valley. This region, it will be recalled, was bounded by the Blue Ridge Mountains on the east and the Alleghenies, or more specifically, the North Mountains, on the west. The Valley runs in a general northeast-southwest direction and extends approximately 155 miles from Harpers Ferry to Lexington.

The Federal Department of West Virginia included the Shenandoah Valley, and in the spring of 1864 Major General Franz Sigel headed the Union army in this region. He had stationed part of his force in the Kanawha River section under Brigadier General George Crook and had kept the remainder at his own headquarters in the lower end of the Valley. As the Shenandoah River flows north before it unites with the Potomac at Harpers Ferry, when one speaks of the Lower Valley, he means that part farthest north.[1]

An important aspect of the Shenandoah Valley region was the fact that several well-traveled railroads passed through its confines. At its northern approach the Baltimore and Ohio system followed the Potomac to Harpers Ferry, where it crossed to the Virginia side, and then left the river, only to return to it later. Running from Baltimore and Washington to Wheeling, this road was the main route of communication between Washington and the West. Farther south, a Confederate line, the Virginia Central |now the Chesapeake and Ohio|, crossed the Shenandoah Valley at Staunton, entered the Blue Ridge Mountains at Rockfish Gap, and then passed through Charlottesville and Gordonsville before reaching Richmond. Still farther south, and, although not strictly speaking in the Shenandoah Valley but close enough to be affected by military operations in it, was the Virginia and Tennessee line |now the Norfolk and Western|. This was Richmond's direct connection with the West.[2]

Another Federal artery of communication and transportation was the Chesapeake and Ohio Canal. This artificial waterway was not as important to Union success as was the railroad because it was generally closed to navigation during the winter months when ice extended from bank to bank. However, the slow-moving canal boats, pulled by mules, hauled vast quantities of supplies from the western terminal, Cumberland, to Washington — 186 miles away. The Confederate counterpart of this waterway was the James River and Kanawha Canal, which afforded water transportation between Lynchburg and the Southern capital.

The military problem confronting General Sigel in 1864 was to protect the Federal arteries and, if possible, to disrupt transportation over the Confederate lines. In accordance with his instructions from General Grant, he sent General George Crook to try to burn the bridge which conducted the Virginia and Tennessee Railroad over the New River and also to destroy the Confederate salt works at Saltville. Sigel hoped to distract attention from Crook's objective by leading another Federal column up the Valley to Staunton, where it could threaten the Virginia Central.

General Crook delegated the task of destroying the salt works to his able cavalry leader, Brigadier General William W. Averell, while he marched his infantry to the place where the railroad bridge was located. Averell had some minor success but was prevented from destroying the salt works because of the strength of the Confederate guard. Crook was more successful. He defeated an enemy force under Generals W. E. Jones and Albert G. Jenkins at the Battle of Cloyd's Mountain and caused the death of Jenkins. After this victory he marched to Newbern, burned the railroad bridge there, and then returned to Union, in present West Virginia.

General Sigel attempted to carry out his part of the Federal program by starting out on April 30 for the Upper Valley. Passing through Winchester, Strasburg, Woodstock, and Mount Jackson, he learned of the presence of a Confederate force at New Market led by Major General John C. Breckinridge. The resulting Battle of New Market on May 15 added new laurels to the cadet corps of the Virginia Military Institute and forced Sigel to flee down the Valley to Cedar Creek, near Strasburg. The Union commander at Washington, General Henry W. Halleck, informed Grant of this disappointment in the following words: "Sigel is in full retreat on Strasburg. He will do nothing but run; never did anything else."[3]

The feeling that Sigel was not the man for the job prompted

Halleck to write Grant three days later that President Lincoln would appoint Major General David Hunter to succeed Sigel if Grant so desired. The lieutenant general very promptly replied: "By all means I would say appoint General Hunter, or anyone else, to the command of West Virginia."[4] Accordingly, on May 19 the necessary orders were given making David Hunter the successor to Sigel.[5]

The new commander in the Valley soon revealed that his force was one to make the Confederate authorities take notice. Moving rapidly up the Valley, General Hunter met and defeated at Piedmont on June 5 a body of Confederates under Brigadier General William E. Jones, causing the latter's death. The following day he entered Staunton, where he captured and paroled 400 sick and wounded Confederate soldiers. In addition, he seized large quantities of commissary and ordnance stores and destroyed all the railroad bridges, factories, and workshops in the town. To add to the destruction of this region, General Crook, entering from the west, tore up the tracks of the Virginia Central line. Crook and Averell joined Hunter at Staunton on June 8, thus increasing his command by 10,000 men.[6] He now had a total force of about 18,000.

In order to meet this new threat which was becoming increasingly serious, General Lee sent General John C. Breckinridge with a small force to Lynchburg. At the same time the Confederate chieftain learned that General Sheridan was off on a cavalry raid to the west to join Hunter. Consequently, Lee dispatched Major General Wade Hampton, Stuart's successor, to pursue Sheridan with Southern troopers. Hampton, moving on a shorter arc, reached the Virginia Central Railroad ahead of Sheridan and at the Battle of Trevilian Station, near Louisa Court House, on June 11, forced Sheridan to abandon his plan to join Hunter and to return to the east.[7]

In the meantime, while Hampton was checking Sheridan, Hunter had entered Lexington. He found it weakly defended by Confederates who persisted in firing at the Federals from some buildings in the town, including those of the Virginia Military Institute. Hunter retaliated by ordering the burning of that famous school. Although Washington College |now Washington and Lee University| escaped this type of destruction, it did suffer the loss of George Washington's statue, which some of the Federals removed from a hall, loaded in their wagons, and later transported to Wheeling. According to one of the Union officers, Washington's statue was taken "to rescue it from the degenerate sons of worthy sires."[8]

Hunter did not stop with ordering the burning of the Virginia Military Institute buildings. Because he found a proclamation from ex-Governor John Letcher of Virginia, who lived in Lexington, urging the people to resist the Federals, Hunter ordered that Letcher's home be given the torch. Thus the Federal commander inaugurated a series of burnings of private homes destined to provoke General Jubal Early to retaliation later on.[9]

Although General Hunter delayed his advance to allow a supply train of 200 wagons to catch up with him at Lexington, he sent General Averell ahead to scout and destroy. Hunter arrived at Buchanan on June 14, where he found that Confederate cavalry under Brigadier General John McCausland had destroyed the bridge across the James River. Unfortunately, the town caught fire from the bridge, and the Federals had an opportunity to repay the South for what Gordon's Confederates had done at Wrightsville, Pennsylvania the year before. Although the Federal troops helped extinguish the fire at Buchanan, they did not succeed in doing so until eleven private dwellings had been devoured by the flames.

With Hunter marching toward Lynchburg from Buchanan, the situation was becoming extremely critical from the Confederate point of view. It was unthinkable that Lynchburg with its network of transportation facilities, including railroads and a canal, its factories, its hospitals, and its garrison of militia and convalescent soldiers should fall to the Federals. Lee realized the need for immediate action, and in his extremity he turned to Jubal Early. He had decided to detach the entire Second Corps from the Army of Northern Virginia and send it under the command of Old Jube to dispose of the Federal threat to Lynchburg.

General Early, it will be recalled, had succeeded General Ewell as the head of the Second Corps of the Army of Northern Virginia. In line with his added responsibilities, Old Jube was promoted to lieutenant general, the normal rank held by a corps commander in the Confederate army. His new rank was to be effective May 31, 1864.[10]

At the time General Lee detached the Second Corps to go to the aid of the Lynchburg defenders, it numbered only about 8,000 muskets. It had suffered severe losses in the Wilderness and especially at Spotsylvania, where it had lost most of General Edward Johnson's division, including that officer himself. Of the twelve brigadier generals in the corps at the beginning of the Wilderness fighting, only one was still in command of the same troops. Generals Ramseur and Gordon had been made major generals, whereas all the others had been killed, captured, or wounded. Divisions were now about the size of brigades, and brigades were no larger than regiments were normally.[11] With this depleted corps, plus what little help he could obtain from the weak garrison of Lynchburg, Early expected to turn back Generals Hunter, Crook, and Averell with their 18,000 men.

Old Jube's selection for this important task was due to several circumstances. For one thing, the heavy fighting of the preceding six weeks had taken such a heavy toll of Lee's able officers that narrowing down of the field necessarily resulted. Then, too, General Early's military star had been rising ever since the First Battle of Bull Run. In the subsequent fighting he had made mistakes, as had other generals, but the overall picture was one of credit. He had been described as a "man of independent mind, entirely self-reliant and with an aptitude for strategy."[12] He was bold and aggressive. According to President Jefferson Davis, General Lee and he agreed that, in the absence of Stonewall Jackson, "Early was the living man who like Jackson could be relied on to carry out the purpose intrusted to him without asking for additional instructions."[13] Finally, Old Jube had fought in the Shenandoah Valley so much that he knew its topography well — an important consideration.

Since the Valley campaign of 1864 was destined to be General Early's greatest military exploit, it might be worth-while to digress long enough to describe his physical appearance at this time. A contemporary described him as follows:

> General Early is about six feet high, and but for a stoop of the shoulder, caused by rheumatism, would be of fine figure. He is about 50 years of age, apparently well preserved, and a person who would be singled out in a crowd. A large white felt hat, ornamented by a dark feather, and an immense white, fulled cloth overcoat, extending to the heels, give him a striking and unique appearance. His face is remarkable, and none could be more expressive of pertinacity and resolution. 'The will to do — the soul to dare,' are unmistakably stamped on every lineament and expressed in every feature. The massive head, the broad, high forehead, the dark, piercing eye, the well cut nose, the compressed lips and thick set jaws are characters in which nature has written self-reliance and inflexible determination.[14]

On June 12 Lee gave Early verbal orders to hold the Second Corps and two battalions of artillery in readiness to move to the

Valley. The Confederate chieftain later gave Old Jube written instructions. Early in the morning of June 13 the Second Corps left the vicinity of Gaines' Mill for Lynchburg. At this time it consisted of three infantry divisions, led by Major Generals John B. Gordon, Robert E. Rodes, and Stephen D. Ramseur. The artillery battalions were those of Lieutenant Colonels Carter Braxton and William Nelson. Brigadier General Armistead L. Long accompanied Old Jube as Chief of artillery.[15]

After marching over eighty miles in four days, Early's troops arrived at the Rivanna River near Charlottesville. This record compares favorably with that made by Jackson's "foot cavalry" in the Valley in 1862. In fact, some of the old Stonewall Brigade were now serving under Old Jube. Early rode ahead of his men into Charlottesville in order to communicate with Breckinridge, who was feverishly attempting to strengthen the weak defenses of Lynchburg. He contacted Breckinridge on June 16 and instructed him to see that the employees of the Orange and Alexandria Railroad cooperated in having rolling stock available at Charlottesville to transport the Second Corps to Lynchburg. With characteristic zeal Early called for "promptness, energy, and dispatch." He informed his subordinate, "I have authority to direct your movements, and I will take the responsibility of what you may find it necessary to do. I will hold all railroad agents and employees responsible with their lives for hearty co-operation with us."[16]

In spite of his strenuous efforts to locate enough rolling stock to move his army to the threatened city, General Early was not able to get his men in motion until the morning of the 17th. Even then only enough transportation was available for about half his infantry. He, therefore, ordered Ramseur's division and part of Gordon's on board and then obtained a place for himself on the front train. The railroad and its equipment were in such poor shape that it took most of the morning for part of Early's army to negotiate the sixty miles separating Charlottesville from Lynchburg.

Old Jube arrived at Lynchburg at one o'clock in the afternoon and immediately contacted Breckinridge. Much to his surprise, he found the latter in bed, suffering from an old injury received when his horse was killed under him at Cold Harbor. Fortunately, Major General D. H. Hill was then in the city, and Breckinridge suggested that he be appointed to succeed him. Old Jube telegraphed Richmond to have the change of commanders approved.[17] He also noted with satisfaction that one of his former brigade commanders,

Harry Hays, was then in Lynchburg and was available for limited duty, as he had only partially recovered from a wound received at Spotsylvania.

Learning that Hunter was approaching from the direction of Bedford, Early, accompanied by Hill, rode out to survey the Lynchburg defenses. Old Jube noticed that a nondescript army of defenders was manning the works. This included Breckinridge's two small infantry brigades, the cadet corps of the Virginia Military Institute, dismounted cavalry which had been with General Jones at Piedmont, reserves, and invalids from the Lynchburg hospitals. His keen eye also observed that the Confederate defense line was so close to the town as to expose the latter to enemy artillery fire. Consequently, he ordered a new line to be established in front of this, and he directed his own troops to occupy it.[18]

The appearance of Early and the van of the Second Corps has been described by Major John W. Daniel, who had served on Old Jube's staff until wounded in the Wilderness. Major Daniel commented as follows of the effect that the appearance of these reinforcements had on the weak force assembled to check Hunter:

> . . . As Hunter's skirmishers were pushing close to the town, and as the cavalry were falling back before them, a few pieces of artillery near the toll-gate, under Lieutenant Carter Berkley, were doing their best to stop the oncomers. In this condition Tinsley, the bugler of the Stonewall Brigade [Second Corps], came trotting up the road, sounding the advance, and behind him came the skirmishers of Ramseur's Division with rapid strides. Just then the artillerists saw through the smoke the broad, white slouch hat and the black feather of 'Old Jube,' who rode amongst them and looking toward the enemy, exclaimed: 'No buttermilk rangers after you now, damn you' . . . .[19]

General Hunter began the Battle of Lynchburg when he sent his infantry against a small, badly mounted and poorly armed force of Confederate cavalry commanded by Brigadier General John D. Imboden, which had taken position on the Bedford road about four miles out. The Federals easily drove back their outnumbered foes, and as Imboden's command was retiring, Early's men moved into position. Aided by the two pieces of artillery already on hand, Old Jube's veterans succeeded in checking the Federal skirmishers. The artillery belonging to the Second Corps had not arrived from Charlottesville. Hunter then opened a heavy artillery fire on the Confederates, but nightfall prevented further fighting.[20]

As Old Jube did not have the remainder of his infantry, to say

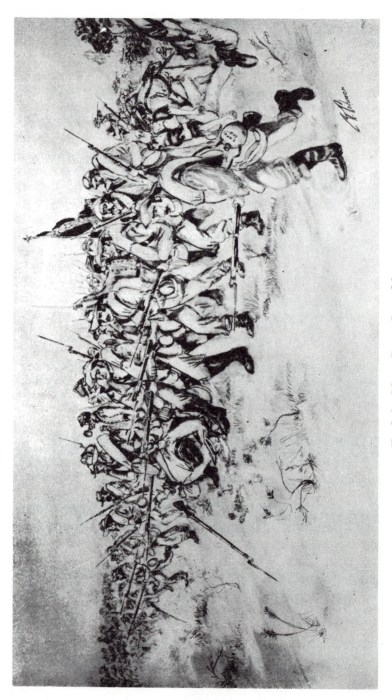

Early's Men Save Lynchburg

190

nothing of his artillery, during the morning of the 18th he remained on the defensive. Hunter had a much stronger force, and Early did not want to jeopardize the safety of the city until he had a reasonable assurance of success. Hunter demonstrated vigorously with his infantry, artillery, and cavalry in the morning, while he attacked in force in the afternoon. None of these efforts succeeded in gaining him entrance into the city. During this day Early had been reinforced by the arrival of Major Generals Arnold Elzey and Robert Ransom from Richmond. Elzey was to assume charge of Breckinridge's force, while Ransom was to head all the cavalry. When the remainder of Early's infantry arrived by train from Charlottesville, Old Jube made plans to assume the offensive at daylight on June 19.

General Hunter supposed that Early's forces outnumbered him two to one and, being short of ammunition, determined to withdraw. Sending off his baggage and supply trains first, he waited until dark before dispatching the bulk of his army. He quite naturally wished to take advantage of the darkness to conceal his movements. By midnight the last line of pickets retired to join the main army, which had preceded it on the road to Bedford.[21] The Battle of Lynchburg was over, and Old Jube had earned the title "Savior of Lynchburg."

As soon as Early learned that Hunter had retreated, he started the Second Corps in pursuit. He caught up with the Federal rear guard at Bedford and drove it back on the main force. Hunter continued his withdrawal through Buford's Gap in the Blue Ridge Mountains, to Bonsack's Station on the Virginia and Tennessee Railroad, thence to Salem. Old Jube pursued as far as Hanging Rock, in Roanoke County, where, finding his quarry still elusive, he suspended the pursuit. Hunter made good his escape into West Virginia, using the route which led through New Castle, White Sulphur Springs, and Lewisburg.[22]

CHAPTER 19

Old Jube Scares Abe Lincoln

After disposing of General Hunter's threat to Lynchburg, General Early determined to assume the offensive. Hunter's withdrawal into the Kanawha Valley of West Virginia stripped the Shenandoah Valley of most of its Federal defenders — hence that favorite route of threatening Washington was wide open. Lee had given Old Jube discretionary orders to move against Washington or return to the Army of Northern Virginia at Petersburg and, as might be expected from a man of adventurous temperament, Early chose the more daring alternative.[1]

Lee had two principal reasons for wanting Early to move down the Shenandoah Valley toward Washington. One was that by creating a diversion in that region Old Jube would possibly relieve the unrelenting pressure which Grant was exerting on Lee at Petersburg. Lee hoped that a Confederate demonstration against the Federal capital would so alarm Northern public opinion that it would force Grant to detach some of his own troops from Petersburg and send them to protect Washington. The strategy of relying upon Northern fears for the safety of Washington to help Confederate forces elsewhere had succeeded in the past and might do so again.

The second reason why Lee wanted Early to move northward was the hope that a successful diversion would insure success for a bold Confederate scheme to release several thousand prisoners of war held in the Federal prison at Point Lookout, Maryland. Point Lookout is located at the tip of the peninsula where the Potomac River enters the Chesapeake Bay. Lee believed such a scheme practicable and in several letters to President Davis he emphasized its desirability.[2] Because the Confederates could never obtain the necessary shipping to cross the Potomac to Point Lookout and because there was insufficient time to contact the prisoners, this plan had to be abandoned.[3]

After Early failed to catch Hunter at Hanging Rock, he allowed his weary men to rest for a day. They had just traveled

192

sixty miles in three days over very rough roads, and some had not eaten much for several days. He also wanted to give his wagons and artillery an opportunity to catch up with the main body. Therefore, from his headquarters at Botetourt Springs General Early on June 22 gave the Second Corps its first day of rest since leaving Lee's army.[4]

Realizing the importance of pushing on before the Northern authorities could recover from Hunter's defeat, Early set his force in motion the following day. Passing through Buchanan and Lexington, where some of the troops marched by Stonewall Jackson's grave, the main body reached Staunton on the 27th. Early arrived in that city the day before and spent his time reorganizing his force and obtaining supplies.

The army which Old Jube assembled in Staunton for the Valley campaign of 1864 consisted of four infantry divisions: those of Rodes, Gordon, Ramseur, and John Echols. The infantry which Brigadier General Echols headed was Breckinridge's old command, and after being led by Generals Arnold Elzey and J. C. Vaughn, it was handed over to Echols. The army's cavalry component, consisting of Ransom's division, included the brigades of Bradley T. Johnson [formerly William E. Jones'], W. L. Jackson, John McCausland, and John D. Imboden.

Besides the artillery pieces which the cavalry had, Early's artillery numbered about forty guns, many of which were 12-pounder Napoleons. This branch was headed by Brigadier General Armistead L. Long, whose three battalions included the batteries of Nelson, King, Braxton, and McLaughlin. In order to give Breckinridge a command commensurate with his rank and ability, Early assigned him something resembling a corps command. He received the two divisions of Gordon and Echols. The other two infantry divisions and the cavalry were directly under Early's orders.[5] The entire force consisted of 10,000 infantry and about 4,000 cavalry and artillery.[6]

One unfortunate condition which boded ill for the future of Early's little army concerned Gordon's division. This body was composed of what had been many diversified elements, and the resulting consolidation did not improve an already sagging *esprit de corps*. This lack of pride in one's organization was bound to impair its efficiency as a fighting unit. Concerning Gordon's command, a Confederate inspector had the following to say in his report dated August 21:

> . . . The discipline in this command is lax. It will be remembered that York's brigade is composed of the discordant

fragments of Hays' and Stafford's brigades, and that Terry's is made up of the remnants of the Stonewall, Jones', and Steuart's brigades, formerly of Johnson's division, comprising the remains of fourteen regiments. Both officers and men bitterly object to their consolidation into one brigade. Strange officers command strange troops, and the difficulties of fusing this incongruous mass are enhanced by constant marching and frequent engagements. Evans' brigade has lost by casualty so many and such valuable officers as to interfere seriously with its good management. . . .[7]

Another handicap confronting Old Jube was the fact that many of the troops, particularly in Breckinridge's command, were from the mountainous sections of the Confederacy and only lukewarm in their zeal for the Southern cause. They were willing to fight for the Stars and Bars when their own homes were in immediate danger, but the farther they got from their native mountains, the more they deserted. This problem became so serious that Early had to address a special note to Breckinridge concerning it.[8]

Still another hindrance to the success of the expedition was the fact that about half the infantry, even including company officers, were almost barefooted. Remembering the suffering of his unshod troops on the hard macadam roads of the Valley in 1862, Early sent word to Richmond requesting that shoes be dispatched immediately to Staunton. As they had not arrived by the time he was ready to leave, he left some wagons behind to bring them and on June 28 resumed the northward march.[9]

Confident of his ability to lead a successful expedition across the Potomac and deal effectively with the superior forces he knew the Federals could bring against him, Early expressed his feelings in a letter to Lee written on June 30 in New Market. In it he requested his chieftain to continue to threaten General Grant. This, of course, was desirable to keep the Federals guessing all along the line. When one considers the obstacles confronting a small Southern army north of the Potomac at this time, he cannot help but admire the courage and aggressiveness of Old Jube. It was the manifestation of this pugnacious spirit on the part of leaders like Lee, Jackson, Stuart, Early, and others that made the war last so long.

The boldness of Early's expedition in 1864 has been aptly phrased by one of Old Jube's staff members, Henry Kyd Douglas, as follows:

Jackson being dead, it is safe to say no other General in either army would have attempted it against such odds. . . .

The audacity of Early's enterprise was its safety; no one who might have taken steps to oppose or cut him off would believe his force was so small.[10]

When Early's troops reached Winchester on July 2, their commander received a communication from General Lee instructing him to remain in the Lower Valley until fully prepared to cross the Potomac and, in the meantime, to wreak destruction on the Baltimore and Ohio Railroad, as well as the Chesapeake and Ohio Canal. Accordingly, Old Jube sent a cavalry force under McCausland to burn the railroad bridge at Back Creek and then move by North Mountain depot to Haynesville on the Martinsburg-Williamsport road. At the same time he ordered Bradley Johnson's troopers to move through Middleway and Leetown to Kearneysville. At the latter place Johnson was to cross the railroad and proceed to Haynesville to unite with McCausland. Old Jube hoped that this movement would cut off the retreat of the Federal garrison in Martinsburg, whose commander was the discredited "Flying Dutchman", Franz Sigel.

Early sent his infantry under Breckinridge directly against Martinsburg from Winchester. He accompanied the remainder of this branch, the divisions of Rodes and Ramseur, on the route that Johnson's troopers had taken through Middleway and Leetown.[11]

As soon as Sigel's pickets warned him of Early's approach, that Federal officer began sending off or destroying supplies to prevent their capture by the Confederates. Sigel then retreated to Shepherdstown, crossed the Potomac, and later made his way to Maryland Heights — opposite the town of Harpers Ferry.

Meanwhile Bradley Johnson's cavalry had encountered a strong Union force led by Colonel James A. Mulligan at Leetown and after some initial success had been pushed back upon Rodes' and Ramseur's infantry divisions. As the latter troops had marched twenty-four miles before arriving at Leetown, Early did not make them engage Mulligan. That night, July 3, Mulligan withdrew to Shepherdstown, where he joined Sigel, and all the Federals crossed the Potomac.[12]

Early followed up these successes by sending Rodes' and Ramseur's divisions against the Federal garrison at Harpers Ferry. Attacking from the direction of Charles Town on July 4, the Confederates forced the defenders back to their riflepits on Camp Hill. Finally, because of the mounting pressure on his lines, the Union commander at Harpers Ferry, Brigadier General Max Weber, evacuated the town, crossed the river, and established his command in a strong position on Maryland Heights. There Sigel joined him and, since that position dominates Harpers Ferry, they were able to make the town untenable for the Confederates.

While Early had been clearing the Valley of its Federal defenders, his various subordinates had been systematically destroying miles of the Baltimore and Ohio Railroad and thus interrupting traffic over that important Union means of transportation. Some appreciation of the magnitude of this phase of Early's offensive against the railroad is afforded by the following quotation:

> For two weeks Confederate troops removed selected segments of the track, cut telegraph wires, and destroyed bridges, culverts, buildings, and rolling stock. They extended their depredations as far east as Monocacy Junction. . . .
>
> Between Harpers Ferry and Cumberland also, Early struck a heavy blow. Company losses included twenty-seven open culverts between Harpers Ferry and Martinsburg, a half mile of track at Quincy Siding, trestling of the Opequon and Rattling bridges, a part of the Pillar bridge near Martinsburg, and all platforms between Martinsburg and Hancock. The railroad bridges at the mouths of Pattersons Creek, the South Branch of the Potomac, and Back Creek likewise fell victim to Confederate thoroughness. Not until Early had withdrawn from Maryland did the Baltimore and Ohio gain a respite. . . .[13]

General Early had become master of the Valley by July 4 and had contemplated using Harpers Ferry as a jumping-off place to reach Washington — only about sixty miles to the southeast. However, when the defeated Federal forces in the Lower Valley gathered behind the strong defenses of Maryland Heights, he was forced to abandon this plan. As he did not want to expend the time and effort required to assault the Union position, he demonstrated against the bluecoats there and then determined to cross the Potomac at Shepherdstown and push on to Frederick, Maryland.

After he had crossed the river into Maryland, Early was in a favorable position to interfere with transportation on another artery, the Chesapeake and Ohio Canal. He sent troops to destroy the aqueduct which carried the canal over Antietam Creek, at the mouth of that stream. In addition, his men put out of commission the locks and canal boats which they found at that location.[14]

As Old Jube's army had received the badly-needed shoes by the evening of July 7, it was ready to push on through the gaps in South Mountain to Frederick and Washington. It started across this range the next day and on July 9 was in Frederick.[15]

Upon entering Maryland, Early issued strict orders against

pillaging or waging war upon the civilian population. He instructed responsible officials to make requisition upon the inhabitants for such supplies as the army needed to sustain itself, but he expected them to pay for these or give certificates redeemable by the Confederate Government later. To enforce his commands in regard to molesting civilians, Old Jube promised that any malefactors would be arrested and summarily punished.

However, Early's qualms concerning civilian welfare in this hostile section of Maryland did not deter him from making demands on the inhabitants for his army, especially in the case of two rival cities, Hagerstown and Frederick. On July 6 Old Jube sent McCausland to levy a contribution of $20,000 on Hagerstown, and three days later he demanded $200,000 from Frederick. As both cities were very similar in size and wealth, it was not understood why Hagerstown escaped so lightly. Early explained later that he had ordered McCausland to collect the same amount, $200,000, from Hagerstown, but that the cavalry officer mistook his figures for $20,000, and the mistake was not discovered until it was too late to correct it.[16]

At any rate, when General Early rode into Frederick to collect the $200,000 levy, he held the city in his grasp and was in position to seize or destroy what he wished. As the Federals had established a depot there, Old Jube considered it a legitimate military target. In vain did Mayor William G. Cole protest that the sum demanded was excessive and that a municipality of only 8,000 souls with an assessable basis of $2,200,000 could ill afford such an outlay. Early was obdurate.

The mayor and city council hurriedly passed the necessary authorization and obtained the entire sum from the city's five banks. In later years the municipality assumed the full debt and reimbursed the banks for the loan. All subsequent efforts by Frederick to have the United States Government reimburse the city failed. Consequently, the unfortunate community had to pay a grand total of over $600,000 principal and interest, during the subsequent eighty-seven years. The last payment on this debt was made on October 1, 1951.[17]

All of this Confederate activity in the Lower Valley had created great alarm in the North. In a communication which Halleck at Washington sent to Grant at City Point [on the James] on July 3 he expressed concern over reports that Early was moving toward the Potomac. Halleck concluded his telegram with the following cynical comment about his subordinates in the threatened part of the Valley: "The three principal officers on the line of the road are Sigel, Stahel, and Max Weber. You can, therefore, judge what probability there is of a good defense if the enemy should attack the line in force."[18]

Grant's reply indicates that the Intelligence Department of the Union army was not functioning properly, for as late as July 3 he stated that Early's corps was then at Petersburg and that the threat to the Potomac line could not be serious.[19]

In order to check Early's invasion of Maryland President Lincoln called upon the governors of New York, Pennsylvania, and Massachusetts to supply him with hundred-day volunteers. In addition he ordered Hunter back to the Valley. He also issued a proclamation on July 7 setting aside the first Thursday in August to be observed by the people of the United States as a day of national humiliation and prayer. In this proclamation the President carried out the will of Congress as expressed in a concurrent resolution passed by that body on July 2. In this statement the Federal political leaders, after requesting the President to set aside the day for prayer, expressed the hope that the people would convene at places of worship:

> . . . to confess and repent of their manifold sins; to implore the compassion and forgiveness of the Almighty, that, if consistent with His will, the existing rebellion may be speedily suppressed . . .; to implore Him, as the Supreme Ruler of the World, not to destroy us as a people, nor suffer us to be destroyed by the hostility or connivance of other nations. . . .[20]

By July 5 General Grant began to feel more concerned about the situation in the Lower Valley, for he offered to send an entire corps from his army if such a large force would be needed to repel the invaders. General Halleck thought that Grant's dismounted cavalry would be sufficient. Grant responded by sending the dismounted cavalry and Ricketts' division of infantry from the Sixth Corps, with the promise of the remainder of the corps if needed.[21]

Another individual very much interested in developments now unfolding was Major General Lew Wallace, better known as the author of *Ben Hur,* but in July, 1864 Federal commander of the Middle Department with headquarters at Baltimore. As soon as he learned about Early's crossing the Potomac, he gathered together a motley army composed of part of the Baltimore garrison, home guards, hundred-day militia, and a small force of cavalry. Since he did not know whether Old Jube would move against Washington or Baltimore, Wallace posted his force at Monocacy Junction, about three miles from Frederick. At this point the Frederick-Baltimore and Frederick-Washington turnpikes are close to each other, and the Baltimore and Ohio Railroad crosses the Monocacy River, a branch of the Potomac.

In order to ascertain the whereabouts of the Confederates, Wallace sent a small cavalry force under Lieutenant Colonel David D. Clendenin to reconnoiter west of Frederick. The Federal horsemen encountered Bradley Johnson's Confederates, who drove them back to Frederick. Fortunately for Wallace, Ricketts' division from Grant's army arrived at Baltimore in the evening of July 7 and immediately marched to Monocacy Junction.

The Battle of Monocacy began in the morning of July 9 when Early's artillery opened on the few enemy pieces across the river. Since Wallace had a strong position and Old Jube was unfamiliar with the terrain, the Confederate general delayed his attack. He had decided not to assault frontally but to try to turn one of the flanks of the enemy. To do this, he would have to discover a suitable place for fording the stream.[22]

While Early was trying to find a place where the Monocacy could be crossed with the least danger from enemy fire, McCausland had led his troopers across at a ford about a mile downstream. The bold, young cavalry general then had his men dismount and, leaving some to hold the horses of the others, he boldly assailed the left flank of the Federal line. Much to the surprise of the Confederates, they were greeted with a heavy fire from the rifles of Ricketts' division, which was defending that part of Wallace's line. Apparently, McCausland had not expected such resistance, for he did not know that the Federal defenders had been reinforced by the veterans from Grant's army. After a fierce struggle the Southern troopers fell back.

As soon as Early saw McCausland advance, he decided to send Gordon's division, which was nearest the ford, to aid the cavalrymen turn the Federal left flank. Gordon gave the necessary orders to his men. He had hoped to be able to cross the river and form his lines before Wallace would become aware of what was taking place on the Federal left, but the Union commander saw what was happening and changed his front to repel the infantry attack.[23]

The intrepid Gordon found his way barred by many obstacles. Not only were Wallace's bluecoats expecting him, but before the Confederates could reach the Federal lines, they would have to cross the river, climb fences, and try to maintain a battle line through fields full of grain-stacks. All of this time they would be exposed to enemy fire, and since the Unionists were behind breastworks, the Southerners found poor targets in their front.

Gordon was somewhat critical of Early for not using the

other Confederate divisions to support him, but he determined to do the best he could under the circumstances. As soon as Gordon's infantrymen reached the first fence, they received a volley which tore great holes in their ranks. Those that survived climbed over and pushed on. Some were even thoughtful enough to make gaps in the fence through which their comrades could pass more easily. These men negotiated the field containing the grain-stacks and came to the second fence. By now they were close to the enemy's first line. The very fury of the Confederate attack forced these Federals back upon their supporters.

Gordon had formed his division in échelon from the right, with Evans' brigade meeting the enemy first, followed by the brigades of York and Terry. Brigadier General Clement A. Evans was severely wounded early in the fighting. Other officers were unhorsed, but the men in the ranks pressed on. Brigadier General Zebulon York, in charge of Hays' and Stafford's Louisiana brigades, moved to the left of Evans' men and forced the Federals back to their third line.[24]

Gordon decided to throw Terry's brigade, which had not been engaged, against this third line of Federals. Although these troops advanced with great spirit, they were not able to drive the enemy from their position. Not wishing to risk a frontal assault, Gordon dispatched two staff officers to seek reinforcements. When he received word that it would be some time before support could reach him, he determined to act without it. He instructed Brigadier General Terry to have his brigade change front and attack the enemy's right, while he used his other two brigades to assault the front. This offensive all along the line forced Ricketts' men out of their position into headlong retreat. Early's other divisions crossed the Monocacy and participated in the pursuit. The Battle of Monocacy was over.[25]

In his official report of this engagement General Gordon called attention to its sanguinary character by stating that he was an eye-witness to the fact that the flow of blood from the killed and wounded was so great that it reddened a little stream more than a hundred yards below the scene of fighting.[26]

General Early did not desire to be encumbered with additional prisoners and, accordingly, abandoned the pursuit. Wallace's defeated troops fled along the Baltimore pike. The Confederate commander reported his entire loss to be between 600 and 700,[27] while his Federal opponent suffered casualties of almost 2,000,[28] although this number was reduced to about 1300 by the return of some of the missing.[29] Wallace's force at the beginning of the battle numbered an estimated 6035,[30] while Early had his entire army at hand, although he did not use part of it.

In the meantime Early's cavalry had been extremely active. The Confederate troopers held possession of the fords across the Potomac with small detachments, while the main body was sending back a long procession of livestock. In addition, they collected great quantities of supplies, including such things as shoes, clothing, grain, bacon, etc. Led by a Marylander, Bradley T. Johnson, one force occupied Westminster, Towsontown, and Reisterstown, and tore up the Northern Central Railroad at Cockeysville.

Another Marylander, Major Harry Gilmor, operating near his home-town of Baltimore, led a force of Confederate troopers against the Philadelphia, Wilmington, and Baltimore Railroad. At Magnolia Station these raiders stopped two trains near the bridge across the Gunpowder River and set them on fire. Then they backed one of the flaming trains on the bridge and thus ignited that structure. They captured General W. B. Franklin on one of the trains, but as he was not closely guarded, he escaped. Naturally Gilmor's raid temporarily cut communication between Washington and the North.[31]

Early's defeat of Wallace at the Battle of Monocacy with the consequent removal of the last important Federal force between the Confederates and Washington stirred the North to renewed efforts of defense. On July 10 Baltimore citizens were manning the trenches protecting their city. The Federal capital's defending force was augmented by the addition of 2,500 dismounted cavalrymen from Sheridan's corps. To protect the ferry and railroad at Havre de Grace, the Union authorities sent one hundred convalescents from Washington. Martial law was proclaimed in Annapolis, and Grant sent one of his better officers, Major General E. O. C. Ord, from the Richmond-Petersburg area to command at Baltimore.[32] In the resulting confusion it it not surprising that frightened Northerners believed Early's little army to be much larger than it actually was.

CHAPTER 20

Old Jube Scares Ulysses Grant

After winning the Battle of Monocacy, General Early pushed his little army on to Washington. At daybreak on the morning of July 10 his columns began the march over the hot and dusty road. He left Ramseur's division at the Monocacy to protect Confederates engaged in destroying the Baltimore and Ohio Railroad bridge across that stream. After this had been accomplished, Ramseur brought up the rear of the main body. Meanwhile the van covered thirty miles before it bivouacked four miles from Rockville.[1]

Wishing to capitalize upon the defenseless condition of the capital and the chaos which prevailed everywhere, Old Jube awakened his men from their slumbers and started them at dawn on the morning of the 11th. He sent McCausland's cavalrymen along the Georgetown pike toward Tenallytown, where that enterprising officer took position on the right of the line Early established before Washington. Preceded by Imboden's troopers under Colonel George H. Smith, the main body turned to the left at Rockville in order to reach the Seventh Street road running past Silver Spring into the capital. Colonel William L. Jackson's cavalry rode on the left flank.

Unfortunately for Early's plans, it seemed as if Nature had conspired to rob him of the fruits of victory. There had been a severe drought in that region which made the roads extremely dusty. In addition, the weather was excessively hot. Old Jube reported that the heat was noticeable even at a very early hour in the morning. The result of the hot weather and dusty roads, plus the fatiguing marches of the preceding days, was a great increase in the number of stragglers. In spite of the fact that Early's veterans had traveled all the way from Cold Harbor to Lynchburg and then from Lynchburg to Frederick, they could not endure the conditions facing them on the morning of the 10th of July, 1864. Many fell by the wayside from sheer exhaustion or heat prostration. Their officers were unable to make them keep up with their com-

202

mands. Naturally this delayed the approach to Washington.[2]

The defenses of the Federal capital consisted of an elaborate network of fifty-three forts which occupied a perimeter of thirty-seven miles all around the city. The forts were connected by trenches and defended by twenty-two batteries which boasted an armament of six hundred and forty-three guns and seventy-five mortars. Sometimes there was a dearth of soldiers to man the defenses, and this was especially true in June and early July, 1864.[3] Grant's losses in the Wilderness fighting had been made up only by stripping the Federal capital of most of its garrison.

In order to appreciate fully the problem confronting Jubal Early's little army of tired and dusty Confederates, it seems desirable to give a few more details concerning Washington's defenses. Perhaps those who are so prone to criticize Old Jube for not being more aggressive at this point are not aware of the magnitude of his task. A more complete description of the Federal defense system at Washington follows:

> Every prominent point, at intervals of eight hundred to one thousand yards, was occupied by an inclosed field-fort, every important approach or depression of ground, unseen from the forts, swept by a battery for |sic| field-guns; and the whole connected by rifle-trenches which were in fact lines of infantry parapets, furnishing emplacement for two ranks of men, and affording covered communication along the line, while roads were opened wherever necessary, so that troops and artillery could be moved rapidly from one point of the immense periphery to another, or, under cover, from point to point along the line. The counterscarps were surrounded by abatis; bomb-proofs were provided in nearly all the forts; all guns not solely intended for distant fire placed in embrasures and well traversed. All commanding points on which an enemy would be likely to concentrate artillery to overpower that of one or two of our forts or batteries were subjected not only to the fire, direct and cross, of many points along the line, but also from heavy rifled guns from distant points unattainable by the enemy's field-guns. With all these developments, the lines certainly approximated to the maximum degree of strength which can be attained from unrevetted earthworks. Inadequately manned as they were, the fortifications compelled at least a concentration and an arraying of force on the part of the assailants, and thus gave time for the arrival of succor.[4]

Before Grant's reinforcements arrived in Washington, the total number of Federal defenders was approximately 17,900. These consisted of 1819 infantry, 1834 artillery, and 63 cavalry north of the Potomac, and 4064 infantry, 1772 artillery, and 51

cavalry south of the river. In addition, there were in Washington
and Alexandria about 3900 effectives and 4400 Veteran Reserves.
Since an adequate portion of this entire force would not be available for repelling an enemy attack at a given point, the city's fortifications would be undermanned. Besides, many of those occupying the defenses were government civilian employees who did not
know how to fire the guns.[5]

As Early's cavalry under Colonel Smith approached Washington from the north along the Seventh Street road, it encountered a
small force of Federal troopers which it drove off. Smith then
dismounted his men and employed them as skirmishers. Old Jube,
riding ahead of his infantry, arrived in sight of Fort Stevens,
defending that part of the Union line, about noon. He noticed with
satisfaction that the works were feebly manned.[6]

Rodes' division was leading Early's infantry and, as soon as
it came up, Old Jube ordered it to send out skirmishers and occupy
the fort. Before this could be done, the Confederates noticed a
blue column filing into the earthworks, and soon after skirmishers
were seen in front. At almost the same time batteries from Fort
Stevens and its neighbors opened fire on the Southerners.

According to one of Old Jube's soldiers, when these big artillery shells came screeching high above their heads, the Confederates laughed out loud at the poor marksmanship of the "Melish,"
as the Union defenders were called. This inability to handle the
big guns in the forts convinced many of the attackers that the
Federals were the much-despised militia who were probably un-
trained and badly frightened. One joker suggested that perhaps
the Union artillerymen were trying to destroy Old Jube's wagon
train far to the rear.

The Confederates were so contemptuous of this artillery fire
that they brought up a battery of twenty-pound Parrott field pieces
and placed it in an open field, in full view of the enemy who was
about 400 yards away. Early's men were soon knocking up red
dirt all about the big Federal guns while the enemy "continued to
aim at the moon and the stars. The report of these, our biggest
guns, sounded like firecrackers or popguns in comparison."[7]

After the Unionists had begun to fire from Fort Stevens, Early
saw that his plan of gaining possession by surprise would have to
be abandoned. Before he could risk an assault, he would have to
reconnoitre to see if such an attack had any possibility of succeeding. He therefore directed Rodes to send out skirmishers to drive
those of the enemy back into the fort. When this was accomplished,
Old Jube made a thorough inspection of the fortifications defend-

Fort Stevens Today

ing the capital, and what he saw convinced him that they were exceedingly strong.[8]

The afternoon of the 11th was spent in making this reconnaissance and in giving his weary men an opportunity to come up and rejoin their units. General Early estimated that not more than one-third of his total force would have been able to attack the Union fortifications that afternoon. Some of Old Jube's subordinates, including the brave division commander, General Ramseur, felt that the men in the ranks could advance no farther.[9]

After darkness had arrived on that fateful day, General Early held a council of war with his division commanders, Generals Breckinridge, Rodes, Gordon, and Ramseur. He pointed out the necessity for doing something immediately, for, as they all realized, the longer the little Confederate army remained north of the Potomac, the more dangerous its position became. Old Jube reminded his subordinates that Federal activity would soon close the passes of South Mountain and the fords of the upper Potomac.[10]

The Confederate officers jokingly offered to place General Breckinridge at the head of a column which would escort him to the Senate chamber and seat him again in the Vice-President's chair. He had previously served in that capacity under President James Buchanan. Early, however, had made other plans, for he intended to storm the Union lines at daybreak the next morning. He would not do so if he received any subsequent information which would make such an assault impracticable. During the night General Bradley Johnson informed his commander that he had obtained unmistakable reports that two corps from Grant's army had arrived in Washington and that the rest of the Army of the Potomac would probably follow. This startling information caused Old Jube to postpone an attack until he could examine the Federal works again. When he did so, at daylight on the morning of July 12, he saw the parapets lined with blue-coated troops. He, therefore, reluctantly abandoned offensive plans.[11]

Naturally this threat to the Federal capital created considerable excitement in the city. Rumors were flying thick and fast. Officers and couriers rode furiously up and down the streets, swarming around the War Department. A Union soldier described the scene as follows:

> Washington was in an uproar. In the morning we heard that Early was at a certain point. At night he was reported as being fifty miles from there. To-day his army was alleged to number 30,000 men. On the morrow pale-faced, anxious men, solemnly asserted that certain information had been received

at the War Department that at least 50,000 veteran soldiers were marching with Early. Late at night, on July 9th I was at Willard's Hotel. An excited man walked rapidly in and told the group in which I was talking that our army, under General Lew Wallace, had been disastrously defeated on the Monocacy by General Early, and that our disordered troops were in full retreat on Baltimore. Later on we heard that Wallace's army had been annihilated. Still later, that the government's books, records, and money were being packed in boxes preparatory to its flight to New York. . . .[12]

Meanwhile, the Federal military authorities had been busy trying to obtain badly-needed reinforcements for their threatened capital. On the very evening of Wallace's defeat at the Monocacy they were heartened by a communication from Grant announcing that he had ordered the remainder of the Sixth Corps to Washington. It will be recalled that one division of this organization, the Third, commanded by Brigadier General James B. Ricketts, had already been sent to join General Wallace at the Battle of Monocacy. Grant stated that they could also have the Nineteenth Corps, which was due to arrive at Fortress Monroe from New Orleans. Finally, the commanding general volunteered to go to Washington in person if his services were needed.[13]

The next day, July 10, President Abraham Lincoln requested, but did not order, Grant to leave part of his army to hold the lines at Petersburg and bring the rest to Washington. The President seemed to feel that the emergency was great enough to warrant Grant's personal appearance at the Federal capital. However, it will be noted, he was careful to leave the final decision with Grant.[14] Lincoln had at last learned the lesson of not interfering with his military commanders in the field.

The commanding general of the Union army replied to Lincoln's request by informing the President he did not think it necessary for him to come in person to deal with Early. Grant pointed out that he had sent a whole corps |the Sixth| under an excellent officer, Major General Horatio G. Wright, as well as 3,000 dismounted cavalry. He further stated that one division of the Nineteenth Corps, 6,000 strong, was on its way to Washington from Fortress Monroe. Finally, he revealed that General David Hunter was at last returning from West Virginia and would have 10,000 additional troops in Early's rear. Grant concluded this dispatch with the optimistic belief that Early would never return to Virginia with much of his army.[15]

About the same time that General Early was approaching Fort Stevens on the Seventh Street road in the early afternoon of

July 11, General Wright, with the vanguard of the Sixth Corps, reached the wharves at the foot of Sixth Street. These reinforcements from Grant's army had traveled by steamer down the James, into the Chesapeake Bay, and up the Potomac to the threatened capital. A huge crowd, including President Lincoln, was on hand to welcome these veterans. Displaying their insignia, which was the Greek cross, the bluecoats disembarked and moved to the city's outskirts, where they occupied some of the defenses.

At almost the same time that the Sixth Corps arrived in the capital, the advance of the Nineteenth Corps came into sight. Although the bulk of this organization came too late to aid in the city's defense, the vanguard of about 650 participated in the honor of saving the capital. By Tuesday morning, July 12, the entire First and Second divisions of the Sixth Corps — numbering 10,000 effectives — had arrived, and Washington was saved.[16]

On July 12 Early kept the bulk of his army in front of Fort Stevens and engaged in some skirmishing. Shots were exchanged between Union pickets from the Sixth Corps and Confederate sharpshooters hidden by numerous trees. In the middle of the afternoon General Wright sent out a brigade to reconnoiter in force. Supported by the big guns of the fort, the veterans from Grant's army drove back Early's skirmishers from the immediate front. Old Jube had already decided that the odds against him were too heavy and that he should retire if he wanted to save his little army and its captured supplies.

While skirmishing was taking place before Fort Stevens, President Lincoln, along with Cabinet officers and other important civilian personnel, witnessed the fighting from the breastworks. In order to gain a better view, Lincoln mounted the parapet and stood at the side of General Wright. As the position was swept by the bullets of Confederate sharpshooters, Wright was very much concerned about the safety of the Chief Executive and suggested that he move to a less exposed position. Although an officer, a surgeon, was shot three feet from Lincoln, the President still remained. Finally Wright politely ordered him to withdraw, as he had cleared the parapet of everyone else. When Lincoln still hesitated, Wright's young aide, Lieutenant Colonel Oliver Wendell Holmes, felt impelled to shout to the President, "Get down, you fool!"[17]

As Early had decided to withdraw, he ordered Bradley Johnson's cavalry to abandon the plan to liberate the Confederate prisoners at Point Lookout. Johnson had already left for this purpose and had to be recalled. Apparently the Federal authorities learned about the contemplated rescue, for they alerted the guard at the prison. In addition, there was a general mixup in the Confederate plans.

After skirmishing with the Unionists in the afternoon of July 12, about dark Early ordered a retreat. His force took the route by Rockville and Poolesville to White's Ford on the Potomac. Using this passageway across that stream, the Second Corps and its brave commander reentered the Old Dominion. With the exception of four hundred men wounded at Monocacy, who had to be left at Frederick, Early had not only saved his army but also brought off his prisoners and captured supplies.[18]

It is idle to speculate whether or not General Early could have captured Washington on July 11 before the arrival of the reinforcements from Grant's army. Many of his critics have asserted that if he had not consumed so much time marching from the Upper Valley to Washington, he could have obtained possession of the capital. However, in this connection, it should be remembered that Grant had a responsibility for the defense of the capital and was expected to detach from his army at Petersburg whatever troops would be needed. It is unlikely that he would have been allowed to strip Washington's defenses to make good his losses in the Wilderness if he had not promised to return those soldiers when needed. If this is true, then, with the Federals controlling the Virginia waters, he could quickly send reinforcements to the capital by steamer.

When Early saw Union soldiers marching into the defenses of Fort Stevens on July 11, he believed them to be part of the Sixth Corps. He had already fought Ricketts' division of that corps two days before at Monocacy, and he knew that the remainder of that body was expected in Washington. Besides, from his own account and from the reports of his subordinates, it appears that Early's men were too exhausted to push on into the city that afternoon.[19]

If Old Jube had attacked Fort Stevens as soon as he approached it on the 11th and, regardless of loss, had pushed on, it is quite possible that he could have entered the city. However, he would still have had to defeat the Sixth Corps and part of the Nineteenth between the fort and the city itself. Unless he could have beaten all the Federal troops within Washington, he might have found himself surrounded in the Union capital. As one observer has remarked, it was like putting his head into a noose. Even if Old Jube could have entered the city, it seems most probable that his little army could not have held it very long against the forces which the Federals could bring against him.

In this phase of Early's Valley campaign occurred several burnings of private residences. Some of Bradley Johnson's troopers, without any authorization from Old Jube, set fire to Governor Augustus W. Bradford's home near Baltimore.[20] The Governor had previously offered his home as a suitable place where lookouts and vedettes might be stationed to give warning of the approach of the Confederates.[21]

Another home which was burned at this time belonged to Montgomery Blair, Lincoln's Postmaster General, located near Silver Spring. Although General Early was blamed for causing the destruction of this mansion, he denied he was responsible and claimed that he never knew who had done it.[22] According to one account, it was burned by some stragglers from Early's army on the night of July 12.[23] However, another story blamed the burning on shells from Federal guns. Lieutenant Joshua Lee of Company I, 53 North Carolina Infantry, of Rodes' division, stated that on three occasions he extinguished fires which Union shells had caused in the mansion. When the house caught fire a fourth time, the Confederate officer and his command had withdrawn.[24]

An amusing incident occurred to one of Early's sharpshooters on the retreat from Washington. Having been instructed by Gordon to capture any horse he could find and to take it back to Virginia, this particular Confederate soldier saw a group of saddled horses grazing along the roadside. Selecting one that he thought would make a good mount, he was about to grab it when he looked at the ground and saw General Early himself fast asleep. As he recognized his commander's animal and did not want to deprive him of his mount, the Southern sharpshooter selected another one which, he later learned, belonged to Major Edwin L. Moore, an assistant inspector general. Not desiring to be found riding the horse of this member of Early's staff, the soldier traded the animal for another one at the nearest farmhouse. The horse which he obtained was an old family horse and was very dear to its owners. The soldier tried to inform the farmer that he was getting a much better animal in return but did not succeed in proving his point. At any rate, he took the old family horse in exchange for that belonging to Major Moore and rode it into Virginia, where he turned it over to the quartermaster. He was never able to find out whether or not Old Jube's assistant inspector general regained his steed.[25]

CHAPTER 21

Back to the Old Dominion

Jubal Early's corps rested near Leesburg before resuming the march to the Shenandoah Valley. While it was advancing toward Snicker's Gap in the Blue Ridge on July 16, a small brigade of Federal cavalry attacked its wagon trains near Purcellville and captured 117 mules and horses, 82 wagons, and 62 prisoners.[1] This was the only instance in which Old Jube was forced to part with his spoils of the Maryland campaign. Infantry from Rodes' and Ramseur's divisions beat off this attack and managed to capture a gun and a caisson while doing so.

The Confederates crossed the Shenandoah River at Snicker's or Castleman's Ferry and skirmished with a body of Federals there on the 18th. In this engagement, which is known locally as the Battle of Cool Spring, Early's men drove the enemy back to the east side of the river and inflicted 422 casualties on the bluecoats. Old Jube's losses were between 200 and 300.[2]

Learning that Brigadier General William W. Averell and his cavalry had joined Major General David Hunter in returning to the Valley from West Virginia and that Averell was moving from Martinsburg to Winchester, General Early felt impelled to take position where his supply wagons would be more protected. As long as he remained in the Berryville-Castleman's Ferry region, his trains were exposed to Federal excursions from Harpers Ferry and Martinsburg. By marching up the Valley to Strasburg, Old Jube could place his wagons in a safe position and then deal with the enemy. On the night of the 19th he proceeded to put this plan into effect.[3]

On the march back to the Valley Brigadier General J. C. Vaughn's force, which had been serving as infantry, received horses and resumed its original role as cavalry. Vaughn had been watching Averell and on July 20 reported to General Ramseur that the Federal cavalry leader was at Stephenson's Depot with a small force. Ramseur marched his division to deal with this threat and while moving by flank found himself suddenly attacked by

Averell at the head of a strong Federal force.[4] The Union cavalryman had formed his line of battle before Ramseur arrived in sight.
The assault was made with such vigor that it broke the back of
Hoke's brigade. When the veterans of this organization fled from
the enemy, their panicky movements infected the troops of Robert
Johnston. In spite of Ramseur's valiant efforts to rally his men,
he could not do so. In the ensuing debacle he lost four guns, 73
dead, and 130 wounded.[5]

For this unfortunate defeat General Ramseur was subjected
to much criticism. Early believed that his able subordinate had
not taken the necessary precautions in advancing but he did not
heap additional coals on the fire. However, Confederate authorities in Richmond were inclined to blame the brave general and,
after newspaper critics had had their say, General Rodes wrote an
official report of the whole affair to his former corps commander,
General Ewell, in which he completely exonerated his friend Ramseur.[6]

General Early was farther up the Valley, at New Market,
when he received the news of General Ramseur's unfortunate
experience at Stephenson's Depot. He immediately went toward
Winchester with Rodes' division to repair the damage. Arriving
at the latter town, he discovered that General Averell had withdrawn a short distance. Old Jube did not attack, however, as he
received word that a large Federal column was moving through
Berryville. Instead, he carried off his sick and wounded, as well
as supplies, to Newtown [now Stephens City]. Later he retired
across Cedar Creek and took position near Strasburg.[7]

The Second Corps did not remain inactive long. Hardly had
its commander given the necessary orders for a much-needed rest
than he received information which made him assume the offensive again. The news which Old Jube obtained was that part of
the force which had pursued him from Washington was returning
to that city. Although he did not know the details of this movement, he later learned that General Grant believed the little Confederate army eliminated as a threat. He had, therefore, ordered
the Sixth Corps to return to Washington, where it would be sent
by steamer to Petersburg.[8] The Federal commanding general
hoped to use this unit to launch an attack on Lee before Early's
corps could rejoin the Army of Northern Virginia. However,
subsequent events proved that Lee had not recalled Old Jube.

On July 24 Early's corps moved down the Valley to attack the
Federals remaining in that neighborhood, and the Battle of Kernstown resulted. The opposing enemy force under General George

Crook consisted of the Army of West Virginia and included the consolidated forces of Averell, Hunter, and Sigel.[9]

Early's tactics at Kernstown consisted of moving Ramseur's division to the left in order to turn Crook's right flank and at the same time moving the remainder of his infantry along the Valley Pike. He sent his cavalry in two columns. One was to move to the right along the road from Front Royal to Winchester and the other was to proceed to the left, west of town, and rejoin the first column north of the city. Early expected that the union would cut off the retreat of the Federal force opposing him at Kernstown.

While Old Jube was driving back Crook's skirmishers, he noticed that the Federal left flank was exposed. Crook had sent Averell, whose cavalry defended the Union left, against Old Jube's wagon trains at the rear. Seeing his opportunity, the Confederate corps commander did not wait for Ramseur to complete the flank movement around the Federal right. Instead, he directed Breckinridge to move Echols' division, now led by Brigadier General G. C. Wharton, around the Federal left flank.[10]

This plan worked admirably. Breckinridge advanced the division under cover of some ravines and struck Crook's left flank in open ground. The force of the Confederate attack doubled up the Federal line and threw it into considerable confusion. At the same time Early advanced his other divisions against Crook's center and right. The bluecoats were unable to withstand all of this pressure and soon broke into headlong retreat.

Early's infantry and artillery pursued the fleeing Federals into Winchester and on beyond. Rodes' division did not stop until it reached Stephenson's Depot, which is four miles northeast of Winchester. As this body had been camped near Strasburg, it marched twenty-seven miles that day. Unfortunately for Old Jube's hopes of even more complete victory, his cavalry failed to equal the record of the infantry and artillery. It did not obey his orders, and since the Valley Pike was a wide macadamized road and the country was open, Crook escaped with his artillery and most of his wagons. Finally one of Old Jube's cavalry columns burst upon the fleeing Federals along the pike and caused a stampede among the teamsters. As a result, the bluecoats had to burn and abandon many wagons and caissons.[11]

Crook's losses in the Battle of Kernstown were probably about 1200, whereas Early's were light.[12] Old Jube reported capturing between 200 and 300 prisoners including Colonel James A. Mulligan, who was mortally wounded. In addition, Early recovered some of his officers whom Averell had captured from Ramseur in the fighting at Stephenson's Depot on July 20. Among this group was Brigadier General Robert D. Lilley.

Because it had marched so far and had fought so strenuously at Kernstown, General Early's infantry was unable to press the chase very far the following day. It did, however, advance to Bunker Hill, twelve miles from Winchester on the road to Martinsburg. Early managed to keep his inefficient cavalry force in pursuit of the fleeing Federals who kept moving through Martinsburg to Williamsport. At the latter place, the defeated remnants of Crook's army crossed the Potomac and eventually took refuge behind the strong fortifications on Maryland Heights at Harpers Ferry.[13]

General Early believed that if his cavalry had been more efficient he would have captured or destroyed the greater part of General Crook's army at the Battle of Kernstown. General Robert Ransom, who was supposed to be in charge of Old Jube's cavalry, had been in such bad health that he was unable to take active command in the field. Old Jube complained that all of his operations in the Valley had been impeded because he did not have an efficient and energetic cavalry commander.[14] In Generals John McCausland, Bradley Johnson, and John Imboden, Early had some able and bold horsemen, but there was no consolidated command to the cavalry. In this connection Dr. Douglas S. Freeman has the following to say:

> These men's troopers had proved themselves raiding forces of varying discipline and hardihood; but they were not, and without an able leader, a strong disciplinarian, they could not be, a unified body of fighting men in the sense that Hampton's or Sheridan's troopers were. Although Early already had monitory evidence of the feebleness of his cavalry, he did not have the aptitude, if indeed he had the time, to improve that arm.[15]

The defeat of General Crook at Kernstown left Early in undisputed possession of the Lower Valley once again. The same day that witnessed Crook's crossing the Potomac found Early's infantry at Martinsburg. The next two days, July 27 and 28, Old Jube spent in destroying anew the Baltimore and Ohio Railroad in the Martinsburg vicinity. Much of the damage he had caused to this line on his advance toward Washington had been repaired, so he thus had another good opportunity to put that important means of transportation for the North out of commission again.[16]

Meanwhile Early's activity in the Lower Valley after his return from Washington had set Federal telegraph wires humming once more. In a communication to Grant's Chief of Staff, Assistant Secretary of War, Charles A. Dana, expressed the disappointment of the Lincoln Administration with the inability of the Federal generals to prevent Early's escape from the Washington area with most of his plunder.[17] Evidence that the Confederates were not the only ones having cavalry trouble is furnished by a dispatch which General David Hunter sent Secretary of War, Edwin M. Stanton, on July 24 stating that the Second Brigade of Federal cavalry had stampeded. An hour later Hunter notified the War Department head that a report from Martinsburg revealed that the cavalry had "behaved disgracefully."[18] In order to bolster discipline in the Union forces General Halleck sent the following telegram to General Hunter at Harpers Ferry on July 25:

> The Secretary of War directs me to say that summary punishment, by drum-head court-martial, should be imposed upon those of your command who are guilty of cowardice in the face of the enemy.[19]

Finally, Early's victory at Kernstown, as well as his other successes since returning to Virginia, caused Grant to change his plans for another offensive against Lee at Petersburg. It will be recalled that Grant, believing Early to be in retreat, had ordered the Sixth Corps to return to his army in the Petersburg-Richmond area. At the same time he had directed the Nineteenth Corps to take up temporary position in Washington, after which he expected it to join him. However, Grant was so much concerned with this new threat from Early that he ordered both the Sixth and the Nineteenth Corps, as well as six regiments of cavalry, back to the Valley. At the same time he directed that all Federal troops arriving in the Chesapeake Bay from the Gulf of Mexico Department be sent directly to Washington, instead of to his army at Petersburg.[20] Thus Early's effort to create a diversion in the Valley was succeeding beyond the hopes of his most optimistic supporters.

CHAPTER 22

Retaliation in Kind

When General Jubal Early returned to Martinsburg after his victory at Kernstown, he learned that since he had last been in that region, a new type of warfare had been inaugurated — war against civilians. The offender in these cases was Major General David Hunter, who had been in charge of the Federal troops in the Lower Shenandoah Valley since his return from West Virginia after Early had driven him from Lynchburg. From his headquarters at Harpers Ferry Hunter issued orders which resulted in the destruction of three beautiful mansions in Jefferson County and almost caused the burning of one in Berkeley County.

During the Civil War the rights of private citizens suffered from time to time by acts of officers on both sides. These liberties with private rights usually consisted of false arrest and imprisonment, robbery, commandeering of property, and infringements of a like nature. Although they were sometimes excused on the grounds of military necessity, for the most part, they were condemned by higher authority. Generally speaking, officers on each side tried to respect private property in the enemy's country. A good example of General Early's ideas along this line is furnished by his handling of his division in the Gettysburg campaign, especially in his attitude toward the city of York, Pennsylvania. However, two notable exceptions to the above statements are found in the persons of Major General David Hunter and his successor in the Valley, Major General Philip H. Sheridan. Both seemed to go to extremes to cause civilians unnecessary discomfort.[1]

In the chapter dealing with the Lynchburg campaign an account of Hunter's destruction at Lexington has been given. It will be recalled that he ordered the burning of the Virginia Military Institute, as well as Ex-Governor John Letcher's home. Not content with this, he engaged in similar activities while he was marching toward Lynchburg. When Hunter retreated from that city over part of the same route, his pursuer, Early, had an opportunity to witness some of the destruction. Old Jube's description of what he saw follows:

> The scenes on Hunter's route from Lynchburg had been truly heart-rending. Houses had been burned, and women and children left without shelter. The country had been stripped of provisions and many families left without a morsel to eat. Furniture and bedding had been cut to pieces, and old men and women and children robbed of all clothing except what they were wearing. Ladies' trunks had been rifled and their dresses torn to pieces in mere wantonness. Even negro girls had lost their little finery. We now had renewed evidences of outrages committed by the commanding general's orders in burning and plundering private houses. We saw the ruins of a number of houses so destroyed.[2]

When Early was threatening Washington, it will be recalled, the home of Governor Augustus W. Bradford near Baltimore was burned by Confederate troopers under Bradley Johnson. Although Johnson was serving under Early, there is no evidence that Old Jube was in any way connected with this deed. Certainly he did not order it, and it is doubtful if he anticipated such an act. Later the home of Montgomery Blair, near Silver Spring, was likewise leveled by flames, and Old Jube was blamed for it even though he disclaimed responsibility. It is interesting to note that in later years the war crimes trials of World War II revealed that a higher commander was held responsible for his subordinates whether he knew what they were doing or not.

When Hunter returned to the Lower Valley and established himself at Harpers Ferry, he continued his war against civilians. Some of the responsibility for this type of warfare may be placed on Grant, but it will be noted in the following dispatch from Halleck to Hunter, dated July 17, that Grant is quoted as opposing the burning of homes. According to Halleck, Grant wrote him as follows:

> . . . If Hunter cannot get to Gordonsville and Charlottesville to cut the railroads he should make all the valleys south of the Baltimore and Ohio road a desert as high up as possible. I do not mean that houses should be burned, but every particle of provisions and stock should be removed, and the people notified to move out. . . . [Grant] wants your troops to eat out Virginia clear and clean as far as they go, so that crows flying over it for the balance of the season will have to carry their provender with them.[3]

In spite of Grant's opposition to the burning of private houses, as stated above, Hunter that very same day, July 17, issued orders to one of his officers to burn two nearby homes. According to these commands, Captain F. G. Martindale, of the First New York (Lincoln) Cavalry, was to take a body of troopers to Charles Town and "burn the dwelling-house and out-buildings of Andrew Hunter, not permitting anything to be taken therefrom except the family."[4] After doing this, Martindale was instructed to proceed to Martinsburg and accord the same treatment to the home of Charles J. Faulkner, Sr.[5]

Captain Martindale lost no time in executing General Hunter's orders. He led his Federal cavalrymen to the beautiful home on the edge of Charles Town occupied by Andrew Hunter and his family. Andrew, a first cousin of the Union general, was a prominent lawyer who had served the Commonwealth of Virginia as special prosecutor when John Brown and his fellow-raiders were tried at Charles Town for murder and treason in 1859. Martindale carried out his orders to the letter, for he did not permit Andrew Hunter's family to save either their clothing or family portraits from the flames.[6] Andrew was taken prisoner to Harpers Ferry, held for a month, and then discharged without any explanation. At the time he was taken into custody, he was wearing a gold ring that years before had been given him, as an evidence of affection, by his "Cousin David."[7]

After destroying the Hunter home in Charles Town, Captain Martindale led his troopers to Martinsburg, where he planned to burn "Boydville," the beautiful home of Charles J. Faulkner. When Mrs. Faulkner received the sad tidings from the Federal officer, she asked for an hour's delay. According to one account, she was allowed to communicate with General G. W. Cullum, Halleck's Chief-of-Staff and a friend of the family. Cullum was asked to request President Lincoln to spare the fine old place. Anxious moments intervened before a courier arrived just in time with the following message from the President:

> The property of Charles J. Faulkner is exempt from the order of General David S. Hunter for the burning of the residences of prominent citizens of the Shenandoah Valley in retaliation for the burning of the Governor Bradford's house in Maryland by the Confederate forces.[8]

Another prospective victim was not so fortunate. On July 19 Captain Martindale took his command to Shepherdstown, where he sought "Fountain Rock," the beautiful home of Alexander R. Boteler.[9] The latter had been active in Virginia circles as a member of the Whig Party. He was representing his district in the

United States House of Representatives in 1861 and, although bitterly opposed to Virginia's secession, he cast his lot with his native state once the decision had been made. During the Civil War he served in the Confederate Congress and also on the staffs of Generals Thomas J. Jackson and J. E. B. Stuart.

Although Colonel Boteler and his wife were not at "Fountain Rock" when the raiding party arrived, the home was not unoccupied. The persons living there then were their two daughters, Helen and Mrs. David Shepherd, a widow with three children, the eldest five years old and the youngest, eighteen months.[10]

When Captain Martindale showed the residents General Hunter's orders to destroy their home, they pleaded to be allowed to save some of their personal property. They succeeded in saving only a few articles. While some of the Federal troopers plundered the house of silver, spoons, forks, cups, and whatever else they wanted, others obtained straw from the barn and carried it inside the dwelling. They piled furniture on the floor, sprinkled it with kerosene brought along for the purpose, and set it on fire. Within twenty minutes the house was a mass of flames.

Helen Boteler, who was a devoted student of music, begged in vain for her piano. While the fire was engulfing the adjoining room and the smoke rolled about her, she seated herself at this instrument, struck a few chords, and then sang Charlotte Elliott's hymn, "Thy Will Be Done." As the flames had now come closer, she calmly closed the piano, locked it, and went outside.

In addition to the stone mansion, which was entirely destroyed along with its contents including Colonel Boteler's fine historical manuscript collection, most of the outbuildings were given the torch.[11] One, a pigeon-house, escaped and was later selected by one of the Boteler girls as a place where she would at least have a roof over her head.

After completing the destruction of the Boteler property, the Federals rode to "Bedford," the nearby home of Edmund J. Lee, a first cousin of the Confederate commanding general. Although Lee was away in Clarke County, his wife, Henrietta, and two young children met the raiders. Mrs. Lee had been sick in bed but arose and tried to persuade Captain Martindale not to destroy her home. In vain she told him that it was her own home, an inheritance from her father, a Revolutionary soldier, and that the Federal army was surely not waging war on women and children. Martindale was not moved by her entreaties and gave the necessary orders to his troopers. Before long the house and most of its contents were consumed. Mrs. Lee's indignation was so great that the next day she wrote a scathing rebuke to General Hunter. Because of the incisive language used so forcibly, it is here reproduced in its entirety:

Shepherdstown, Va., July 20, 1864

General Hunter:

Yesterday your underling, Captain Martindale, of the First New York Veteran Cavalry, executed your infamous order and burned my house. You have had the satisfaction ere this of receiving from him the information that your orders were fulfilled to the letter, the dwelling and every outbuilding, seven in number, with their contents, being burned. I, therefore, a helpless woman whom you have cruelly wronged, address you, a Major General of the United States Army, and demand why this was done? What was my offence? My husband was absent — an exile. He has never been a politician or in any way engaged in the struggle now going on, his age preventing. This fact your chief-of-staff, David Strother, could have told you.

The house was built by my father, a Revolutionary soldier, who served the whole seven years for your independence. There was I born; there the sacred dead repose. It was my house and my home, and there had your niece, Miss Griffith, who lived among us all this horrid war up to the present moment, met with all kindness and hospitality at my hands. Was it for this that you turned me, my young daughter, and little son out upon the world without shelter? Or was it because my husband is the grandson of the Revolutionary patriot and 'rebel,' Richard Henry Lee, and the near kinsman of the noblest of Christian warriors, and greatest of generals, Robert E. Lee? Heaven's blessing be upon his head forever! You and your Government have failed to conquer, subdue, or match him; and disappointed rage and malice find vent on the helpless and inoffensive.

Hyena-like you have torn my heart to pieces! for all hallowed memories clustered around that homestead; and demonlike, you have done it without even the pretext of revenge, for I never saw or harmed you. Your office is not to lead, like a brave man and soldier, your men to fight in the ranks of war, but your work has been to separate yourself from all danger, and with your incendiary band steal unaware upon helpless women and children, to insult and destroy. Two fair homes did you yesterday ruthlessly lay in ashes, giving not a moment's warning to the startled inmates of your wicked purpose; turning mothers and children out of doors, your very name is execrated by your own men for the cruel work you give them to do.

In the case of Mr. A. R. Boteler, both father and mother were far away. Any heart but that of Captain Martindale (and yours) would have been touched by that little circle, comprising a widowed daughter just risen from her bed of illness, her three fatherless babies — the eldest five years old — and her heroic sister. I repeat, any *man* would have been touched at the sight but Captain Martindale! One might as well hope to find mercy and feeling in the heart of a wolf bent on his prey of young lambs, as to search for such qualities in his bosom. You have chosen well your agent for such deeds, and doubtless will promote him.

A colonel of the Federal Army has stated that you deprived forty of your officers of their commands because they refused to carry out your malignant mischief. All honor to their names for this, at least! They are *men,* and have human hearts and blush for such a commander! I ask who that does not wish infamy and disgrace attached to him forever would serve under you? Your name will stand on History's pages as the Hunter of weak women, and innocent children; the Hunter to destroy defenceless villages and beautiful homes — to torture afresh the agonized hearts of widows; the Hunter of Africa's poor sons and daughters, to lure them on to ruin and death of soul and body; the Hunter with the relentless heart of a wild beast, the face of a fiend, and the form of a man. Oh, Earth, behold the monster! Can I say 'God forgive you'? No prayer can be offered for you! Were it possible for human lips to raise your name heavenward, angels would thrust the foul thing back again, and demons claim their own. The curse of thousands, the scorn of the manly and upright, and the hatred of the true and honorable, will follow you and yours through all time, and brand your name infamy! infamy!

Again, I demand why have you burned my house? Answer as you must answer before the Searcher of all hearts; why have you added this cruel, wicked deed to your many crimes?

Henrietta B. Lee.[12]

Among the Northern sympathizers who disapproved of Hunter's ruthlessness in the Valley was John W. Garrett, President of the Baltimore and Ohio Railroad. As has been pointed out, Garrett's line had been serving the Union as the most important transportation link between Washington and the West. As a result, it had suffered severely whenever Confederates approached its right of way. About the same time that Hunter was giving the torch to those beautiful homes in Jefferson County Garrett learned from a railroad employee at Harpers Ferry that Hunter planned to burn Charles Town if he found guerrillas there. The railroad executive also learned that because neighboring Clarke County had polled only two votes against the secession ordinance in 1861, Hunter said he would burn every house in that county.[13]

In a letter to Secretary of War Stanton dated July 18 Garrett quoted the above intentions of Hunter and added that if they were carried out, the border region could expect retaliation by Confederate authorities. Of course, the railroad president was thinking particularly in terms of destruction to his line, for he was having a very difficult time keeping traffic moving over it because of Confederate attacks.[14]

General Jubal Early at his camp near Martinsburg was very much impressed by the type of warfare which General Hunter was then waging against the private citizens of the Lower Valley. As the same thing had happened in other parts of the South, he came to the conclusion that "it was time to open the eyes of the people of the North to this enormity, by an example in the way of retaliation."[15] Old Jube accordingly formulated his plans.

Early's idea was to send Confederate soldiers to some of the nearby Federal towns to force collection of sums of money which he would turn over to those Southern families which had suffered because of Hunter's policy. It will be recalled that the Confederates had collected $200,000 from Frederick and $20,000 from Hagerstown during Early's advance to Washington, although this money was turned over to the Confederate Government and not used to indemnify private citizens. If the Northern towns did not raise the ransom money which Old Jube demanded, they were to be given the torch.

Early selected Chambersburg, Pennsylvania as the first victim. He chose it because he thought it was large enough to pay the ransom and also because it was near the Maryland border. Also, since it was north of Mason and Dixon's Line, there was no mistaking its allegiance to the Union.[16]

Consequently, on July 28, 1864, General Early requested General John McCausland to come to his headquarters at Martinsburg so that he could acquaint his bold young cavalry officer with his plan. Old Jube directed McCausland to take his own brigade of cavalry, the brigade commanded by General Bradley T. Johnson, and Captain William G. McNutty's battery of artillery by way of Clear Spring and Mercersburg to Chambersburg. Upon reaching the latter city, McCausland was to read a proclamation which Early had prepared for its citizens. This announcement would inform the Pennsylvanians that they must pay $100,000 in gold or $500,-000 in greenbacks if they wanted their city spared. If they did not comply with these terms, McCausland was to arrest fifty of their leading citizens and cause their community to be set on fire.

Early directed McCausland then to return by the way of McConnelsburg to Hancock, Maryland, from which place he was to proceed to Cumberland to collect a similar amount. If the residents of that Maryland city did not raise the stated sum, McCausland was to burn it and destroy the machinery of its coal pits. After accomplishing this, the Confederate cavalry leader was expected to recross the Potomac into West Virginia and destroy the Baltimore and Ohio Railroad, as well as Federal defenses, near New Creek Station. Finally, he was to collect all the horses, cattle, and other supplies available, return to Winchester, and then report to Old Jube in person.[17]

No sooner had McCausland received his orders from Early than he began to execute them. With a total force of about 4,000 men, he set out on July 29 for the Potomac, which he crossed at McCoy's Ford. Passing through Clear Spring, he reached Mercersburg in the evening. He halted at the latter place long enough to feed the horses and collect stragglers before beginning a night march to Chambersburg. Reaching his first objective about daylight July 30, he brushed aside weak opposition furnished by a small body of home guards and soon became master of the town.

Leaving most of his command at the city's outskirts, General McCausland with his staff and about 500 troopers entered Chambersburg at 5:30 o'clock on the morning of July 30. The officers rode to the Franklin Hotel, where they ordered breakfast. Then some of the general's staff rode up the main street to inform residents that McCausland wished to see the town's officials so he could make clear his demands upon them. As they were unable to find any of the community's officers, they accosted an ordinary resident, J. W. Douglas, to act as messenger to others.[18]

Douglas informed some of his fellow-citizens of the Confederate order, but, unfortunately, he was unable to convince them that the grey-clad troopers were serious. Declaring that the Southerners were merely trying to scare them, some of the Chambersburgers went into their houses or shops. Others laughed outright. Finally, a Confederate officer read to those before him the following proclamation from General Early:

> Hd Qrs Advance Forces CS Army
> July 29, 1864

To the Municipal Authorities of
   Chambersburg, Pennsylvania

> The houses of Andrew Hunter Esq. Alexander R. Boteler Esq and Edmund I. |sic| Lee Esq., citizens of Jefferson County Virginia having been burned by order of the officer commanding, the Federal Forces, in the Department called the 'Department of Virginia,' I have directed that your town pay for the

said houses to be handed over to the owners the sum of $100,-
000 in gold or $500,000 in current Northern funds.

In default of the payment of this money your town is
directed to be laid in ashes in retaliation for the burning of
said houses, and other houses of citizens of Virginia by Federal authorities.

J. A. Early
Lt General[19]

Official
    T Rowland

As the reading of Old Jube's orders failed to impress the
town's citizens that the Confederates were in earnest, McCausland
spoke to them as follows: "Are you sure you have seen your public
men? I should be very sorry to carry out the retributive part of
my orders. Can't you ring the courthouse bell and call the citizens
together and see if the money cannot be raised?"[20]

Although Douglas remonstrated that the courthouse was
locked and the janitor could not be found, the problem of gaining
access to the building was solved by a few blows from musket
butts. Shortly afterwards the vigorous clanging of the bell informed the Pennsylvanians of the threat of their town. When some
more of the residents gathered at the courthouse, McCausland
vainly tried to convince them of the urgent need for their attempting to raise the money. After he saw that they were still unim-
pressed, he informed them that he would wait six hours before
carrying out the punitive part of his orders.[21]

While time was running out for saving the town from the
torch, many of the residents approached the Confederate cavalry
commander. Some were willing to pay the money, but others were
not. McCausland urged them again to comply and told them very
plainly that he would have to burn Chambersburg if they did not
pay the ransom. Some claimed there was not that much money
in the town; others said they would not pay five cents. McCausland
believed they were stalling for time, as many of them knew that
a strong Federal cavalry force under General Averell was coming
to their relief.

When the six-hour ultimatum expired at about eleven-thirty
o'clock and the town's residents had still made no move to raise
the amount demanded, or any amount, McCausland ordered the
application of the torch. After removing the inhabitants from
their homes and shops near the center of the settlement so as to
prevent loss of life, the Confederates entered the buildings, broke
the furniture into splinters, piled it in the middle of the floor, and

set it on fire. When the conflagration became general, this procedure was abandoned, for one house would cause its neighbors to burn.[22] Soon the whole center of the settlement was in flames. Besides private homes, the flames engulfed a bank, town hall, courthouse, hotel, two churches, many stores, and several mills. Altogether 527 buildings, valued at $313,294.34, were destroyed, and, in addition, $915,137.24 worth of personal property fell victim to the flames.[23]

An interesting sidelight on the burning of Chambersburg was the refusal of Colonel William E. Peters, commanding the 21st Virginia Cavalry regiment, to execute McCausland's command. When this officer received a verbal order from McCausland to burn the town, and the latter had ridden off without waiting for a reply, he asked Bradley Johnson if he had understood his commander properly. After Johnson replied in the affirmative, Colonel Peters remarked that he would not obey the order — that he would break his sword and throw it away before he would obey it. He added that there were only defenseless women and children in Chambersburg.

Johnson then directed his unruly subordinate to collect his men and withdraw from the city. Peters complied. While he was a short distance away, he received a written communication from McCausland inquiring if he had understood the order to burn the town, and, if so, why had he not obeyed it. The disobedient colonel replied that he had understood the instructions perfectly, but that he would not heed them. The result of this show of rebellion against authority for the sake of a principle caused Colonel Peters to be placed under arrest. However, on the return trip from Pennsylvania the arrest was lifted, and he was restored to command of his regiment. The reason for this relaxation of discipline was the proximity of General Averell with two brigades of Federal cavalry. In the presence of the new threat, this was no time for the Confederates to be deprived of the services of one of their gallant officers. After the war Colonel Peters taught Latin at the University of Virginia for forty-six years.[24]

Some of the Confederates, both officers and enlisted men, regretted the burning of Chambersburg. They did not feel that they should make war on defenseless women and children. Others, however, felt that this form of retaliation was not only just but also necessary to deter the Federals from such policies in the future. A good example of this attitude is furnished by an incident which occurred on the Confederate withdrawal. A few miles from town some of the troopers halted at a prosperous-looking farm establishment to water their horses. After one of them had returned and had mounted his steed, he noticed that the farmer's huge barn was on fire. When some of the Southern cavalrymen demanded in angry tones why two of their body had committed such vandalism, one of the culprits replied, "Why, _____ it, they burnt our barn."[25]

After firing the town, McCausland realized there was no time to tarry. His scouts had informed him that a strong Federal force under Averell was approaching. Consequently, he ordered the troopers to mount and leave the burning city. One of them, Lieutenant Calder Bailey, had become so drunk that he was left behind and was subsequently beaten to death by clubs at the hands of the irate Pennsylvanians.[26]

Leaving Chambersburg, the Confederates rode to McConnellsburg, where they spent the night. Early in the morning of July 31 they were in the saddle on the road to Hancock. McCausland's demand that this town raise $30,000 under threat of being destroyed aroused so much resentment from Marylanders in his command that for a brief period it looked as if the Confederates were going to fight among themselves. However, the arrival of Averell's troopers reunited the Southerners against the common foe.[27]

After a skirmish with the Federal cavalry McCausland led his command to Cumberland. Finding the city's defenses too strong, he skirmished a while and then withdrew during the night to Old Town, Maryland, where he hoped to ford the Potomac. First he had to overcome opposition from a Federal fort and an armored train. He succeeded in doing this, crossed the river, and moved against the Baltimore and Ohio Railroad at New Creek. Succeeding in taking only one of the protecting forts, he withdrew to Romney and then to Moorefield in the South Branch Valley.

At Moorefield McCausland gave his weary troopers a much-needed rest. About daylight on August 7 his rear guard under Johnson received a surprise attack from the aggressive Averell. The Federal cavalry captured Johnson's pickets and prevented them from giving the alarm to their sleeping comrades. As a result, the Confederate troopers were taken completely by surprise and were unable to offer resistance. In this disastrous encounter their losses included 420 prisoners, all their artillery, 678 horses, 150 men killed, wounded, or missing, as well as much equipment.[28] The remnants of this cavalry command made their way as best they could back to the Shenandoah Valley. They were in such bad shape that General Early, in writing about the Moorefield debacle, commented that the affair "had a very damaging effect upon my cavalry for the rest of the campaign."[29]

General Early never regretted his part in the destruction of Chambersburg. He assumed full responsibility for the act and saw no reason to retire from his position that retaliation was necessary. In a letter written to Edward Bok in 1882 he had the following to say in this connection:

. . . The town of Chambersburg was burned on the same day on which the demand on it was made by McCausland and refused. It was ascertained that a force of the enemy's cavalry was approaching, and there was no time for delay. Moreover, the refusal was peremptory, and there was no reason for delay unless the demand was a mere idle threat.

I had no knowledge of what amount of money there might be in Chambersburg. I knew it was a town of some 12,000 inhabitants. The town of Frederick, in Maryland, which was a smaller town than Chambersburg, had in June [sic] very promptly responded to my demand on it for $200,000. Some of the inhabitants who were very friendly to me expressed the regret that I had not made it $500,000. There was one or more National banks at Chambersburg, and the town ought to have been able to raise the sum I demanded. I never heard that the refusal was based on the inability to pay any sum. The value of the houses destroyed by Hunter with their contents, was fully $100,000 in gold, and at the time I made the demand the price of gold in greenbacks had very nearly reached $3.00 and was going up very rapidly. Hence it was that I required the $500,000 in greenbacks, if the gold was not paid, to provide against any further depreciation of the paper money.

I would have been fully justified, by the laws of retaliation in war, in burning the town without giving the inhabitants the opportunity of redeeming it.

For this act I alone am responsible, as the officers engaged in it were simply executing my orders and had no discretion left them. Notwithstanding the lapse of time which has occurred and the result of the war, I see no reason to regret my conduct.[30]

In spite of the disaster to his cavalry at Moorefield, which greatly weakened that already irresponsible arm of the service, General Early's second expedition north of the Potomac had created almost as much consternation there as his first had earlier that month. He had strengthened the Federal determination to keep the Sixth and Nineteenth Corps from rejoining Grant at Petersburg and, in addition, he had seriously damaged the Baltimore and Ohio Railroad and the canal. In fact, he had created such a disturbance that Grant was determined to rid himself of this menace once and for all.[31]

CHAPTER 23

Sheridan Defeats Early at Winchester

While General Early's cavalry was returning from the Chambersburg campaign, events were transpiring which caused the war in the Shenandoah Valley to assume greater proportions. As soon as the Confederate authorities in Richmond discovered that General Grant had sent additional troops from Petersburg to the Valley, they decided to reinforce Old Jube.[1] Consequently General Lee gave the necessary orders for Kershaw's division of infantry and Fitz Lee's division of cavalry to join Early. As Kershaw's troops belonged to the First Corps, Lee sent General R. H. Anderson, who had succeeded the wounded Longstreet, to head these reinforcements.

Although Anderson ranked Old Jube, Lee did not intend for him to take charge of all the Confederate troops in the Valley. Instead, he decided to leave Early with the Second Corps west of the Blue Ridge and to keep Anderson, for a while, east of those mountains. By doing this, Lee thought Anderson's presence would cause the Federals to retain part of their forces near Washington.[2]

Naturally Early was glad to get these additional troops. The arduous campaigning of the preceding two months had greatly depleted his little army. He was also pleased to note that he still retained Lee's confidence; otherwise, Anderson might have succeeded him. The addition of Fitz Lee's troopers was especially welcome, for Early's cavalry had been by far his weakest arm of service, as has been pointed out. Not only were Old Jube's horsemen small in numbers, but also they had poor equipment, ill-fed horses, and, worst of all, an independence of spirit that militated against all forms of discipline. Some extent of the demoralization of Early's cavalry is afforded by the following excerpt taken from General Bradley Johnson's report of the Chambersburg raid:

> It is due to myself and the cause I serve to remark on the outrageous conduct of the troops on this expedition . . . . Every crime in the catalogue of infamy has been committed, I believe, except murder and rape. Highway robbery of watches

228

and pocket-books was of ordinary occurrence; the taking of breast-pins, finger-rings, and earrings frequently happened. Pillage and sack of private dwellings took place hourly . . . . At Chambersburg, while the town was in flames, a quartermaster, aided and directed by a field officer, exacted ransom of individuals for their houses, holding the torch in terror over the house until it was paid . . . . Thus the grand spectacle of a national retaliation was reduced to a miserable huckstering for greenbacks . . . . In Virginia a lieutenant knocked down and kicked an aged woman who has two sons in the Confederate army, and after choking the sister locked her in a stable and set fire to it . . . . I tried, and was seconded by almost every officer of my command, but in vain to preserve the discipline of this brigade, but it was impossible . . . .[3]

One of Early's cavalry commanders, John D. Imboden, informed him on August 9 that a large Federal army was then assembling at Harpers Ferry. The officer reported that this force included three corps and a new commander. The head of this formidable threat to the Confederates in the Lower Valley was Major General Philip H. Sheridan, who had been serving Grant as the head of the Cavalry Corps.[4]

In order to confuse the new Federal commander in the Valley, Early embarked upon a program of ceaseless maneuver. By marching and countermarching all over the neighboring terrain, Old Jube created the impression that his army was much stronger than it actually was. His favorite trick in this connection was to make a long night march to the rear and then come back the next day with the flags flying and drums beating.[5] This stratagem of having his army appear as reinforcements to itself undoubtedly explains some of Sheridan's caution in the first month of his new command.

When Lee heard that Sheridan had gone to the Valley with his main cavalry force, he determined to send Wade Hampton with another division of troopers to reinforce Early.[6] Unfortunately for Old Jube, the activity of Federal cavalry under Brigadier General David Gregg caused Lee to keep Hampton near Petersburg.[7]

If General Hampton could not proceed to the Valley, it was quite apparent that something would have to be done to try to improve the cavalry there. General Robert Ransom, who had been put in charge of Early's troopers, was so incapacitated that he was unable to serve in the field. Subsequently, Ransom received orders to report to Richmond, while Lunsford L. Lomax was promoted to major general and given the unenviable task of trying to improve the efficiency of Early's cavalry.[8]

During the time that Old Jube was engaged in all of this

Lieutenant Sam H. Early, Jubal Early's Brother

marching and countermarching, along with some occasional skirmishing, he was forming the wrong opinion of his adversary. He did not know that Grant had ordered Sheridan to wait a while and build up his strength before moving against him. Consequently, Early concluded that Sheridan was excessively cautious, even timid, and Old Jube became somewhat over-confident.[9] In acquiring this frame of mind about Sheridan's lack of initiative, Early was not prepared for such an aggressive campaign as the Federal commander launched when he was ready.

An interesting contrast is furnished by Generals Early and Sheridan, who were to play the major roles in the drama beginning to unfold in the Valley. One writer has expressed the differences in the two commanders as follows:

> The qualities, the character and ability, of the two commanders . . . were at once sharply different and identical. The resemblance lay in the fact that they were both extremely capable Generals; they fought their men successfully; their tactics were successful. The differences were more significant — each represented almost completely the virtues and defects of the region he fought for, the place of his birth. Early was nearly as rapid and decisive in his movements, his swift forays and skillful withdrawals, as Stonewall Jackson and General John H. Morgan; his initiative and bravery were indomitable. He was, in the manner of the South, romantic; there was a color of splendor, an aspect of the spectacular, in whatever he accomplished. His maneuvers, the battles he fought, were invariably stirring; there was about Early, except at the last, the sound of bugles, the high incentive of silken and honorable colors. But at the end his romantic bravery, his utter valor, came to nothing; the sound of the bugles was, after all, only a sound; the colors were silk.
>
> General Sheridan, conversely, was, for his period, wholly commonplace, almost drab, in his proceedings. It is necessary to repeat, to remember, that Sheridan was a professional soldier. He was a fighter with a consuming silent ambition placed within the bounds of organized warfare, subjected to the restraints of discipline. He attained to moments of splendor, supremely at the Battle of Cedar Creek, but they had no part in the basic reality of his preoccupation and victories. It was inevitable, representing the North, that Sheridan would succeed, just as Early — a part of the South — was addressed to disaster. His autobiography, compared to the dry paragraphs, the precise awkward phrases, of Sheridan's memoirs, is vivid with a bitter conviction and vitality; yet at the last that availed him nothing; Sheridan, the Union, without visible glory, but with an overwhelming weight of men and metal, drove the Confederate forces from their valleys and moun-

tains and plains, utterly defeating their cause. It was, to a great degree, a combat between the individualism of the past and the largely anonymous masses that were coming to represent the necessities and aspirations of the future.[10]

The force which Sheridan had been assembling at Harpers Ferry in August to expel the Confederates from the Valley was a formidable one. His command was subsequently called The Army of the Shenandoah and included the Sixth Corps, part of the Nineteenth, Crook's corps, Torbert's division of cavalry, and Lowell's provisional brigade of cavalry. In September, just before the Battle of Winchester, Sheridan boasted a command totaling about 48,000 effectives. For field duty he could assemble about 40,000, which included more than 6400 cavalry.[11]

To oppose this strong army at the Battle of Winchester Early had Breckinridge's, Rodes', Gordon's, and Ramseur's divisions of infantry, Carter's division of artillery, and Lomax's and Fitz Lee's divisions of cavalry. The infantry numbered about 8,500, the artillery about 750, and the cavalry, about 2,900, thus making a total of approximately 12,150.[12] This figure does not include Kershaw's division which did not participate in the Battle of Winchester because Lee had ordered its return to Petersburg.

Although Early and Sheridan engaged in a large number of skirmishes in August and early September, no decisive contest occurred until the Battle of Winchester was fought on September 19. Unfortunately for Old Jube, he had been weakened when Lee ordered Anderson to return to Petersburg with Kershaw's division. The latter body of troops left Early on September 14 and was proceeding toward Front Royal on the way to the James.[13] In addition to the infantry division, Lee also deprived Early of Cutshaw's battalion of artillery.[14] Sheridan heard about this diminution of Early's army, and with his own force stronger than ever, he determined to attack Old Jube between Opequon Creek and Winchester.

Learning that a force was engaged in repairing damage to the Baltimore and Ohio Railroad at Martinsburg, Early took Gordon's division and some cavalry there on September 18. Instead of seeing the railroad repairmen, he met Averell's division of cavalry, which he drove off in the direction of Charles Town. After this skirmish he brought Gordon's division back toward Winchester, and it bivouacked at Bunker Hill. Rodes' and Breckinridge's divisions occupied positions near Stephenson's Depot,[15] while Ramseur's troops were slightly east of Winchester on the Berryville pike.

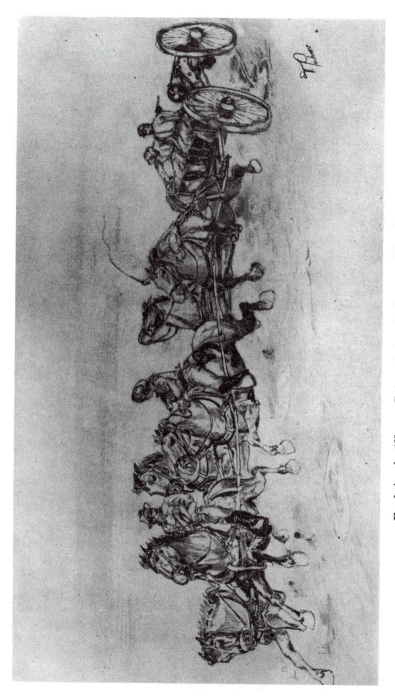

Early's Artillery Going into Action at Winchester

Early placed his cavalry to protect his flanks, with Fitz Lee picketing the left side and Lomax the right.[16]

The Battle of Winchester or the Opequon, as it is sometimes called, began on the morning of September 19 when Sheridan crossed the Opequon Creek on the Winchester-Berryville road. The Union officer planned to move his main force, preceded by a division of cavalry, along this road, while he sent his other two divisions of troopers to Stephenson's Depot.

As soon as Early's cavalry pickets had been driven back along the Winchester-Berryville road, and he realized that the main Federal force was advancing against Ramseur's division, Old Jube directed Gordon to come to the aid of Ramseur. At the same time he sent for the infantry divisions of Rodes and Breckinridge.[17] He then posted his artillery where he thought it could render the most assistance and sent a small cavalry force to protect Ramseur's left flank until Gordon should arrive.

Gordon arrived first, at about ten o'clock in the morning, and shortly thereafter Rodes appeared with three of his brigades. Gordon occupied the Confederate left, Rodes the center, and Ramseur the right. As soon as Early realized that Sheridan was trying to hold Ramseur in front and then move around the Confederate left, Old Jube determined to try to outflank Sheridan by moving around the Federal right.[18]

Early's able division commanders, Gordon and Rodes, had already decided to attempt this maneuver, and before Old Jube's orders reached them, they had put their men in motion. While they were advancing under fire, a shell fragment knocked Rodes from his horse and gave him a mortal wound.[19] Aided by excellent support from Nelson's and Braxton's batteries, Rodes' and Gordon's men pressed forward.

On the extreme left of the Confederate line, however, Evans' brigade of Gordon's division received a severe check and had to withdraw. This retirement exposed seven pieces of Braxton's artillery to enemy musket fire and unless the bluecoats could be driven back, the guns might be lost. The situation was saved when the artillerymen stood their ground and used canister on the Federals. About the same time Battle's brigade of Rodes' division, which had been delayed, appeared and attacked vigorously. Losing heavily, the Federals retired.[20]

When the veterans of Rodes' and Gordon's divisions continued the attack, they threw the bluecoats into great confusion and drove them from the field. The battle seemed to have been won, especially when John C. Breckinridge belatedly arrived on the scene with his three brigades. He had been delayed because he had to repel a Federal cavalry attack along the Opequon. Early placed one of these brigades on the left and the remaining two on the right, where his line was the weakest.[21]

No sooner had Old Jube made these dispositions than he noticed with surprise that the cavalry on his left was retiring in great confusion before a strong body of Federal troopers. To meet this new threat, he ordered Breckinridge's men to the extreme left. Aided by strong artillery fire, Breckinridge succeeded in repelling the Federal cavalry force, which had advanced to the rear of Early's left flank. At the same time Old Jube's infantrymen managed to repel a strong Federal attack made by Crook's division against the Confederate left, nearer the front.

Unfortunately for Early, the infantrymen of Gordon's, Rodes', and Ramseur's divisions, who had been fighting so magnificently, became alarmed by the sound of firing on their left. Thinking that they had been outflanked, they withdrew to the rear. Their officers were unable to get them to make a stand until they had reached the rifle-pits constructed earlier in the war on the edge of Winchester. Having gained these earthen breast-works, Old Jube was determined to stay there and fight it out. According to Gordon, Early was "one of the coolest and most imperturbable of men under fire and in extremity."[22]

While Old Jube was bravely beating off Federal attacks on his left and center, he received the disconcerting news that the bluecoats were turning his right flank. There was now nothing to do but order a general withdrawal, and he reluctantly gave the necessary commands. No sooner had the troops begun to retire than Early discovered that the force supposed to be turning his right was Ramseur's division of his own army, which was merely moving back to keep in line with the other Confederates on its left.[23]

Relieved to make this discovery and still hopeful of checking the enemy, Early tried to get his men to return to the trenches they had just left. Some of them obeyed his orders, but others felt that the battle was lost and retreated pell-mell through Winchester. A near-panic seized some of them. Old Jube directed Ramseur's division, which had maintained its organization, to move east of the town and form a new battle line on its southern outskirts. After the other Confederates had fled through Winchester, they saw Ramseur's men in their new line and received new courage. Forming on it, they managed to check the Federal advance until nightfall, when they retired to Newtown [Stephens City].

While Early's defeated troops were making their way through

Winchester, they were seen by Mrs. John B. Gordon, who tried in vain to rally them. When she discovered that they belonged to her husband's division, she ran into the street, and, disregarding her personal safety, made further useless efforts to check the rout. In fact she lingered there so long that she barely escaped capture by the hotly-pursuing Federals.[24]

Like many other officers' wives, Mrs. Gordon desired to follow the army so as to be near her husband. As might be expected from a bachelor like Old Jube, he had no patience whatsoever with the problems of married men. He would never approve a leave for a man to get married, for he felt that all soldiers should remain single as long as the war lasted. He used to say that every officer who married either proved himself utterly worthless or straightway got killed.[25] Mrs. Gordon's persistence in keeping up with the army once led Old Jube to exclaim, "I wish the Yankees would capture Mrs. Gordon and hold her till the war is over!" As the wagons were being parked at night near Winchester, Early noticed a conveyance different from all others. When his quartermaster informed him that one was Mrs. Gordon's, Old Jube shouted, "Well, I'll be damned! If my men would keep up as she does, I'd never issue another order against straggling."[26]

Early continued his retreat to Strasburg and on beyond to Fisher's Hill, which he considered the only place where he could make a successful stand. His losses at Winchester had been heavy. He reported the number of killed, wounded, and missing among his infantry and artillery to be 3,611.[27] He does not give his cavalry losses but Dr. Freeman estimates them to be about 1,000.[28] Thus, in this one battle Old Jube's total casualties approximated two-fifths of his entire force. It mattered not that his opponent, Sheridan, had suffered even greater losses.[29] Sheridan, like Grant, could afford to sustain heavy casualties, whereas Early, like Lee, knew there was no hope for a large number of replacements.

Besides losing many enlisted veterans at the Battle of Winchester, General Early was deprived of the services of some of his best officers. It has already been related how General Rodes was mortally wounded while gallantly leading his division into the thickest of the fighting. In addition, Old Jube had lost Brigadier General A. C. Godwin, who commanded Hoke's old brigade. Fitz Lee received a wound in his thigh from a Minié ball and was thus incapacitated at the very time when Early needed his services to help Lomax reorganize the cavalry. Finally, Colonel George S. Patton, grandfather of the famous American general of the same name in World War II, was left in the hands of the Federals, mortally wounded. He had been commanding Echols' brigade of Breckinridge's division.[30] Losses like these were serious indeed for a little army that would be pitted against Sheridan's strong force in future battles.

In spite of his defeat, Early was still full of fight. On the retreat to Strasburg he was planning his defense line at Fisher's Hill and hoped to turn on the enemy and recover some of the lost ground. As he and Breckinridge were riding along, thinking of their recent defeat and realizing the tremendous odds confronting them, as well as the whole Confederacy, Old Jube retained his sense of humor. Before the war he had been an old-line Whig who opposed so-called Southern rights to own slaves in the Federal territories, whereas Breckinridge, a Southern Democrat, had been loud in his demands for these rights. On the retreat to Strasburg after the Battle of Winchester Old Jube could not refrain from remarking to his gloomy companion, "Well, Breckinridge, what do you think of our rights in the territories now?"[31]

In connection with the Battle of Winchester, a story has been preserved about a woman who kept a toll gate across the Valley Pike which she lowered when Sheridan's army was approaching. When she demanded the usual fee for raising the gate, Sheridan paid for himself and staff but told her that he could not pay for his whole army. Although she allowed his troops to pass, she counted each soldier as he marched by. After the war she is said to have collected the toll from the United States Government for those to whom she had extended credit.[32]

CHAPTER 24

Old Jube Makes Enemies in the Confederacy

After the Battle of Winchester Jubal Early's weary and dispirited little army occupied a defensive position at Fisher's Hill, just south of Strasburg. As their brave but unfortunate commander realized, this was the best defensive position between Winchester and Staunton. At Fisher's Hill the Main Valley, which is twenty miles wide farther north, narrows to only four miles because of the beginning of Massanutten Mountain. This range is about half-way between the Blue Ridge on the east and North Mountain on the west and divides the region into the Main Valley and the Luray or Page Valley. By throwing a line across the four-mile stretch from North Mountain to Massanutten Mountain and by posting a force in the Luray Valley, Old Jube hoped to check his victorious opponent.

General Early realized that he might have difficulty holding Sheridan if that enterprising Federal commander should attempt to force his way through with the bulk of his strong army. However, the only alternative was to retreat southward up the Valley to one of the gaps in the Blue Ridge opposite Charlottesville or Gordonsville. Although he realized that his force was too small to occupy and defend successfully even the short line at Fisher's Hill, Early hoped that if he made a show of a stand there, Sheridan might not attack.[1] In that he was doomed to disappointment.

No sooner had Old Jube taken up position at Fisher's Hill than he sustained another serious blow. Major General John C. Breckinridge received orders from Richmond to return immediately to the Department of Southwest Virginia, where he had formerly been.[2] Breckinridge had served Early well, and it was with regret that Old Jube released this fine officer and his troops. The pill was sweetened somewhat by the promise of the Richmond authorities to return Kershaw's division of infantry and Cutshaw's battalion of artillery, as well as more cavalry. These troops, it will be recalled, had left Early to rejoin Lee but had proceeded no farther than Culpeper when they received orders to return to the Valley.[3]

238

Unfortunately for Old Jube, they did not arrive in time to help check Sheridan at Fisher's Hill.

General Early's most pressing problem was the reorganization of his command after the losses sustained at Winchester and the return of Breckinridge to Southwest Virginia. He transferred Ramseur to the command of Rodes' division and advanced Brigadier General John Pegram, who had been at the head of a brigade, to lead Ramseur's old division.[4] The corps commander then gave his third divisional head, General Gordon, the troops known as Wharton's division. Brigadier General W. C. Wickham received Fitz Lee's cavalry division.[5]

While Early was occupying the Fisher's Hill position, he also gained possession of a signal station on the end of Three Top Mountain, a branch of Massanutten Mountain. From this commanding position one could see the movements of friend and foe alike. No wonder that the station changed hands many times. In August General Lee had sent Old Jube a copy of the Federal alphabet which had been deciphered by some of the Confederate signal corps men. At the same time Lee informed Early that the enemy was able to read messages sent by Confederates.[6]

Old Jube determined to use the latter information to confuse Sheridan about the size of his army. When he discovered that the Federals were reading his signals, he instructed his men to flag to himself the following message:

Lieut. Gen. Early, Fisher's Hill, Va.

Be ready to advance on Sheridan as soon as my forces get up, and we can crush Sheridan before he finds out that I have joined you.

J. Longstreet

Since Sheridan supposed Longstreet to be with Lee at Petersburg, this bogus message caused great consternation among the Federal authorities. Grant at Petersburg, Halleck at Washington, and Sheridan in the Valley wrote to each other frequently in an effort to discover the whereabouts of Longstreet's corps.[7]

When Early went into position at Fisher's Hill on September 20, he placed Wharton's division on the extreme right, then Gordon's, Pegram's, and Ramseur's troops, respectively. As his force of infantry was too small to occupy the four-mile line, he had to use his cavalry also. Accordingly, he ordered Lomax to dismount the greater part of his troopers and hold the extreme left. Even then the line was too long for Old Jube's little army and was, consequently, thinly held.[8] In order to prevent Federal cavalry from moving up the Luray Valley, crossing the mountain, and getting in his rear, Early posted Wickham's troops at a narrow pass near Millford.

General Sheridan followed up his victory at Winchester by pushing on to Strasburg and on September 21 occupying a strong position facing Early at Fisher's Hill. After making a thorough reconnaissance, the Federal commander decided to try again the tactics that had proved so successful at Winchester; that is, to turn Early's left flank with Crook's command. Simultaneously he would send Brigadier General Alfred T. A. Torbert's cavalry up the Luray Valley, past the Confederate right flank, so that it could cross the Massanutten farther south, get in Early's rear, and thus cut off his escape.[9]

At first Early believed Sheridan would not attack, but when he saw the Federal troop movements, he changed his mind. Realizing that his force was too weak to withstand a determined assault, Old Jube gave orders for his army to withdraw after dark. However, he was not allowed to occupy his lines that long.

Early on the morning of September 22 General Crook began Sheridan's flanking movement. He marched his men to the Federal right toward Little North Mountain. Using the wooded area to conceal his movements, he moved along this eminence until he had moved around Early's left flank. Then he rushed his men across the intervening space where they surprised and quickly routed Lomax's undependable, dismounted troopers, who were defending Early's extreme left. Simultaneously Sheridan advanced his lines in front.[10]

True to his nature, Ramseur tried to check the Federal flanking movement by moving his men to the left. Pegram likewise cooperated. Unfortunately for the Confederates, these changes produced considerable confusion, which was just the opportunity for Sheridan to hurl his full strength against Old Jube's front. The weak Confederate line was broken in many places, and the veterans of the Second Corps ran like panicky recruits.

According to one Confederate officer, Captain S. D. Buck of the 13th Virginia Infantry, the defending Confederates were quite nervous and were very much afraid of Sheridan's cavalry. This arm of the Federals was well-mounted, well-equipped, well-officered, and well supplied with picked soldiers. They were so much superior to Early's troopers that Old Jube's infantrymen knew any contest between them could end only one way. Hence the foot-soldier had a horror of being outflanked and then ridden down by Sheridan's fast-flying horsemen.[11]

When Early's infantrymen first heard fighting on their left, they suspected what was happening but, nevertheless, changed front to meet this new threat. While awaiting the attack, they witnessed a lone dismounted cavalryman going the length of the line informing each command that the Confederates were being flanked. This naturally increased the insecure feeling of some of the men. Just as General Pegram began moving one of his brigades to face the Federals on their left, a North Carolina brigade fell back. Although they had not even seen the enemy, these Carolinians — usually excellent soldiers — got the impression that Pegram was trying to save his old brigade and was going to allow them to be captured.

While the North Carolina brigade was fleeing to the rear, General Early rode up and, without hesitation, commanded the 13th Virginia Infantry regiment to fire into those who were going toward the rear. His soldiers refused to kill their panic-stricken comrades. Old Jube, assisted by General Pegram and other officers, made brave but futile efforts to stem the tide. The whole Confederate army seemed to have but one objective — to reach the Valley Pike and put as much space as possible between General Sheridan's dreaded cavalry and themselves.[12]

A few officers and men — braver than the rest — did try to rally the demoralized army. One of these, Lieutenant Colonel A. S. "Sandy" Pendleton, Early's adjutant general who had also served on Stonewall Jackson's staff, was shot from his horse and mortally wounded while trying to post a small force to check the enemy. Another officer, a Captain Carpenter, who had saved two artillery pieces from his battery did not hesitate to risk the loss of these two by unlimbering and firing at the Federals from a new position.[13]

Another kind of valiant but fruitless bravery was displayed by Colonel E. M. Atkinson of the 26th Georgia regiment. In spite of the hail of enemy bullets, he tried to bring off an artillery piece that had been abandoned by its former users. The noble infantry colonel grabbed hold of one of the wheels of the gun and implored the fleeing soldiers to help him bring off the gun to safety. Most of them passed him by, but finally one, I. G. Bradwell of the 31st Georgia regiment, stopped to help. Together Atkinson and Bradwell tugged at the wheels of the heavy gun, but they made rather poor progress. Finally, when the Federals kept getting nearer and nearer, Bradwell believed discretion the better part of valor and deserted the colonel. By fleeing, Bradwell lived to fight again, but by remaining with the gun, Atkinson was captured and sent to a Federal prison.[14]

Early's artillery, as usual, fought magnificently at Fisher's Hill. Both officers and men remained with their guns as long as there was any possibility of checking the bluecoats. Displaying remarkable coolness and fighting to the very last, they kept firing until Old Jube himself had to ride among them and order them to retire. Even then, some of the artillerymen served their guns too long, for Sheridan's army was able to overrun many batteries and succeeded in capturing twelve pieces.[15]

While Sheridan's main force had been engaged in breaking Early's lines at Fisher's Hill, the Federal cavalry in the Luray Valley had not been so successful.[16] It will be recalled that Sheridan had sent his cavalry commander, General Torbert, into the Luray Valley in hopes it would go far enough south, cross the Massanutten, and gain the main Valley Pike in Early's rear, thus insuring the capture of most of his force. Old Jube had anticipated such a move and, consequently, had dispatched General Wickham with Confederate troopers to defend the smaller valley. Wickham seized a narrow gorge south of Millford Creek and was able to frustrate all enemy efforts to get past him.[17]

General Early reported his infantry and artillery losses in the fighting at Fisher's Hill as 1,235 in killed, wounded, and missing. He did not give his cavalry losses in this engagement but stated that they were slight.[18] General Sheridan did not report all of his casualties for the Battle of Fisher's Hill alone, but from the combined records, he seems to have lost about 500 in killed, wounded, and missing.[19]

After his defeat at Fisher's Hill Early withdrew up the Valley through Woodstock to Mount Jackson. He halted at the latter place to drive back a pursuing cavalry force, then retired to Rude's Hill, between Mount Jackson and New Market. When Sheridan would bring up infantry to outflank him, Old Jube would retire again. This kept up until he reached Port Republic, where the badly needed reinforcements were to join him.[20]

Naturally, General Early was greatly disappointed at his failure to check the victorious Federals. In writing to Lee at Petersburg, Old Jube had the following to say:

> . . . The enemy's immense superiority in cavalry and the inefficiency of the greater part of mine has been the cause of all my disasters. In the affair at Fisher's Hill the cavalry gave way but it was flanked. This could have been remedied if the troops had remained steady, but a panic seized them at the

idea of being flanked, and without being defeated they broke, many of them fleeing shamefully. The artillery was not captured by the enemy, but abandoned by the infantry.

My troops are very much shattered, the men very much exhausted, and many of them without shoes . . . .[21]

General Lee's reply to his corps commander in the Valley was that he was sending back Kershaw's division and that he thought the addition of these fine troops would enable Early to win a victory. Lee suggested that his subordinate's tendency to fight his battles by divisions instead of with his whole corps might have had something to do with the reverses. Unfortunately, Lee did not appreciate the odds against which Old Jube was fighting and thought that Sheridan's strength was much less than Early knew it to be. In this same letter Lee estimated Sheridan's infantry as numbering only 12,000,[22] whereas Sheridan, himself, reported he had 32,624 infantry present for duty in addition to 4,815 comprising the Military District of Harpers Ferry. To oppose Early's feeble cavalry divisions Sheridan reported that he had 6,465 troopers present for duty.[23] As has been pointed out before, these Federal horsemen were picked men and with their fine mounts and equipment were much the superior of Early's disorganized, inefficient horsemen.

Although Early's Valley campaign of 1864 was not over, according to Dr. Douglas S. Freeman, strategically this chapter which began with the march to Lynchburg ended with the defeat at Fisher's Hill. In summarizing Old Jube's accomplishments to date, that eminent author writes:

> Force and results considered, it was a chapter as full of honor as of disaster. Early had succeeded in drawing from the Army of the Potomac the whole of the VI Corps, which was an infantry force larger than his own total strength, had occupied Sheridan and one Division of cavalry from James River, and had compelled the Federals to consolidate against him the troops of Crook and of Averell who might have been engaged in attacks on Confederate supply lines. This was a remarkable achievement for a command that at no stage of operations counted more than 13,000 infantry and about 3,700 cavalry. These were the outside figures when Kershaw was in the Valley. Without Kershaw, but counting Fitz Lee, Early never had more than 10,200 infantry and 3,700 cavalry, a force steadily and swiftly reduced. Sheridan, as noted already, had 40,000.[24]

Early's recent reverses furnished ammunition to the many enemies and critics he had made in the Confederacy. He was not the type of individual, like Lee, who endeared men to him. He was a very exacting commander who could see no excuse for dereliction of duty. According to General D. H. Hill in a letter written after the war, Old Jube was unpopular only with those soldiers who did not do their duty.[25] Besides the demands which Early made on his troops, he increased his unpopularity with some by his biting sarcasm and stinging remarks. He had many admirers, both in the North and South, but he also had many enemies who used his military defeats to discredit him and, eventually, to cause his removal.

One of Early's chief critics who indulged in efforts to discredit him was William Smith, at that time Governor of the Commonwealth of Virginia. Smith had formerly served as an officer under Early and had obtained and nurtured a dislike for his former commander. In a communication to General Lee, dated October 6, Governor Smith, admitting "some little unfriendliness in my relations with General Early," stated his belief that Old Jube should be relieved as Commander of the Confederate forces in the Valley. He added that he had received a letter from an officer serving under Early and the communication revealed a startling state of affairs in the Second Corps.[26]

The letter from Governor Smith's informant blamed General Early for marching his men in cold weather unnecessarily and in not being considerate generally of their well-being. It stated further that the army did not believe Old Jube was a safe commander and had no respect for him. It cited the loss of twenty-five pieces of artillery in the field as being proof of Early's incapacity and expressed the opinion that most of his troops desired his removal from command. To these indictments the Governor added his own, namely, that outside of being brave and patriotic, Old Jube had no other qualities for independent command whatsoever.

General Lee's reply to the state's Chief Executive was a frank endorsement of his commander in the Valley. He stated his belief that Early had ably conducted the military operations in the Valley, but that he could only ascertain the validity of the other charges by communicating with Early's complaining officer. To get in touch with him, Lee would have to know his name.[27]

Governor Smith wrote General Lee another letter in this regard but refused to give him any names. Lee's reply again upheld Early and quoted General Breckinridge, who had served under Old Jube, as speaking in high terms of the corps commander's capacity and energy during the time Breckinridge was associated with him.[28] As Breckinridge was the man Smith recommended for Early's successor in the Valley, it may be that the Governor decided to drop the matter, for there is no evidence of additional complaint on his part.

General Lee sent the Governor's letters, as well as copies of his replies, to the Confederate Secretary of War, James A. Seddon. The latter refused to endorse the Governor's position and forwarded the communication to President Jefferson Davis. Davis returned the correspondence to the Secretary of War with the statement that his views concerning Early's ability to command were the same as General Lee's. The President concluded his note with the remark that he had received a very favorable report of Old Jube's military ability from an officer who was wounded while serving under him at Winchester.[29]

Although Governor Smith's charges did not succeed in having General Early relieved of command at this time, they did cast the finger of suspicion at Old Jube. The Chief Executive was a popular figure in Virginia, and his opposition to Early caused many persons to wonder if a change of commanders should be made.[30]

This feeling against Old Jube also took the form of a charge that he had been intoxicated at the Battle of Winchester. A correspondent of the Savannah *News* wrote a letter to that journal stating that at Winchester Early had ridden over the field with a bottle in his hand from which he drank quite frequently. Subsequently, James L. Orr of South Carolina introduced a resolution in the Confederate Senate instructing the Military Committee to inquire into the causes of the reverses in the Valley. Senator Orr intimated that the defeats were due to the excessive use of ardent spirits, while another member of that body, Benjamin H. Hill of Georgia, remarked that perhaps the type used was apple-brandy.

As soon as Old Jube heard about this, he wrote to the Chairman of the Senate Military Committee demanding a complete investigation to prove or disprove the disparaging remarks made about him. However, in the meantime General Breckinridge, who had gone to Richmond, and whose service with Early made him a qualified witness, indignantly denounced the whole accusation as being entirely false. The Senate refused to act on Orr's resolution, and the matter was dropped.[31]

General Early later wrote that on the day of the Battle of Winchester he had taken but one drink which was given him by General Rodes. Old Jube pointed out that, although he had no flask of his own, he did possess at Winchester a pair of black field-glasses which he used quite frequently to observe the enemy's movements. This may have accounted for the impression he gave that he was continually taking a drink from a bottle.[32]

The charge of intoxication during the Valley campaign of 1864 has been made so often against General Early that some mention should be made of it. According to one account, he had at his headquarters an ambulance in which a barrel of brandy and a Negro cook were the only baggage. Old Jube himself said, "I had never at any time carried any spirit about my person, and very rarely had any with my luggage."[33] When a member of his staff heard the tale about the brandy, he contradicted it in the following terms:

> ... This is not true. During the time I served on his staff, there never was an ambulance at Head Quarters, and a barrel of brandy was never seen there. He had a Negro man, who came with him when he entered the service and remained with him to the end, who served in the double capacity of cook and body servant.[34]

Early undoubtedly would take a drink occasionally, as many other soldiers exposed to the elements day after day would indulge themselves, but there does not seem any substantiation to the charges that during the Valley campaign of 1864 he was drunk and hence unfit to be in command. Most of his accusers were enemies or critics who had received a tongue-lashing for some gross neglect of military duty. Unfortunately for his career, the very fact that he was accused of being a drunkard caused tongues to wag and finally, when he had suffered further defeats, to result in his removal.

Although Old Jube's enemies might question his sobriety and his military prowess, they could not criticize him for lacking devotion to the Confederate cause. He was always thinking about what he could do with such a small army. Even when he attended church, his mind was on his assigned task, as is proved by an incident related by one of his officers.

According to Major Henry Kyd Douglas, one of Early's staff members, he and his chief attended a church service one Sunday in the Valley. The minister, who was speaking of the dead of the centuries, asked his listeners what they would do if the dead came marching back to earth by thousands and tens of thousands. Old Jube, who had been thinking of his feeble little army and the hopelessness of reinforcements, remarked to Douglas, "I'd conscript every damned one of them."[35]

CHAPTER 25

The Sun of Middletown

After General Early's defeat at Fisher's Hill he continued retreating up the Valley for the purpose of effecting a junction with his promised reinforcements and reorganizing his scattered command. His men were in bad shape. Many lacked shoes; few had sufficient clothing to protect them from the elements. The following description of one of Jubal Early's soldiers killed in the Valley campaign of 1864 gives a good picture of the kind of men he had:

> His feet, wrapped in rags, had coarse shoes upon them, so worn and full of holes that they were only held together by many pieces of thick twine. Ragged trousers, a jacket, and a shirt of what used to be called 'tow cloth,' a straw hat, which had lost a large portion of both crown and rim, completed his attire . . . . A haversack hung from his shoulder. Its contents were a jack-knife, a plug of twisted tobacco, a tin cup, and about two quarts of coarsely cracked corn, with, perhaps, an ounce of salt, tied in a rag.[1]

Not only were Early's troops lacking many of those things which provided for their physical comfort but, what was perhaps more important, in the fall of 1864 an increasingly large number suffered a decline in morale. This was due partly to the hard marching over the rough roads, discomfort from improper clothing, insufficient food, dejection from military reverses, and, finally, a growing realization of the hopelessness of the cause for which they were fighting. Concerning this, one of Old Jube's soldiers wrote as follows:

> I found the morale of the army very bad. It was not disaffection or disloyalty to the cause for which they had so long fought, but they reasoned this way: 'We are confronted with an army four times that of our own; Lee is besieged at Richmond and Petersburg; Sherman is marching through Georgia; we are cut off from the Trans-Mississippi Department; our ports are blockaded; our army is daily diminishing, with no material for recruiting; our families are in want and destitu-

247

One of Old Jube's Veterans in 1864

248

tion at home, while the Federal government has abundant resources at home and all Europe from which to recruit their armies.' With these conditions, they felt and maintained that there was no hope for our success. As sensible men, then, why should they sacrifice their limbs or lives for a hopeless cause, however righteous? This was plain to every sensible man . . . .

Many of the rank and file expressed the belief, and it was a frequent assertion, that our army would not repel an attack with the same composure and courage as formerly . . . . hence the almost universal opinion among the soldiers that we were liable to break the first time we were vigorously attacked.[2]

The significant part of the preceding quotation is the last sentence which contains the statement that at the first sign of a determined attack by the enemy the Confederates were likely to break into headlong retreat. Unless Jubal Early could overcome this feeling of resignation to defeat, he could not expect his little army in the Valley to accomplish much.

An interesting sidelight to the composition of Old Jube's force in October, 1864 is the revelation that it contained several women soldiers. Edmund Ruffin's diary for October 29 contains an entry that two young women, named Molly and Mary Bell, had been found serving in Early's army and had been brought to Richmond. They had disguised themselves in male attire and enlisted in the Confederate army in 1862. One had been advanced to the rank of sergeant, while the other had been made a corporal. As soon as it was discovered that they were of the "gentler" sex, they were sent to Richmond and detained in Castle Thunder, pending final disposition of their cases.[3]

Although the exploits of women who served the Confederacy as spies, such as Belle Boyd and others, have been well publicized, it is not known to what extent members of that sex served in the, ranks as soldiers in the field. Another instance of this sort was reported by G. N. Saussy, who was a Confederate prisoner at Point Lookout, Maryland, for eighteen months. He stated on one occasion the Federals brought to that prison a female Confederate soldier named Jane Perkins, who had been serving as a member of the Pittsylvania, Virginia, Battery.[4]

Jubal Early's promised reinforcements joined the main army at Brown's Gap in the Blue Ridge Mountains. This was the same secluded retreat to which Stonewall Jackson had withdrawn after his successful Valley campaign in 1862. The additions to Old Jube's army consisted of Cutshaw's battalion of artillery, Kershaw's division of about 2,700 muskets, which arrived on September 26, and, later, on October 5, Rosser's brigade of cavalry, numbering about 600.[5] It is needless to add that Early gladly welcomed these additions to his depleted command, which he said almost made up for his losses at Winchester and Fisher's Hill. As soon as his force had rested, he planned to strike Sheridan again. His defeats and consequent withdrawal had in no way curbed his aggressive instincts.

While Early was at Brown's Gap getting his force ready for a renewal of the struggle, Sheridan had been creating havoc in the Upper Valley. Acting on instructions which Grant had given him earlier to make the Shenandoah Valley a barren waste,[6] he had sent his troops in all directions from the main Valley Pike. They concentrated principally on burning barns, mills, and farm equipment and in driving off livestock so that the region would not be able to provide supplies for the Confederacy. In some cases they burned private dwellings.[7]

Because one of Sheridan's officers, Lieutenant John R. Meigs, was killed near Dayton on October 3, the Federal commander ordered that all the houses within an area of five miles be burned. He stated the reason for such retribution was that the perpetrators were "bush-whackers" or irregular Confederate partisans who had their homes in the vicinity, where they had been sheltered. However, according to the statement of a Confederate soldier, Meigs was killed in a fair fight with regular Confederate soldiers and the one responsible for his death was not a guerrilla but Private George W. Martin of Company H, 4th Virginia Cavalry. Martin, with two companions, was on a scouting expedition when his party met Meigs and two other Federals. In the ensuing contest it fell to the lot of Martin to engage Meigs, and he succeeded in shooting the Union officer and giving him a mortal wound. Because Lieutenant Meigs was the son of Major General Montgomery C. Meigs, Quartermaster General of the Federal Army, the incident attracted much attention. After the war ended, General Meigs offered a reward of $1,000 for the one responsible for his son's death, which caused Martin to seek exile in a secluded section of Missouri.[8]

Sheridan remained in the Harrisonburg vicinity with his infantry but sent his cavalry out on destructive raids. General Torbert entered Staunton September 26, where he destroyed supplies belonging to the Confederate Government. He then pressed on to Waynesboro to wreck the Virginia Central Railroad bridge and the tunnel through the Blue Ridge. He succeeded in destroying the bridge but was prevented by Early's infantry from demolishing the tunnel.[9] On the 29th Sheridan dispatched Merritt's and Custer's divisions of cavalry toward Piedmont in order to devastate that region.[10] Because of these incursions into the countryside, numerous skirmishes took place. However, none were particularly important.

As a result of his successful march up the Valley to Harrisonburg and beyond, Sheridan became overconfident. He believed that Early's little army was too demoralized to offer further effective resistance and had left the Valley entirely. Consequently, he advised Grant to transfer the Sixth and Nineteenth Corps to Petersburg. He felt that with Early disposed of for good, Crook's force would be sufficient to hold the Valley for the Federals.[11] Grant was more cautious, though, for he advised his subordinate to retain the Nineteenth Corps but to send the Sixth Corps and one division of cavalry to him.[12] It was very fortunate for Sheridan that he had all of those troops when Early assaulted him at Cedar Creek on October 19. A Confederate attack near Strasburg on the 13th caused Sheridan to send to Front Royal for the Sixth Corps to return to the Valley.

Although Early's cavalry under Rosser and Lomax received a bad beating from Torbert's Federal troopers at Tom's Brook on October 9, Old Jube was ready to lock horns with Sheridan once again. He was still skeptical of his horsemen, in spite of the fact he had Rosser's famous Laurel Brigade. This organization was confident of its ability to redeem cavalry fortunes in the Valley, but Old Jube was probably not surprised at the outcome of the Tom's Brook affair. The Southerners lost about 330 prisoners, eleven guns, ambulances, caissons, and even the headquarters wagons of Rosser, Lomax, and Wickham.[13] Some of the troopers were driven twenty miles by the Federals. No wonder Old Jube once dryly remarked, "The laurel is a running vine."[14]

The news that Sheridan was sending the Sixth Corps to Grant was all that Early needed to resume the fighting. As Sheridan had retired down the Valley just north of Strasburg, where he had fortified himself behind Cedar Creek, Old Jube followed. On October 13 the Confederates reached Fisher's Hill and occupied their former defense line there, about a mile south of Strasburg.

Early took part of his command to reconnoiter in force and advanced to Hupp's Hill, between Strasburg and Cedar Creek. An artillery exchange and an infantry skirmish between a Federal division and Confederate brigade resulted in the repulse of the bluecoats and the wounding of Brigadier General James Conner. Colonel George D. Wells, who commanded the Federal division, fell into Old Jube's hands, mortally wounded.[15] A more important consequence of this skirmish was the revelation of Early's army in force, which caused Sheridan to recall the Sixth Corps on the way to join Grant. The cavalry division intended for the Union commanding general likewise returned to Cedar Creek. Old Jube would have been better off at the Battle of Cedar Creek if he had not caused Sheridan to get these reinforcements.

Early's position at Fisher's Hill was daily growing more serious. Because of Sheridan's thorough work of devastation, Old Jube could not draw supplies from the surrounding countryside but instead had to haul them all the way from Staunton. As the supplies which he had brought along with him were rapidly becoming exhausted, he had either to attack or retreat. Because of his aggressive nature, he chose the former alternative.

In planning for an assault on Sheridan's lines to drive the Federals from their position, General Early was convinced that a frontal attack was impossible. The North Fork of the Shenandoah River and Cedar Creek made an offensive against that portion of the Federal lines inadvisable. The only a l t e r n a t i v e was a flank movement. Because he was suffering badly from rheumatism and general poor health, Old Jube was unable to make the steep ascent up Three Top Mountain to the signal station. Instead he sent General Gordon and Captain Jed Hotchkiss to this choice viewing-place on the Confederate right. At the same time he ordered General Pegram to move to the left to see how the Federals had placed their forces opposite that flank.[16]

From Hotchkiss and Gordon's viewing-place on Three Top Mountain the two Confederate officers could look down into both camps. They viewed the dispositions which Sheridan had made of his forces and saw the opportunity to attack the left side of the Federal line. They envisioned the possibility of moving infantry along the base of Three Top, near the river, to a crossing below Cedar Creek. They realized that such a movement would involve two crossings of the Shenandoah because of its winding course but that their troops would emerge into a dense woods near the Union camp. They also noted with satisfaction that the enemy had posted troops to defend the Federal right but that the left was virtually unprotected, except for a few cavalrymen.

As soon as Hotchkiss and Gordon returned and reported the result of their mountain-climbing, Old Jube made his plans. Calling his division commanders before him, he unfolded his offensive intentions and the best way of carrying them out.

According to the corps commander's directions, Gordon was to

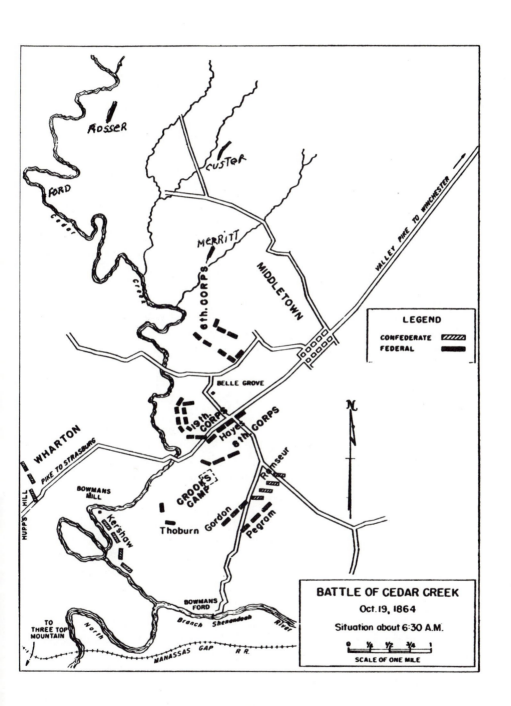

ROSSER

CUSTER

FORD

MERRITT

6th CORPS

MIDDLETOWN

VALLEY PIKE TO WINCHESTER

Cedar Creek

LEGEND

CONFEDERATE
FEDERAL

BELLE GROVE

19th CORPS

Hayes

8th CORPS

WHARTON

PIKE TO STRASBURG

Ranseur

HUPPS HILL

BOWMANS MILL

CROOKS CAMP

Kershaw

Thoburn Gordon

Pegram

TO THREE TOP MOUNTAIN

North

BOWMANS FORD

Branch Shenandoah River

MANASSAS GAP R.R.

BATTLE OF CEDAR CREEK

Oct. 19, 1864

Situation about 6:30 A.M.

0   ¼   ½   ¾   1

SCALE OF ONE MILE

253

lead the three divisions of the Second Corps on the movement to the right, march at night around the base of the mountain, cross the Shenandoah, and get in position near the house of one J. Cooley in the enemy's rear. There he was to deploy, cross the Valley Pike, and head for "Belle Grove," a stone house which was the headquarters of Sheridan. General William H. Payne's cavalry was to try to capture Sheridan himself.[17]

Kershaw was to cooperate by leading his division through the town of Strasburg, crossing Cedar Creek at Bowman's Mill, and striking the left of the Federals whom Gordon would attack. Wharton was directed to march up the Valley Pike so as to obtain the bridge across Cedar Creek and then assault those Unionists facing him. Rosser was to move with his own cavalry and Wickham's brigade on the Confederate left, while Lomax was to take his troopers to Front Royal and then strike the enemy along the Valley Pike.[18]

The plan was somewhat complicated and bold to say the least but not impossible to execute successfully. With Early's inferiority in numbers and equipment and Sheridan's strong position back of Cedar Creek, a frontal assault could not be considered. The strength of the two armies in the Battle of Cedar Creek was approximately the same as when they faced each other at Winchester one month previous, which meant that Sheridan had a better than three to one superiority. When Pegram reported to Early after his reconnaissance on the Confederate left, Old Jube learned that the enemy was strongly posted on that side. Consequently, the only thing that remained for Early to do was to execute the daring flanking movement to the right.

After Early's division commanders had heard his explanation of the plans for the proposed attack, they were very enthusiastic about its chances of success. They were quite anxious to redeem their reverses in the Valley and believed this surprise offensive would afford them an opportunity to do so. Old Jube reaffirmed his confidence in his subordinates but reminded them that if one failed, he could expect the criticism he deserved.

As Gordon's men had to traverse the longest and most difficult road, they set out first. Leaving behind canteens, swords, and any other equipment likely to betray their movements by its clinking, they marched into the darkness. They proceeded in Indian file along a narrow path at the foot of the mountain, crossed the Shenandoah on a bridge, and moving along the river bank, reached a position opposite Bowman's Ford. This would be their second crossing of the stream. Although it was still dark, they were able to discern a few Federals on their horses in the middle of the river guarding the ford.[19]

Meanwhile the remainder of the Confederate army had been carrying out its part of the program. At one o'clock on the morning of October 19 Kershaw's and Wharton's divisions moved along the Valley Pike to Strasburg. Then, Kershaw marched to the right toward Bowman's Mill, along Cedar Creek, while Wharton led his division along the Valley Pike to Hupp's Hill. Old Jube had instructed his chief of artillery, Colonel T. H. Carter, to move his batteries to Hupp's Hill and Wharton to support the guns with his infantry. Because the rumbling of the wheels would reveal the movement to the enemy, Carter did not bring up his pieces until the firing had commenced.

General Early accompanied Kershaw's division, which was thus occupying the center of the Confederate line. About three-thirty o'clock he came in sight of the Federal camp fires. As the moon was shining, he was able to see the enemy's camp fairly well. While waiting for the selected hour, Old Jube pointed out the Union position to his officers and instructed them how he wanted them to attack. He directed Kershaw to cross over Cedar Creek as quietly as possible, form his division in column of brigades, and then advance against the breastworks.[20]

At four-thirty Kershaw's men marched across the creek. While they were forming their columns on the other side of the stream, they heard firing on the left, where Rosser's troopers were engaging the Federals. Far to the right they heard more shots, which were caused by Gordon's men driving in the Union pickets at Bowman's Ford. At exactly five o'clock, the agreed upon time for the attack, they moved against the enemy line, swept over it, and caused the Federals to fall back in great confusion. The Southerners captured seven guns in this sector, which they immediately turned upon their former owners. The Unionists who were thus assaulted and driven from their position belonged to Colonel Joseph Thoburn's division of Crook's Army of West Virginia or the Eighth Corps as it was sometimes known.

No sooner had Kershaw launched his successful attack than Early rode to the rear to see if his artillery had arrived on Hupp's Hill. He noted with satisfaction that his able officer in charge of that arm was already putting in appearance and was preparing to engage the enemy. It required only a few minutes for Colonel Carter to place the guns in position and send shells screeching across the Federal position. Before long he had the satisfaction of seeing the enemy withdraw from the high ground in front.[21]

While Old Jube's dependable artillery was doing its part, Gordon's infantrymen were moving against the left flank of Crook's forces. They were partly concealed by a fog, and the first intimation the Eighth Corps had of an attack on their left flank was when Gordon's men burst upon them. After Kershaw had assaulted one of his divisions in front, General Crook, aided by other officers, attempted to form a new line along the pike. For the basis of it he employed his Second Division under Colonel Rutherford B. Hayes and Kitching's provisional division.

Unfortunately for the Union corps commander, when Gordon's Confederates suddenly appeared on the left of this line, the Federals gave way. They were already somewhat unnerved by Kershaw's rout of their comrades, and the attack from another quarter was all that was needed to cause them to flee. In doing so, they uncovered the position of the Union Nineteenth Corps, which was posted to the right and rear of Crook's original line. As the Nineteenth Corps was exposed to a galling enfilading fire that took in reverse its entire line of works, it had to retire. It abandoned eleven guns to the advancing Confederates.[22]

At the beginning of the Battle of Cedar Creek Major General Horatio G. Wright was in command of the Union army. Sheridan had gone to Washington to confer with Federal authorities and did not return to Winchester until the afternoon of the 19th. As Wright was normally in charge of the Sixth Corps, the command of that fine organization devolved upon one of its divisional leaders, Brigadier General James B. Ricketts.

After the rout of the Eighth and the Nineteenth Corps, the Sixth Corps of the Union army tried to stem the Confederate advance. As its main function had been to act as reserve, it had occupied a position in the rear, from whence it could move to reinforce any part of the front that the Southerners might attack. The Sixth Corps was soon exposed to the combined fire from Gordon's corps and Kershaw's division. Although General Ricketts was wounded and the whole corps forced back, it did manage to form a line which checked the Confederate advance.[23]

When Early perceived the success all along the line, he ordered Wharton's division and the artillery to move forward. Riding in advance of this part of his army, he met Gordon on a hill. Gordon reported that he had linked up with Kershaw and that they were vigorously pressing on after the retreating bluecoats. He also revealed that he had captured many pieces of artillery, much camp equipment, and a large number of prisoners. Leaving

Old Jube, the able subordinate returned to take charge of his troops.

A heavy fog now appeared, which, augmented by smoke from the firing, made observation practically impossible. Early rode forward to a more favorable position for reconnoitering. On his way he met Generals Ramseur and Pegram, who informed him that their divisions, after driving back part of the Sixth Corps, were then facing the whole of that body. They also stated the existence of a gap in the Confederate line on their right and asked for reinforcements to fill it. As Wharton's division had no immediate opponent, Old Jube sent it to plug the gap. It did so but then moved out in front, where it received a heavy fire from the Sixth Corps. This caused Wharton to withdraw and align his division with that of Pegram.[24]

In spite of the fact that the Sixth Corps was not routed, it was unable to maintain the second defensive line it occupied, which was directly west of Middletown. Although these Federal veterans fought hard, they finally had to yield their position because of the destructive artillery fire which Colonel Carter's gunners were pouring into them. They retired in good order to a position northwest of Middletown, where they established their third position of the day and where they were joined by elements from the other two corps. According to one artilleryman of the Sixth Corps, who had fought in a number of battles, Early's batteries at Cedar Creek were the best he had ever met in any of the engagements.[25] Old Jube's cavalry might leave much to be desired, but his artillery came through gloriously time after time.

While Early's little army had been winning such a great victory, the fog began to disappear and was succeeded by a bright sun. As Old Jube surveyed the defeat of the Federals all along the line, he could not conceal his joy, and he paraphrased Napoleon Bonaparte at the Battle of Austerlitz by exclaiming, "The sun of Middletown, the sun of Middletown!"[26]

It was the hour of Jubal Early's most brilliant victory. His planning and handling of his little army during the surprise attack on the strong Federal force were brilliant and compare favorably with the strategy and tactics employed by Stonewall Jackson in the same valley more than two years before. Too weak to assail Sheridan's Federals in front, Early had surprised them completely by his bold flank attack. As a result of the morning's activities, he could claim credit for having routed two whole corps of the Union army, forced a third from two defensive positions, and captured over 1300 prisoners, eighteen guns, besides numerous small

arms, wagons, and supplies of all kinds.[27] It seemed incredible
that his weak force had been able to do so much, especially with
such small losses as he had sustained.

It was now about nine-thirty in the morning. Determined to
follow up his advantage, Early sent Lieutenant Mann Page of his
staff with orders to Generals Gordon and Kershaw to assault the
enemy's right flank. When the lieutenant returned, he informed
Old Jube that Kershaw had stated his division was so scattered it
was impossible for him to attack. Page had not even delivered
the order to General Gordon, for the staff officer noted Gordon's
men were not in condition to carry out Old Jube's orders.

As the Federals had established their third defense line, which
was across the Valley Pike about two miles north of Middletown,
and had sent a heavy force of cavalry against the Confederate
right flank, Early rode to Middletown to meet this threat. He
posted the divisions of Pegram and Wharton, along with the brigade of Wofford, where they would face the cavalry, and these
troops repulsed several attacks by the bluecoated troopers. The
only cavalry which Old Jube had on his right consisted of Brigadier General William H. Payne's brigade of about 300 men. Since
Lomax had not arrived, Early sent word for him to come to Middletown as quickly as possible but, through some mistake, this
message was never received by Lomax. Rosser's troopers were
protecting the Confederate left.[28]

Early finally succeeded in getting Ramseur's, Kershaw's, Pegram's, and Gordon's divisions in line for an attack. Ordering all
of them against the third Federal defense position, Old Jube kept
his eyes on an enemy cavalry force on the Confederate left. As
the country was relatively open and hence advantageous for cavalry activities, he had to watch that a strong body of Union troopers
did not get around his flank and fall upon his rear. When Early
saw Gordon advancing on the Confederate left, he instructed him
not to assault the Federal line if he found it too strong to be
carried successfully. When his skirmishers reported a Federal line
of battle behind breastworks, Gordon decided not to press on.[29]

At this point Early determined to halt his whole army. In
doing so, he has been severely criticized for what General Gordon
calls the "fatal halt at Cedar Creek." In Gordon's book, entitled
Reminiscences of the Civil War, that officer devoted a whole chapter to criticizing his chief for failure to push on. He amassed a
considerable amount of evidence to show that Early erred in stop-
ping at this time. In some cases he refuted some of Old Jube's
statements, but as Early had died before Gordon's book appeared,

there was no way for him to reply to the statements made by Gordon.

General Early's reason for not pressing on after his victory in the morning seems perfectly valid. It was simply the condition of his troops, who were badly disorganized, hungry, tired, and worn out from the day's activities. Many had left their commands to plunder the captured Federal camps. Gordon later minimized the number of those engaged in this breach of discipline and insisted that they were not soldiers from the ranks but disabled ones who had not been fighting.[30] It must be admitted that General Gordon collected some very good evidence to support his contention.

On the other hand, General Early has considerable support for his statement that a number of his troops had left their commands to engage in plundering the Federal camps. According to Captain Samuel D. Buck, of the 13th Virginia Infantry regiment, fully one-third of Early's force left ranks to obtain clothing and other supplies.[31] He stated on another occasion that in the afternoon of that day Old Jube did not have 5,000 men in line because of straggling and absenteeism.[32] Another participant in this engagement, a Captain Benson, of the 17th Mississippi Volunteer regiment, stated that the Confederates could not resist the temptation of breaking ranks to plunder and that consequently, "this weakened our lines considerably."[33]

Still another Confederate, Joseph D. Shewalter, who served as a courier in Old Jube's army, stated that the Confederates were so starved that many left the ranks to obtain something to eat from the abundant stores in the Federal camp. Among the latter were three barrels of whiskey, whose contents were quickly absorbed by some of the men. The resulting drunkenness did not improve their discipline. Shewalter also revealed that they would not obey their officers when ordered to return to the battle front.[34]

Major Samuel J. C. Moore, who was Early's adjutant general, also upheld Old Jube's position in regard to the amount of straggling at Cedar Creek. According to Major Moore, one of Early's staff members sent back to order up artillery observed that the Federal camp through which Gordon's men had just passed was "swarming with men who had left the ranks to engage in plunder."[35] When he reported this to his chief, Old Jube sent other officers to induce the men to return to their commands. Other evidences could be gathered concerning the straggling and its effect on Early's defeat later in the day, but it is not necessary to devote more space to it. Of course, Old Jube and his officers were to blame for not controlling their men better.

Besides the desire to plunder the Federal camp, the Confederates were worn out with the marching and fighting. It will be recalled that many of them had been up all the previous night and had been engaged in a hard march, followed by the surprise attack. In the latter they had pushed the Federals back about three miles. The Confederate lines were somewhat disorganized by the fighting, and it would take time to straighten them out.

It is difficult to believe that a man as aggressive by nature as Early would hold back when he had a chance to inflict irreparable damage on the enemy. The whole planning of the Cedar Creek attack shows Old Jube's daring, and he could be expected to press on as long as there was any chance for success. That he did not do so must be due to the fact that his army was in no position to continue the attack.

Regardless of his r e a s o n for failing to press on after the victory of the morning, General Early formed his lines just north and west of the village of Middletown. This ended the first phase of the day's fighting, which had begun at daybreak and ended at about nine-thirty in the morning. The lull in the contest lasted from nine-thirty in the morning until about three-thirty in the afternoon, when the Federals launched a successful counterattack and drove the Southerners from the field.[36]

Determined to keep what he had already gained, Old Jube ordered that the prisoners, captured artillery, and other abandoned supplies be taken to the rear. Federal cavalry tried to break his lines on the right, but he managed to frustrate these efforts. Unfortunately, his own troopers had not been able to strike in force the enemy infantrymen fleeing along the Valley Pike. The only horsemen he had on that thoroughfare were Payne's 300 troopers. Rosser had attacked Custer on the extreme left of the Confederate line, while Lomax was so engaged at Stony Point and Newtown that he never did reach the main battlefield but returned to Luray Valley. Consequently, while Early's cavalry again failed him, the Federal troopers were free to aid in holding the Valley Pike.[37]

Meanwhile events had been transpiring in the Winchester vicinity which were destined to turn Old Jube's brilliant victory of the morning into a disastrous defeat in the afternoon. The much-publicized "Sheridan's Ride" had begun and, like a snowball, was gathering momentum, as well as Union stragglers, on the way to the battlefield. As has been related, General Sheridan, believing his army safe behind Cedar Creek, had left General Wright in command and had gone to Washington to confer with the Federal authorities. Completing his business in the capital on the morning of October 17, he took the noon train to Martinsburg. He did not think it necessary to rejoin his army immediately and attended to some business there before riding to Winchester, where he spent the evening of the 18th. Even when he heard artillery firing in the direction of Cedar Creek, he was not disturbed, for he believed it resulted from a reconnaissance.

Two hours later this feeling of smug security gave way to one of concern. The continued firing made too much noise to indicate a mere reconnaissance. Hastily mounting his horse and accompanied by his staff, the Federal commander rode toward Cedar Creek. Just south of Winchester, he was amazed to see part of his troops, with some wagons, fleeing from Early's attack. It took but a few minutes to order his men to park the vehicles, turn about, and form for a counterattack. He used a reserve brigade at Winchester as a nucleus to rally his men. Spreading this unit out on both sides of the Valley Pike, Sheridan attempted to check the bluecoats fleeing through the fields, as well as along the road. His efforts were successful. Encouraged by their leader's example, hundreds of fugitives ended their retreat and followed him to Middletown.[38]

When General Sheridan reached the front, he devoted his efforts toward establishing a strong line of battle. Noticing the thin rank of Confederates opposed to him and realizing the strength of his own command, he determined to collect every man he could and, supported by his strong cavalry force, to hit Early with everything he had. By doing so, he might recover some of the lost prestige.

About three-thirty that afternoon, Sheridan was ready. Using the Sixth Corps as a steadying influence, he organized his line of battle so that it presented a strong front. He placed Merritt's troopers on the left flank and Custer's on the right. He knew that in the open country before him his cavalry could sweep around Early's sides, or, if Old Jube should extend himself so as to make his lines too thin, the Federal horsemen could break through. Of course Sheridan also planned to use the infantrymen of the Sixth and Nineteenth Corps between the cavalry divisions. He left the remnants of Crook's undependable corps in reserve.[39]

Meanwhile, Early had not been inactive. When he discovered that he was unable to continue the pursuit, he placed his depleted army in a position of defense. In the reorganization after the morning advance the positions of the various divisions had changed. The Confederate infantry from left to right consisted of the divisions of Gordon, Kershaw, Ramseur, Pegram, and Wharton, respectively. Far to the left was Rosser's brigade of cavalry, while closer in, on the right, was Payne's small force of troopers.

Because of his fear of being outflanked by the Federal cavalry, Early stretched his lines so much that they were very thinly held. Although some of his infantrymen were posted behind stone walls, they were not strong enough to repulse the overwhelming force Sheridan was preparing to send against them. Gordon pleaded for reinforcements to strengthen the weak Confederate left, but there were no reserves, and Old Jube needed the remaining troops to hold the other parts of the line. The best he could do was to order three batteries into position to try to bolster the left.[40]

Sheridan's counterattack in the late afternoon was launched first against the weak Confederate left. His troops found and quickly exploited a gap between two of Gordon's brigades, Evans' and York's. Before long they succeeded in putting to flight the whole of Gordon's division. Some of the best troops in Early's army, fearing a cavalry flanking movement and believing their situation hopeless, broke and ran to the rear. The retreat of Gordon's men unnerved the Confederates on their right, who belonged to Kershaw's and Ramseur's divisions. Before long they were in retreat. The enemy was not putting pressure on this part of the line, but Kershaw's and Ramseur's veterans seemed greatly afraid of being outflanked. They soon became panicky.[41]

Early and his officers did everything they could to rally the disorganized Confederates. His dependable artillery commander, Colonel Carter, added to his laurels by the courageous way his men stuck with their guns and fired into the advancing bluecoats. The artillery, aided by some infantry which had rallied, checked the enemy for a brief period. The repulse was only temporary. While bravely attempting to restore the shattered line, General Ramseur received a mortal wound. Deprived of his leadership, his troops were unable to continue their stand. When Sheridan pressed on again, the Confederates fell back all along the line. The retreat of their left degenerated into a rout. With one mad rush the dispirited troops fled to the rear to gain the safety of their original position on Fisher's Hill. The men would not listen to their officers' entreaties, threats, or appeals. They were terrorized by the thought of the enemy's cavalry running over them.[42]

Sheridan relentlessly pushed his advantage. Capturing scores of prisoners, his infantry followed as far as Cedar Creek, but his cavalry went on beyond Strasburg. Aided by the fact that a bridge across a brook between Strasburg and Fisher's Hill had broken down, the Federal troopers fell upon the mass of blocked guns, caissons, ambulances, and wagons. The Confederates were so demoralized that they abandoned everything and were content with merely trying to save their lives. Considerable materiel of war thus fell into the hands of the hard-riding bluecoated troopers.

When he failed to prevent the rout of his army, General Early rode back to his original position at Fisher's Hill with the hope of trying to form a defense line there. The only organized group he had left was the body of Federal prisoners and its guard. He quickly sent these farther south, and he succeeded in saving them intact. The whole group reached Richmond a few days later. Although many stragglers made their way back to Fisher's Hill, it was impossible to form them into organized commands. The only thing that saved the defeated army from complete annihilation was the fact that Sheridan did not pursue all the way to Fisher's Hill. Fortunately for Old Jube, darkness came to his rescue. Leaving Rosser's cavalry at Fisher's Hill to cover the retreat, Early moved the infantry which he could collect to New Market. There he could compute the extent of his losses and also lick his wounds.[43]

Old Jube's little army had suffered a great deal as a result of Sheridan's victory at Cedar Creek. His killed and wounded amounted to about 1860, while his losses in prisoners numbered from 1000 to 1200. He lost twenty-three pieces of his own artillery, as well as all of that which he had captured from the Federals in the morning.[44] In addition, he was deprived of the services of the gallant Dodson Ramseur, who had been mortally wounded and had to be left in the enemy's hands. One of his able brigadier generals, Cullen Battle, had been wounded by a bullet in the knee. Earlier in the fighting on October 13, Brigadier General James Conner suffered a leg wound that made amputation necessary. Early's loss of regimental and company officers was also very heavy.

One of the guns captured by Sheridan was a long black rifle-cannon which the Confederate authorities had managed to send to Old Jube. As this artillery piece was on its way to the Valley, some pessimistic person had written on it in large white letters the following inscription: "Respectfully consigned to General Sheridan through General Early."[45]

Sheridan had not emerged from his victory at Cedar Creek entirely unscathed. In his official report of the battle, in which he believed Early's infantry to number 25,000 when Old Jube attacked, the Federal commander stated his loss in killed and wounded to be between 3000 and 4000.[46] Subsequent reports revealed that he lost not only 4,074 killed and wounded in this battle but an additional 1,591 who were captured or missing. Thus the total amounted to 5,665.[47]

When General Early had an opportunity to get his breath at New Market, he was naturally very despondent. Reporting to General Lee of the disaster at Cedar Creek, he attributed his defeat to the bad conduct of his troops. By this he meant both the plundering of the Federal camp and the panic that spread among his men after Sheridan had delivered his counterattack. The remainder of his letter to his chief shows that, although discouraged, Old Jube was still willing to do what he could for the cause he believed to be right. He wrote as follows:

> It is mortifying to me, general, to have to make these explanations of my reverses. They are due to no want of effort on my part, though it may be that I have not the capacity or judgment to prevent them. I have labored faithfully to gain success, and I have not failed to expose my person and to set an example to my men. I know that I shall have to endure censure from those who do not understand my position and difficulties, but I am still willing to make renewed efforts. If you think, however, that the interests of the service would be promoted by a change of commanders, I beg you will have no hesitation in making the change. The interests of the service are far beyond any mere personal considerations, and if they require it I am willing to surrender my command into other hands . . . .[48]

General Early may have failed to administer a serious defeat to General Sheridan at Cedar Creek, but he had caused his opponent severe losses and had shown the folly of sending Federals from the Valley to reinforce Grant. Even though Old Jube's army had been routed completely, if Sheridan diminished his strength and Early received reinforcements, that aggressive old fighter might repeat the attempt which had come so close to succeeding at Cedar Creek. In fact, as long as Lee kept Early in the Valley and gave him anything resembling an army, it would be risky for the Federal authorities to minimize the threat.

From July 1 to October 20 Early and his little force had put out of action a total of 14,500 Federals — roughly a whole army corps. This number was as large as Early's infantry force had ever been. The odds which Old Jube was facing were not known in 1864, and he could not publish them without exposing his own sadly-deficient force. Even General Lee did not know Sheridan's strength and in underestimating Early's opponent, Lee committed his greatest mathematical miscalculation of the war.[49]

Nor could the Southern people appreciate the difficulties confronting Early's command. They could only see that he had "failed" at Washington, had "failed" at Winchester, had "failed" at Fisher's Hill, and had "failed" at Cedar Creek. He had "failed" in the same valley in which Stonewall Jackson had succeeded so brilliantly in 1862. Old Jube's critics did not take into consideration the changed conditions in 1864 with the Confederacy on the wane and with a capable Federal general in command of a consolidated army in the Valley. All they could use to evaluate Early's worth were military victories which were too few to satisfy the public thirst. Before long the murmur of discontent with Old Jube's military prowess was to develop into a thunderous roar for his removal.

The story is told of an incident at Cedar Creek. After Early's defeat a hard-bitten old Confederate was captured, disarmed, and taken to the rear of the Union lines, a prisoner of war. "Sergeant," he said to the man in charge of the Union guard detail, "jest a few more of us rebels up there and we would have whipped h__l outta you Yanks!" The Federal, disliking such talk, took him to the company commander. "Cap'n," said the Confederate, "jest a few more of us rebels and we'd a beat h__l outta you Yanks." The captain, also annoyed, took him to regimental headquarters, where he repeated his tactless remark. The colonel decided to make an example of such a captive and had him taken at once to the commanding general for official reprimand:

"What's this all about?" demanded General Sheridan, assuming his most formidable attitude. When he was told that the Federal officers did not like the captive's talk, the general asked the Confederate what he had said. "Gen'l, I said if we'd jest had a few more rebels at Cedar Creek, we'd have whipped the devil outta you Yanks." "Sir," replied the Union commander, "that is treason against the Government of the United States! You will either take the oath of allegiance at once or I will have you shot within the hour!"

The old Confederate took the oath of allegiance to the United States Government. Then laying his hand confidentially on Sheridan's arm, he is said to have whispered, "Now, general, if there had been jest a few more of them dam rebels back there at Cedar Creek, they'd have whipped h__l outta us Yanks, wouldn't they?"

CHAPTER 26

The Old Soldier Fades Away

After the Cedar Creek disaster General Early brought the remnants of his command into camp at New Market, where he attempted to reorganize them once again. He used the occasion to give a sharp lecture on their recent conduct.[1] He blamed them for his failure to pursue the Federals after he had administered such a defeat to Sheridan's army in the morning. He realized after the engagement that, whatever the reason for his failure to pursue, he had erred grievously in not exploiting to the fullest his success. In sending Jed Hotchkiss to Richmond with dispatches to General Lee, Old Jube instructed his able cartographer not to tell the commanding general that the victorious Confederates should have pushed on at Middletown, for Early later believed they should have done so.[2]

While his infantry spent the remainder of October resting at New Market, Early's cavalry under General Lomax on October 25 repulsed an attempt by Brigadier General William H. Powell's Federal troopers to force the narrow pass at Millford in the Luray Valley.[3] After his failure to participate in the main fighting at Cedar Creek, Lomax had withdrawn to Millford, where he could cover Early's right flank. Old Jube, with the main army, was on the other side of Massanutten Mountain.

At New Market a few reinforcements joined Early's little army. They consisted of about 250 cavalrymen under Brigadier General G. B. Cosby, who had been detached from Breckinridge's Department of Southwestern Virginia, as well as a few hundred convalescents and conscripts.[4] Learning from his scouts that Sheridan had withdrawn his army to Kernstown and, believing that this movement presaged the sending of reinforcements to General Grant, Early moved down the Valley once more on November 10. His force soon crossed Cedar Creek and advanced toward Middletown.

On November 12 General Sheridan sent his strong cavalry force to meet the Confederate troopers. Merritt's and Custer's divisions moved against Rosser's command, while Powell, advancing along the Front Royal pike, marched against Lomax. Rosser was so hard pressed that Early had to reinforce him with Lomax's cavalrymen. Powell, seeing his opportunity, fell upon McCausland's brigade at Cedarville and completely routed it, capturing two pieces of artillery. After these cavalry setbacks, Early withdrew southward, for he did not feel strong enough to attack Sheridan's main force with any hope of success. His men reached New Market November 14. Old Jube had ascertained that Sheridan had not sent any troops to Grant.[5]

After the return to New Market, Early's army was weakened by the transfer of Kershaw's division to its proper corps at Petersburg and the return of Cosby's troopers to Southwest Virginia. Grant believed these movements meant that Early's whole army had left the Valley and, therefore, directed Sheridan to send him the Sixth Corps if this turned out to be the case. Sheridan had learned the lesson at Cedar Creek that as long as Early had an army of any size, it was necessary to respect its aggressive leader. Consequently, before weakening himself to strengthen Grant, he sent his cavalry up the Valley to determine the true state of affairs.

When the two divisions of Federal troopers drove in Early's cavalry pickets at Mount Jackson on November 22, Old Jube had to bring up his infantry to the rescue. After discovering that the Confederates were still very much in evidence in the Valley, the Union troopers withdrew. Sheridan thereupon requested permission to retain the Sixth Corps with him for the present.

Meanwhile, Old Jube had been contemplating another strike at the Baltimore and Ohio Railroad. Traffic had been restored over this artery, and Early hoped to interfere with it and create concern back of Sheridan's lines On November 27 he sent Rosser with two brigades of cavalry, his own and Payne's, across Great North Mountain to New Creek, a fortified post along the railroad. The Confederate troopers arrived at their destination on the 29th, surprised the garrison, and captured the entire post. Among the spoils were about 430 prisoners, 500 horses, 100 ambulances and wagons, and four pieces of artillery. They destroyed everything they could not carry off. The unfortunate commander of the Federals at New Creek, Colonel George R. Latham, was subsequently courtmartialed for his alleged "cowardice and disloyalty."[6] On his return, Rosser brought off several hundred cattle and sheep from Hampshire and Hardy counties.[7]

Another Confederate cavalryman, Lieutenant Colonel John S.

Mosby, with a relatively small band, caused Sheridan considerable annoyance during the autumn of 1864. Mosby's Rangers, as the group was called, consisted, for the most part, of men who had lived in the Lower Shenandoah Valley and hence were familiar with every bypath. With never more than a few hundred troopers and many times with only a handful, Mosby concentrated on attacking Sheridan's wagon trains, surprising pickets at the fords, gaining valuable information about the enemy, and helping the Confederate cause in numerous other ways. Early later spoke critically of Mosby's Rangers as being injurious to the Confederacy because they created so much disorganization and dissatisfaction among the regular Southern troops.[8] However, the fact remains that in the latter part of 1864 Mosby's men helped Early by causing so much trouble for Sheridan.

One of the most interesting of Colonel Mosby's exploits during this period was the famous "Greenback Raid" on the Baltimore and Ohio Railroad. Learning that a number of Federal paymasters had left Washington with money for Sheridan's army, Mosby determined to intercept their train between Duffields Depot and Kearneysville, in Jefferson County. As Mosby's men comprised an independent command, they received no regular pay from the Confederate Government, and they were always on the lookout for an opportunity to replenish their empty pockets.

On the night of October 13 about seventy of the rangers arrived at the chosen spot and prepared to stop the train. Using strong fence rails, a detail of twenty succeeded in raising one side of the track some distance above the level of the roadbed. As the railroad was double-tracked, both lines were torn up. A short time before, the rangers had disturbed only one track and were greatly chagrined to witness a train go thundering past on the track that remained untouched.[9]

Unknown to Mosby, the train he was attempting to rob had passed this point in safety before his command reached the railroad. However, luck was with him, for two Federal paymasters had missed their train and were compelled to take the next one. While the Southerners were waiting for the object of their raid, they were startled by their guard's sudden announcement, "The Yankees are coming!" Running for their horses, the troopers were astonished to receive no rain of bullets. Closer examination revealed that the guard had been frightened by a sow and her pigs running through the dry autumn leaves. Thoroughly disgusted, the raiders resumed their former positions, while Mosby swore at the guard and threatened to send him back to the regular army—a thing greatly dreaded by all the rangers.

Early in the morning of October 14 a distant rumble disturbed the stillness of the night. Presently the headlight of a locomotive came into view as a fast westbound train approached. When the wheels reached the elevated track, a grinding noise resounded and the engine tumbled over on the other track. Although the locomotive was completely wrecked, the ten coaches did not receive much damage, and the passengers escaped with a general jolting.

As soon as the train stopped, Mosby's men went through the cars. One of the rangers, J. West Aldrich, was engaged in this when he noticed a dark object between two seats. Further examination revealed it to be General David C. Ruggles, one of the Union paymasters. A little later Aldrich's foot struck an object on the floor. He picked it up and discovered that it was a paymaster's strong box containing more than $100,000. In the meantime, another ranger, Charles H. Dear, had captured General Edwin L. Moore and $68,000 additional. As most of the money was in greenbacks, this name was given to the raid.

Mosby ordered the passengers out of the cars so that he might set fire to the wooden coaches. A little difficulty arose when a group of westbound German immigrants refused to leave their seats. An interpreter explained that as these Germans had purchased through tickets, they were determined to remain aboard until they arrived at the end of the line. Mosby then gave vent to his impatience by ordering his men to scatter newspapers in the aisle and to "burn the d__d Dutch up if they didn't disgorge and leave the car." It is perhaps needless to add that when the flames spread through the wooden coach, the immigrants poured out like bees from a hive.

As many Union soldiers were not far away, the rangers determined to leave. In the light of the burning train they put their prisoners, who were Federals on furlough, behind them on horseback and departed. Before long they had placed the Shenandoah River between them and the scene of the raid. Agreeing to meet the following day at Bloomfield, in Loudoun County, the command separated. At the appointed time and place they divided the money among themselves, each receiving about $2,000. As Mosby refused to take any of the money, his devoted followers later bought him a fine thoroughbred horse. The Federal paymasters were sent to Richmond as prisoners of war and another drama in Mosby's career was ended. For a time greenbacks were plentiful in the Lower Valley.[10]

Colonel Mosby's activities had caused so much embarrassment to the Federal authorities that Grant had earlier ordered Sheridan to send a division of cavalry through Loudoun County "to destroy and carry off the crops, animals, negroes, and all men under fifty years of age capable of bearing arms. In this way you will get many of Mosby's men." He also instructed the Federal commander in the Valley to hang without trial any of Mosby's men whom he captured.[11]

At that time because of Early's activity in the Lower Valley Sheridan was unable to spare a division of cavalry. However, he passed on to his subordinates Grant's instructions to hang Mosby's men, and one of them, Brigadier General George A. Custer, proceeded to carry them out. Meeting a small body of rangers near Front Royal, he managed to capture six. Within a short while he ordered all of them executed, some being shot and others being hanged. His colleague, Colonel William H. Powell, extended the noose to another one of Mosby's men a short time later. Powell hanged the Confederate at the side of a public road and placed a placard on him which read as follows: "This would be the fate of Mosby and all his men."[12]

Mosby was not one to overlook such deeds. When he had captured a number of Federals from Custer's and Powell's commands, he selected a group to draw lots to see which ones would be the victims of the gallows to atone for their generals' mistakes. On the first drawing a fifteen-year-old drummer boy was chosen. Mosby released him, and the drawing proceeded until the required number was obtained. He then ordered a subordinate to take the prisoners out on the Berryville-Winchester road and hang them. The Confederate to whom these orders were given found the hanging process somewhat slow and after disposing of some of the Federals in this manner, he ordered the remainder to be shot.

Mosby then informed Sheridan of what Custer and Powell had done and what he had done in retaliation. The Confederate ranger concluded his communication to the Union officer with the following sentence: "Hereafter any prisoners falling into my hands will be treated with the kindness due to their condition, unless some new act of barbarity shall compel me reluctantly to adopt a course of policy repulsive to humanity."[13]

Although Sheridan's reply is not to be found in the *Official Records,* there is no evidence that the hanging of Mosby's men continued.

On November 27 Sheridan felt he could spare the troopers for an expedition against Mosby's men and ordered General Wesley

Merritt to take a whole cavalry division east of the Blue Ridge. Although the Federal commander enjoined his subordinate against burning dwellings, he directed him to "consume and destroy all forage and subsistence, burn all barns and mills and their contents, and drive off all stock in the region. . ."[14] Merritt did not succeed in finding Mosby's Rangers, but he reported that he drove off 5,000 to 6,000 head of cattle, 3,000 to 4,000 head of sheep, 1,000 hogs, and 500 to 700 horses. In addition, he destroyed a number of barns, mills, and huge quantities of hay. Most of this damage was done in Loudoun County.[15]

General Merritt was more considerate of a particular homestead on the western side of the Blue Ridge Mountains in Clarke County. This one, named "Springfield," belonged to Colonel Josiah W. Ware, a paroled Confederate prisoner of war. When Merritt encamped on the estate, Ware displayed true Southern hospitality by inviting the Federal officer to be his guest at the mansion-house. Ware had to inform his guest that because of the scarcity of food, the Federal officer would have to furnish his own provisions. Merritt accepted this offer but graciously informed his host that he and his family must be his guests in turn.

Thus a bargain was struck. With supplies from the Union commissary brought to the Ware kitchen, the family entertained the Federal officer in the beautiful dining-room. This arrangement proved so satisfactory that when Merritt had to leave a few days later, there was sincere regret on both sides. Before departing, he informed Colonel Ware that he would take steps to see that the property was not molested by Union soldiers.

The Ware family did not realize at the time how much this parting promise would mean to them. Not long afterwards some of Mosby's men killed a Union picket, and the order was given to destroy four of the most imposing homes in the vicinity. The Ware home was one of those on the list.

The Union soldiers approached the house while Colonel Ware was absent and immediately set fire to it. Mrs. Ware sent for the officer in command and informed him of General Merritt's guarantee of protection. The officer asked to see the paper but was told that the guarantee was verbal. When the mistress of the house offered to try to find Merritt to procure a written statement, the Federal officer replied, "Madam, the word of a lady is sufficient." Not desiring to burn the home but merely carrying out his orders, he was glad to escape from his unpleasant duty. It took only a moment to give the necessary orders to extinguish the fires and thus save the house from destruction.[16]

Two other homes in the neighborhood had no such protection and were burned to the ground. They were named "Hawthorn" and "Hill and Dale." A fourth one, known as "Arcadia," was selected for destruction and the Federals placed dry hay on the porch. However, just before they applied the torch, a group of Mosby's Rangers appeared and drove off the arsonists.[17]

When December arrived, the weather was too bad for infantry campaigning in the Shenandoah Valley, and Lee recalled the Second Corps to Petersburg, where it was still possible to maneuver. As soon as Grant learned about this movement, he directed Sheridan to send him the Sixth Corps.[18] Early then posted a signal party on Three Top Mountain and cavalry pickets at New Market while he took his remaining infantry, Wharton's division, his artillery, and his cavalry into winter quarters at Staunton. Sheridan's force was transferred to other sectors until the only infantry he had left consisted of the Nineteenth Corps.[19] Except for cavalry skirmishes, fighting in the Valley virtually ceased during the remainder of 1864.

After the new year dawned, several minor exploits occurred in the Lower Valley. On the Federal side of the ledger, Lieutenant Colonel Edward W. Whitaker of the First Connecticut Cavalry, selected 300 men to accompany him on a 140-mile round trip across mountains, swollen streams, and hazardous roads. He hoped to capture Major Harry Gilmor, a Baltimorean whose aggressive cavalry exploits in behalf of the Confederacy had earned Jubal Early's gratitude. Piloted by Major Henry H. Young, Sheridan's valuable Chief of Scouts, the blue-clad troopers left their camp near Winchester early on the morning of February 4, 1865. Crossing several mountains, they passed through Wardensville and about midnight approached Moorefield, in the South Branch Valley of the Potomac.[20]

Major Young made untiring efforts to ascertain the whereabouts of Gilmor and finally arrived at a house owned by a man named Randolph, about three miles from Moorefield. Becoming suspicious of the large number of horses in the stable, Young inquired of a Negro woman what soldiers were there. When she replied, "Major Gilmor is upstairs," he ordered his men to surround the house. In this manner he captured not only Gilmor but his cousin, who had just arrived from Baltimore. He turned his prisoners over to Colonel Whitaker, who successfully eluded all pursuit and led his troop back to its Winchester camp.[21]

Not to be outdone by this daring exploit, Early's men struck back a few weeks later. Because of the importance of the Federals captured, this incident received hearty acclaim throughout the Southland. It was one of the few opportunities for the expiring Confederacy to rejoice in the discouraging days of 1865. Specifically, this incident was the removal of two Federal generals, Benjamin F. Kelly and George Crook, from their hotels in Cumberland by a handful of men led by Lieutenant Jesse C. McNeill of the famous McNeill Rangers. The latter body had been organized in 1862 by the new commander's father, Captain John H. McNeill, for scout duty in the South Branch Valley. The elder McNeill had been mortally wounded in October, 1864 and his son elevated to the position of command. While Jubal Early was the Confederate commander in the Valley, the rangers had cooperated with him. It was Old Jube who made the official report to General Lee about the raid on Cumberland.[22]

The plan originated in the mind of John B. Fay, a Cumberland native who was one of McNeill's Rangers. For some time this Confederate soldier had been discussing the proposed raid with Lieutenant McNeill and had made two trips into Cumberland to obtain the vital information necessary to assure the success of the undertaking. By the middle of February, 1865, McNeill's men were ready to strike.[23]

With only sixty-three troopers, most of whom belonged to his own command, Lieutenant McNeill left his camp near Romney in the afternoon of February 20 and set out for Cumberland, about thirty miles distant. The difficulties confronting this small band were so great as to discourage all but the most courageous. A snowstorm had blanketed the countryside and created huge drifts; the temperature was so cold as to penetrate the overcoats of the men; and it was necessary to cross several mountains and one river. Once the city was reached, the rangers had to make their way among its Federal garrison, numbering about 8,000, find the quarters of the two generals, and then attempt to force the prisoners to accompany them on the return trip. Meanwhile, the raiders could expect a vigorous pursuit from Union cavalry.

With McNeill heading the advance, the Confederate troopers arrived within a few miles of their destination before they encountered the enemy. A single shot from the pistol of the partisan leader caused the surrender of three Federal pickets, one of whom attempted to challenge the Confederate advance. Although McNeill ordered his prisoners to give the countersign, they stubbornly refused until he threatened to hang one and choke the words out of him. The terrified Unionist believed discretion to be better than valor, for he obediently revealed that the countersign was "Bulls Gap."[24]

Fortunately for the Confederates, the Federal reserve picket squad, about a mile away, had not heard the pistol shot, and, disarmed by the countersign, soon joined their three colleagues as prisoners. Not wishing to be encumbered with them on the trip into the city, McNeill destroyed their arms, ordered them to remain at their post, and paroled them. He felt he could accomplish his mission before these enemy soldiers could give the alarm in case they wanted to violate their word.

As it was still dark, the bold raiders were able to keep their true identity secret while they entered the city containing its thousands of sleepers. To confuse the few bluecoats they met on the streets, they sang Federal songs, joked with the enemy, and successfully passed as Union cavalry returning after a night of hard marching. General Kelly was believed to be staying at the Barnum Hotel, whereas Crook was said to be at the Revere House. Luckily for McNeill, the two hostelries were only about a hundred yards apart.[25]

McNeill sent a small squad after each general, and it was but a short while before his men returned with their two distinguished prisoners who had been captured in bed. Taking time only to destroy the telegraph wires and instruments, the Confederates left the heart of the city to begin their hazardous return trip. Besides the two generals, they had also taken a few other captives, as well as headquarters flags. McNeill did not know that two future Presidents of the United States, Brigadier General Rutherford B. Hayes and Major William McKinley, were late arrivals at these hotels, or he would undoubtedly have added to his list of distinguished captives.[26]

With the prisoners mounted on captured horses and surrounded by the daring raiders, the little body made its way out of the city toward the Potomac. They passed two picket posts who allowed them to proceed without molestation.

According to one account, when a Federal picket inquired, "What's up?", McNeill could not r e f r a i n from replying, "O, old Granny Kelley [sic] has had a bad dream that the Rebs are after him and is sending us out in this bitter weather to scout the other side of the river. He's a regular old granny. Don't you wish Grant would relieve him, and put Crook in command?" The Federal picket, never dreaming that General Kelly was within ten feet of him and was thus listening to every word, agreed that a change of commanders in the Cumberland district was highly desirable. General Crook, who could appreciate the humor of the incident even though a prisoner, could not resist giving Kelly a nudge when the Federal picket suggested that he replace his superior officer.[27]

Although the Federals organized a hot pursuit shortly after the raiders had left Cumberland and day had finally broken, they were unable to rescue their officers. They came in sight of their quarry and pressed hard on McNeill's rear guard but eventually had to relinquish the pursuit.

By taking a circuitous route McNeill led his little band and its captives back into the Shenandoah Valley, where he delivered the prisoners to General Early at Staunton. Old Jube arranged for his high-ranking guests to be served a bountiful supper and provided with comfortable beds. Later he sent them to Richmond.

During the excitement in Cumberland after the results of the daring raid became known, Miss Mary Clara Bruce, who afterwards married General Kelly, appeared on a theatre stage in an entertainment. When she began to sing, "He Kissed Me When He Left," a drunken soldier in the audience shouted, "No, I'll be damned if he did — McNeill didn't give him time!" The singer retired from the stage and refused to appear again.[28]

In the early part of the year 1865 General Early's little army in the Valley was so depleted in numbers that he felt impelled to go to Richmond to talk the situation over with General Lee. The Confederate chieftain informed his discouraged subordinate that he had left him with the small command which remained in order to give the enemy the impression that a much larger force was still in the Valley. Lee encouraged Early to do the best he could under the circumstances. With his desire to serve the dying cause strengthened by his visit to the Confederate capital, Old Jube returned to his winter quarters at Staunton.[29]

Because of a great drought which ruined the corn crop in the Valley the preceding summer and Sheridan's systematic destruction of other grains and hay, there was very little sustenance for the cavalry and artillery horses attached to Early's command. As Old Jube found it impossible to get the harassed Richmond authorities to furnish sufficient forage, he sent his horses to other localities. In making this disposition of his forces, he dispatched Fitz Lee's two brigades to the Richmond-Petersburg area and Lomax's troopers to the counties of Pendleton, Highland, Bath, Alleghany, and Greenbrier. He solved the problem for Rosser's brigade by ordering it to be temporarily disbanded and the men to take their horses to their homes.[30]

A Young Confederate

With the artillery the story was practically the same. Early retained Nelson's battalion at Staunton but sent the officers and men of the other battalions, under General Long, to Lee, where they could be used to man stationary batteries. In the case of Lieutenant Colonel King's artillery, Old Jube ordered that the men and horses be taken into southwestern Virginia where supplies were more plentiful than in the Shenandoah Valley.[31]

When Major General John C. Breckinridge was made Confederate Secretary of War, General Lee issued an order on February 20 which extended Early's command over the Department of Southwestern Virginia and East Tennessee. Breckinridge had formerly been in charge of Confederate forces in this area.[32]

Toward the end of February events occurred which required the immediate presence not only of all these troops but any additional ones which Early could get his hands on. On February 20 General Grant had written to his able lieutenant in the Valley, General Sheridan, instructing him to move on Lynchburg with his cavalry so as to destroy transportation facilities in the neighborhood of that important city. The Federal chieftain even expressed the hope that after he had accomplished this, Sheridan might be able to march to the south and join hands with Major General William T. Sherman, who was pushing northward from the Carolinas, leaving behind him a devastated countryside and ruined transportation facilities. Grant informed Sheridan that if he could succeed in carrying out his part of the Union strategy, other movements were then transpiring which would "leave nothing for the rebellion to stand upon."[33]

General Sheridan soon proceeded to carry out Grant's orders. With a strong cavalry force numbering over 10,000, plus some sections of artillery, he left Winchester on February 27. He pushed on rapidly without opposition until he reached Mount Crawford, where General Rosser, with a hastily assembled body of troopers, attempted to bar the way. Sheridan easily brushed aside this feeble opposition and then marched to Staunton, which he found evacuated by the Confederates. Ascertaining that Early had moved his little army to Waynesboro, the Federal leader gave orders to proceed there. Once again he was about to join battle with his old antagonist but this time the odds were so much in his favor that he could not lose.

On the morning of March 2 Early and Sheridan opposed each other for the last time. Early had managed to assemble a little force consisting of Wharton's two infantry brigades, Nelson's battalion of six guns, and Rosser's cavalry brigade. His infantry probably did not number more than 1,000, his cavalry not more than 100, and his artillery even less than the latter figure. Old Jube had not intended to make his final stand at Waynesboro but had taken position on a ridge west of the town in order to allow time for the removal of five guns without horses and other supplies in the vicinity. He hoped that by presenting a bold front, he would accomplish these objectives and then retreat to Rockfish Gap in the Blue Ridge Mountains.[34]

Such was not to be the case. General George A. Custer sent three Federal cavalry regiments around Early's left flank and at the same time struck hard at the Confederate front. With hardly a show of resistance the soldiers defending the left of Old Jube's line gave way, and soon his entire force was in the utmost confusion. Everyone seemed to have but one objective — to put the South River between the hard-charging Federal troopers and himself. In vain did Early and his officers attempt to stem the tide. Their efforts to rally their broken commands not only failed utterly but almost resulted in their capture. As it was, the Federals took practically everything that had formerly belonged to Early's army, including his own baggage wagon.

The rout was complete. Sheridan reported the capture of 1600 prisoners, which figure may have been somewhat exaggerated unless Early's original strength was larger than he estimated it to be. In addition the Federals took eleven pieces of artillery, 200 wagons loaded with supplies, and seventeen battle-flags.[35] Sheridan sent the prisoners under strong guard back to Winchester. Although Rosser attempted to release his comrades by attacking the column near Mount Jackson, he was unable to do so and was driven off after suffering some losses. The Confederate generals at Waynesboro, including Early himself, fled into the mountains and escaped.[36]

An interesting sidelight to the flight of Early and his staff after the rout at Waynesboro concerned Dr. Hunter McGuire, formerly Stonewall Jackson's and now Old Jube's medical director and chief surgeon. Attempting to reach a wooded area along with his colleagues on Early's staff, McGuire tried to get his horse to jump over a rail-fence, but the animal fell sprawling, throwing its rider to the ground. As soon as the medical officer got upon his feet, he found himself looking into the barrel of a Federal carbine. Retaining his presence of mind, he did not attempt escape as his comrade, Colonel William H. Harman, did in Waynesboro for which he lost his life. Instead, McGuire made a peculiar sign or signal to his Federal captors. As soon as he had done this a Union officer rode up and informed the other bluecoats, "This man is my prisoner. Let him alone." He then took McGuire to the rear, where he introduced him to Sheridan and his staff.[37]

Because of McGuire's prominence and the general hopelessness of the whole Confederate cause, he was promptly paroled. As the battle of Waynesboro was over and the weather was cold and rainy, he suggested to his Federal captor that they seek a good warm meal at the home of a lady friend, a Mrs. Gallaher. The Unionist gladly complied and soon he and McGuire were partaking of the Southern woman's hospitality. While they were enjoying the meal, their hostess revealed that Federal troops were robbing her smokehouse and were setting fire to nearby buildings, thus endangering her own home. It took only a few minutes for McGuire's captor to put an end to the looting and burning by giving the necessary orders to the Union soldiers. After the two guests had finished their interrupted meal, they thanked Mrs. Gallaher and rode away.

Apparently the reason for the Federal officer's interest in McGuire at the time of his capture was the fact that both were Masons. He had recognized the sign which the Confederate surgeon had made at the time his horse fell. Later in Mrs. Gallaher's home he had noticed a picture on the wall containing Masonic inscriptions and insignia. When he inquired about the picture, he was told that Mrs. Gallaher's absentee husband was also a Mason. Hence his fraternal instinct prompted him to safeguard the home and possessions of another Mason, even though he was on the opposing side during the war.[38]

The affair at Waynesboro in which General Early lost almost his entire command ended his fighting for the Confederacy. With a small group of attendants he made his way across the Blue Ridge Mountains toward Charlottesville but was forced to make a wide detour when he discovered Federal troops in possession of that city. He then proceeded to Gordonsville, from which place he set out for Richmond. While approaching the Confederate capital with a small escort, he was almost captured by a force of Federal cavalry sent after him, but he finally eluded the enemy and made his way into the city.[39]

Although General Lee's confidence in Jubal Early remained unimpaired after the disasters in the Valley and the Confederate chieftain desired him to return there, such was not to be the case. Ever since Old Jube had begun to suffer defeats from Sheridan's overpowering forces, a persistent demand arose in the Southland for his scalp. His biting sarcasm and quick wit had continued to make him unpopular, and the humiliation at Waynesboro gave his enemies the opportunity they desired. They overlooked the change in the general situation of the Confederacy and continued to harp on the theme that Early had failed so miserably in the same Shenandoah Valley where Stonewall Jackson had succeeded so brilliantly. Consequently the demand for Old Jube's removal now became such a loud outcry that Lee was forced to yield to the public clamor.

While Old Jube was trying to organize a Confederate force in southwest Virginia, where Lee had sent him, he received a telegram on March 30 from his beloved commander instructing him to turn the troops in that part of the state over to Brigadier General John Echols and those in the Shenandoah Valley over to Major General Lunsford L. Lomax. In the same communication Lee informed Early that he would address a letter to him at his Franklin County home.[40] Still accustomed to obeying orders, Old Jube sorrowfully bade adieu to his small band of associates and headed for Rocky Mount.

On his way home General Early contracted a severe cold and cough which produced a hemorrhage in his lungs. This illness necessitated his remaining at Marion, in Smythe County, for several days. When he was able to resume his journey in an ambulance a few days later, he received the news of General Lee's surrender at Appomattox. He could hardly believe his ears, for it seemed impossible that the cause for which he and his comrades had sacrificed everything had been abandoned. While Old Jube, prostrate in mind and body, was lying in the ambulance, his first reaction to the news of Lee's capitulation at Appomattox was to swear violently and, turning in his uneasy bed with a groan to exclaim, "Blow your horn, Gabriel!"[41]

No doubt Early's incredulity upon hearing the news from Appomattox was comparable to that of many other Confederates of all ranks. An example of the confidence which the Southern soldiers had in Lee is illustrated by an anecdote which Major General Fitzhugh Lee told on himself after the war. It will be recalled that he was a cavalryman and, in general, the cavalry was not popular with the infantry, for the foot-soldiers felt that their mounted companions got most of the breaks.

According to Fitz Lee, he was riding away from Appomattox after the surrender when he met an old infantryman who, he later learned, had been visiting his home in North Carolina. The Confederate cavalry officer reported the following conversation as having taken place:

"Ho, there," cried General Lee, "where are you going?"

"I've been off on a furlough and am now going back to join General Bob Lee," replied the soldier.

"You needn't go back but can throw your gun away and return home, for Lee's surrendered."

"Lee's surrendered?"

"That's what I said," said Fitz.

"It must have been that damned Fitz Lee, then. Rob Lee would never surrender." Whereupon the old soldier shouldered his musket and, with a look of contempt, walked on.[42]

In spite of the news from Appomattox Early decided to proceed to his home before determining his future course. After he arrived in his native county, he received the long-delayed letter from General Lee explaining the reasons why the Confederate chieftain had relieved him from command. It read as follows:

Headquarters C. S. Armies
30th March, 1865

Lieut General J. A. Early
Franklin County, Va.

General,

My telegram will have informed you that I deem a change of commanders in your department necessary, but it is due to your zealous and patriotic services that I should explain the reasons that prompted my action. The situation of affairs is such that we can neglect no means calculated to develop the resources we possess to the greatest extent and make them as efficient as possible. To this end it is essential that we should have the cheerful and hearty support of the people and the full confidence of the soldiers, without which our efforts would be embarrassed and our means of resistance weakened. I have reluctantly arrived at the conclusion that you cannot command the united and willing co-operation which is essential to success. Your reverses in the Valley, of which the public and the army judge chiefly by the results, have, I fear, impaired your influence, both with the people and the soldiers, and would add greatly to the difficulties which will, under any circumstances, attend our military operations in Southwestern Virginia. While my own confidence in your ability, zeal, and devotion to the cause is unimpaired, I have nevertheless felt that I could not oppose what seems to be the current of opinion, without injustice to your reputation and injury to the service. I therefore felt constrained to endeavor to find a commander who would be more likely to develop the strength and resources of the country and inspire the soldiers with confidence; and to accomplish this purpose, I thought it proper to yield my own opinion and to defer to that of those to whom alone we can look for support.

I am sure that you will understand and appreciate my motives, and that no one will be more ready than yourself to acquiesce in any measures which the interests of the country may seem to require, regardless of all personal considerations.

Thanking you for the fidelity and energy with which you have always supported my efforts, and for the courage and devotion you have ever manifested in the service of the country,

I am, very respectfully and truly,
Your obedient servant,

R. E. Lee,
General.[43]

CHAPTER 27

The Unreconstructed Rebel

When Jubal Early arrived in Franklin County after having received news of the surrender at Appomattox, he was suffering again from his old ailment — rheumatism. While he was recovering, he learned that several groups of Federal soldiers were looking for him.[1] As one of these parties approached the house near Rocky Mount where Old Jube was believed to be hiding, the Confederate general was perhaps saved by the devotion of a faithful Negro. Upon inquiring from the colored man Early's whereabouts, the Federals were told that he had just left the house and gone in "dat direction." Quickly they set out after him. Much later they learned that their quarry had escaped for good and managed to do so because he had departed in the opposite direction from that indicated by the Negro.[2]

In spite of his sickness General Early concluded that his home county was not a safe place. B e c a u s e of his relief from command, he did not consider himself included in the surrender terms given Generals Robert E. Lee and Joseph E. Johnston. Too proud to ask for an individual parole and still desiring to fight for the Confederacy, he determined to make the long journey to the Trans-Mississippi Department, where he hoped General E. Kirby-Smith was still defending the Stars and Bars. Procuring a horse and accompanied by three young men, one of whom was his nephew, the ailing, tragic figure left Virginia to pass through the Carolinas, Georgia, Alabama, and Mississippi. While in Alabama, the little band learned that General Kirby-Smith had also surrendered. Two of Early's companions then changed their plans and left him. Thus, he and his nephew continued their westward journey by themselves. The overwhelming desire to get away from the rule of his hated conquerors influenced Old Jube considerably in this decision.[3]

The Mississippi River loomed as a formidable barrier, for all the principal crossings were well-guarded by Federal soldiers. As Early had a horse with the initials "U. S." branded on him, he

Early in Disguise as an Exile

realized the folly of attempting to fool his would-be captors. He had determined to try to swim his horse across the river but was persuaded to use a passing steamboat for that purpose. Suspicious that this vessel might be carrying Federal soldiers, Old Jube was willing to risk his steed but not his own person. His skepticism proved justified, for the boat did contain a party of about thirty Union cavalrymen, who, recognizing the familiar brand, seized Early's horse, saddle, and bridle. Old Jube and his nephew crossed by a small boat. The younger man, being sick, joined a party of Missourians going home, and thus Early was left to continue his journey by himself.[4]

The refugee succeeded in obtaining another horse, which he rode until he reached the upper waters of the Brazos River. Unfortunately this animal was so broken down that Early was forced to give him a rest. As the general himself was sick again, he looked for a place to stay. Luck was with him, for in that region lived an ex-Confederate who had lost a leg fighting in Virginia. This veteran proved to be a good Samaritan indeed. Not only did he provide Old Jube with a place to stay but, in addition, he undertook to collect a sum of money from his neighbors for the exile. As a result of his efforts, he thus obtained several hundred dollars in gold, which he gave to Early. Although the general was badly in need of funds for a trip out of the country, he was reluctant to accept this pecuniary aid, but the way in which it was presented convinced him that his new friends really wanted to help him. He, therefore, accepted their present. He does not enlighten us concerning the name of his host at this time.

Early remained in this vicinity until October 6, when in improved health he took leave of his benefactor. Because of the danger from robbers and Mexican guerrillas, he concluded it unwise to cross the Rio Grande into Mexico but, instead, decided to go to Galveston and get on board a ship leaving the country. On the way to the seaport he met Major Thomas P. Turner, the former commandant of Libby Prison in Richmond. At Galveston he was fortunate enough to meet another unnamed friend, who obtained passage for the two refugees on a Federal vessel bound for Liverpool. In addition, Early, along with Turner, received a present of 500 dollars in gold, which was raised by generous Texans. William S. Sellers of Galveston was the leader of this group which came to the aid of the two needy Confederate officers. Even the Northern skipper of the ship, who knew the identity of his prominent passengers, refused to take any of their scanty funds to pay for their passage.[5]

Before long Early and Turner reached an island in the Bahamas, which was under the control of the British Government and inhabited almost entirely by Negroes. Their black hosts accorded them every respect and made their nine-day sojourn on the island a pleasant one. The Negro authorities quartered the Confederate exiles in the Government House, which, apparently, was the most comfortable lodging-place there. Early described his visit with some trace of humor, for he noted the unusual situation when two Confederate officers took drinks and touched glasses with a "great black Negro fellow, who would have brought at least $2,000 in gold in the New Orleans market before the war."[6] Although their hosts did not know the guests were ex-Confederate officers, Early learned later that the Southern lost cause was not unpopular in the Bahamas.

General Early then obtained passage on a schooner bound for Nassau in the Bahamas. Needing some clothes, he purchased a gray suit, for which he was able to get some Confederate buttons. He then sailed for Havana, Cuba, where he arrived on December 10. At the latter place he heard rumors concerning the possibility of a war between the United States and France over Napoleon III's attempt to establish a puppet regime in Mexico. The French emperor's efforts to maintain the unfortunate Maximilian in that country were a clear violation of the Monroe Doctrine. If war resulted, Old Jube was determined to take up arms once more against the United States. With high hopes he left Havana for Mexico.[7]

Early spent three months in the country south of the Rio Grande and hence had ample opportunity to learn the true state of affairs. He was much disappointed with what he saw. It was quite obvious that Maximilian's Government was very unpopular with the native Mexicans and had to be sustained entirely by French soldiers. He was convinced that if Napoleon withdrew his troops, Maximilian would have to leave also. While there, he received an offer of $150 a month to serve the puppet government as inspector of surveys, but he declined. Old Jube stated that he had no desire to be mistaken for a Frenchman by the Mexicans and perhaps be shot. He was so disappointed with conditions in Mexico that he wrote a public letter to the New York *News* advising Americans to stay out of the troubled country to the south.[8]

Early used his time in Mexico to write his memoirs of the Shenandoah Valley campaign during the last year of the Civil War. He was extremely anxious to do this while the events were still fresh in his mind and while he would be able to communicate with other officers to corroborate facts about which he was uncertain. In order that he would be able to get in touch with them more easly and, desiring better facilities for publishing his writings, he determined to move to Canada. Consequently, he returned to Havana to await a vessel northward bound. While in Cuba he received a communication from his brother Sam containing over $400, which greatly supplemented his meager purse. As there was no direct communication between Cuba and Canada, he proceeded to St. Thomas, where he was able to obtain passage on a steamer headed for Halifax, Nova Scotia, on July 3, 1866.[9]

The voyage from Cuba to Canada was made without incident, and the latter part of July General Early made his way to Niagara, where he remained on the Canadian side of the falls. He soon found himself in a congenial atmosphere, for Niagara was then the temporary home of General John C. Breckinridge, ex-Senator James M. Mason, and other former Confederate leaders. As Breckinridge was planning to leave shortly for Europe because of the health of his wife, Old Jube used this opportunity to have his former lieutenant read and criticize the manuscript of the Valley campaign. He was extremely anxious to have this pamphlet as accurate as possible so that the true picture of his last great assignment would be left to posterity.[10]

In due course of time Early succeeded in getting his pamphlet published in Canada. Consisting of 130 pages, it first appeared in 1866 and was republished a year later. It has the distinction of being one of the first narratives of the war by a prominent Confederate general. Because of an unusual incident that attended the publication, it received a great deal of unexpected publicity.

During the winter of 1865-1866 a newspaper in Lynchburg, entitled the Lynchburg *Virginian,* published a copy of the letter which General Lee had written to General Early relieving him from command. No sooner had it appeared than the Federal officer in charge of that district informed the editor of the *Virginian* that the letter belonged to the United States Government and demanded that he give it up. Because the editor had used a copy of the letter, and not the original, he was, consequently, unable to comply.

It so happened that the original communication was then in General Early's hands and since the refugee was in Canada, there was no way to force relinquishment of the desired epistle. As one might suspect, Old Jube was not inclined to oblige the government of his former adversaries, and when he heard about the demand on the editor of the *Virginian,* he uttered a few oaths and penned the following rebuke to the United States authorities:

This demand for General Lee's private letter to me, and the attempt to enforce it, by military power, show how wide has been the departure from the original principles of the United States Government, and to what petty and contemptible measures that Government, as at present administered, resorts in domineering over a disarmed and helpless people. I have the pleasure of informing the Hon. Secretary of War, and the keeper of the 'Archive Office,' that the original letter is in my possession, beyond the reach of provost marshals and agents of the Freedmen's Bureau, or even Holt with his Bureau of Military Justice and suborners of perjury.[11]

Naturally this open defiance of the United States Government was hailed throughout the South, then in the throes of so-called Reconstruction, but Early's book was not as well received as he had hoped it would be. As has been pointed out before, he was not a popular man and had never tried to make himself one. His former companions-in-arms could only recall the succession of defeats that seemed to be his luck everywhere he went in the gloomy days of 1864-1865. Just about the time that Early's memoirs appeared from the press, Dabney's narrative of Stonewall Jackson's Valley campaign of 1862 was published.[12] The reading public, especially a critical one, could not view Early's record in 1864 in the same light that it could Jackson's in 1862.

This letter which General Early wrote to the Federal authorities is but one example of the hatred which he felt toward his late conquerors — a hatred that was destined to increase with the passing years. It is doubtful if there was anyone in the South who could qualify any better for the title of "Unreconstructed Rebel" than Jubal Early. When it is recalled how bitterly he opposed the secession of Virginia at the Convention in 1861, this uncompromising attitude after the war seems all the more remarkable. No wonder that Fitz Lee once said of him in connection with the Civil War, "When Early drew his sword in that conflict he threw the scabbard away and was never afterward able to find it."[13]

General Early was even unable to concede that General Grant's terms at Appomattox were generous. In this view he differed with most of his former comrades, including his good friend Jefferson Davis. Old Jube believed that although Lee was not then in condition to give battle he could have abandoned his trains and artillery, escaped into the nearby mountains, and then made his way to the southwest to join the Confederates in the Trans-Mississippi Department. Early thought that Grant was so anxious to have the glory of Lee's surrender and was so fearful of not obtaining it that he would consent to any terms necessary to attain this objective. In supporting his contention, Old Jube mentioned Grant's failure later to support President Andrew Johnson's liberal Reconstruction policy and Grant's first official act as President to remove the Union General Winfield S. Hancock and replace him with General Phil Sheridan as Military Commander of New Orleans.[14]

Nor was Old Jube's opinion of the assassinated President Lincoln much better. In a letter to a certain T. C. Reynolds written from Canada in December, 1867, Early criticized Mrs. Lincoln for having been the recipient of $30,000 worth of shawls, laces, drapes, etc. and stated that this was due to the President's influence in awarding government contracts and making appointments. He also felt that the report of Lincoln's administrator showing the ex-President to have had an estate of more than $100,000 after the payment of all debts, proved the former poor lawyer guilty of malfeasance in office.[15]

As for Lincoln's successor in the White House, Andrew Johnson of Tennessee, General Early had difficulty finding words strong enough to express his contempt. He regarded Johnson as a "miserable, cowardly renegade" and a traitor to the Southland from which he came. He blamed Johnson for executing the Radical Reconstruction Bill of March 2, 1867, even though the President had attempted to prevent its passage by use of the veto. In referring to the struggle between Johnson and the Radical Congress over Reconstruction in general, Old Jube wrote as follows: "The fight between him and the Radicals has been surely a fight over different schemes of wrong to the South, and I trust they will impeach, convict, and hang him. Justice will be done then on one traitor though it might not be for the right reason."[16]

Early's opinion of Ulysses S. Grant did not change when the successful Union general was nominated by the Republicans for the Presidency in 1868 and seemed sure of victory over his Democratic opponent, Governor Horatio Seymour of New York. In writing to his brother Sam concerning the probability of Grant's election in 1868, he displayed remarkable political sagacity and prognostication. In this letter Old Jube referred to Grant as "a man of too little sense and too little character to be anything else than a mere tool in the hands of others."[17]

When General Early left the United States in 1865, he had made up his mind never to return unless he could come back under the Confederate flag. In a letter to his friend and former cavalry leader, General Thomas L. Rosser, written from Cuba in 1866, he stated:

. . . My hatred of the infernal Yankees is increasing daily, if possible, and I do not speak to any of them that I meet. My motto is still 'War to the death,' and I yet hope to have another chance at them. Whenever war arises between the U. S. and any other power, I shall be in, and God forbid that I meet any Confederates on that side.[18]

Two full years after he was relieved from command by General Lee, Early still felt vengeful toward his conquerors. Even though he was then living in Canada and thus free from molestation by those "infernal Yankees," he could not help sharing the misfortunes imposed upon the ex-Confederacy by Radical Reconstruction. He suggested to his former comrades in arms that, rather than continue submission to "the cowardly fiends who rule in Washington," they should, if possible, take up arms once more and fight until they would be exterminated. Old Jube regretted that his ill health and age prevented him from assisting them in this mad scheme. He even expressed a desire to join the Indians in the West and lead a band of "20,000 or 30,000 Commanches and Apaches through Kansas, Nebraska, Iowa, and across the Mississippi" so that he could "leave a trail behind that would not be erased in this century. . . ."[19]

In spite of his feelings toward those in control of the United States Government, after a few years in exile General Early realized that the only sensible thing for him to do was to return to the land of his birth. He was getting older, his health was becoming worse, and, what bothered him most of all, was that he had no means of earning a living in Canada or in any other foreign country. In spite of the simple, unostentatious life he was leading, he had no regular means of support. His relatives, and especially his brother Sam, sent him varying sums of money from time to time and that source constituted his principal income. Old Jube was greatly disturbed by the fact that he was such a burden on his family and on one occasion he expressed regret that he had not died on the battlefield fighting for the cause he believed to be right. He felt that it was unfair to his in-laws for his brothers to send part of the family income to maintain him in idleness "a pensioner on the bounty of those whose means are limited." Therefore, Old Jube wrote his brother Sam in July, 1868 to come to Canada if possible to help him decide on his future plans.[20]

Sam's reply was for his brother to remain in Canada for the present as he believed that a Federal indictment for treason was then pending against Old Jube. Subsequent investigation revealed that the Confederate general, with about thirty others, had been indicted first in the district court in Norfolk in 1865 and later in the Federal Circuit Court in Richmond. Although these court papers were then dormant, Early was apprehensive lest the Federal authorities revive them upon his return to the United States.[21] He was anxious to have some kind of guarantee that he would not be molested.

That guarantee was soon forthcoming. On December 25, 1868 President Andrew Johnson issued a proclamation promising a full and unconditional pardon for all those who had fought against the United States during the Civil War.[22] Since this action settled the question concerning the status of those ex-Confederates who had been excepted from previous proclamations, General Early determined to avail himself of its provisions. However, he could not refrain from commenting on it as follows:

> ... Looking upon this proclamation as a final acknowledgment by the government of its inability to hold us responsible under the laws and Constitution as they stood for our resistance to its usurpations and encroachments, I accept it in that light, and not as a pardon for any offense committed. I think I can now return without any compromise of principle, and it is certainly a great deal better for me to do so than to remain a burden in the hands of friends who have to submit to the ills of Yankee rule in order to be able to furnish the means on which I live.[23]

When Jubal Early heard about this Presidential proclamation, he was living in Drummondville, Ontario. He had moved to this little town, about a mile from Niagara Falls, so as to avail himself of its quiet atmosphere and cheapness of living. However, he soon made his plans to return to the United States. Since his ailing father was then living in Lexington, Missouri, with son Robert, Jubal determined to proceed directly from Canada to Missouri and then to Virginia. On February 2, 1869 he left Ontario, and, passing through Michigan and Illinois, arrived in Lexington, Missouri five days later. He had originally expected to visit friends in New Orleans before returning to Virginia, but he felt he could not afford this extra expense.[24] Although he had considered settling elsewhere, like many Virginians, he had finally decided to spend his remaining years in the Old Dominion. After visiting with his relatives in Missouri for a few months, he found himself once more in the state of his birth. He had been away from it about four years.

Once back home General Early tried to decide the best means of making a living. Although his letters and papers do not shed

Memorial Arch at Lynchburg

much light on all of his business pursuits after the war, it is possible to piece together a few details. He considered opening a Virginia agency for the Carolina Life Insurance Company, of which his friend Jefferson Davis was president. In January, 1870 he inquired about the possibility of his obtaining such employment. He received a favorable reply and was told he could have the agency if he wanted it, but a careful study of the existing manuscripts for this period of his life does not reveal whether or not he became an insurance agent.[25]

Presumably Jubal Early earned his living from 1870 to 1877 by returning to his civilian profession — law. He did not engage in a large general practice but took a few special cases only. He lived in Lynchburg rather than Rocky Mount, because the larger city seemed to offer better opportunities to a man beginning anew the earning of a livelihood during those dark days of Reconstruction.

At any rate, General Early's financial difficulties were solved when on Feb. 17, 1877 he, along with General P. G. T. Beauregard, was appointed a commissioner to supervise the principal drawings of the Louisiana State Lottery. As his connection with this enterprise was of such importance to himself and friends that it occupied most of the remaining years of his life, it will be discussed in more detail in the succeeding chapter. It is only necessary here to repeat that his salary as commissioner of the Lottery was sufficiently large to enable him to support himself adequately, as well as to help many of his friends in need.

Even though Jubal Early returned to his native state and submitted to the authority of the United States Government, he retained bitter feelings toward his late conquerors. He still felt as he did when he was in Canada and expressed his sentiments in a letter to General D. H. Hill. Referring to the passage in the Scripture requiring one to forgive his enemies Old Jube said: "I am clearly of opinion that the Yankees furnish an exception. At any rate, if my salvation depends upon my being able to love them, I fear I shall be lost . . . . there is scarce a night of my life that I do not dream of being engaged in battle with the Yankees. I wish it was not all a dream."[26]

Several incidents occurred in 1875 which show very clearly that General Early's views had in no way changed since his return to Virginia. In August of that year he received a communication from a group of Bostonians inviting him to be present at a meeting to be held the following month in Faneuil Hall to form a new political organization known as the "National Union Party,"

pledged to bring about "Reconciliation and Honest Government."
The invitation included an offer to pay Old Jube's expenses to
Boston, as well as provide a suitable reception for him. Early replied that for business reasons he would be detained in Virginia the
whole month of September, and hence would be unable to accept.
He also took the occasion to impress upon the Bostonians the futility of trying to form a new party, and he expressed the opinion
that the Democratic Party was the only one "whose principles and
policy can give any hope of a restoration of the rights of the
States and a return of the Federal government to its ancient integrity. . . ."[27] Therefore, he felt he could not support any movement designed to supplant it.

In fact, after General Early returned to Virginia from his
exile in Canada, he voted regularly for the Democratic candidates
in every national, state, and city election. This is contrary to the
popular but erroneous belief that he never voted at all after the
war.[28] As the Whig Party, which he had supported before the war,
was no more, he shifted his allegiance to the Democrats. He believed that in doing this he was protesting against Radical Reconstruction and everything that the Republican Party then espoused.

On another occasion Early received an invitation from the
City Council of Boston to attend the dedication of the Army and
Navy monument on Boston Common and participate in the hospitality of that New England metropolis. This, too, he declined. In
doing so, Old Jube expressed his thanks for the honor and then
concluded with a characteristic statement:

> . . . While I fully appreciate the fraternal and harmonizing
> spirit which prompts our Northern friends to condone the of-
> fences of their 'erring Southern brethren,' yet I have not ar-
> rived at that happy frame of mind which would enable me in-
> dividually to perform, with becoming grace, the part of the
> erring Southern brother returning in a contrite mood to the
> 'house of his father's.'[29]

The same year that General Early declined the Boston invitation to assist in the formation of a new national party brought him
still another communication from the camp of his erstwhile opponents. This was from the Elisha B. Smith Post, Grand Army of
the Republic, of Norwich, New York which invited the ex-Confederate general to attend as a special guest the semi-annual encampment of the Union veterans. As an added attraction the
Northerners planned to put on a dramatic performance entitled
"The Spy of the Shenandoah." Since the play included a reference
to the Battle of Cedar Creek, General Early would be treated to

the sight of a former Union soldier impersonating himself. The one selected to play the part of Old Jube was Elmore Sharpe, who was the Chaplain of the Elisha B. Smith Post.[30]

Although there is no evidence to indicate that Old Jube took advantage of the opportunity to see the Battle of Cedar Creek played by Northerners on a stage, the invitation afforded much amusement to his friends. One of them, General Fitz Lee, could not refrain from writing Old Jube as follows:

> . . . I too have received an invitation to go on to your Elisha B. Smith banquet. I am almost sorry now I have declined the invitation, because the sight of a chaplain personating General Early is alone worth the price of the trip. I don't see what you have done to merit all that. . .when the selection had to be made of a few persons to personate you the minds of the whole post instinctively turned towards their chaplain — and with one voice they all exclaimed — 'There art the man!'[31]

Another incident which showed the feelings entertained by General Early after the war occurred in connection with the parade and unveiling of a statue of Stonewall Jackson in Richmond on October 26, 1875. When Old Jube heard that the Virginia authorities had agreed to allow several companies of Negro soldiers to participate in the parade, he exploded and condemned the proposal in vigorous protests to Generals Henry Heth and James L. Kemper. The fact that Kemper was then Governor of the Old Dominion did not lessen the sting of the sharp rebuke Early made. As Old Jube had suggested the name of Heth for the position of chief assistant marshal for the parade, he felt, to some degree, responsible for Heth's acts in that capacity.[32]

Early's objection was based on the assumption that since Negro troops had fought against the Confederacy, to allow Negro companies to participate in a parade honoring Stonewall Jackson would be "an indignity to the memory of Jackson and an insult to all Confederates who shall attend the inauguration of the statue. . . ." He also objected to the possibility that members of that race might assemble in Capitol Square in such numbers as to make it impossible for white people to attend the exercises there. Finally, the unreconstructed one informed his friends that if the Negro soldiers were allowed in the parade, "the sun shall not shine on me in Richmond on the day when such an outrage shall be committed. . . ."[33]

Governor Kemper's reply was equally as sharp in tone. He pointed out that officers of several Negro volunteer companies, as

well as some ministers of that race, had approached him about the
possibility of allowing Richmond Negroes to show their respect
and admiration for Stonewall Jackson by marching in the parade
honoring him. Kemper emphasized the humble spirit with which
the Negro leaders had come to him, and, after consulting with other
ex-Confederates, he had agreed to allow their companies to occupy
a place toward the rear of the parade. Defending his stand as the
only proper one to further better relations between the two races,
the Governor wrote Early that the program would be carried out
as planned and that if Old Jube were coming with the intention of
influencing others to his way of thinking, then it would be better
for him to remain in Lynchburg on the day of the parade.[34] Although Early's reply to this communication is not available, it is a
safe bet that he was not in Richmond at the unveiling of Jackson's
Statue in Capitol Square.

General Early's devotion to the cause for which he had fought
continued to grow as the years passed. After the war he always
appeared only in suits of Confederate gray, some of which were
furnished free by a Charlottesville clothing concern. Even in 1886
the old fighter, as active with the pen as he had formerly been with
the sword, felt impelled to protest against the appearance of a
model representing the proposed statue of General Lee to be
erected in Richmond. On this occasion he again directed his communication to the Governor of Virginia, who at that time was his
old friend, Fitz Lee. The following excerpt from Early's letter is
typical:

> . . . If the picture is a fair representation of the model, it
> is an abomination. The idea of representing General Lee on a
> bob tail horse, looking like an English jockey is revolting, and
> if such a monument should ever be erected in my life time, I
> should feel like collecting the survivors of the 2nd Corps, and
> going to Richmond to blow up the thing with dynamite. . . .[35]

Although General Early was anxious to assist in memorializ-
ing the Confederate heroes by suitable monuments, he was not
willing to do so if the builders had to go beyond the borders of the
Confederacy for their materials. On one occasion he was ready to
contribute generously to a monument to General Lee until he
learned that granite from Maine had been used in its construction.
In spite of the entreaties of his friends to overlook this seemingly
unimportant objection, Old Jube would not budge an inch and
stubbornly refused to have any part in the undertaking.[36]

General Early was a very popular speaker after the war and
was always ready to state his views frankly. He spoke at numerous

reunions for Confederate veterans and, as might be expected, he continued to sound the praises of the lost cause. He had no use at all for those former veterans who had gone over to the enemy after the war, and on one occasion he referred to the former daring cavalry leader, Colonel John S. Mosby, as a ranger "whose idea was that the highest motive that can influence a soldier is the desire for plunder, and whose *post bellum* history is in accordance with his war experience — still fighting for plunder."[37] He also spoke disparagingly of General Longstreet, who, like Mosby, had turned Republican after the war and had become a good friend of General Grant.

General Early obtained much pleasure from attending these reunions of former Confederate comrades and, when his health permitted, was generally on hand at any important meeting. His stooped figure, his beard, his black, piercing eyes, and his gray clothing made him a conspicuous figure. He was usually called upon for a speech, and he generally obliged. On one occasion, while he was addressing an audience at the Montgomery, Alabama, Exposition, he concluded with the following typical humorous remark:

> . . . The Confederate soldiers fought over four years in defence of their country, and in defence of a principle which they believed right, and which was right. The army of Northern Virginia never was defeated. It simply wore itself out whipping the enemy."[38]

Early was asked to deliver the principal address on Confederate Memorial Day at the Stonewall Cemetery, Winchester, Virginia, on June 6, 1889. In the course of his remarks, he extolled the characters of those men who had given their lives for the Southern cause and praised those that had remained true to their ideals after hostilities had ceased. On this particular occasion, he seemed more moved than usual, and concluded in the following strong language:

> . . . If ever I repudiate, disown, or apologize for the cause for which Lee fought, and Jackson died, may the lightning of Heaven blast me, and the scorn of all good women and true men be my portion; and I re-iterate now, what I have often said before, that the Confederate who has deserted since the war is infinitely worse than one who deserted during the war, for the former has gone over to the enemy at no personal risk to himself, and simply from motives of gain, while the latter took his life in his hands, knowing that he would be shot if captured, and in a number of cases he was tempted to leave the service to go to the assistance of his family, which he was induced to believe was starving at home.[39]

CHAPTER 28

Taps

In the period after the Civil War Jubal Early undertook to defend the Southern cause against all critics. In his zeal to make his position clear, he remained loyal to his friends, Robert E. Lee and Jefferson Davis, and engaged in sharp verbal battles with some of the other ex-Confederate officers. His tongue and pen were directed especially against those two prominent Southerners who joined the ranks of the Republican Party, James Longstreet and John S. Mosby, but he also became involved in controversies with Generals John B. Gordon, William Mahone, and Thomas L. Rosser. His quarrels with the latter trio were largely over details in connection with some of his military campaigns.

In August, 1869, General Early received an invitation to lecture to the newly-organized Southern Historical Society in New Orleans. The records do not reveal whether he accepted, but they do indicate that he was greatly interested in the work being done by this organization. Although he later became a vice-president of this group, it never seemed to function successfully, and he determined to devote his efforts to the formation of another society.[1]

In October, 1870, General Bradley T. Johnson wrote Early asking his former commander to help form a "Society of the Army of Northern Virginia to preserve our old friendships, to collect materials for the history of the army, and to cherish the names and fame of our dead comrades." As Old Jube was then in process of calling upon Confederate veterans to join him in erecting a suitable memorial to General Lee, Johnson thought that the proposed society could assist in this undertaking.[2]

General Early heartily approved of the idea and went to Richmond to be present at the first meeting of the Society of the Army of Northern Virginia. Assembling in a theatre on November 4, a number of Lee's former officers and soldiers met and elected permanent officials. Much to his own surprise, Old Jube was elected president. Among his other war comrades chosen to positions of leadership in the organization were Generals George E. Pickett, Edward Johnson, Dabney Maury, and William Smith.[3]

The society went on record favoring the formation of similar groups in each Southern state. These, in turn, were to be authorized to establish sub-associations, which were expected to collect the muster rolls and names of all ex-Confederate soldiers, living and dead. After this material had been assembled, it was to be forwarded to the state organization and from it to the general association. It was thus hoped that Colonel Charles S. Venable, the recording secretary of the general organization, would become, in time, the custodian of all the aggregated historical records of the sub-associations in the various states.[4]

Apparently the Society of the Army of Northern Virginia and its affiliated groups did not succeed in becoming a repository for the collection of historical data dealing with the South. The state organizations were more interested in assembling the material relating to their respective states than they were in preserving the history of the South as a whole. After a few years, due partly to the general disorganization of all Southern state institutions after the war, they declined in popularity and were barely able to maintain a skeleton staff to carry on their work. Consequently Jubal Early felt that steps should be taken to form a new organization which would "collect, collate, and preserve the materials for a history of the late war from a Southern standpoint."[5]

In August, 1873, General Early and a few interested friends met at the Montgomery White Sulphur Springs in Virginia and launched the movement for the reorganization of "The Southern Historical Society." At its first meeting the new body announced its plans to preserve the history of the Confederacy as a whole without giving an undue importance to the part played by any particular state. For the present it planned to have a Baltimore organ entitled the *Southern Magazine* to publish the articles which it sponsored, and later it hoped to have its own periodical. From a modest beginning the new organization grew until it became much stronger than any of its predecessors. Through its journal, *Southern Historical Society Papers,* it revealed to a surprised public many unknown facts about the Southern struggle for independence, and it has continued to exercise a great influence over historians writing about that conflict. For a number of years General Early served as its president.

In December, 1876, General Early received a letter from his friend and former comrade-in-arms, General P. G. T. Beauregard, offering him a position as commissioner to supervise the principal drawings of the Louisiana State Lottery Company. Beauregard had been chosen as one of the commissioners and had been authorized to select a colleague.[6] According to one account, the position offered Old Jube had previously been tendered to two other ex-Confederate officers. General John B. Hood refused this opportunity to add materially to his means because he did not want his name to be associated with a business of so dubious a character.[7] Then General Wade Hampton was approached and had accepted conditionally, but his nomination and subsequent election to the Governorship of South Carolina caused his declination.[8]

As the offer from Beauregard carried with it the promise of "liberal compensation" for his services, Early was very much interested. Although he was by no means destitute, he was anxious to augment his uncertain income by any honest means that presented itself. He did not want to call upon his brothers and other members of his family for any more financial aid, and the income from his law practice, though increasing, was not enough to afford him that security which every man desires. Besides this, his generous nature made him desire to give liberally to requests for financial assistance which he was continually receiving from less fortunate persons. He was particularly sympathetic with ex-Confederates who had difficulty reestablishing their businesses in the post-war South.

In spite of the desire to add to his income, General Early's honesty impelled him to seek further information from Beauregard regarding the characters of those in charge of the lottery. Because the company managing the enterprise had been chartered in 1868 by bribing a corrupt Louisiana Legislature and had not enjoyed too enviable a reputation in the succeeding years, Old Jube had his doubts.[9] Beauregard's assurances that the managers of the lottery at that time were respectable, honest men were enough to convince Early to give the offer a try.

Consequently, on February 17, 1877, Jubal A. Early and P. G. T. Beauregard appended their signatures to a contract offered by the Louisiana State Lottery Company accepting the position of commissioners to supervise the principal drawings to be held in New Orleans each year. Their starting salary was to be a minimum of $5,000 annually for each, with the possibility of an increase if they were engaged to superintend additional drawings. The honest intentions of the two Confederate generals caused the contract to contain an opportunity for them to withdraw from the agreement if they should discover any frauds in the enterprise.[10]

The Lottery Company employed Early and Beauregard in

order to obtain the confidence of the American public in the integrity of its principal drawings. In this expectation it was not disappointed for both of these ex-Confederate generals enjoyed the respect of the Southern people. Both were known to be men of integrity, and the public felt reassured when the two commissioners attended the drawings in person, kept a careful watch on all the proceedings, and then certified that the project had been conducted honestly. That the company was satisfied with its investment in the two new employees is proved by the fact that it decided later to get them to supervise the monthly lottery drawings in addition to the principal ones. For all of his work with the company Early reported in December, 1881 that he received an annual salary of $10,000 plus $150 a month for expenses.[11]

During the succeeding years the operations of the Lottery Company drew attacks from leading citizens in all parts of the United States, for many tickets were sold outside of Louisiana. Charges of fraud and corruption were hurled against it time after time, and it was necessary for the two commissioners to rise in its defense. The company contributed liberally to charitable and educational enterprises, but this generosity only served to give its opponents additional ammunition, for they could claim that it was trying to cover up its wicked activities under the guise of charity. The Lottery Company also became involved in lawsuits, lobbying activities, and various attempts to propagandize the public into supporting the gamble.

A bitter struggle was waged by the defenders and opponents of the Lottery Company when a convention met in New Orleans in 1879 to draw up a new state constitution. After the arguments had been made, pro and con, a compromise was reached with the adoption of Article 167 of the Constitution of 1879. This required the Louisiana State Lottery Company to yield its monopoly privileges but allowed it to continue to operate until January 1, 1895.[12]

Although the Lottery Company enjoyed a period of prosperity in the decade of the 1880's, dark days were ahead. Anti-lottery sentiment had been crystallizing so much in the nation as a whole that the United States Congress passed an act on September 19, 1890 denying the use of the postal system to lottery promoters. Not to be outmaneuvered, the Louisiana Lottery officials tried to conduct their business through the express companies and even offered to pay express charges on orders of five dollars or more. However, they had to abandon their substitute for the mails when three of the leading express companies denied lotteries the use of their channels.[13]

Those conducting the lottery also tried to have the company's charter extended beyond the 1895 deadline by means of a state constitutional amendment, but the Louisiana voters by an over- whelming vote rejected any extension.[14] Hence, unable to operate successfully against adverse Federal and state legislation, the Louisiana State Lottery Company held its last drawing in Decem- ber, 1893, after which it moved to Honduras to continue its ac- tivities.[15]

General Early continued to serve as commissioner almost as long as the company operated in Louisiana. Although careful research does not reveal the exact date that he severed his con- nections with it, an account of a drawing held March 11, 1890 reveals that Old Jube was still actively assisting Beauregard to supervise the drawings.[16] It is sufficient to state that he remained on the payroll of the Lottery Company long enough to amass a relatively good fortune, which not only made him completely independent financially but also made it possible for him to share his good fortune with others.

There is no lack of examples concerning General Early's generosity to those in need. Being a man of extremely simple tastes, not interested in money, he lived a plain existence even when he was receiving more than $10,000 a year from the Lottery Company. When the Federal Government allowed him a pension for his services in the Mexican War, he transferred the entire amount to his old Negro body servant who had been with him in that conflict. It is hardly necessary to add that this pension was sufficient to provide for all of the material comforts for the faith- ful old servant until he died. When another Negro servant, who worked for him in Lynchburg after the Civil War, became ill, Old Jube provided him with every care and attention. In spite of this, the Negro died. As members of the servant's own race had shunned him while he was sick, in order to punish them for their neglect Old Jube would not allow them to attend the funeral.[17]

General Early was especially generous in contributing to help his former Confederate friends and their relatives when financial aid was needed. He also aided materially in the erection of numerous monuments and memorials to Southern heroes. His letters and papers in the Library of Congress contain many com- munications from persons grateful for a contribution. Among them is one from Mrs. Thomas J. Jackson thanking him for giving her $1000 for the support and education of her grandchildren.

Another one was from the Governor of Virginia expressing his appreciation for $1000 which Old Jube had given to erect a monument to General Robert E. Lee in Richmond. He likewise donated $200 to aid in establishing a monument to General Beauregard in New Orleans.[18] Still another $200 contribution from him went to the Confederate Memorial Association in Lynchburg. One of his former soldiers in the Valley campaign, who later became a minister in Frederick County, Maryland, even asked Early for a donation to help build a rectory, but whether or not Old Jube honored this unusual request is not shown by the available records.[19]

Jubal Early's friends went to him not only for money after the war but also for advice. Ironically enough, his advice was sometimes sought in connection with marital matters. In view of the fact that he was a bachelor, this seems all the more remarkable. On one occasion the wife of Jefferson Davis wrote him to find out his attitude toward the announcement of the approaching marriage of her daughter, Winnie, to Alfred Wilkinson of New York. Mrs. Davis explained that originally her husband had opposed the match but after Winnie's health gave way under the strain, he had become reconciled to her marrying a Northerner.[20]

In her letter to General Early, dated April 20, 1890, Mrs. Davis tried to offset the birthplace of her prospective son-in-law by stating that Wilkinson was a states' rights Democrat, a child of six years when the Civil War began, and a Southern sympathizer. She also revealed that he was a graduate of Harvard and, as a successful businessman, was capable of providing for Winnie's every comfort. Besides all this, he was in love with Winnie and she with him.

Unfortunately neither the Early Papers nor the Davis Papers reveal the reply of General Early to this request for advice. Old Jube received a letter about the same time from General L. L. Lomax, President of Virginia Agricultural and Mechanical College at Blacksburg, asking him to use his influence to break off the engagement because Wilkinson was a New Yorker.[21] In view of General Early's feeling about Northerners even as late as 1890, one is perhaps justified in surmising that he could not bring himself to the point where he would sanction a marriage between Jefferson Davis' daughter and a "Yankee", and he probably wrote Mrs. Davis disapproving of the match. Whether he did so or not is open to question, but the fact remains that the engagement was broken off. Of course, many other Southerners expressed their opposition to the match in no uncertain terms.

General Early had a narrow escape from death on September

30, 1890, when the walls of a brick building fell in on him and several Negro assistants. A fire had destroyed part of the building in which he kept some of his books and papers. While the old general was rummaging around trying to salvage what he could, the outer walls caved in and buried him and his servants under a mass of heavy timbers and bricks. It is believed that the timbers fell over him in such a way as to protect him from the bricks. As soon as the accident was discovered by a Lynchburg resident, the fire bells were rung and a large crowd assembled. The rescuers feared that the brave old soldier had fought his last battle and, consequently, were greatly relieved when he and his companions emerged, unhurt, from the wreckage.[22] According to Dr. Douglas S. Freeman, whose father was one of the volunteers helping with the rescue, Old Jube emerged from the debris and remarked, "Uh, I didn't know there were that many bricks between me and hell."[23]

General Early's narrow escape from death caused a flood of letters and telegrams to be sent congratulating him on his survival. The concern which his friends and former Confederate comrades expressed at this time indicates that Old Jube still occupied a position of respect. One of the most interesting comments he received came from Fitz Lee and was worded as follows:

> In connection with all other Armies except the Army of the Potomac, I rejoice at the narrow escape you made the other day. It is hard to kill you infantry fellows, at least it was during the War. If that had been a cavalryman he would never have been where you were because it was so close to danger. He would have gone to the rear as he used to do when the fighting began. I wish hereafter you would walk out in the middle of the street, never carry a brick in your hat or go near brick buildings, and join the Catholic Church because · the Pope was the only one that recognized the Southern Confederacy; and be happy.[24]

Although General Early recovered from this experience, he was not so fortunate almost four years later. On February 16, 1894, as he was walking down the stone steps of the post office building in Lynchburg, he slipped and fell. He was soon on his feet again and was inclined to minimize the incident, but that evening he suffered severely from shock. The attending physician could not discover any bruises or broken bones but realized the seriousness of the shock to a person as old as his patient was. The old soldier did not want to die and tried to rally just as he had attempted to rally his dispirited troops during the war, but his great heart ceased beating on March 2.[25]

Taps

On March 5, 1894, Lynchburg and Virginia paid homage to Jubal Anderson Early. The funeral service for the brave old soldier was held in the Episcopal Church by the Rev. T. M. Carson, one of the Confederate chaplains who had served under Early. While the Virginia State Flag hung at half-staff over the Capitol at Richmond and while the Governor and Legislature paid respect to his memory, persons from all walks of life were crowding into the church and the adjacent expanse outdoors. Among the thousands of mourners were many of the ragged veterans who had followed the fallen leader in the Valley campaign of 1864. One of these grizzled old soldiers could not resist the temptation to step forward and kiss the brow of the gray-clad figure in the coffin.[26]

After the services at the church the procession moved to Spring Hill Cemetery, where on an elevated lot — in full view of the mountains he loved so well — the mortal remains of Jubal Early were laid to rest. After a detachment of the Richmond Howitzers and one from the Virginia Military Institute had fired a last salute, a bugler sounded taps. This was on almost the same spot where Old Jube's bugler, Tinsley, had given the signal to attack Hunter in 1864.[27]

That attack had been successful. So now was Old Jube launched forth in memory for those following on History's page! His grand old spirit ever lives! His indomitable courage, his loyalty and devotion to duty, his military and forensic ability, his integrity of character, his keen wit and humor, his forthrightness, his consecration to a righteous cause, his impulsive generosity, his triumphs, his heartaches, his colorful career — all make richer the heritage that is ours.

FOOTNOTES

CHAPTER 1

Young Jube

1. Jubal A. Early *Scrapbook.*
2. *Ibid.*
3. *Genesis,* 4:21.
4. R. H. Early, *Lieutenant-General Jubal Anderson Early, C. S. A.* p. xvii.
5. Statement of Judge A. H. Hopkins of Rocky Mount, Virginia to author, Sept. 12, 1951.
6. R. H. Early, *The Family of Early Which Settled upon the Eastern Shore of Virginia and Its Connection with Other Families,* pp. 107-108.
7. *Ibid.,* pp. 18-24.
8. *Ibid.,* pp. 63-67.
9. *Ibid.,* pp. 106-108.
10. United States Military Academy *Records* in the Adjutant General's Office, National Archives.
11. *Ibid.*
12. Jubal A. Early *Scrapbook.*

CHAPTER 2

The Bluffs Above The Hudson

1. Roswell Park, *A Sketch of the History and Topography of West Point and the U. S. Military Academy,* pp. 6-7.
2. *Official Register of the Officers and Cadets of the United States Military Academy,* 1834, pp. 11-12.
3. F. A. Mitchel, *Ormsby MacKnight Mitchel, Astronomer and General,* p. 20; *Regulations of the U. S. Military Academy at West Point,* 1832, pp. 25, 38; A. E. Church, *Personal Reminiscences of the Military Academy from 1824 to 1831,* p. 21.
4. *USMA Regulations,* pp. 27-29, 38-39.
5. *USMA Post Order Book,* 1833-1837, pp. 49-50.
6. *Ibid.*
7. *Ibid.,* p. 83.
8. *USMA Regulations,* p. 13.
9. *Ibid.,* p. 12.
10. Douglas S. Freeman, *R. E. Lee, a Biography,* Vol. I, p. 57.
11. *USMA Regulations,* p. 7; *USMA Post Order Book,* 1833-1837, pp. 125, 135-136.

12. *USMA Staff Records No.* 1, 1818-1835, p. 534.
13. *Ibid.,* pp. 539-540.
14. *USMA Register,* 1834, p. 19.
15. R. H. Early, *Lieutenant General Jubal Anderson Early, C. S. A.,* p. xviii.
16. Hervey Allen, *Israfel, the Life and Times of Edgar Allan Poe,* Vol. I, pp. 280-281. Quoted by special permission of Rinehart and Company, Publishers.
17. *USMA Register,* 1826, p. 3; *Ibid.,* 1827, p. 19; *Ibid.,* 1828, p. 19; *Ibid.,* 1829, p. 19.
18. Letter from Samuel H. Early to Jubal A. Early, June 2, 1834, in Jubal A. Early *Papers,* Vol. I, Library of Congress.
19. *USMA Regulations,* p. 13; *American State Papers.* Class 5. Military Affairs. Vol. 5. pp. 212-213.
20. Park, *op. cit.,* pp. 97-98, 105.
21. *USMA Staff Records No.* 1, 1818-1835, p. 552.
22. *USMA Library Circulation List,* 1833-1837.
23. *USMA Staff Records No.* 2, 1835 *to* 1842, pp. 14-15; *USMA Register,* 1835, pp. 10-11.
24. *USMA Register,* 1835, pp. 16, 19.
25. Walter Harrison, *Pickett's Men: A Fragment of War History,* p. 33.
26. *USMA Regulations,* p. 22.
27. *USMA Post Order Book,* 1833-1837. [Page not numbered].
28. *USMA Regulations,* pp. 9-10; Freeman, *op. cit.,* p. 69.
29. Copy of letter from Jubal A. Early to Joab Early, Nov. 8, 1835 in Jubal A. Early *Papers,* Vol. I, Library of Congress.
30. *USMA Staff Records No.* 2, 1835 *to* 1842, p. 32.
31. *Ibid.,* pp. 43-44; *USMA Register,* 1836, pp. 9-10.
32. *USMA Register,* 1836, p. 24.
33. R. H. Early, *op. cit.,* p. xviii.
34. *Confederate Veteran,* Vol. XXVI, No. 10, p. 430.
35. *USMA Register,* 1837, p. 3; Park, *op. cit.,* p. 79.
36. *USMA Staff Records No.* 2, 1835 *to* 1842, pp. 61-62; G. W. Cullum, *Biographical Register of the Officers and Graduates of the United States Military Academy from* 1802 *to* 1840. Vol. I, pp. 518-520.
37. *USMA Register,* 1837, pp. 2, 6-8; *USMA Post Order Book* 1833-1837 [Page not numbered], under date of June 8-12, 1837.
38. *USMA Register,* 1837, p. 24; *USMA Post Order Book* 1833-1837 [Page not numbered] under date of Oct. 2, 1836, Oct. 8, 1836, and March 6, 1837.
39. *USMA Register,* 1834, 1835, 1836, 1837.
40. Cullum, *op. cit.,* p. 529; R. H. Early, *op. cit.,* p. xviii.

CHAPTER 3

War and Peace

1. Grant Forman, *Indian Removal,* pp. 316-317.
2. *American State Papers,* "Military Affairs", Vol. VII, p. 454.

3.   George A. McCall, *Letters from the Frontiers*, pp. 299-306.
4.   R. H. Early, *Lieutenant General Jubal Anderson Early, C. S. A.*, pp. xviii-xix.
5.   U. S. Senate *Document*, No. 507, 25th Congress, 2nd Session, pp. 5-6; John T. Sprague, *The Origin, Progress, and Conclusion of the Florida War*, pp. 203-212.
6.   U. S. Senate *Document*, No. 507, 25th Congress, 2nd Session, p. 8; R. H. Early, *op. cit.*, p. xix.
7.   Sprague, *op. cit.*, p. 198.
8.   U. S. Senate *Document*, No. 507, 25th Congress, 2nd Session, pp. 8-12; Sprague, *op. cit.*, pp. 199-202.
9.   R. H. Early, *op. cit.*, pp. xix-xx.
10. Jubal A. Early *Scrapbook*.
11. *Ibid.*
12. *Ibid.*
13. George W. Cullum, *Biographical Register of the Officers and Graduates of the U. S. Military Academy from 1802 to 1840*, Vol. I, p. 529; R. H. Early, *op. cit.*, p. xx.
14. Letter from Jubal A. Early to James N. Ellis, Sept. 11, 1839, in Jubal A. Early *Papers*, Virginia Historical Society Library.
15. Letter from James N. Ellis to Jubal A. Early, Sept. 21, 1839, in Jubal A. Early *Papers*, Library of Congress.
16. Jubal A. Early *Scrapbook*.
17. Samuel S. Early, *A History of the Family of Early in America*, p. 24.
18. Jubal A. Early *Scrapbook*.
19. Letter from Jubal Early to James K. Polk, May 18, 1846, in Jubal A. Early *Papers*, Duke University Library.
20. Letter from William M. Treadway to Jubal Early, Dec. 9, 1846, in Jubal A. Early *Papers*, Vol. 2, Library of Congress.
21. Millard K. Bushong, *A History of Jefferson County, West Virginia*, p. 92.
22. Letter from Jubal A. Early to John F. Hamtramck, Jan. 15, 1847, in Jubal A. Early *Papers*, Duke University Library.
23. Letter from Jubal A. Early to Joab Early, Feb. 27, 1847, in Jubal A. Early *Scrapbook*, Library of Congress.
24. Jubal A. Early *Scrapbook*.
25. R. H. Early, *The Family of Early*, p. 116.
26. Jubal A. Early *Scrapbook*.
27. R. H. Early, *The Family of Early*, p. 116.
28. *Ibid.*

CHAPTER 4

The Terrapin from Franklin

1.   James G. Randall, *The Civil War and Reconstruction*, p. 183.
2.   *Ibid.*, pp. 184-185.
3.   Charles H. Ambler, *West Virginia the Mountain State*, p. 306.
4.   Henry T. Shanks, *The Secession Movement in Virginia, 1847-1861*, pp. 144-150.

5. *Ibid.,* pp. 145, 170.
6. *Ibid.,* p. 154.
7. Millard K. Bushong, *A History of Jefferson County, West Virginia,* p. 101.
8. *Richmond Enquirer,* March 7, 1861.
9. Shanks, *op. cit.,* p. 158.
10. *Ibid.,* p. 159.
11. *Ibid.,* pp. 159-160.
12. Ambler, *op. cit.,* pp. 314-315.
13. James D. Richardson, *A Compilation of the Messages and Papers of the Presidents,* Vol. VII, p. 3209.
14. *The Daily Richmond Enquirer,* Feb. 21, 1861.
15. *Ibid.,* Feb. 25, 1861.
16. *Richmond Enquirer,* March 7, 1861.
17. Jubal A. Early *Papers,* Vol. 3, Library of Congress.
18. Shanks, *op. cit.,* pp. 178-179, 182-190, 263.
19. Ambler, *op. cit.,* pp. 319-320.
20. *Richmond Enquirer,* April 23, 1861.
21. *Ibid.,* April 25, 1861.
22. Richardson, *op. cit.,* p. 3214.
23. *Richmond Enquirer,* April 18, 1861.
24. R. H. Early, *Lieutenant General Jubal Anderson Early, C. S. A.,* p. vii.
25. *Confederate Veteran,* Vol. XL, No. 4, p. 128.
26. Letter from John Otey Taylor to Jubal A. Early, dated April 1, 1861, in Jubal A. Early *Papers,* Vol. 3, No. 388, Library of Congress.
27. Letter from G. B. Greer to Jubal A. Early, dated April 25, 1861, in Jubal A. Early *Papers,* Vol. 3, No. 393, Library of Congress.
28. *Daily Richmond Examiner,* April 18, 1861.
29. Shanks, *op. cit.,* pp. 212-213.
30. Letter from Jubal A. Early to John Letcher, dated May 2, 1861, in Jubal A. Early *Papers,* Virginia Historical Society Library.
31. R. H. Early, *op. cit.,* pp. 1-2.

CHAPTER 5

In the Nick of Time

1. R. H. Early, *Lieutenant General Jubal Anderson Early, C. S. A.,* p. 2.
2. *Richmond Enquirer,* June 18, 1861; Jubal A. Early *Papers,* Vol. 3, No. 423, Library of Congress.
3. Matthew F. Steele, *American Campaigns,* Vol. I, p. 144.
4. *Official Records,* Series I, Vol. II, pp. 473, 478.
5. Douglas S. Freeman, *Lee's Lieutenants,* Vol. I, p. 59.
6. *Ibid.,* pp. 63-64; *Official Records,* Series I, Vol. II, pp. 474-475.
7. Thomas J. Goree *Papers,* Department of Archives, Louisiana State University.

8. R. H. Early, *op. cit.*, pp. 16-20.
9. *Ibid.*, pp. 21-22.
10. *Battles and Leaders of the Civil War*, Vol. I, p. 188; Steele, *op. cit.*, p. 139.
11. *Official Records*, Series I, Vol. II, p. 394.
12. Freeman, *op. cit.*, pp. 71-72.
13. *Battles and Leaders*, Vol. I, pp. 191-192.
14. R. H. Early, *op. cit.*, pp. 26-28.
15. *Ibid.*, p. 47.

CHAPTER 6

On the Peninsula

1. Matthew F. Steele, *American Campaigns*, Vol. I, p. 191.
2. *Battles and Leaders of the Civil War*, Vol. I, p. 252.
3. James G. Randall, *The Civil War and Reconstruction*, pp. 276-277.
4. Steele, *op. cit.*, p. 193.
5. *Ibid.*, pp. 193-194.
6. *Official Records*, Series I, Vol. XI, Pt. III, p. 130.
7. *Battles and Leaders*, Vol. II, pp. 169-170.
8. Douglas S. Freeman, *Lee's Lieutenants*, Vol. I, pp. 177-178.
9. *Official Records*, Series I, Vol. XI, Pt. I, p. 606.
10. Freeman, *op. cit.*, pp. 181-182.
11. *Official Records*, Series I, Vol. XI, Pt. I, p. 613.
12. D. H. Hill *Papers*, No. 126.
13. *Ibid.*
14. R. H. Early, *Lieutenant General Jubal Anderson Early, C. S. A.*, p. 73.
15. Freeman, *op. cit.*, pp. 185-188.
16. *Ibid.; Official Records*, Series I, Vol. XI, Pt. I, p. 538.
17. R. H. Early, *op. cit.*, p. 73.

CHAPTER 7

In Defense of Richmond

1. James G. Randall, *The Civil War and Reconstruction*, p. 291.
2. *The Advanced Engineer Manual*, Vol. II, p. 76.
3. Randall, *op. cit.*, pp. 292-293.
4. *Ibid.*, pp. 295-299.
5. *Confederate Veteran*, Vol. V, No. 12, p. 594.
6. *Confederate Archives*, Chap. 6, File No. [Vol.] 724, p. 10.
7. R. H. Early, *Lieutenant General Jubal Anderson Early, C. S. A.*, pp. 75-77.
8. *Ibid.*, p. 78.
9. Matthew F. Steele, *American Campaigns*, Vol. I, p. 208.
10. *Battles and Leaders of the Civil War*, Vol. II, p. 392.
11. R. H. Early, *op. cit.*, p. 83.
12. *Battles and Leaders*, Vol. II, pp. 315, 317.

13. Randall, *op. cit.*, pp. 301-303.
14. *Ibid.*, p. 301.
15. *Confederate Veteran*, Vol. XXI, No. 10, p. 471.

CHAPTER 8

Recommended for Promotion

1. *Official Records*, Series 1, Vol. XII, Pt. III, pp. 473-474.
2. Matthew F. Steele, *American Campaigns*, Vol. I, p. 239.
3. *Ibid.*, pp. 239-241.
4. Kenneth P. Williams, *Lincoln Finds a General*, Vol. I, pp. 254-256.
5. G. F. R. Henderson, *Stonewall Jackson and the American Civil War*, p. 398.
6. *Official Records*, Series 1, Vol. XII, Pt. III, pp. 918-919.
7. *Ibid.*, Series 1, Vol. XI, Pt. III, p. 334.
8. Letter from Jubal A. Early to Col. R. H. Chilton, July 23, 1862, in Jubal A. Early *Scrapbook*.
9. *Official Records*, Series 1, Vol. XI, Pt. III, pp. 664-665.
10. Douglas S. Freeman, *Lee's Lieutenants*, Vol. II, p. 14.
11. *Ibid.*, p. 21.
12. *Official Records*, Series 1, Vol. XII, Pt. II, p. 227.
13. *Battles and Leaders of the Civil War*, Vol. II, p. 496.
14. R. H. Early, *Lieutenant General Jubal Anderson Early, C. S. A.*, p. 94.
15. *Ibid.*, pp. 94-96.
16. *Official Records*, Series I, Vol. XII, Pt. II, p. 230.
17. R. H. Early, *op. cit.*, p. 97.
18. Douglas S. Freeman, *op. cit.*, pp. 33-35.
19. *Ibid.*, pp. 35-36.
20. R. H. Early, *op. cit.*, pp. 98-99.
21. Douglas S. Freeman, *op. cit.*, pp. 38-40.
22. *Ibid.*, pp. 40-41.
23. R. H. Early, *op. cit.*, pp. 101-102.
24. *Confederate Veteran*, Vol. XII, No. 3, p. 117.
25. *Official Records*, Series I, Vol. XII, Pt. II, p. 180.
26. *Ibid.*, p. 139.
27. *Ibid.*, p. 183.
28. *Ibid.*, p. 227.

CHAPTER 9

Another Bull Run

1. *Official Records*, Series I, Vol. XII, Pt. II, p. 552.
2. John W. Thomason, Jr., *Jeb Stuart*, pp. 220-224.
3. *Official Records*, Series I, Vol. XII, Pt. II, p. 650.
4. *Ibid.*, p. 670.
5. Douglas S. Freeman, *Lee's Lieutenants*, Vol. II, p. 99.
6. Matthew F. Steele, *American Campaigns*, Vol. I, p. 245.
7. *Ibid.*, p. 246.

8. R. H. Early, *Lieutenant General Jubal Anderson Early, C. S. A.,* pp. 120-121.
9. *Official Records,* Series I, Vol. XII, Pt. II, p. 671; Percy G. Hamlin, *Old Bald Head,* p. 129.
10. Steele, *op. cit.,* p. 247.
11. R. H. Early, *op. cit.,* pp. 122-125.
12. *Official Records,* Series I, Vol. XII, Pt. II, p. 671.
13. *Ibid.,* p. 509.
14. *Ibid.*
15. Steele, *op. cit.,* pp. 251-252.
16. William Wood, *Captains of the Civil War,* p. 239.
17. Steele, *op. cit.,* p. 249.
18. Wood, *op. cit.,* pp. 241-242.
19. *Ibid.*
20. R. H. Early, *op. cit.,* pp. 126-127.
21. *Official Records,* Series I, Vol. XII, Pt. II, p. 566; Steele, *op. cit.,* p. 250.
22. Steele, *op. cit.,* p. 250.
23. *Ibid.,* p. 251.
24. *Official Records,* Series I, Vol. XII, Pt. II, pp. 714-715.
25. *Ibid.,* pp. 715-716.
26. *Ibid.,* Pt. III, pp. 796-797.
27. *Ibid.,* p. 798.
28. Kenneth P. Williams, *Lincoln Finds a General,* Vol. I, p. 359.

CHAPTER 10

Old Jube Heads a Division

1. *Battles and Leaders of the Civil War,* Vol. II, p. 605.
2. Letter from Jubal A. Early to D. H. Hill, Aug. 2, 1885, Nos. 176-181 in D. H. Hill *Papers.*
3. *Battles and Leaders,* Vol. II, p. 552.
4. *Ibid.,* p. 551.
5. *Official Records,* Series I, Vol. XIX, Pt. II, pp. 601-602.
6. Matthew F. Steele, *American Campaigns,* Vol. I, pp. 263-264.
7. Douglas S. Freeman, *Lee's Lieutenants,* Vol. II, pp. 173-174.
8. Henry Kyd Douglas, *I Rode with Stonewall,* pp. 151-152.
9. *Southern Historical Society Papers,* Vol. VII, p. 437.
10. R. H. Early, *Lieutenant General Jubal Anderson Early, C. S. A.,* pp. 135-136.
11. *Official Records,* Series I, Vol. XIX, Pt. I, pp. 528, 955, 966.
12. Douglas, *op. cit.,* p. 162.
13. *Confederate Veteran,* Vol. XXII, No. 10, p. 437.
14. *Official Records,* Series I, Vol. XIX, Pt. I, p. 955.
15. *Ibid.,* pp. 583-584.
16. Steele, *op. cit.,* p. 267.
17. *Confederate Veteran,* Vol. XI, No. 7, p. 328.
18. Steele, *op. cit.,* p. 268.
19. Freeman, *op. cit.,* pp. 207-209.
20. *Official Records,* Series I, Vol. XIX, Pt. I, pp. 969-970.

21. *Ibid.,* pp. 971-972.
22. Steele, *op. cit.,* p. 271.
23. *Ibid.,* p. 272.
24. *Ibid.*
25. *Official Records,* Series I, Vol. XIX, Pt. I, p. 419.
26. *Ibid.,* pp. 419-421.
27. *Ibid.,* p. 982.
28. *Ibid.,* pp. 204, 348-349.
29. Millard K. Bushong, *A History of Jefferson County, West Virginia,* pp. 157-158.
30. *Battles and Leaders,* Vol. II, p. 693.
31. Steele, *op. cit.,* p. 279.

CHAPTER 11

Jubal's Boys Get Hill Out o' Trouble

1. Matthew F. Steele, *American Campaigns,* Vol. I, p. 284.
2. Douglas S. Freeman, *Lee's Lieutenants,* Vol. II, pp. 259-260.
3. *Official Records,* Series I, Vol. XIX, Pt. I, p. 149.
4. *Ibid.,* p. 821.
5. *Ibid.,* p. 956.
6. Freeman, *op. cit.,* pp. 264, 266.
7. Steele, *op. cit.,* pp. 285-286.
8. Kenneth P. Williams, *Lincoln Finds a General,* Vol. II, pp. 472-475.
9. Steele, *op. cit.,* pp. 289-291.
10. D. H. Hill *Papers,* Nos. 176-181.
11. *Confederate Veteran,* Vol. XXXIII, No. 1, p. 21.
12. *Ibid.,* Vol. XXV., No. 11, p. 492.
13. R. H. Early, *Lieutenant General Jubal Anderson Early, C. S. A.,* p. 477.
14. Steele, *op. cit.,* pp. 293-294.
15. *Ibid.,* p. 295.
16. *Official Records,* Series I, Vol. XXI, p. 71.
17. *Confederate Veteran,* Vol. XIII, No. 10, p. 459.
18. Freeman, *op. cit.,* pp. 354-355.
19. *Official Records,* Series I, Vol. XXI, pp. 663-664.
20. *Battles and Leaders of the Civil War,* Vol. III, p. 140.
21. *Official Records,* Series I, Vol. XXI, pp. 663-665.
22. Steele, *op. cit.,* p. 298.
23. *Ibid.,* pp. 298-299; *Official Records,* Series I, Vol. XXI, p. 287.
24. Steele, *op. cit.,* p. 299.
25. *Confederate Veteran,* Vol. XI, No. 2, p. 57.
26. *Official Records,* Series I, Vol. XXI, p. 356.
27. *Ibid.;* Steele, *op. cit.,* p. 300.
28. Williams, *op. cit.,* p. 826.
29. Letter from Jubal A. Early to D. H. Hill, August 2, 1885, in D. H. Hill *Papers,* Nos. 176-181.

CHAPTER 12

Old Jube Helps Defeat Hooker

1. R. H. Early, *Lieutenant General Jubal Anderson Early, C. S. A.,* pp. 184-185.
2. *Confederate Archives,* Chap. I, Vol. 86, p. 3.
3. R. H. Early, *op. cit.,* p. 188.
4. *Official Records,* Series I, Vol. XXI, p. 994.
5. *Ibid.,* pp. 1004-1005.
6. R. H. Early, *op. cit.,* p. 190.
7. Kenneth P. Williams, *Lincoln Finds a General,* Vol. II, pp. 551-552.
8. Matthew F. Steele, *American Campaigns,* Vol. I, pp. 329-330.
9. *Official Records,* Series I, Vol. XXV, Pt. 2, p. 320.
10. *Ibid.,* p. 696; *Battles and Leaders of the Civil War,* Vol. III, p. 238.
11. Steele, *op. cit.,* p. 331.
12. Douglas S. Freeman, *Lee's Lieutenants,* Vol. II, p. 603.
13. R. H. Early, *op. cit.,* p. 197.
14. Freeman, *op. cit.,* pp. 604-605.
15. *Official Records,* Series I, Vol. XXV, Pt. I, pp. 811-812.
16. *Ibid.;* R. H. Early, *op. cit.,* pp. 200-201.
17. R. H. Early, *op. cit.,* p. 203.
18. *Official Records,* Series I, Vol. XXV, Pt. I, pp. 813-814.
19. R. H. Early, *op. cit.,* pp. 205-206.
20. *Ibid.,* p. 207.
21. *Official Records,* Series I, Vol. XXV, Pt. I, p. 816.
22. R. H. Early, *op. cit.,* p. 208.
23. *Official Records,* Series I, Vol. XXV, Pt. I, p. 1001.
24. *Ibid.*
25. R. H. Early, *op. cit.,* pp. 226-227.
26. *Official Records,* Series I, Vol. XXV, Pt. I, pp. 802, 828.
27. R. H. Early, *op. cit.,* pp. 229-230.
28. *Ibid.,* p. 233.
29. *Official Records,* Series I, Vol. XXV, Pt. I, p. 802.
30. *Confederate Veteran,* Vol. I, No. 7, p. 209.

CHAPTER 13

Old Bald Head and Old Jube Cooperate

1. Matthew F. Steele, *American Campaigns,* Vol. I, p. 353.
2. *Ibid.,* pp. 353-354.
3. *Ibid.,* pp. 354-355.
4. *Battles and Leaders of the Civil War,* Vol. III, p. 438.
5. R. H. Early, *Lieutenant General Jubal Anderson Early, C. S. A.,* p. 237.
6. *Official Records,* Series I, Vol. XXVII, Pt. II, p. 440.
7. *Ibid.,* p. 171.
8. *Ibid.,* p. 440.
9. *Ibid.,* pp. 462-463.

10. *Ibid.,* p. 501; *Southern Historical Society Papers,* Vol. VII, pp. 202-203.
11. *Official Records,* Series I, Vol. XXVII, Pt. II, p. 463.
12. *Ibid.,* p. 442.
13. Douglas S. Freeman, *Lee's Lieutenants,* Vol. III, pp. 26-27.
14. *Official Records,* Series I, Vol. XXVII, Pt. II, p. 171.

CHAPTER 14

In the Enemy's Country

1. *Official Records,* Series I, Vol. XXVII, Pt. 2, p. 442.
2. *Ibid.,* pp. 693-697.
3. *Ibid.,* Pt. 3, p. 374.
4. *Ibid.,* Pt. 2, pp. 464-465.
5. R. H. Early, *Lieutenant General Jubal Anderson Early, C. S. A.,* pp. 255-256.
6. John B. Gordon, *Reminiscences of the Civil War,* pp. 145-146.
7. *Official Records,* Series I, Vol. XXVII, Pt. 2, pp. 465-466.
8. Gordon, *op. cit.,* pp. 143-144.
9. *Official Records,* Series I, Vol. XXVII, Pt. 2, p. 466.
10. Jubal A. Early *Scrapbook.*
11. *Ibid.*
12. Gordon, *op. cit.,* p. 147.
13. *Ibid.,* p. 148.
14. *Official Records,* Series I, Vol. XXVII, Pt. 2, pp. 467-468.
15. R. H. Early, *op. cit.,* p. 265.
16. *Confederate Veteran,* Vol. XI, No. 9, p. 396.
17. Matthew F. Steele, *American Campaigns,* Vol. I, pp. 360-361.
18. *Ibid.,* p. 364.
19. *Ibid.,* pp. 365-366.
20. *Ibid.,* pp. 366-367.
21. *Official Records,* Series I, Vol. XXVII, Pt. 2, p. 444.
22. *Ibid.,* p. 445.
23. Gordon, *op. cit.,* p. 151.
24. *Ibid.,* pp. 152-153.
25. *Official Records,* Series I, Vol. XXVII, Pt. 2, p. 469.
26. *Ibid.,* p. 445.
27. Gordon, *op. cit.,* p. 157.
28. Douglas S. Freeman, *Lee's Lieutenants,* Vol. III, pp. 92-94.
29. *Official Records,* Series I, Vol. XXVII, Pt. 2, p. 445.
30. *Ibid.,* pp. 318-319.
31. Freeman, *op. cit.,* pp. 171-173.
32. Kenneth P. Williams, *Lincoln Finds a General,* Vol. II, pp. 690-691.
33. Freeman, *op. cit.,* pp. 122-124.
34. *Official Records,* Series I, Vol. XXVII, Pt. 2, p. 470.
35. *Ibid.*
36. *Ibid.*
37. *Ibid.,* p. 447.
38. *Ibid.,* p. 556.

39. *Ibid.*, pp. 480-481.
40. R. H. Early, *op. cit.*, pp. 274-275.
41. Jubal A. Early *Papers,* Vol. 14, No. 2993, Library of Congress.
42. *Official Records,* Series I, Vol. XXVII, Pt. 2, pp. 447-448.
43. *Ibid.*, p. 448.
44. *Battles and Leaders of the Civil War,* Vol. III, pp. 423-425.
45. *Official Records,* Series I, Vol. XXVII, Pt. 2, pp. 471-472.
46. *Ibid.*, p. 472.

CHAPTER 15

Commanding the Second Corps

1. R. H. Early, *Lieutenant General Jubal Anderson Early, C. S. A.,* pp. 303-304.
2. *Official Records,* Series I, Vol. XXIX, Pt. 1, p.427.
3. R. H. Early, *op. cit.,* pp. 304-306.
4. *Official Records,* Series I, Vol. XXIX, Pt. 1, pp. 619-620.
5. *Ibid.*, p. 621.
6. *Ibid.*, pp. 622-624.
7. *Ibid.*, p. 624.
8. *Ibid.*, p. 625.
9. Douglas S. Freeman, *Lee's Lieutenants,* Vol. III, p. 269.
10. Percy G. Hamlin, *Old Bald Head,* p. 162.
11. *Official Records,* Series I, Vol. XXIX, Pt. 1, p. 895.
12. *Ibid.*, p. 833.
13. R. H. Early, *op. cit.,* p. 321.
14. *Official Records,* Series I, Vol. XXIX, Pt. 1, pp. 834-835.
15. *Ibid.*, p. 835.
16. Freeman, *op. cit.,* p. 277.
17. Hamlin, *op. cit.,* p. 162.

CHAPTER 16

Early Forms a Dislike for Cavalry

1. *Official Records,* Series I, Vol. XXIX, Pt. 1, p. 920.
2. *Ibid.*, p. 970.
3. *Ibid.*, p. 928.
4. William E. Eisenberg, *The First Hundred Years Roanoke College* 1842-1942, pp. 97-98.
5. R. H. Early, *Lieutenant General Jubal Anderson Early, C. S. A.,* pp. 327-328.
6. *Ibid.*, p. 329.
7. *Official Records,* Series I, Vol. XXIX, Pt. 1, p. 931.
8. R. H. Early, *op. cit.,* pp. 330-331.
9. *Ibid.*, p. 331.
10. *Official Records,* Series I, Vol. XXIX, Pt. 1, p. 922.
11. *Ibid.*, Pt. 2, pp. 889-890.
12. *Ibid.*, Vol. XXXIII, p. 7.
13. *Ibid.*, p. 8.

14. *Ibid.,* p. 43.
15. *Ibid.,* pp. 43-45.
16. *Official Records,* Series I, Vol. XXIX, Pt. 1, p. 970.
17. *Ibid.,* Series I, Vol. XXXIII, pp. 1066-1067.
18. *Ibid.,* p. 1086.
19. *Ibid.,* p. 1168.
20. *Ibid.,* p. 1167.
21. *Ibid.,* p. 1168.
22. *Ibid.,* pp. 1166-1167.
23. *Ibid.,* p. 1166; R. H. Early, *op. cit.,* p. 341.
24. Percy G. Hamlin, *Old Bald Head,* pp. 167-168.
25. *Ibid.,* p. 168.

CHAPTER 17

Early Misses a Golden Opportunity

1. *Official Records,* Series I, Vol. XXXVI, Pt. 1, p. 198.
2. *Ibid.,* p. 915.
3. Douglas S. Freeman, *Lee's Lieutenants,* Vol. III, p. 345.
4. Matthew F. Steele, *American Campaigns,* Vol. I, pp. 470-471.
5. *Ibid.,* pp. 473-474.
6. *Ibid.,* pp. 475-476.
7. John B. Gordon, *Reminiscences of the Civil War,* p. 239.
8. *Ibid.,* pp. 240-241; *Official Records,* Series I, Vol. XXXVI, Pt. 1, p. 1070.
9. *Official Records,* Series I, Vol. XXXVI, Pt. 1, pp. 189-190.
10. *Ibid.,* p. 1062.
11. Gordon, *op. cit.,* p. 243.
12. *Ibid.,* pp. 243-244.
13. R. H. Early, *Lieutenant General Jubal Anderson Early, C. S. A.,* p. 348.
14. *Official Records,* Series I, Vol. XXXVI, Pt. 1, p. 1071.
15. Gordon, *op. cit.,* p. 258.
16. R. H. Early, *op. cit.,* p. 349.
17. *Official Records,* Series I, Vol. XXXVI, Pt. 1, pp. 1077-1078.
18. Gordon, *op. cit.,* p. 250.
19. R. H. Early, *op. cit.,* p. 351.
20. *Ibid.,* p. 352.
21. Steele, *op. cit.,* p. 496.
22. R. H. Early, *op. cit.,* p. 356.
23. *Ibid.,* p. 358.
24. *Official Records,* Series I, Vol. XXXVI, Pt. 1, p. 1074.
25. *Ibid.*
26. *Official Records,* Series I, Vol. LI, Pt. 2, p. 975.
27. R. H. Early, *op. cit.,* p. 363.
28. *Official Records,* Series I, Vol. XXXVI, Pt. 2, p. 627.
29. James G. Randall, *The Civil War and Reconstruction,* p. 543.
30. R. H. Early, *op. cit.,* pp. 363-364.
31. *Battles and Leaders of the Civil War,* Vol. IV, p. 182.
32. Randall, *op. cit.,* pp. 547-549.

CHAPTER 18

Savior of Lynchburg

1. George E. Pond, *The Shenandoah Valley in* 1864, p. 9.
2. *Ibid.*
3. Matthew F. Steele, *American Campaigns*, Vol. I, p. 470.
4. *Official Records,* Series I, Vol. XXXVII, Pt. 1, p. 492.
5. *Ibid.*
6. *Ibid.,* pp. 94-96.
7. *Official Records,* Series I, Vol. XXXVI, Pt. 1, p. 796.
8. Pond, *op. cit.,* p. 30.
9. *Official Records,* Series I, Vol. XXXVII, Pt. 1, p. 97.
10. *Confederate Archives,* Chapter I, Vol. 94, p. 440.
11. R. H. Early, *Lieutenant General Jubal Anderson Early, C. S. A.,* pp. 371-372.
12. Douglas S. Freeman, *Lee's Lieutenants,* Vol. III, p. 524.
13. Jubal A. Early *Papers,* Vol. 10, Nos. 1982-1983, Library of Congress.
14. Richmond *Whig,* October 31, 1864.
15. Jubal A. Early *Papers,* Vol. 4, Nos. 659-665, Library of Congress.
16. *Official Records,* Series I, Vol. XXXVII, Pt. 1, p. 763.
17. D. H. Hill *Papers,* No. 1573.
18. R. H. Early, *op. cit.,* p. 374.
19. Edward M. Daniel, *Speeches and Orations of John Warwick Daniel,* p. 541.
20. R. H. Early, *op. cit.,* pp. 374-375.
21. *Official Records,* Series I, Vol. XXXVII, Pt. 1, p. 100.
22. *Ibid.,* pp. 101-102.

CHAPTER 19

Old Jube Scares Abe Lincoln

1. *Official Records,* Series I, Vol. XXXVII, Pt. 1, p. 766.
2. *Ibid.,* pp. 767-769.
3. John B. Gordon, *Reminiscences of the Civil War,* p. 316.
4. Jubal A. Early *Papers,* Vol. 4, Nos. 659-665, Library of Congress.
5. George E. Pond, *The Shenandoah Valley in* 1864, pp. 46-47.
6. Douglas S. Freeman, *Lee's Lieutenants,* Vol. III, p. 558.
7. *Official Records,* Series I, Vol. XLIII, Pt. 1, p. 609.
8. *Ibid.,* Vol. XXXVII, Pt. 2, p. 600.
9. R. H. Early, *Lieutenant General Jubal Anderson Early, C. S. A.,* p. 382.
10. Henry Kyd Douglas, *I Rode with Stonewall,* pp. 293-294.
11. R. H. Early, *op. cit.,* pp. 383-384.
12. *Official Records,* Series I, Vol. XXXVII, Pt. 1, pp. 175-176.
13. Festus P. Summers, *The Baltimore and Ohio in the Civil War,* pp. 123-124.
14. R. H. Early, *op. cit.,* p. 385.

15. Jubal A. Early *Papers*, Vol. 4, Nos. 659-665, Library of Congress.
16. *Ibid.*, Vol. 11, No. 2270.
17. Richmond *News Leader*, March 19, 1951; Letter from Joseph F. Eisenhauer, 3rd, of Frederick, Md. to author, May 15, 1952.
18. *Official Records*, Series I, Vol. XXXVII, Pt. 2, p. 15.
19. *Ibid.*
20. James D. Richardson, *A Compilation of the Messages and Papers of the Presidents*, Vol. VII, pp. 3422-3423.
21. *Official Records*, Series I, Vol. XXXVII, Pt. 2, pp. 58-60.
22. R. H. Early, *op. cit.*, p. 387.
23. Gordon, *op. cit.*, p. 310.
24. *Official Records*, Series I, Vol. XXXVII, Pt. 1, p. 351.
25. *Ibid.*, pp. 351-352; *Confederate Veteran*, Vol. XXXVI, No. 1, pp. 20-23.
26. *Official Records*, Series I, Vol. XXXVII, Pt. 1, p. 352.
27. *Ibid.*, p. 348.
28. *Ibid.*, pp. 201-202.
29. Freeman, *op. cit.*, p. 564.
30. *Battles and Leaders of the Civil War*, Vol. IV, p. 499.
31. Pond, *op. cit.*, pp. 61-62.
32. *Ibid.*, pp. 60-61.

CHAPTER 20

Old Jube Scares Ulysses Grant

1. *Official Records*, Series I, Vol. XXXVII, Pt. 1, p. 348.
2. *Ibid.*
3. *The United Service*, July, 1889, pp. 37-38.
4. *Battles and Leaders of the Civil War*, Vol. IV, p. 498.
5. *Ibid.*
6. R. H. Early, *Lieutenant General Jubal Anderson Early, C. S. A.*, p. 389.
7. *Confederate Veteran*, Vol. XXXVI, No. 3, p. 95.
8. *Official Records*, Series I, Vol. XXXVII, Pt. 1, p. 348.
9. Douglas S. Freeman, *Lee's Lieutenants*, Vol. III, p. 567.
10. R. H. Early, *op. cit.*, pp. 391-392.
11. *Ibid.*
12. *Southern Historical Society Papers*, Vol. 30, p. 253.
13. *Official Records*, Series I, Vol. XXXVII, Pt. 2, p. 134.
14. *Ibid.*, p. 155.
15. *Ibid.*, pp. 155-156.
16. *Ibid.*, p. 258.
17. Margaret Leech, *Reveille in Washington*, 1860-1865, p. 343.
18. R. H. Early, *op. cit.*, pp. 394-395.
19. *Ibid.*, pp. 391-392; Freeman, *op. cit.*, p. 567.
20. *Official Records*, Series I, Vol. XXXVII, Pt. 2, p. 194.
21. *Ibid.*, p. 179.
22. R. H. Early, *op. cit.*, p. 395.
23. *Confederate Veteran*, Vol. XIX, No. 7, p. 336.

24. *Ibid.,* Vol. XVIII, No. 8, p. 376.
25. *Ibid.,* Vol. XX, No. 12, p. 561.

CHAPTER 21

Back to the Old Dominion

1. *Official Records,* Series I, Vol. XXXVII, Pt. 2, p. 369.
2. R. H. Early, *Lieutenant General Jubal Anderson Early, C. S. A.,* p. 396.
3. *Official Records,* Series I, Vol. XXXVII, Pt. 2, p. 597.
4. R. H. Early, *op. cit.,* pp. 396-397.
5. *Official Records,* Series I, Vol. XXXVII, Pt. 1, p. 327.
6. *Ibid.,* p. 353.
7. R. H. Early, *op. cit.,* pp. 397-398.
8. *Official Records,* Series I, Vol. XXXVII, Pt. 2, p. 422.
9. R. H. Early, *op. cit.,* p. 399.
10. *Ibid.*
11. George E. Pond, *The Shenandoah Valley in* 1864, pp. 96-97.
12. *Official Records,* Series I, Vol. XXXVII, Pt. 1, pp. 288-290; R. H. Early, *op. cit.,* p. 400.
13. R. H. Early, *op. cit.,* p. 400; *Official Records,* Series I, Vol. XXXVII, Pt. 1, p. 347.
14. R. H. Early, *op. cit.,* p. 400.
15. Douglas S. Freeman, *Lee's Lieutenants,* Vol. III, p. 568.
16. R. H. Early, *op. cit.,* p. 401.
17. *Official Records,* Series I, Vol. XXXVII, Pt. 2, p. 427.
18. *Ibid.,* pp. 429-430.
19. *Ibid.,* p. 436.
20. *Ibid.,* pp. 445-446.

CHAPTER 22

Retaliation in Kind

1. Millard K. Bushong, *A History of Jefferson County, West Virginia,* pp. 171-172.
2. R. H. Early, *Lieutenant General Jubal Anderson Early, C. S. A.,* p. 380.
3. *Official Records,* Series I, Vol. XXXVII, Pt. 2, p. 366.
4. *Ibid.,* p. 367.
5. *Ibid.*
6. Bushong, *op. cit.,* pp. 172-173.
7. Henry Kyd Douglas, *I Rode with Stonewall,* p. 297.
8. Willis F. Evans, *History of Berkeley County, West Virginia,* pp. 263-264.
9. Bradley T. Johnson *Papers.*
10. Bushong, *op. cit.,* p. 173.
11. *Ibid.*
12. *Ibid.,* pp. 174-176.
13. *Official Records,* Series I, Vol. XXXVII, Pt. 2, pp. 374-375.
14. *Ibid.*

15. R. H. Early, *op. cit.,* p. 401.
16. Edward Bok, *The Americanization of Edward Bok,* p. 209.
17. James E. Brown, "Life of Brigadier General John McCausland" in *West Virginia History, a Quarterly Magazine,* for July, 1943, p. 275.
18. Jubal A. Early *Scrapbook.*
19. Bradley T. Johnson *Papers.*
20. Jubal A. Early *Scrapbook.*
21. *Confederate Veteran,* Vol. XI, No. 10, p. 445.
22. *Ibid.,* Vol. XVII, No. 11, p. 560.
23. Brown, *loc. cit.,* p. 277.
24. *Southern Historical Society Papers,* Vol. XXX, pp. 266-268.
25. *Confederate Veteran,* Vol. XVII, No. 11, pp. 560-561.
26. Brown, *loc. cit.,* p. 277.
27. George E. Pond, *The Shenandoah Valley in* 1864, p. 104.
28. *Official Records,* Series I, Vol. XLIII, Pt. 1, p. 84.
29. R. H. Early, *op. cit.,* p. 405.
30. Bok, *op. cit.,* p. 209.
31. Pond, *op. cit.,* p. 109.

CHAPTER 23

Sheridan Defeats Early at Winchester

1. *Official Records,* Series I, Vol. XLII, Pt. 2, p. 1170.
2. *Ibid.,* Series I, Vol. XLIII, Pt. 1, p. 1006.
3. *Ibid.,* pp. 7-8.
4. R. H. Early, *Lieutenant General Jubal Anderson Early, C. S. A.,* p. 406.
5. "Recollections of Jubal Early by One Who Followed Him" in *The Century Magazine,* Vol. 70, May-October, 1905, [n. p.].
6. *Official Records,* Series I, Vol. XLIII, Pt. 1, pp. 995-996.
7. *Ibid.,* p. 999.
8. *Ibid.,* p. 993.
9. R. H. Early, *op. cit.,* p. 415.
10. Joseph Hergesheimer, *Sheridan a Military Narrative,* pp. 162-163. Quoted with special permission from Houghton Mifflin Company, Publisher.
11. *Official Records,* Series I, Vol. XLIII, Pt. 1, pp. 60-61.
12. R. H. Early, *op. cit.,* pp. 415-416.
13. *Official Records,* Series I, Vol. XLIII, Pt. 1, p. 1027.
14. R. H. Early, *op. cit.,* p. 413.
15. *Ibid.,* p. 419.
16. *Ibid.,* p. 414.
17. *Official Records,* Vol. XLIII, Pt. 1, p. 554.
18. R. H. Early, *op. cit.,* p. 421.
19. John B. Gordon, *Reminiscences of the Civil War,* p. 321.
20. *Official Records,* Vol. XLIII, Pt. 1, p. 555.
21. *Ibid.*
22. Gordon, *op. cit.,* p. 317.
23. R. H. Early, *op. cit.,* pp. 425-426.

24. Gordon, *op. cit.,* p. 320.
25. Jubal A. Early *Scrapbook.*
26. Gordon, *op. cit.,* p. 319.
27. *Official Records,* Series I, Vol. XLIII, Pt. 1, p. 555.
28. Douglas S. Freeman, *Lee's Lieutenants,* Vol. III, p. 581.
29. *Official Records,* Series I, Vol. XLIII, Pt. 1, pp. 112-118.
30. *Ibid.,* p. 597.
31. Jubal A. Early *Scrapbook.*
32. Statement of Professor W. B. Hackley to author on September 16, 1952.

CHAPTER 24

Old Jube Makes Enemies in the Confederacy

1. R. H. Early, *Lieutenant General Jubal Anderson Early, C. S. A.,* p. 429.
2. *Ibid.,* pp. 429-430.
3. *Official Records,* Series I, Vol. XLIII, Pt. 2, pp. 877-880.
4. *Ibid.,* p. 877.
5. R. H. Early, *op. cit.,* p. 429.
6. *Official Records,* Series I, Vol. XLIII, Pt. 1, pp. 1009-1010.
7. *Confederate Veteran,* Vol. XL, No. 8, p. 305.
8. *Official Records,* Series I, Vol. XLIII, Pt. 1, p. 556.
9. George E. Pond, *The Shenandoah Valley in* 1864, pp. 175-176.
10. R. H. Early, *op. cit.,* p. 430.
11. *Confederate Veteran,* Vol. II, No. 11, p. 338.
12. *Ibid.*
13. *Ibid.*
14. *Ibid.,* Vol. XXV, No. 3, p. 109.
15. *Official Records,* Series I, Vol. XLIII, Pt. 1, p. 556.
16. *Ibid.,* p. 48.
17. *Ibid.,* p. 428.
18. *Ibid.,* p. 556.
19. *Ibid.,* p. 59.
20. *Ibid.,* p. 556.
21. *Ibid.,* p. 558.
22. *Ibid.,* pp. 558-559.
23. *Ibid.,* p. 61.
24. Douglas S. Freeman, *Lee's Lieutenants,* Vol. III, p. 585.
25. Jubal A. Early *Papers,* Vol. 12, Nos. 2461-2462, Library of Congress.
26. *Official Records,* Series I, Vol. XLIII, Pt. II, p. 894.
27. *Ibid.,* p. 895.
28. *Ibid.,* p. 897.
29. *Ibid.,* p. 893.
30. Freeman, *op. cit.,* p. 587.
31. Marcus J. Wright *Papers,* Folder No. 10-F.
32. *Ibid.*
33. *Ibid.*
34. Jubal A. Early *Scrapbook.*
35. Henry Kyd Douglas, *I Rode with Stonewall,* p. 324.

CHAPTER 25

The Sun of Middletown

1. E. Merton Coulter, *The Confederate States of America,* 1861-1865, note on p. 449.
2. *Confederate Veteran,* Vol. X, No. 4, p. 165.
3. William and Mary College Quarterly Historical *Magazine,* Vol. XXIII, No. 1, p. 36.
4. *Confederate Veteran,* Vol. VI, No. 11, p. 536.
5. *Official Records,* Series I, Vol. XLIII, Pt. 1, p. 576; R. H. Early, *Lieutenant General Jubal Anderson Early, C. S. A.,* p. 435.
6. *Official Records,* Series I, Vol. XLIII, Pt. 2, p. 202.
7. *Ibid.,* p. 308.
8. *Confederate Veteran,* Vol. XXII, No. 3, p. 128.
9. *Official Records,* Series I, Vol. XLIII, Pt. 2, p. 209.
10. *Ibid.*
11. *Ibid.,* p. 250.
12. *Ibid.,* p. 327.
13. *Ibid.*
14. Henry Kyd Douglas, *I Rode with Stonewall,* p. 314.
15. R. H. Early, *op. cit.,* p. 437.
16. *Ibid.,* p. 438.
17. R. H. Early, *op. cit.,* pp. 440-441.
18. *Ibid.*
19. John B. Gordon, *Reminiscences of the Civil War,* p. 337.
20. R. H. Early, *op. cit.,* pp. 442-443.
21. *Ibid.,* p. 443.
22. George E. Pond, *The Shenandoah Valley in* 1864, pp. 227-228.
23. *Ibid.,* p. 229.
24. R. H. Early, *op. cit.,* pp. 443-445.
25. Jubal A. Early *Papers,* Vol. 14, Nos. 2816-2818, Library of Congress.
26. Douglas S. Freeman, *Lee's Lieutenants,* Vol. III, p. 603.
27. *Official Records,* Series I, Vol. XLIII, Pt. 1, p. 561.
28. R. H. Early, *op. cit.,* p. 446.
29. *Ibid.,* p. 447.
30. Gordon, *op. cit.,* pp. 365-368.
31. *Confederate Veteran,* Vol. II, No. 3, p. 76.
32. *Ibid.,* Vol. XII, No. 1, pp. 23-24.
33. *Ibid.,* Vol. XXVII, No. 10, p. 390.
34. *Ibid.,* Vol. XXXI, No. 3, p. 88.
35. S. J. C. Moore, "The Battle of Cedar Creek or Belle Grove" in Jubal A. Early *Notes,* p. 6.
36. *Ibid.,* p. 9.
37. Pond, *op. cit.,* pp. 232-233.
38. *Ibid.,* p. 235.
39. *Ibid.,* p. 237.
40. Moore, *loc. cit.,* p. 6.
41. *Official Records,* Series I, Vol. XLIII, Pt. 1, p. 562.

42. *Ibid.*
43. R. H. Early, *op. cit.*, p. 450.
44. *Official Records*, Series I, Vol. XLIII, Pt. 1, p. 564.
45. Gordon, *op. cit.*, p. 331.
46. *Official Records*, Series I, Vol. XLIII, Pt. 1, p. 34.
47. *Ibid.*, p. 137.
48. *Ibid.*, pp. 563-564.
49. Freeman, *op. cit.*, p. 611.

CHAPTER 26

The Old Soldier Fades Away

1. R. H. Early, *Lieutenant General Jubal Anderson Early, C. S. A.*, p. 451.
2. *Official Records*, Series I, Vol. XLIII, Pt. 1, p. 582.
3. *Ibid.*, Pt. 2, p. 909.
4. *Ibid.*, pp. 902-904; R. H. Early, *op. cit.*, p. 453.
5. R. H. Early, *op. cit.*, pp. 453-454.
6. *Official Records*, Series I, Vol. XLIII, Pt. 2, pp. 746, 780.
7. R. H. Early, *op. cit.*, p. 455.
8. *Confederate Veteran*, Vol. XXXIV, No. 4, p. 157.
9. Millard K. Bushong, *A History of Jefferson County, West Virginia*, pp. 182-183.
10. *Ibid.*, pp. 183-184.
11. *Official Records*, Series I, Vol. XLIII, Pt. 1, p. 811.
12. *Ibid.*, Pt. 2, p. 920.
13. *Ibid.; Confederate Veteran*, Vol. XIV, No. 2, p. 68.
14. *Official Records*, Series I, Vol. XLIII, Pt. 2, p. 679.
15. *Ibid.*, p. 730; *Ibid.*, Pt. 1, pp. 671-673.
16. *Confederate Veteran*, Vol. XXXIX, No. 12, p. 446.
17. Statement of Benjamin Crampton of Berryville, Virginia, to author on December 28, 1954.
18. *Official Records*, Series I, Vol. XLIII, Pt. 2, p. 765.
19. George E. Pond, *The Shenandoah Valley in* 1864, p. 249.
20. *Official Records*, Series I, Vol. XLVI, Pt. 1, p. 456.
21. *Ibid.*
22. *Ibid.*, pp. 471-472.
23. J. W. Duffey, *Two Generals Kidnaped and a Race for a Prize*, pp. 3-6.
24. Duffey, *op. cit.*, p. 9.
25. *Confederate Veteran*, Vol. XII, No. 9, p. 437.
26. Duffey, *op. cit.*, p. 12.
27. *Confederate Veteran*, Vol. XII, No. 9, p. 437.
28. Duffey, *op. cit.*, p. 16.
29. R. H. Early, *op. cit.*, p. 459.
30. *Ibid.*
31. *Ibid.*, p. 460.
32. R. H. Early, *op. cit.*, p. 461.
33. *Official Records*, Series I, Vol. XLVI, Pt. 1, p. 48.
34. R. H. Early, *op. cit.*, p. 462.

35. *Official Records,* Series I, Vol. XLVI, Pt. 1, p. 476.
36. Pond, *op. cit.,* p. 253.
37. *Confederate Veteran,* Vol. XXXI, No. 2, p. 47.
38. *Ibid.*
39. R. H. Early, *op. cit.,* pp. 464-465.
40. *Ibid.,* p. 466; Jubal A. Early *Papers,* Vol. 4, No. 700, Library of Congress.
41. Jubal A. Early *Scrapbook.*
42. *Confederate Veteran,* Vol. IV, No. 1, p. 23.
43. Jubal A. Early *Papers,* Vol. 4, No. 701, Library of Congress.

CHAPTER 27

The Unreconstructed Rebel

1. Jubal A. Early *Papers,* Vol. 8, No. 374A, Library of Congress.
2. Statement of Judge A. H. Hopkins of Rocky Mount, Va. to author on September 12, 1951.
3. Letter from Jubal Early to a certain Goode dated June 8, 1866, in Jubal A. Early *Papers,* Duke University Library.
4. *Ibid.*
5. *Ibid.*
6. *Ibid.*
7. *Ibid.*
8. Jubal A. Early *Papers,* Vol. 4, No. 725, Library of Congress.
9. Letter from Jubal A. Early to Sam H. Early, dated May 30, 1866 in Jubal A. Early *Papers,* Vol. 4, Nos. 728-729, Library of Congress.
10. Letter from Jubal A. Early to Sam H. Early, dated Aug. 8, 1866, in Jubal A. Early *Papers,* Vol. 4, Nos. 735-736, Library of Congress.
11. Douglas S. Freeman, *The South to Posterity,* pp. 70-71.
12. *Ibid.*
13. Jubal A. Early *Scrapbook.*
14. Letter from Jubal Early to Jefferson Davis, dated April 20, 1885, in Jefferson Davis *Papers.*
15. Letter from Jubal Early to T. C. Reynolds dated December 11, 1867, in Jubal A. Early *Papers,* Duke University Library.
16. Letter from Jubal Early to D. H. Hill, dated March 27, 1867, in D. H. Hill *Papers,* Nos. 585-588.
17. Letter from Jubal Early to Sam H. Early, dated Nov. 3, 1868, in Jubal A. Early *Papers,* Vol. 5, Nos. 808-809, Library of Congress.
18. Letter from Jubal Early to Thomas L. Rosser, dated May 10, 1866, in Jubal A. Early *Papers,* University of Virginia Library.
19. Letter from Jubal Early to D. H. Hill, dated March 27, 1867, in D. H. Hill *Papers,* Nos. 585-588.
20. Letter from Jubal Early to Sam H. Early, dated July 27, 1868, in Jubal A. Early *Papers,* Vol. 5, Nos. 796-797, Library of Congress.

21. Letter from Jubal Early to Sam H. Early, dated Sept. 6, 1868, in Jubal A. Early *Papers*, Vol. 5, Nos. 800-801, Library of Congress.

22. James D. Richardson, *A Compilation of the Messages and Papers of the Presidents*, Vol. VIII, p. 3906.

23. Letter from Jubal Early to Sam Early, dated Dec. 27, 1868, in Jubal A. Early *Scrapbook*.

24. Letter from Jubal Early to Sam H. Early, dated Feb. 11, 1869, in Jubal A. Early *Papers*, Vol. 5, Nos. 825-826, Library of Congress.

25. Letter from Jubal Early to Jefferson Davis, dated Jan. 26, 1870, in Jubal A. Early *Papers*, Vol. 5, No. 871, Library of Congress; also Letter from Jefferson Davis to Jubal Early, dated April 16, 1870, in Jubal T. Early *Papers*, Vol. 5, Nos. 888-889, Library of Congress.

26. Letter from Jubal Early to D. H. Hill, dated Dec. 4, 1866, in D. H. Hill *Papers*.

27. Letter from Jubal Early to Russell H. Conwell, dated Aug. 30, 1875, in Jubal A. Early *Scrapbook*.

28. Jubal A. Early *Scrapbook*.

29. *Ibid.*

30. Letter from Elmore Sharpe to Jubal Early, dated July 14, 1875, in Jubal A. Early *Papers*, Vol. 7, No. 1446, Library of Congress.

31. Letter from Fitz Lee to Jubal Early, dated Aug. 9, 1875, in Jubal A. Early *Papers*, Vol. 7, Nos. 1451-1452, Library of Congress.

32. Letter from Jubal Early to Henry Heth, dated October 22, 1875, in James L. Kemper *Executive Papers*, July-December 1875, in Virginia State Library.

33. *Ibid.*

34. Letter from James L. Kemper to Jubal Early, dated October 22, 1875, in Jubal A. Early *Papers*, Vol. 8, Nos. 1483-1485, Library of Congress.

35. Letter from Jubal Early to Fitzhugh Lee, dated March 27, 1886, in Fitzhugh Lee *Executive Papers*, No. 367, Virginia State Library.

36. Letter from Fitzhugh Lee to Jubal Early, dated July 30, 1889, in Jubal A. Early *Papers*, Vol. 14, Nos. 2907-2908, Library of Congress.

37. Letter from Jubal Early to Major H. B. McClellan, dated Feb. 2, 1878, in Jubal A. Early *Papers*, Virginia Historical Society Library.

38. Jubal A. Early *Scrapbook*.

39. Jubal A. Early *Papers*, Vol. 8, Nos. 1511-1512, Library of Congress.

CHAPTER 28

Taps

1. Letter from Jubal A. Early to Henry B. Dawson, dated Oct. 25, 1873, in Jubal A. Early *Papers,* U. S. M. A. Library, West Point.

2. Letter from Bradley T. Johnson to Jubal A. Early, dated Oct. 25, 1870, in Jubal A. Early *Papers,* Vol. 5, Nos. 893-896, Library of Congress.

3. Jubal A. Early *Scrapbook.*

4. *Ibid.*

5. Letter from Jubal A. Early to Henry B. Dawson, dated October 25, 1873, in Jubal A. Early *Papers,* U. S. M. A. Library, West Point.

6. Letter from G. T. Beauregard to Jubal A. Early, dated Dec. 10, 1876, in Jubal A. Early *Papers,* Vol. 8, No. 1649, Library of Congress.

7. John P. Dyer, *The Gallant Hood,* p. 317.

8. Letter from Wade Hampton to G. T. Beauregard, dated Nov. 19, 1876, in Jubal A. Early *Papers,* Vol. 8, No. 1648, Library of Congress.

9. Letter from G. T. Beauregard to Jubal A. Early, dated January 3, 1877, in Jubal A. Early *Papers,* Vol. 9, Nos. 1660-1661, Library of Congress.

10. Jubal A. Early *Scrapbook.*

11. Letter from Jubal A. Early to J. Cabell Early, dated Dec. 23, 1881, in Jubal A. Early *Papers,* Vol. 11, Nos. 2266-2267, Library of Congress.

12. Berthold C. Alwes, "The History of the Louisiana State Lottery Company", in The Louisiana Historical *Quarterly,* Vol. 27, No. 4 (October, 1944), p. 39.

13. *Ibid.,* p. 115.

14. *Ibid.,* p. 133.

15. *Ibid.,* p. 136.

16. *Ibid.,* p. 54

17. Jubal A. Early *Scrapbook.*

18. Jubal A. Early *Papers,* Vol. 15, No. 3064, Library of Congress.

19. Letter from C. Randolph Page to Jubal Early, dated April 21, 1890, in Jubal A. Early *Papers,* Vol. 14, 2953, Library of Congress.

20. Letter from Varina Davis to Jubal A. Early, dated April 20, 1890, in Jubal A. Early *Papers,* Vol. 14, Nos. 2950-2952, Library of Congress.

21. Letter from L. L. Lomax to Jubal A. Early, dated April 3, 1890, in Jubal A. Early *Papers,* Vol. 14, No. 2948, Library of Congress.

22. Jubal A. Early *Scrapbook.*
23. Letter from Dr. Douglas S. Freeman of Richmond, Va. to author, dated August 20, 1952.
24. Letter from Fitz Lee to Jubal A. Early, dated Oct. 2, 1890, in Jubal A. Early *Scrapbook.*
25. Jubal A. Early *Scrapbook.*
26. *Ibid.*
27. *Ibid.*

BIBLIOGRAPHY
Manuscript Material

James L. Kemper, *Executive Papers, July-December,* 1875. Virginia State Library, Richmond, Va.

Fitzhugh Lee *Executive Papers,* 1886. Virginia State Library, Richmond, Va.

Scrapbook of Manuscripts, Clippings, Pictures, Etc., Relating to Jubal A. Early, Dated Mainly 1833 to 1930. Library of Congress, Washington, D. C.

The Papers of Jefferson Davis. Louisiana Historical Association Library, New Orleans, La.

The Notes of Jubal A. Early. In possession of Miss Henrianne C. Early, Washington, D. C.

The Papers of Jubal A. Early. Duke University Library, Durham, N. C.

The Papers of Jubal A. Early, 1829-1911. 15 vols. Library of Congress, Washington, D. C.

The Papers of Jubal A. Early. United States Military Academy Library, West Point, N. Y.

The Papers of Jubal A. Early. University of Virginia Library, Charlottesville, Va.

The Papers of Jubal A. Early. Virginia Historical Society Library, Richmond, Va.

The Papers of Thomas J. Goree. Louisiana State University Library, Baton Rouge, La.

The Papers of Daniel Harvey Hill. Virginia State Library, Richmond, Va.

The Papers of Bradley T. Johnson. Duke University Library, Durham, N. C.

The Papers of Marcus J. Wright. University of North Carolina Library, Chapel Hill, N. C.

United States War Department Archives. Photostats of the *Confederate Archives.* The National Archives, Washington, D. C.

Printed Material

Allen, Hervey, *Israfel, the Life and Times of Edgar Allan Poe.* 2 vols. New York, N. Y. 1927.

Alwes, Berthold C., "The History of the Louisiana State Lottery Company" in *The Louisiana Historical Quarterly,* Vol. 27, No. 4. October, 1944.

Ambler, Charles H., *West Virginia the Mountain State.* New York, N. Y. 1940.

American State Papers. Class V., Military Affairs. Vol. V. Washington, D. C. 1860.

Battles and Leaders of the Civil War. 4 vols. New York, N. Y. 1887-1888.

Beukema, Herman, *The United States Military Academy and Its Foreign Contemporaries.* West Point, N. Y. 1941.

Bok, Edward, *The Americanization of Edward Bok.* New York, N. Y. 1920.

Boynton, Edward C., *History of West Point and its Military Importance during the American Revolution: and the Origin and Progress of the United States Military Academy.* New York, N. Y. 1863.

Bushong, Millard K., *A History of Jefferson County, West Virginia.* Charles Town, W. Va. 1941.

Church, Albert E., *Personal Reminiscences of the Military Academy from 1824 to 1831.* West Point, N. Y. 1879.

Confederate Veteran. 40 vols. Nashville, Tenn. 1893-1932.

Coulter, E. Merton., *The Confederate States of America.* Vol. VII in *A History of the South* series. Baton Rouge, La. 1950.

Cram, T. J., Recollections Jotted Down during Half a Century's Active Service — Four Years as a Cadet — Forty-Six Years as an Officer in the United States Army (MS).

Cullum, George W., *Biographical Register of the Officers and Graduates of the U. S. Military Academy from 1802 to 1840.* Vol. 1. New York, N. Y. 1879.

Daily Richmond *Examiner.* 1861.

Daniel, Edward M., *Speeches and Orations of John Warwick Daniel.* Lynchburg, Va. 1911.

Dictionary of American Biography (edited by Allen Johnson and Dumas Malone). 20 vols. New York, N. Y. 1928-1936.

Douglas, Henry Kyd, *I Rode with Stonewall.* Chapel Hill, N. C. 1940.

Duffey, J. W., *Two Generals Kidnaped and A Race for a Prize.* 3rd Edition. Washington, D. C. 1927.

Dyer, John P., *The Gallant Hood.* New York, N. Y. 1950.

Early, Jubal A., *A Memoir of the Last Year of the War.* 1866.

Early, R. H., *Lieutenant General Jubal Anderson Early, C. S. A. Autobiographical Sketch and Narrative of the War between the States.* Philadelphia, Pa. 1912.

_____, *The Family of Early Which Settled upon the E a s t e r n Shore of Virginia and Its Connection with Other Families.* Lynchburg, Va. 1920.

Early Samuel S., *A History of the Family of Early in America.* Albany, N. Y. 1896.

Eisenberg, William E., *The First Hundred Years Roanoke College, 1842-1942.* Strasburg, Va. 1942.

Evans, Willis F., *History of Berkeley County, West Virginia.* Wheeling, W. Va. 1928.

Foreman, Grant, *Indian Removal.* Norman, Okla. 1932.

Freeman, Douglas S., *Lee's Lieutenants: a Study in Command.* 3 vols. New York, N. Y. 1943-1944.

_____, *R. E. Lee, a Biography.* 4 vols. New York, N. Y. 1934.

_____, *The South to Posterity.* New York, N. Y. 1939.

Gordon, John B., *Reminiscences of the Civil War.* New York, N. Y. 1904.

Hamlin, Percy Gatling, *Old Bald Head (General R. S. Ewell) the Portrait of a Soldier.* Strasburg, Va. 1940.

Harrison, Walter, *Pickett's Men: a Fragment of War History.* New York, N. Y. 1870.

Henderson, G. F. R., *Stonewall Jackson and the American Civil War.* Authorized American Edition. New York, N. Y.

Hergesheimer, Joseph, *Sheridan a Military Narrative.* New York, N. Y. 1931.

Leech, Margaret, *Reveille in Washington, 1860-1865.* New York, N. Y. 1941.

McCall, George A., *Letters from the Frontiers.* Philadelphia, Pa. 1868.

Mitchel, F. A., *Ormsby MacKnight Mitchel, Astronomer and General.* New York, N. Y. 1887.

Moore-Willson, Minnie, *The Seminoles of Florida.* New York, N. Y. 1910.

Official Register of the Officers and Cadets of the United States Military Academy. 1826-1829; 1833-1837. West Point, N. Y.

Park, Roswell, *A Sketch of the History and Topography of West Point and the U. S. Military Academy.* Philadelphia, Pa. 1840.

Pond, George E., *The Shenandoah Valley in 1864.* Vol. XI in *Campaigns of the Civil War* series. New York, N. Y. 1883.

Randall, James G., *The Civil War and Reconstruction.* New York, N. Y. 1937.

Regulations of the U. S. Military Academy at West Point. New York, N. Y. 1832.

Richardson, James D., *A Compilation of the Messages and Papers of the Presidents.* 20 vols. New York, N. Y. 1897-1929.

Richmond *Dispatch.* 1881.

Richmond *Enquirer.* 1861.

Richmond *News Leader.* 1951.

Richmond *Whig.* 1864.

Shanks, Henry T., *The Secession Movement in Virginia, 1847-1861.* Richmond, Va. 1934.

Smith, Francis H., *West Point Fifty Years Ago.* New York, N. Y. 1879.

Southern Historical Society Papers. 39 vols. Richmond, Va. 1876-1919.

Sprague, John T., *The Origin, Progress, and Conclusion of the Florida War.* New York, N. Y. 1848.

Steele, Matthew F,, *American Campaigns.* 2 vols. Harrisburg, Pa. 1943.

Summers, Festus P., *The Baltimore and Ohio in the Civil War.* New York, N. Y. 1939.

The Advanced Engineer Manual. Vol. II. 5th Edition. Harrisburg, Pa. 1938.
The Century Magazine. 1905.
The Daily Richmond *Enquirer.* 1861.
The Encyclopedia Americana. 1939 Edition. Vol. 24. New York, N. Y. 1939.
The United Service. 1889.
The War of the Rebellion: A Compilation of the Official Records of the Union and Confederate Armies. 70 vols. in 128 books. Washington, D. C. 1881-1901.
Thomason, John W., Jr., *Jeb Stuart.* New York, N. Y. 1946.
United States Military Academy Library Circulation List. West Point, N. Y.
United States Military Academy Post Order Book, 1833-1837. West Point, N. Y.
United States Military Academy *Records* in the Adjutant General's Office. The National Archives, Washington, D. C.
United States Military Academy Staff Records. West Point, N. Y.
United States Senate, *Public Document No.* 507. 25th Congress, 2nd Session. Vol. VI. Washington, D. C. 1838.
West Virginia History, a Quarterly Magazine. Charleston, W. Va. 1943.
William and Mary College Quarterly, *Historical Magazine.* Vol. XXIII, No. 1, 1st series. Williamsburg, Va. 1914-1915.
Williams, Kenneth P., *Lincoln Finds a General: A Military Study of the Civil War.* 3 vols. New York, N. Y. 1949-1952.
Wood, William, *Captains of the Civil War.* Vol. 31 in *The Chronicles of America* series. New Haven, Conn. 1921.

Index

334

Additional Books of Interest published by White Mane Publishing Co., Inc. . . .

Fighting For Time

by Glenn Worthington

with new introduction and additional material by **Brian Pohanka**

384 pp., index, illustrations, maps and dust jacket —
$19.95   (ISBN: 0-932751-03-2)

The Battle of Monocacy, July 9, 1864 — 7500 Yankees against nearly twice that number of Jubal A. Early's Rebels. Written by an eyewitness and out of print for over 50 years.

This remains the only book-length account of the battle that may have saved Washington, by the valiant stand of Union soldiers *"fightin' for time!"*

Fort Lyon to Harpers Ferry:
On The Border Of North And South
With "Rambling Jour", A Civil War Soldier

Compiled and edited by Lee C. Drickamer and Karen D. Drickamer

The Civil War Letters and Newspaper Dispatches of Charles H. Moulton (34th Mass. Vol. Inf.)

273 pp., index, illustrations and dust jacket, with an
introduction by Dennis Frye
$19.95   (ISBN: 0-942597-01-X)

Enlisting in August 1862, Charles Moulton, a twenty-year old Massachusetts corporal, spent most of his Civil War years behind a desk. Fortunately for future generations, those assignments gave Moulton time both to learn and to write about the events and people around him. Perhaps the most significant chapter in Moulton's adventure is his tenure as a provost clerk at Harpers Ferry. With few exceptions, we know little about the important work of the Provost Marshal's organization during the Civil War. Even less is known about Harpers Ferry's wartime role. Moulton's insightful chronicles shed much light on these two important but unfamiliar subject areas.

When War Passed This Way

by W. P. Conrad and Ted Alexander

*A Greencastle Bicentennial Publication in cooperation with
the Lilian S. Besore Memorial Library*

448 pp., index, illustrations, maps and dust jacket —
$24.95   (ISBN: 0-942597-02-8)

When War Passed This Way is the story of the Civil War in the Cumberland
Valley of Pennsylvania and Maryland as seen through the eyes of the community
of Greencastle, Pa. This small border town was located right in the path of some
of the war's major events such as: Union General Robert Patterson's Campaign in
1861; the Confederate invasion of 1862, Robert E. Lee's Gettysburg Campaign of
1863 and the burning of Chambersburg in 1864. Utilizing many previously unpublished
sources, the authors have provided an indepth look at how a civilian population dealt
with adversity during this nation's most tragic conflict. Out of print for several years
and demanding collectors' prices, White Mane Publishing Company, Inc. has made
this best selling book available again, complete with errata sheet.

Visit your local bookstore to obtain these and many other titles of interest
published by White Mane Publishing Co., Inc.

Should your local bookstore be out of stock simply photo-copy the order form
printed on the following page and return it to
White Mane Publishing Co., Inc.

TITLE	PRICE @	QTY.	TOTAL $
Fighting for Time (ISBN 0-932751-03-2)	$19.95		
Fort Lyon To Harpers Ferry (ISBN 0-942597-01-X)	19.95		
When War Passed This Way (ISBN 0-942597-02-8)	24.95		
		Sub-Total	
PA Residents add 6% Sales Tax			
Shipping and Handling ($1.50/book)			

TOTAL AMOUNT ENCLOSED

PAYMENT: ☐ Check enclosed ☐ MasterCard ☐ VISA

Card # _____ Expires _____

Signature _____

Name _____
(PLEASE PRINT)

Shipping Address _____
_____

RETURN ORDER FORM
AND
MAKE CHECKS PAYABLE TO:
WHITE MANE PUBLISHING CO., INC.
P.O. Box 152
Shippensburg, PA 17257